P9-CRO-800

Management Audits

The assessment of quality management systems

Allan J. Sayle

Second edition

Published by

ALLAN J. SAYLE LTD.

British Library Cataloguing in Publication Data

Sayle, Allan J.
Management audits: The assessment of quality management systems
1. Companies. Management Auditing.
I. Title
658.4'03
ISBN 0-9511739-1-X

First published 1981 by McGraw-Hill Book Co(UK) Ltd.
Published by Allan J. Sayle. 1985
Reprint 1985
Reprint 1986
Reprint 1987 (twice)
Second edition 1988
Reprint 1988 (twice)
Reprint 1989 (twice)

Printed in Great Britain

Contents

And in such indexes, although small pricks
To their subsequent volumes, there is seen
The baby figure of the giant mass
Of things to come at large.
William Shakespeare (Troilus and Cressida).

Preface

With a little help from my friends.
John Lennon & Paul McCartney.

In my preface to the first edition of this book, I said that I would welcome a debate on auditing. This is still the case although the intervening period has witnessed little debate. In the ten years that have elapsed since then, there has been an explosion of interest in quality improvement programmes and in management auditing. This has led to a demand for management auditors that has outstripped the available supply of experienced professionals. As things stand, too many auditors believe that their task is to tear apart the auditee and merely to find fault rather than to adopt a helpful and constructive approach.

The advent of contractually required QA programmes has resulted in the attitude whereby many managements view audits as a necessary evil. Accordingly, they have yet to realize that the audit is a valuable management tool which can reveal major opportunities for business improvement and cost reduction, yet to understand how to take advantage of it. I still maintain that the title "management audit" succinctly sums up the purpose and authority behind such activities. Progressive companies are now using all levels of management audit from self audit to the president's audit. As a result, they are reaping the benefits.

Over the last five years, there has been a noticeable convergence of the management audit and the traditional internal audit, as practised by the accountancy profession. This is hardly surprising since, as I have indicated in the past, in many areas they ask similar questions and have the same real concerns about the avoidance of loss. I believe that this convergence will continue until a complete merger occurs, probably within the next ten years. This will be a welcome development because each has much which will benefit the other.

The first edition of *Management Audits* was well received all over the world and I am grateful for the numerous complimentary reviews that it received. I was never satisfied, however, that the first edition was detailed enough and this second edition therefore enlarges on various points. I have included the narration of some additional experiences gained and especially discussions on auditing software projects and computer installations, services, resources' usage, energy usage, safety matters and the conduct of "president's audits" which are increasingly being implemented by progressive companies.

The universal applicability of my "Task Elements" is now widely acknowledged. They remain virtually unchanged except for some minor amendments described in Chapter 5. To assist service functions with their audits, a new task element "SERVICE", which I have used with considerable success when auditing such activities, has been created: this is detailed in Chapter 25.

On the advice of many people, I have retained the original text as far as possible, particularly the case examples and stories which were quite popular. My responses to various questions raised by delegates who have attended my audit training courses worldwide have been incorporated. A common appreciation of the first edition was that one could read about one topic without the need to read the whole book: I have consequently endeavoured to retain this feature which necessarily entails occasional repetition between different chapters. I wish to thank all those people for their constructive remarks.

Most of the QA standards quoted in the first edition have been superseded so I have used current ones to illustrate the pitfalls in wording that can be encountered when auditing against codes, regulations and standards.

As in the first edition, I have refused to fill this book with detailed checklists since I still firmly believe that an auditor must know how to construct his own, according to the objectives of any particular audit: stereotypes do not get real results. However, I have included extra guidance points for the auditor to consider when investigating particular features of the auditee's operation during an audit.

It is my hope that, apart from helping auditors to work more effectively, the book will also benefit those companies who wish to introduce a quality programme since the text indicates quite clearly what companies should do in this respect.

The debts of gratitude that I expressed in the first edition still remain but I must add my appreciation to those many people around the world who have written to me expressing their own appreciation of the audit methods that I use and promote.

Once more the greatest debt is owed to my wife, Lois, who, again, painstakingly prepared the manuscript draft and gave me support and encouragement throughout the preparation of this second edition; also to my Great Dane — Cleo — for regularly reminding me that a good walk refreshes the mind and helps one to work even better.

Allan J. Sayle.
Hampshire, England.

March 1988

1. Audit benefits, audit development and audit costs

Facts do not cease to exist because they are ignored.
Aldous Huxley.

Why audit?

It is proper to deal with this question at the outset. Audits are performed by people and people cost a lot of money to employ. Before deciding to embark on any course, a manager needs to know the justification for committing manpower, time and effort to pursuing it. So what is the justification for performing audits, either within one's own company or that of a supplier?

1. To obtain factual input for management decisions.

   All managerial decisions and plans require factual input. Many companies practise a policy of formulating annual, middle-term and long-term plans. Some managements call their plans ''objectives'' and operate what are commonly known as ''Management By Objectives'' exercises (MBO). These plans are only of value in so far as the data on which they are based is reliable. An audit is one method of gathering factual information based on an unbiased assessment of objective evidence rather than on subjective opinion. Managerial decisions based on this quality of data should be more meaningful for the enterprise than those with a less firm foundation of fact.

2. To obtain unbiased management information.

   Since an audit systematically analyses objective evidence and presents facts rather than value judgements, it corrects preconceived ideas about the status of a company's management systems, procedures, methods and training requirements. This also involves the correction of peculiar notions about whether or not the various parts of the company are working in a manner which is consistent with the policies and objectives delegated from the board of directors. It is common for senior and middle management to see their own operation through rose-coloured spectacles, sometimes to such an extent that any similarity between the official procedure and actual practice is purely coincidental. Senior managements obtain their information through the channels that run upwards through the organization's hierarchy. As the information is passed from level to level, it is inevitably liable to be distorted and filtered before it ever reaches senior management. This can be disastrous in extreme cases and costly at other times. An audit report bypasses a number of management levels and reaches senior management in its original form, giving an undistorted picture of company operations and the effectiveness of the various departments and managers within the organization.

3. To know factually if the company is at risk.

An audit provides vital feedback to management as to whether the organization is meeting its legal and contractual obligations — an increasingly significant benefit in view of recent trends in product liability. This reduces the possibility of customer complaints and expensive litigation. Moreover, it provides even more vital feedback concerning the organization's ability to compete in the future and hence the wisdom or otherwise of becoming involved in contracts and product markets which the organization does not currently have the capacity to satisfy. Many companies contract in their problems from pure ignorance of their real capacity in relation to market and other external factors. The audit also determines whether the company is meeting its contractual and legal obligations within the company to its staff. This includes, inter alia, assessment of safety practices and compliance with employment legislation.

4. To identify areas of opportunity.

The audit analyses objective evidence concerning the effectiveness of the organization and its structure: it can identify the circumstances by which resources and time are utilised ineffectively. This is because a properly conducted management audit challenges decisions and the original basis for them, thus ensuring that the status quo is constantly challenged in the light of changing business and technological circumstances. (Note, the professional auditor challenges decisions and the factors on which they are based but never challenges the person who made them because that is counterproductive to the performance of the audit.)

5. To improve communications and motivation.

Since the audit report reaches senior management directly, it promotes communication between the lowest and the highest levels within the company. It enables employees at all levels to suggest improved methods of operation. The lower echelons are those most closely involved with the actual product and are normally in the best position to see the truth about the practical implementation of the official quality management systems.

All such systems inevitably become outdated and it is often difficult to find the time to update and upgrade them. This tends to result in the systems losing credibility with the lower echelons, who often see them as something imposed from above, without consultation. By consulting people at all levels, an audit can make them feel that they are genuinely involved in managerial decisions, that management is interested in their suggestions and that their opinion is going to reach senior management unexpurgated. This improvement in communication can raise morale and motivation at all levels. If the people's ideas are acted upon as a result of the audit, they may feel more committed to making their suggestions work.

6. To assess individuals' performance based on facts.

An audit produces an unbiased assessment of each individual's training needs and of each individual's effectiveness at his or her job. Many managers do not enjoy the routine of the annual appraisal. They dislike the feeling that they are sitting in judgement on their subordinates, some of whom may perhaps be closer to friends than mere business colleagues. Moreover, where some are concerned, personal feelings may cloud the issue and render the appraisal less than accurate. The audit not only helps to take any personal colouring out of the annual appraisal but also helps to safeguard the subordinate's position, in that any personal dislikes between subordinate and manager will not be taken into account.

7. To assess the status and capability of company equipment.

An audit assists in obtaining an unbiased assessment of the status and capability of equipment throughout the enterprise: its physical condition, its maintenance requirements, its repair and fault history as well as the need for new or modified equipment to perform new procedures. It can also help to show how effective the preventive maintenance or condition monitoring systems are and assess whether or not, in the light of technological advances and competitors' activities, the equipment wastes time and resources (such as manpower, floorspace, or energy) in use. This may be the case for, even though the equipment is still serviceable, it may now represent a liability to the company's competitive position.

8. To assist with training of company staff.

An audit can provide useful training for the personnel who participate as observers. The observers see the various departments' interaction as well as the function and location of each individual department.

Audits and decision making

People at all levels in an organization either make, or are involved in the making of, decisions. The real product of anyone's labours is "the decision". The output of any decision making process is, obviously, only as good as the input. Audits are fact finding activities which examine objective evidence in an unbiased manner so as to provide reliable input for decisions. A central purpose of a management audit is to obtain correct information that will provide essential input to assist the decision making process so that quality problems and costs can be prevented or rectified, avoidable costs being saved.

Decisions are made at all levels in a company. At the highest level, the strategic decision is of vital importance. The greatest failure cost occurs in any company when these decisions go wrong. For example, if an ill-informed board of directors decides to enter a market for which the company possesses neither the product nor the capacity to meet jurisdictional requirements, it does not matter how well the existing product is made or whether it is made right first time, the entire production cost and effort is waste: such a result would reduce profit, could cripple the company and damage the share price.

Audits are unbiased fact finding exercises which substantially improve the quality of decisions by helping to reduce the risks associated with them. Audits provide management information.

The value of audits has been recognised by such management notables as A.P. Sloan[1], Henri Fayol[2] and Harold Geneen[3]. A.P. Sloan was a master at strategic decision making: he built the General Motors empire and from the quotation reproduced in page 3-10, it can reasonably be stated that audits were of considerable importance in assisting Mr. Sloan in that task.

Audits and management problems

All businesses have problems, indeed, within any given organization, all departments continually have problems. The tasks of management at whatever level in the organization are to identify possible sources of problems, to plan preventive action in order to forestall the problems and to solve them, should they arise. If this were not the case, managers would not be needed. When reduced to fundamentals, the vast majority of the problems are, in essence, quality problems. They are problems concerning the quality of work being performed, the quality of work that has been performed, the quality of items being received, the quality of information being communicated, the quality of available equipment, the quality of decisions made.

All quality problems have a cost associated with them. It, therefore, follows that the avoidance, prevention and solving of these problems equates to the prevention and reduction of unnecessary costs. The quality assurance profession refers to these as ''failure costs'', which are avoidable by taking appropriate preventive measures. The old adage of ''an ounce of prevention being worth a pound of cure'' can be rewritten as a ''few cents worth of prevention will save many dollars worth of avoidable costs''. Clearly, the prevention of quality problems must be considered the prime task of management.

The whole philosophy and purpose of quality assurance is to prevent problems before they occur, to identify and correct them swiftly if they should occur, and to uncover the root cause. The accent is on prevention first rather than on actions designed merely to find problems that have occurred. Management audits are central to effective management because they are tools that provide forewarning of situations that will lead to problems: they identify the real root causes and the risks associated with leaving them uncorrected.

Over the years, I have found that there are only six real causes of quality problems. These are discussed in Chapter 18 and consist of:—

LACK OF ORGANIZATION
LACK OF TRAINING
LACK OF DISCIPLINE
LACK OF RESOURCES
LACK OF TIME
LACK OF TOP MANAGEMENT SUPPORT

The management auditor is looking for any of the many symptoms of these real causes of quality problems as well as for avoidable costs.

The following example amply illustrates the cost benefit of performing audits.

> A large utility decided to build a new complex which would cost \$350 million. The design work for this installation was subcontracted, a very small management team being set up within that utility to provide overall control of the design contractor. Several months into the design work, the project manager felt unhappy with the performance of the design contractor and considered having an audit performed. The audit was costed out at approximately \$35,000. The project manager decided that this was too expensive and refrained from proceeding further. As the project progressed, avoidable rework and delays amounted to a \$15 million loss for the utility. This loss would have been totally avoided, had a systems audit had been conducted on the contracting organization at the outset.

Analogies

The word "audit" was in use two thousand years ago to refer to a hearing of oral evidence. Its more modern usage is found in the Oxford English Dictionary, which defines an audit as "an official examination of accounts with verification by references to witnesses and vouchers" and states that to audit is "to make an official systematic examination of [accounts]". Management audits contain several of the characteristics here ascribed to financial audits. To be specific:

- — management audits are official;
- — they are carried out systematically;
- — they verify by referring to objective evidence (such as documents, items made, equipment used).

Management auditors must be independent of the activity being audited. A financial auditor has to **ascertain** that the accounts present a "true and fair view" of the financial state of a company. The management auditor has to **present** a "true and fair view" of the efficacy, status, and implementation of the management systems as well as of the capabilities of the auditee. The value of a properly performed management audit is precisely that it presents a true and fair view, not one that subscribes to palatable fictions. The similarity of the management audit to the financial audit is so great that in some company departments, such as receiving, purchasing and stores, the financial auditor and the management auditor may be asking identical questions.

What is a "management audit"?

A management audit is an independent examination of objective evidence, performed by competent personnel, to determine whether or not the auditee

- — is assisting or is capable of assisting the company to achieve its policies and objectives; and/or
- — is capable of or is assisting the company to fulfil its contractual and legal obligations; and
- — has integrated management systems to do so; and/or,
- — is effectively implementing those systems.

It is also the true and fair presentation of the results of such examination.

When conducting an audit, it is vital constantly to remember that one's aim is

FACT FINDING NOT FAULT FINDING.

Obviously, there will be occasions when faults will be found — but that is a fact! Fact finding denotes the correct attitude, fault finding does not. A management audit is a fact finding exercise which provides management information.

Everybody in every organization has a product. Everybody is responsible for the quality of his or her product and must, therefore, manage both their own work and themselves properly. Effectively this means that everyone is a manager, regardless of whether staff control comes under their delegated responsibilities. This is a basic principle of a company wide quality programme.

At times in this book, the term "quality assurance" may be used interchangeably with "management". This is the result of the author's view that quality assurance, when reduced to fundamentals, equates to elements of good management.

What type of organization should perform management audits?

All companies and enterprises, regardless of size, can benefit by examining their activities and management systems. This applies no less to local government, civil service, commerce and the service industries than it does to manufacturing industry.

Managers often say "I can't afford the time to perform audits because I have too many problems". One must recognise that the vast majority of day-to-day problems are quality problems: performing an audit can lead most speedily to the root cause of problems. When one has problems and time appears to be pressing, this is exactly the right occasion to perform an audit, for this will identify the real causes of those problems, presenting solutions that will prevent their future recurrence. The manager will thereby be presented with real opportunities for improved performance, opportunities which he or she would be foolish to ignore.

Management audits should be tiered. At the highest level is the "President's audit", which is further discussed in Chapter 27. From the senior levels downwards, audits are directed at ascertaining that the subordinate levels are setting and working towards objectives that are consistent with those that have been delegated to them (as well as the matters described above under "What is a management audit?"). Such appraisals also ascertain that the lower echelons are performing their own similar audits properly, an activity which helps to give reassurance that any problems can be identified and corrected promptly or before they occur.

The basic audit is a self audit which places mature responsibility onto one's employees. Since everyone is a manager, it is sensible for each individual periodically to determine the results of his or her efforts and associated needs for improvement. This is where the performance of a "self audit" is most useful. Although the ingredient of independence is lost, the extra values of self discipline and delegated trust fully compensate. Self audits are performed in addition to, not as a substitute for, independent management audits.

The techniques of auditing that are described in this book can be applied on a day to day basis by any person in order to determine the status of activities for which he or she is responsible. The question technique that is described in Chapter 13 can be used for obtaining information concerning such matters as people's needs, decisions, work, items and equipment. The task elements described in Chapters 5 and 25 can be used to guide the conduct of meetings and as an aid to communications in both written and verbal form.

In-house or hired auditors?

A company will inevitably have to consider the value, or otherwise, of employing a permanent staff whose duties will consist solely of auditing. The decision depends upon a number of factors including the size of the company, the product or service supplied and the type and number of contracts with which it is involved. Large companies can generally justify and sustain the cost of in-house auditors as a part of their quality assurance department. Small companies, however, may find it cheaper and more beneficial to hire a management auditor from an external source (a consultant or someone employed by consortium or joint venture partners). The major benefit of outside management auditors is their independence. Other benefits include the experience of other types of systems, the absence of in-bred company habits and freedom from preconceived ideas.

It is also beneficial and cost effective to train people from various parts of the organization to perform audits, thereby gradually obtaining a pool of auditors that the managers can use to audit different departments. In this way, a measure of independence is assured.

Cost of audits

The benefits of management audits discussed here must be weighed against the costs of performing them. The costs consist of:

1. the auditor's time spent preparing, performing, following up and completing the audit.
2. the auditee's time spent participating in and following up the results arising from the audit.
3. overheads.

The greatest costs arise when the audit is performed by untrained or unsuitable auditors, as anyone who has been subject to this experience can testify. Such auditors are unlikely to produce constructive analyses: often they leave a trail of destructive criticism and mayhem in their wake. Hence, good training of management auditors is an important factor in determining the cost of the audit. Sadly, good training has been a rarity in the past. In some cases, people have suddenly been told that they have to perform an audit, without having any system, methods or much idea of what to do let alone what to look for. An auditor can hardly be expected to produce meaningful results if he is not given the tools needed to achieve them.

During the on site portion of the audit, the auditee normally invests at least twice as much as the auditor. This can be simply explained as follows: at any workplace, time is consumed as an auditee employee answers questions and produces objective evidence for the auditor; the escort's time is also taken up just by being present. (It is normal practice to have a knowledgeable escort present at all times, as further discussed in Chapter 23.) Given that a minimum of two of the auditee's people are thus present throughout the audit proceedings, the man hours involved are twice as much, assuming that only one auditor is present. Even when more than one auditor is present, the investment made by the auditee must still be respected.

Accordingly, the audit needs to be conducted professionally. For his investment, the auditee is entitled to a good return, some constructive criticism and valuable conclusions from the audit. Failure to achieve this is costly for both the auditor and the auditee organizations. Ultimately the cost is born by the auditor's organization. The auditee's costs inevitably become incorporated in the unit price of the product and are passed on to the auditor's organization.

Incompetent and ill trained practitioners cause auditing and quality assurance to fall into disrepute. The attitude of many auditors also leads to inadequate results. Some of them revel in their apparent power and abuse the authority vested in them: they are irresponsible. They believe that their job is to search for auditee errors as opposed to evaluating the strengths. Moreover, upon discovering a problem, they tend automatically to think "Let's put another piece of paper into this auditee's operation"; or "Shouldn't we have another procedure for this?" That is wrong: many quality problems disappear when systems are simplified and paperwork is reduced. To suggest the introduction of extra "quality controls" and more paper is short-sighted and can have the opposite effect to the one desired.

The costs of audits mount up quickly and the benefit plummets when the auditors possess the wrong background. In some audit environments, shop floor inspectors are inappropriate as auditors. This is not to denigrate them, they do have a very useful role to play, but it is unreasonable to expect them to audit areas where they have no direct experience of or competence in the techniques and products concerned. Some do fully comprehend contract processes, design processes, sales/marketing, personnel and accounts, but many do not. Regrettably, the trend has been for managements to expect these people to audit such areas, often unassisted. It is an unreasonable demand.

> The North Sea oil industry has instituted more formal auditing since the early 1980s. The audits have, in the vast majority of cases, been performed by a mixture of former shop floor and construction yard inspectors. In reality, because of their backgrounds and inadequate investment in developing the auditors' abilities, many audits have been what I call "Inspection nouveau". Although the North Sea industry has spent a considerable amount of money in the performance of audits over the last several years, in general, they have not, I believe, had good value for that money.

It is always a question of horses for courses. Selection of the right auditor for the task is a primary audit decision, as is discussed in Chapter 3.

Development of audits

Audits, in the form adopted by a number of industries nowadays, were pioneered in the USA and began to develop after the Second World War in the military, nuclear and aerospace industries. These industries have two things in common: firstly that, they are capital intensive and secondly that in the event of malfunction, there is a high safety-related risk. The audit developed as a result of the need to make certain that contracts were being properly performed. The earlier "audits", such as the works surveys performed by various classification societies, concentrated on hardware and the physical and manufacturing capabilities of a company: they were not audits as we understand the term nowadays.

At present, more and more industries are recognizing the benefits of audits as part of a quality assurance programme and it is reasonable to suppose that in the future the technique will spread even further into the field of commerce too. Some industries are already reeling as a result of the frequency and number of audits to which they are subjected by outside organizations. It is conceivable that in the future, a more extensive interchange of audit reports between companies will develop in order to save money and to reduce the number of audits and the problems of multiple assessment. Eventually, an organization such as Dun and Bradstreet may include in their assessment of a company an analysis of the efficacy of the enterprise's quality management systems, based on information gathered by an audit of the enterprise in question. This is already beginning with the advent of assessment "authorities" but problems do exist.

The problem of multiple assessment

The explosion in the number of audits being performed in industry at large has served to highlight even further the problems of multiple assessment, by which several companies operating in the same industry separately audit the same suppliers with resultant excessive costs to them all and to their national economy. To reduce these costs, it would obviously be beneficial if schemes were introduced whereby an assessment of a company by a single organization would satisfy the needs of many. Such schemes are beginning to appear but they require various prerequisites in order to prove themselves acceptable.

A reputable assessment scheme must guarantee consistency in approach by all the organizations authorised to perform assessments; must have strict standards for the selection, vetting and continuous monitoring of those organizations; must have rigid standards for the performance of assessments and the competence of personnel (auditors).

The reputation of individual assessment bodies is directly dependent on the quality of the auditors used and on the consistency of their approach. Rigorous procedures for conducting the assessments, along with utmost integrity in the people involved, are crucial. In the final analysis, however, everything is dependent on the competence and attributes of the assessors, on the quality of training and on the methods of selection of the staff concerned.

Clearly, there is a need for professional training and qualification schemes. Training is only as good as the experience of those who perform it: auditing is a practical subject best taught by experienced practitioners, not by academics. An auditor qualification scheme which is not dependent on verifying the competent performance of the auditor and which does not require observation of the auditor at work, in order to decide whether or not that auditor should be registered, must be regarded as unreliable and lacking.

Britain has recently seen the emergence of various assessment schemes designed to reduce multiple assessment of companies in general. Their major plank is that applicant companies are assessed for compliance with a particular part of the British quality assurance standard BS 5750[4] (identical to the ISO 9000 series of standards). It will take time for these schemes' credibility to become fully established. It is, however, doubtful that they will be of value if they remain based on the current ISO 9000 series since that series leaves too much scope for interpretation, as described in Chapter 6. In short, different customers may have radically different contractual requirements for the interpretation of ISO 9001/9002/ or 9003. Thus, when an assessment body investigates compliance with the standard, it will only be considering AN interpretation — and it will issue a certificate whose validity rests on that interpretation alone: assessment bodies do not, currently, have the authority to impose their interpretation of that standard's words into the auditee's practices or management systems. Accordingly, any company wishing to select a supplier solely on the basis of an assessment body's certificate would be well advised to remain circumspect. This is further discussed in Chapter 2, in the comparison of supplier evaluations, external audits, pre-award surveys and third party assessments.

References:

1. Sloan, Alfred P., *My years with General Motors*, Doubleday & Co. Inc.
2. Fayol, Henri *General and industrial management*, Pitman.
3. Geneen, Harold (with Alvin Moscow), *Managing*, Avon Books, 1984, New York.
4. BS 5750 (1987) Parts 0,1,2,3 *Quality systems.* British Standards Institution, Park Street, London W1A 2BS.

2. Management audit types, depth and scope

Like — but oh! how different!
William Wordsworth.

There are three basic types of management audit and these vary in their depth and scope. It is important for an auditor to be clear about these points in advance because they affect the preparation and structure of the audit team required. The relationship between auditor and auditee will also vary according to the type of audit. It is often easier to have an open discussion when auditing within one's own company than it is when auditing or being audited by another organization.

Types of management audit

Internal audit

This is a management audit performed by a company or a department upon its own systems, procedures and facilities. The auditors may be from the company's own ranks or hired from outside to act on its behalf. The internal audit is a technique whereby the management feels its own pulse and assesses the organization's performance, its needs, its strong points and its failings.

Self audit:

This is a particular type of internal audit performed by an individual upon his or her own systems, procedures and facilities in order to assess his or her performance, needs, strengths and failings.

External audit

External audits are performed by a company upon its own suppliers or sub-suppliers. The auditors may be either from the company's own ranks or hired from an outside source to act on behalf of the company. This type of management audit is performed in order to assess the status of contracts made with the company's suppliers and sub-suppliers, in order to determine whether the company will be receiving what it is paying for. In some cases, the line between the external audit and the internal audit may be rather blurred — as, for example, when the auditing company considers its suppliers as part of its own organization for the duration of the contract, providing technical guidance and support until the contract is fulfilled. This blurring of the boundary between the internal and external audit in no way undermines the basic distinction: where a contract exists, certain implications concerning rights of access and examination of goods necessarily follow.

Extrinsic audit

This type of management audit is performed either by a customer or by a regulatory body or an inspection agency (or their representative). The title also covers such audits as those carried out by a customer on a company's suppliers or sub-suppliers.

Fig. 2.1 Audit Direction

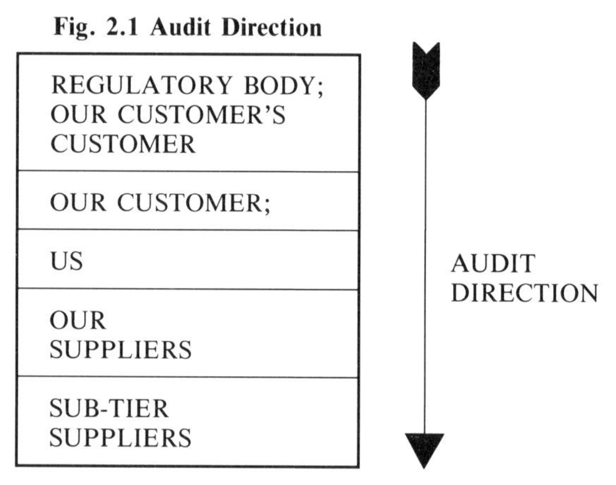

Figure 2.1 shows the relationship between the various participants in audits. The arrow always points in one direction: it is not possible, as well as not done, to audit one's own customer. Anybody who is above "US" on the ladder is an extrinsic auditor: an audit from "US" to a lower rung is an external audit.

Figure 2.2. shows how the various management audits relate to one another. Notice the column marked "Duration". The total duration of a full internal audit is measured in weeks rather than days because the internal auditor is able to go to a greater number of departments by performing a series of partial audits: he is able to examine a greater quantity of objective evidence over a longer period of time than an external or extrinsic auditor ever could. The latter are generally only allocated a number of man days in which to perform the audit in question: this is why the duration of external or extrinsic audits is measured in days rather than weeks. (See also the discussion on time/benefit — Chapter 9, Figure 9.6.) Bearing this in mind, an external/extrinsic auditor will always regard the auditee's internal audits as activities that must be covered. Internal audits not only provide the auditee's management with an

Fig. 2.2 Management audit type, depth and scope

Type	*Auditor organization*	*Auditee organization*	*Scope*	*Depth*	*Duration*
Internal	'Us' = own organization or hired auditor	'Us'	Full, partial or follow-up	Systems or compliance	Weeks
External	'Us' = own organization or hired auditor, consortium partner, joint venture partner	Our supplier, sub-suppliers, etc.	Full, partial or follow-up	Systems or compliance	Days for each supplier
Extrinsic	Our customer, customer's customer, etc., regulatory body	'Us', our supplier, sub-suppliers, etc.	Full, partial or follow-up	Systems or compliance	Days

assurance that all is well and that problems are being foreseen and forestalled, they also create confidence in the customer that someone within the auditee's organization is continually appraising the efficacy of the systems. It follows, therefore, that, if during an external audit the need for corrective action is identified, one must question why the auditee's own internal audits failed to discover this whilst investigating the effectiveness of and genuine authority vested in those internal activities.

Audit depth

Systems audit

A systems audit probes whether or not there are organizational plans and quality management systems in existence and whether these were conceived to enable the various activities of interest to be accomplished as required. It assesses the adequacy of the management systems to meet the particular codes, standard and regulations invoked by a contract (for example an ISO standard, ANSI standard or British standard) or required by virtue of the legislation which applies to those activities and their products. The quality management systems must also have defined the type of objective evidence to be produced as work proceeds, in order to provide information on the results obtained from their implementation. An auditor does not consider such a system to exist unless there is objective evidence — i.e., proof — of its existence. Although some standards require that the quality management systems comprise a "quality assurance manual", others, such as ISO 9001[1], merely ask that they be documented somewhere (e.g., within a procedure, an instruction, a memorandum or a letter).

The systems audit does not ask whether the company complies with a system: it merely ascertains whether or not management has developed the systems needed to meet contractual and legal obligations. The mere provision of a tool is not guarantee that the tool will be used as it should be. The systems audit may be able to suggest improvements to the auditee's proposals but there is no guarantee that those improvements will prove to be effective in practice.

It is advantageous to conduct a systems audit well in advance of the actual starting of an activity. The major purpose of that audit is to determine whether all the necessary organizational controls have been considered and whether the systems are in place, such that the decision to start the activity can be taken in the knowledge that the risk of loss has been minimized. The audit gives management the assurance that it is less likely to put good money after bad and that the methods which will be used to control expenditure of effort, time and resources have been carefully and thoroughly thought through. Such audits are timed so that in the event of inadequacies being identified, it is possible to implement corrective action. This philosophy renders systems audits akin to readiness reviews. Management is well advised only to release resources and expenditure upon the satisfactory outcome of such an audit. Although it makes little sense to commence work using methods which are likely to incur loss, the number of activities launched on such a basis is truly surprising.

Compliance audit

Once it has been established that management has provided a particular system, the compliance audit then investigates whether or not that management system is being implemented. In order to answer this question, the auditor scrutinizes the objective evidence that should be generated by the implementation of the system, assessing whether or not the system is effective. The auditor checks that the auditee works to the letter of the documents which describe the management system. Sometimes auditees do not work to the letter but still achieve the desired result. In this case, the auditor reports this fact as part of the audit report. Only the compliance audit can assess the real efficacy of the quality management systems and determine where improvement is possible or corrective action is needed. The audit may reveal that the auditee's personnel are deviating from the authorized procedure or system. This is not necessarily a bad thing and is further discussed in Chapter 17.

Whereas the compliance audit is performed to verify that activities are being accomplished in accordance with the systems authorized by the auditee's management, it must not be confused with an "inspection". The latter is concerned with product acceptance and release for further processing. The former concerns itself with verifying that management systems are being implemented satisfactorily.

Audit scope

An audit's scope refers to the number of the auditee's activities the auditor wishes to see in order to meet the objectives of his audit. It will vary from audit to audit according to the information required.

Full audit

A full audit (sometimes called a "cradle-to-grave" audit) covers all the activities and departments involved

a) in the execution of a particular contract; or
b) in the development and supply of a particular product line/range including after sales service throughout the lifetime of the product concerned; or
c) company wide.

In the case of a), such audits are very difficult to carry out on a single contract unless the contract has already been completed. (This is, of course, true only in the case of a compliance audit. It is entirely possible to perform a full audit to a system depth). If problems are discovered, it is costly and difficult to resolve them but the lessons to be learned will be of value for the future handling of similar contracts.

Similar remarks can be made in the case of b). Where the particular product line or range is to be made on an on-going basis, areas of opportunity might be identified, after completion of the audit, which will be of benefit for its future supply and customer service.

Partial, mini, or phased audit

This is performed only on certain tasks or departments which are of particular interest. It may cover only those activities up to and including completion of design or it may cover only a special process capability of the auditee, such as heat treatment, other activities (such as buying, design, sales, or planning) being excluded from the partial audit because they are not of equal interest at that time. This is not to say that these other activities will not be audited later nor that they have not been audited on previous occasions.

Follow-up audit

A follow-up audit is performed to verify and assess the efficacy of corrective action taken as a result of a previous audit. These audits are almost always partial audits (see above). However, a follow-up audit is not the only means of verifying the efficacy of corrective action. There are many other perfectly good and, perhaps, more cost effective means of performing follow-up action. This is further discussed in Chapter 21.

Informal audit

Sometimes people want to call an audit "informal". Any auditee, who is told that "This will only be an informal audit", should demand that the audit be formal and on the record. If it is not, he should refuse to participate. By implication, if the audit is "informal", its results are not binding and have no weight. In view of the costs of audits, it is unreasonable to expect an auditee to allocate time and money to participating in such an audit unless assured of some benefit. In any case, the "informal" audit generally ends up by becoming formal if the auditor sees some deficiencies that require corrective action.

> I heard of one quality assurance manager who enjoyed calling certain audits "mini-informal audits". The individual concerned had no real authority and respect within his own company and was afraid to tell an auditee the truth. Many of his suppliers were in very poor shape but because the purchasing department in his company was extremely powerful he was afraid of "rocking the boat". The audits were called "informal" to make them appear more acceptable but they ended up simply causing a lot of annoyance. Having had shortcomings indicated to them, the suppliers' departments could not go to their own managements

demanding corrective action because the audits were "informal". In some cases, there was not even a written audit report and the whole time-consuming process produced absolutely no benefit either to the suppliers or to the auditing company itself.

Unannounced Audit

I was contacted by a company requesting help with one of its customers who had gained access to the premises on the pretext of a visit and a brief meeting. During that visit, the company concerned had brought along a quality assurance auditor who, whilst "looking around", had spotted a few deficiencies which were not to his liking. Thereupon he had issued a couple of corrective action request forms. Since there was no contractual requirement for the implementation of a particular quality assurance programme, the company that had been "audited", naturally, had felt rather perplexed. The issue was resolved by agreeing to institute the actions required providing that formal corrective action requests were rescinded. That auditor's attitude had caused resentment, upset and embarrassment for each organization.

(See also page 14-9 in the discussion concerning "clean-ups").

Supplier evaluations, third party assessments and pre-award surveys

Pre-award surveys

Although the terms "audit","survey" and "assessment" are sometimes used interchangeably, I prefer to reserve the latter two to refer solely to a "quasi-external audit" performed *before* awarding a contract to a supplier. Hence I define a pre-award survey as:

> A visit to a potential supplier's premises for the purpose of assessing both his ability to supply items or services in accordance with the purchaser's anticipated requirements as well as to evaluate the amount of assistance that may be required from the purchaser in order to help that potential supplier comply with the purchaser's economic requirements.

There are two parts to that definition: firstly, the assessment of the supplier's ability; secondly, the amount of assistance. This is deliberate: all potential suppliers can be considered acceptable for the execution of a contract but some will require more support to enable them to comply with the contract requirements than others. A particular potential supplier may be able to deliver product which meets the fitness for purpose requirements, but, in so doing, he may incur excessive failure costs, for which the purchaser will ultimately pay. There may well, therefore, be an opportunity for the purchaser to obtain an even better price by providing assistance to that potential supplier in order to reduce those failure costs. In short, the surveyor is asking the vital question:

"How well would this vendor spend my company's money?"

One must always remember that a supplier does not have any money of his own — he only has his customer's with which, in the event of a contract, he is being entrusted.

In order to evaluate a tender properly and to determine the most economic source, one must consider the amount of effort (i.e. cost) should the contract be awarded. Suppliers have varying capabilities and these will have a cost impact on one's own company throughout the execution of the contract. As part of a pre-award survey, the surveyor must give an estimate of the assistance effort needed. The estimate may be in monetary units, such as dollars, or in an equivalent, such as man days of effort required, according to the company's standard practice. The above describes the difference between purchase price and procurement cost.

Fig. 2.3 Components of supplier evaluation

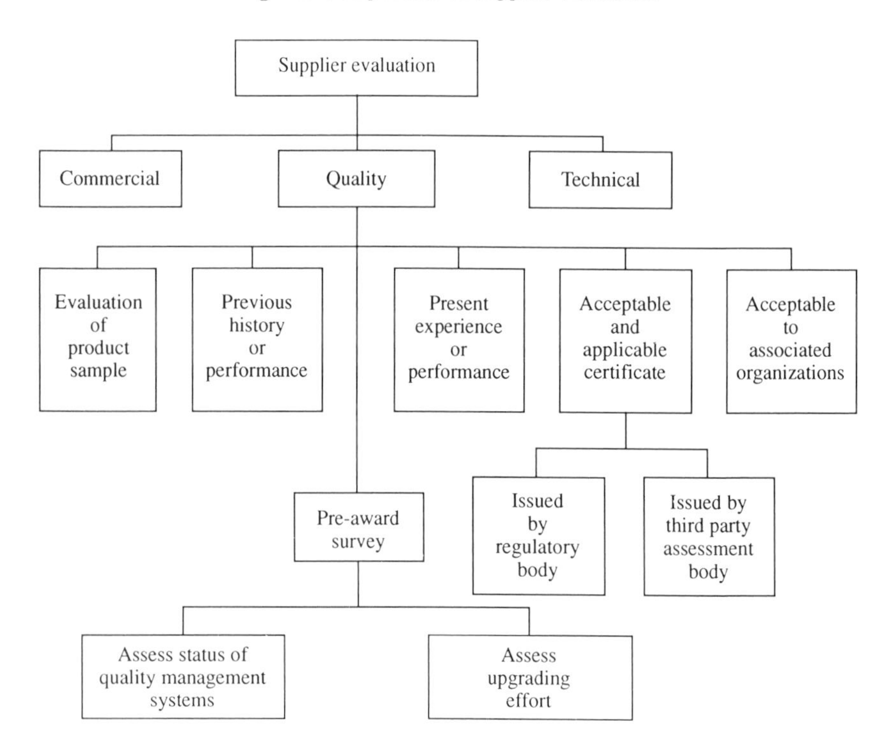

Supplier evaluation

A pre-award survey is not what is sometimes called a "supplier evaluation". A supplier evaluation is an appraisal that also takes into account commercial, quality and technical factors but it does not necessarily involve a visit to the supplier's premises.

A supplier evaluation is:

> an appraisal to determine the ability of a potential supplier to supply items or services in accordance with the purchaser's anticipated requirements as well as of the amount of effort that may be required by the purchaser to administrate the contract concerned.

The quality management aspect of that appraisal may be carried out in a number of different methods, as shown in Figure 2.3.

It should be clear from Figure 2.3, which shows the various components of supplier evaluation, that the process is not akin to an audit: whilst a pre-award survey may be performed as part of a supplier evaluation, the two procedures are not equivalent.

Third party assessments

Third party assessments are performed by organizations that consider themselves both as competent to do so and as authorities in the auditee's field of activity. The purpose is to perform an audit on behalf of the auditee's potential customers, who do not wish or cannot afford the expenditure of surveying or auditing external organizations themselves. The normal outcome of a successful assessment is the issuing of a certificate which states the auditee's compliance with the requirements of a pertinent standard or regulation. The assessment body is engaged by the auditee as an impartial external body to perform this compliance audit. I stress the term compliance audit, for one can hardly consider these particular assessments to have any validity if they are performed before any product has been made.

Any certificate issued by an assessment body is worthless if the audit has gone no further than a systems depth. To make an assessment on the basis of a review of the quality assurance manual and little more than a quick walk around the auditee's premises is obviously unwise, but too many do precisely that. Nobody would feel comfortable, given that the various systems might still be in a state of gestation or have never been implemented.

The essential service provided by an assessment body should be to inform those "whom it may concern" that they can have full confidence that the products furnished by the auditee

a) are fit for purpose;
b) are made strictly in accordance with reliable systems;
c) are economic and reduce the risk of loss to all concerned.

Frequently QA manuals are little more than statements of intent, simply a marketing gimmick which can blatantly mislead the customer, indeed, are intended to do so. Certificates issued by incompetent approval "authorities" likewise serve only to mislead.

The American Society of Mechanical Engineers (ASME) recognised the truth of this latter argument. It insists that, in order to obtain recognition by the ASME, the applicant auditee must produce a qualification piece of work produced by means of the management systems that have been implemented in accordance with a QA manual submitted to and approved by the ASME. ASME have the backing of statutory regulation in the United States which requires all pressure vessels installed and used in the USA to be designed and constructed in accordance with ASME requirements including a quality assurance programme laid down by ASME. Thus, in the modern context of assessments, ASME are not like a normal third party assessment body — they are more akin to a regulatory body and, accordingly, within this book an audit by ASME is considered to be an extrinsic audit and not a third party assessment.

Increasingly, many third party assessments take the form of:

> a visit to a company to assess its ability to supply items or services in accordance with requirements that the company has selected, the assessment being performed by an organisation that has been engaged by the company appraised but which is independent of it.

A major problem is that the assessment body might not have the authority to interpret the meaning of a particular standard's words and must assess strictly against the letter of the standard selected by the company being assessed. There is thus the real risk that the unwary customer could believe the supplier to possess capabilities that the latter does not. For an example of this, turn to the discussion in Chapter 6, "Pitfalls in practice". The wisest advice for any company to adopt when reviewing a certificate issued by a third party assessment body is that of CAVEAT EMPTOR.

The differences between a pre-award survey (PAS), a third party assessment (TPA) and an external audit are summarised in Fig. 2.4. and are discussed as follows:

ITEM 1. A PAS is performed at the discretion of the customer: the internationally recognized QA standards do not require one to be performed. In some industries, however, an external audit is mandatory because the standards require that audits be performed to assess all parts of a quality programme. TPAs are performed at the discretion of the vendor.

ITEM 2. PAS is performed prior to contract placement whereas external audits are performed post contract. This seemingly trite point has implications for the teams involved, (see ITEM 4). TPA can be performed at any time but, to have relevance, it does need to be performed once saleable product has been completely produced. The customer has no knowledge of when and under what circumstances a TPA has been performed.

ITEM 3. A PAS helps a customer to generate his own list of suppliers together with the goods or services for which they are considered acceptable sources. Such a list is generated on the basis of supplier evaluations, a method of which is the PAS. The external audit, on the other hand, may help to remove a supplier from the qualified supplier's list if it reveals that the supplier's performance has been unsatisfactory, that corrective actions have not been taken or that goods and services do not meet the customer's requirements. In the light of such removal, the company's buyers would no longer be authorized to procure goods or services from that supplier.

TPA is a device which the vendor hopes will assist the potential customer to place that vendor on his list of acceptable suppliers.

ITEM 4. Generally, a PAS team comprises representatives from various departments within the customer's company, those representatives being individuals directly involved on the contract concerned. The purchasing department's representative investigates the commercial acceptability of the potential supplier (items such as financial strength, current order book level etc.) and discusses the commercial terms of the proposed contract; the technical specialists (design engineers, scientists, computer programmers and the like) investigate the technical capability of the potential supplier in relation to the product technical requirements; the quality assurance representative(s) assess(es) the supplier's applicable management systems and the production engineer assesses the manufacturing facilities and capabilities. The outcome of the PAS is a consensus of opinion on the part of all members of the survey team which reflects the different standpoints that must be balanced in the supplier evaluation.

For an external audit, the team is primarily restricted to members of the quality assurance department. This is for two reasons. The first of these is that the commercial and technical terms of the contract are of an on-going

Fig. 2.4 Comparison of pre-award surveys, third party assessments and external audits

Pre-award survey	*External audit*	*Third party assessment*
1. Customer discretionary	Mandatory in some industries	Supplier discretionary
2. Prior to contract/purchase order placement	After contract/purchase order placement	Timed to suit supplier, not related to any specific contract
3. Helps to generate customer's qualified supplier list	Might help to 'de-generate' the customer's qualified supplier list	Might help customer to generate his qualified supplier list. Might help an industry to generate its own qualified supplier list
4. Survey team is broader based e.g. buyers, technologists, QA	Audit team generally restricted to QA staff supported by product specialists	Team depends on assessment body's professionalism, available resources and costs agreed with supplier
5. No contractual access right; supplier can refuse	Contractual access right or right of 'examination' of product (depends on law of country)	Supplier has initiated the access and decides extent of access according to scope of assessment
6. Objective evidence is not necessarily 'yours'. It may be considered as being another's proprietary information	Own objective evidence available according to contract status	Objective evidence available depends on state of work, type of product and restrictions imposed by current customers
7. Systems orientated	Systems and/or compliance orientated	Orientation depends upon practices of assessment body
8. Not too deep (generally time limited)	As deep as necessary — can be extended if time short; could be a series of partial audits	Depth depends upon practices of assessment body and costs agreed by supplier

9. Preparation and planning is often not so extensive (depends on contract size, type and value, in-house information, etc.)	Extensive preparation and planning — in-house information on progress and problems is available	Preparation and planning depends on assessment body's practices and costs approved by supplier.
10. Checklist/procedure not required by QA standards	Checklist/procedure mandatory in some industries	Checklist/procedure depends on QA standard the supplier selects and on assessment body's practices
11. Competent/trained surveyors generally not required by QA standards.	Competent/trained auditors mandatory in some industries	Competent/trained assessors depending on QA standard selected and on assessment body's practices
12. Method of reporting aimed at acceptability of the supplier, the content of reports generally not so detailed	Reports aimed at contract/regulatory compliance; reports give details of deficiences	Reports aimed at issuing of a certificate. Deficiences SHOULD lead to non-issue of certificate. Report may be confidential to supplier alone
13. Provides opportunity for additional contract clauses/safeguards or milestones payment conditions	Additional contract safeguards/clauses are difficult and costly to backfit or impose	No guarantee that additional safeguards are not necessary — CAVEAT EMPTOR
14. Report gives levelization estimate for bid adjudication (man-hours, dollars etc.)	Future money value and regulatory/customer requirements cannot be assessed reliably	No guarantee that prudent levelization amounts are not required — CAVEAT EMPTOR

nature whereas the function of the external audit is to assess whether or not contract compliance is being maintained, and can be attained, by the management systems. The second factor — and this is what I refer to as "the two-edged sword principle" — is that the external auditors assess to what extent their own organization is performing in the manner required by the contract (that the correct information is passed on punctually to the supplier, for example, or that the communicating information has been generated in accordance with company policy, that the company has taken its own customers' requirements into account in the contract with which the supplier has to comply). Hence, if a design engineer were to audit the supplier's design department, the audit might reveal his own mistakes and so the basic principle of the independence of the auditor would be violated. In order to protect this principle of the two edged sword, where the lead auditor has decided that specialists are required as part of the audit team in order to conduct the audit properly, he will attempt to obtain that support from persons who are independent of the contract in hand.

TPA teams depend on the assessment body's discretion and professional attitude. They also depend on the requirements of the standard against which the vendor is to be assessed and the terms of reference stipulated by the vendor.

ITEM 5. There is a difference in contractual rights of access. Before a contract has been awarded, the supplier can refuse to have its premises and systems surveyed. The award of a contract changes the situation. Most contracts nowadays contain a contractual right of access to examine the goods being supplied. In some countries, such a clause may not even need to be written into the contract since the law of the land provides for it automatically taking the view that, since the customer is paying for goods or services, part of his property exists within the supplier's facilities and that legally a person has right of access to his own property. This right must not be construed as meaning that the audit team can wander at will over the supplier's facilities. It may, however, amount to the right to examine the goods being supplied and the associated equipment and services utilized in the supply of those goods, and to verify by examination of objective evidence that the goods are what they purport to be. It should be noted that "goods" refers not only to the hardware but also to the software and records that are part of the contract supply and for which the customer is paying.

TPA access is not a problem because it is at the vendor's initiative.

ITEM 6. The PAS team must remember that the objective evidence that they review (or would like to review) is not necessarily their own company's property. This is particularly the case when the supplier has no existing contract with the potential customer. Some objective evidence may relate to another customer's contract and that other customer may consider such objective evidence to be proprietary information. The potential supplier is, therefore, not in a position to divulge details of contracts upon which work is being done or to allow all items to be examined by the survey team. This is particularly true for a company working on defence contracts and governed by the Official Secrets Act. However helpful the potential supplier wishes to be, it may simply not be within his power to disclose sufficient information for the surveyor to decide whether or not there is compliance with the management systems. It may only be possible to review the management systems that are allegedly in effect. In the case of the external audit, the auditor is in a stronger position because, depending on the status of the contract, there will be objective evidence of contract compliance and of compliance with the supplier's own management systems. The amount of objective evidence may not be so great if the external audit is performed shortly after the awarding of the contract. Nonetheless, the auditor will have contractual rights of access to that objective evidence. Furthermore, the external auditor will understand the nature of the objective evidence because he will be (or should be) intimately familiar with the details of his own company's contract. Thus, the pre-award survey tends, perforce, to be more systems oriented while the external audit is systems and compliance oriented (see ITEM 7).

TPA objective evidence is basically whatever is available: this may well have no relevance to a particular customer's needs. There may be restrictions imposed because of the Official Secrets Act or similar limitations.

ITEM 7. A PAS can do little more than assess the potential efficacy of the auditee's quality management systems so that the intended method of operating can be established. (Unless the procurement from the auditee of goods similar/identical to those already in production is being considered.)

The terms of reference for a TPA depend primarily on the vendor: the assessors can only assess compliance within the letter of the standard of interest and cannot consider all permutations of every customer's needs. The status of the quality management system depends on the vendor's interpretation of the standard's requirements as well as on the flexibility and limits of the standard's wording. That interpretation may be consistent with the vendor's business needs and attitude rather than with those of the customer.

The external audit is performed in accordance with the customer's interpretation, if any, of the standard as stated and agreed in the contract.

ITEM 8. The previous point (ITEM 7.) contains implications for the time-scale necessary for the visit to the supplier's facilities. Since the PAS tends to be systems oriented, the examination of objective evidence cannot be too deep, and a time limitation may have to be imposed in the interest of economy. If a company is considering bids from several companies, it becomes very costly to spend a long time surveying each company on the basis of compliance. It is common to find that, at best, the PAS tends to be a "look see". (There are attendant risks in this, particularly when the company has embarked on a Just In Time policy, discussed later in this chapter). The external audit, by contrast, can be as deep as is necessary to get to the truth and, should the time limit run out, it can be extended. The external audit may consist of a series of partial audits and hence the time available for auditing each activity selected may be greater.

TPA depth and time depend on the professionalism of the assessors and upon the vendor's willingness to pay.

ITEM 9. The preparation and planning needed for a PAS are often less extensive than for an external audit although this depends on the type and size of the contract in question and on the other information available in-house concerning the potential supplier. The amount of in-house information available will naturally be greater for an existing, rather than for an unknown, supplier. In the case of an external audit, a certain amount of in-house information concerning the contract progress and problems that have been encountered is available to the auditor for review prior to the audit. The in-house information may be in document form or expressed verbally by other departments who have experience of dealing with the supplier.

TPA preparation and planning depend on the assessors' professionalism and the status of information available from the vendor prior to performance. The assessors' preparation and planning require an investment of time for which the vendor must be willing to pay.

ITEM 10. The internationally recognized QA standards do not require a checklist or procedure to be used for a PAS whereas for an external audit it is often mandatory. The choice of a procedure or checklist for a TPA depends on the professionalism of the assessors and upon whether they conduct their affairs in accordance with a particular standard.

ITEM 11. Some QA standards do not require that trained surveyors perform a PAS whereas only trained and qualified auditors should perform external audits. This limits the choice of personnel to make up the audit team.

The TPA assessors' training and competence level depend on their professionalism and on the standard to which they operate.

ITEM 12. The PAS report states whether or not the supplier is acceptable to the customer. The external audit report goes further, stating whether or not the contract and regulatory requirements have been met and whether or not the supplier's management systems are efficacious in this respect. Any deficiencies revealed by the external audit are included in the report. One major difference between the PAS and the external audit is that the former provides an opportunity for additional clauses and safeguards to be written into the contract. These additions may be of crucial importance and it is both extremely difficult and expensive to try to impose or back-fit such clauses and safeguards after two parties have signed a contract.

The TPA report states whether or not the vendor complies with a standard that he has selected. The usefulness of the assessment report or certificate to any particular customer depends on that customer wanting an identical set of requirements and interpretation of the standard.

ITEM 13. As seen in the definition of PAS, the report should give estimates of the amount of effort required to render assistance to the potential supplier, either in monetary units or in kind, to help bid adjudication. The external audit does not give such estimates: problems already encountered should be noted in other records which will be reviewed for the purpose of future bid adjudication and supplier evaluation. It would be pointless in any case for an external audit to give an estimate of future money costs in view of the wildly variable rates of inflation that will affect them. Furthermore, it is impossible to predict the future requirements of unknown customers and of new or revised codes and standards. Future legislative requirements that have not reached the draft or discussion stage are similarly impossible to foresee.

In the case of external audits, though, there is one exception. If the auditor has found that corrective action is necessary, it may be prudent to include in the audit report a statement which quantifies the monetary equivalent of the risks of allowing the deficient situation to remain uncorrected. This is further discussed in Chapter 17 ''Corrective Action Decision''.

TPA reports are not directed at costs.

Just in Time Justifies Time

The time allocated to the performance of pre-award surveys is normally substantially less than the time assigned to external audits. This can be considerably risky in the case of a company wishing to implement a Just In Time (JIT) type of programme. The financial benefits of JIT have been well documented. There are also, however, considerable attendant costs if the organizations that are supposed to supply a product "just in time" are unable to do so. This means that the management decision to authorize a particular supplier to supply products just in time has to be taken with some care. A cursory review of the potential supplier's activities is inadequate: management must be prepared to allocate the requisite time budget that will be required. Chapter 9 "Audit Preparation" discusses the importance of time budgeting and Fig. 9.6 is a benefit-time curve which illustrates this point. Most pre-award surveys operate at the low end of that curve. For JIT, the time budget in the pre-award situation must greatly exceed that which would be allocated for the normal external audit situation.

The size of team and the constituent members is also affected. Too often pre-award surveys and audits are entrusted to the people "we can spare". In normal circumstances, this is unwise; for JIT decisions, it is foolhardy because they require the involvement of fully trained auditors/surveyors of the highest calibre possible, sourced from the disciplines that are of interest.

References:

1. ISO 9001 *Quality systems — Model for quality assurance in design/development, production, installation and servicing*. Published by the International Organization for Standardization. (ISO).

3. The Audit Decision Process

Before you begin, get good counsel;
then, having decided, act promptly
Caius Sallust.

Information affecting audit decisions

This chapter discusses the decisions that have to be made before preparing and performing a management audit. In order to make the correct decisions, one needs accurate information about the issues listed below.

1. The scope of the contracts involved (those between the customer and the company as well as those between the company and its suppliers).

In simple terms this reduces to asking the question "What is the product?" Auditors must remember

NEVER LOSE SIGHT OF THE PRODUCT.

Each contract may invoke a particular QA standard (such as ISO 9001[1], AS 1821[2] or any other of the QA standards cited throughout this book) or certain regulations to be met. The standard will describe the management systems that have to be developed, documented and implemented as a minimum by the company and its suppliers and thus it tells the auditor some of the things for which he must look. Regulations may be applicable by virtue of the product and the industry to which the organization belongs.

2. The classification of the product that is involved.

Products can be any of those listed in page 6.4 and their associated level of importance can and should be classified. The classification can range from essential, safety related (or dangerous in the case of by-products) to non-essential or non-hazardous. Some products may not need to be audited at all unless they are over-running their budget, in which case, the decision to audit may be taken on economic grounds. The matter is different with products that carry a safety risk unless they are up to standard. Here the company may have no sensible choice but to carry out regular audits to make sure that the terms of the contract are being fulfilled and that the company will not be liable to litigation as a result of defective products, inadequate practices or poor contract performance.

At the time of printing the second edition of this book, the new ISO 9000 series[3] has just been released and, although it alludes to the need for classification of products, it provides no suggested method to help the reader. The weight placed on each of the key criteria that it suggests will be a matter of decision for each company concerned. This raises the prospect of auditors and auditees arguing interminably over what is, essentially, subjective opinion. It is inadvisable for any auditor to get enmeshed in subjective opinion: always work on the basis of objective evidence.

3. The current work status of the product relative to the contract progress and delivery date.

The amount of objective evidence available increases as work and contracts progress. It is unwise to audit only when the delivery or completion date is imminent: if problems call for corrective action at this stage, delivery dates may suffer and the company may run into penalties for late delivery, loss of customer good-will, warranty problems and so on. It is equally unwise to embark on a major new phase of the work unless one is sure that the release of resources entailed is a wise decision.

4. The content of files detailing previous auditee performance.

These files will contain the results of customer complaints, warranty costs, non-conformity reports, quality costs, previous audits and pre-award surveys and hence may indicate likely problem areas or specify corrective action required in the past. In the case of a supplier, the files may also contain that supplier's rating (although not all firms make use of this type of scheme).

5. The audit schedule.

If one has been prepared, it should not only indicate the dates possible for the audit to take place but may also give a clue about the priority assigned to other auditing commitments which may affect the preferred dates.

6. Pending decisions.

Both the internal and the external auditor need this knowledge in order to single out particular activities or management systems that will need to be fully effective in the future and which therefore merit special consideration.

Since audits provide input for management decisions, it makes sense for management to inform the auditor of those decisions which it either wishes or is forced to make as a result of changing circumstances in the business environment. Some decisions are made in response to internal factors. Others are dictated by external circumstances. These factors can have a significant

Fig. 3.1 Major factors in strategic decision making

Internal factors	*External factors*
Staff capabilities Equipment capabilities Technological: — Company state-of-art — Company R & D Product(s) developments Product(s) capabilities Product(s) quality track record Bid enquiries Existing order status Incipient contracts/orders Resource availability: — manpower — equipment — financial Corporate relationships: — subsidiaries — licencees — joint ventures — agents	Legislation: — fiscal — safety — other product liability related Market place: — Competitor activities — Customer expectations — Economic strength Technological: — general state-of-art — competitors' developments Economic: — policies of available sources of finance, in general and towards the company Suppliers: — Availability — Capability — Prices and cost to the company Political

Fig 3.2 Basic internal audit plan for a simple project

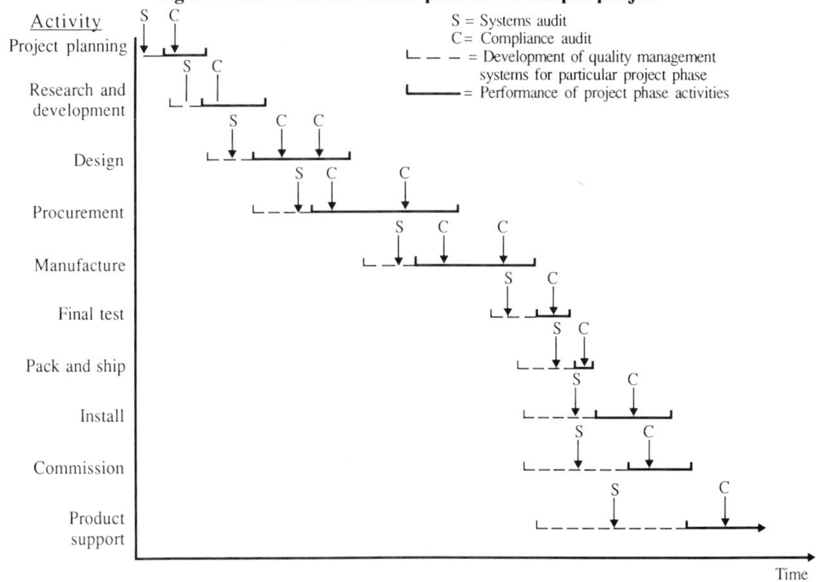

effect on the company's business strategy for survival and are summarized in the Figure 3.1. Auditors must always strive to keep ahead of the business circumstances rather than merely providing a history lesson.

Decisions that must be taken

1. Do we need an audit?

It is not always necessary to perform an audit for every contract or for every item or service involved in it. At the beginning of a major contract with a customer, it is wise to classify the items and services involved according to the necessity or desirability of auditing them and thus to generate an audit schedule for the whole contract. This type of schedule is particularly important for a complex project.

2. What must be the objective of the management audit?

Since the prime purpose of a management audit is to obtain information, it is important to establish clearly exactly what sort of information management expects the audit team to obtain. This knowledge is essential for performing those audit preparation activities described in Chapter 9. Embarking on an audit without knowing the objective is pointless. Managements which sanction the performance of an audit must define both the terms of reference and the objectives. It is poor management which authorizes the expenditure of resources for unknown and undefined benefits thereby giving the auditor a blank cheque. To do so can also cause annoyance for the auditee who has a right to know exactly why the audit has been commissioned. Where there is no clearly defined objective, there can be no purposeful preparation and no meaningful results.

The objective of an audit can be stated in simple terms. There can be several objectives, in which case, each of these needs to be carefully and unambiguously defined. Examples of this could be:

"To determine whether the auditee has documented and implemented management systems that satisfy the requirements of......" or

"To determine whether resources are being properly controlled and to identify those areas which will provide opportunity for cost reduction" or

"To determine whether the management systems comply with the requirements of the Health and Safety at Work Act 1984."

One particular audit that I was engaged to perform had the following objectives defined by the management: "To assess the status and effectiveness of the design department quality management systems in serving the company's needs and to make recommendations, where considered appropriate, for the improvement or simplification of the same".

3. What must be the type, depth, and scope of the management audit?

The classification of the goods or services involved may dictate these answers but it is always worth considering whether or not a series of partial audits might be more beneficial than a full audit. In some cases, either the industry's requirements or the prime contract with the customer will specify that internal, external and extrinsic audits are all to take place. Although extrinsic audits are the customer's or a regulatory body's responsibility, the company must still be aware of them in case it needs to integrate these with other audits.

The type of management audit (internal or external) will be fixed but the actual depth and scope may vary according to the audit objectives and information to be sought. So far as scope is concerned, perhaps a partial audit on a particular phase of the contract, such as design or inspection and testing, may be the best arrangement. The depth may depend partly on the capabilities of the auditee. For example, if the latter has not yet implemented the management systems required, the likely depth would be a systems audit. Later on, when the systems should be working effectively, a compliance audit could be performed.

The depth of the audit is directly affected by the risks involved in not having reliable information available for management to use as the basis for its decisions. If, for example, the company wishes to introduce a Just In Time system with respect to a particular vendor, then the risk of authorising a go-ahead entails accepting that a complete production line may rapidly come to a halt if the vendor is not capable of reliably delivering fault free product whenever required. To obtain confidence that this risk is minimized, the audit will need to take greater samples of the auditee's work than would otherwise be necessary.

4. When is the management audit needed?

To obtain management information in advance of key decision points dictates the need for proper timing so that the full cost benefit potential of an audit may be realised. Figure 3.2 depicts a simple project that passes through various distinct phases. The starting of each phase entails a decision to release resources in the hope that they will not be squandered and that the requisite quality of product will result. The prudent manager would want to be confident that the risks involved in taking such a decision, particularly the risk of loss, have been minimized. Only the performance of a thorough management audit can give that confidence. Sensible advance timing should enable any corrective action that the audit reveals as being required to be properly implemented. Failure costs are thus minimized or totally avoided from the outset. Forewarned is forearmed and appropriate timing of an audit forewarns the manager.

It is essential to plan the audit for the proper work phase. It is useless to perform audits solely when the item is about to be handed over to the customer. As indicated earlier, errors detected at such a late stage are extremely expensive and embarrassing to put right.

Limiting factors such as holiday arrangements or previous auditing commitments may make it impossible to carry out the audit during the period preferred. A request by a customer for an extrinsic audit may also disrupt the planned schedule.

5. What are the risks involved if the audit is postponed and major problems then found during its course?

These are questions that too few managers ask. It is unwise to postpone an audit continually until there is no time left in which to perform it or to correct major problems without incurring considerable expense: to do so is also bad management. Of course, one must ask whether or not it is likely that major problems will come to light during the audit. The answer depends on the previous performance of the auditee. An auditee who has either a poor record or little experience of the product or contract requirements is more likely to suffer from a number of deficiencies, some of which may be major problems. This point must be considered when the audit is scheduled and planned.

6. Who must be sent to perform the audit?

The personal and professional commitments of the auditors are important here. X may be the ideal person to perform the audit but circumstances may none the less dictate that Y is the only person available. The golden rule, however, has to be the question "Who MUST go?" as opposed to "Who can we spare?" The right expertise is essential for the successful conducting of the audit and to obtain the cost benefit required from its accomplishment. That expertise must be provided regardless of the level at which it might be found in the company. If the management is unwilling to make it available from within its own ranks, the alternative is to hire it in from outside. The cost benefit of the audit will dictate that this is advisable.

7. Can the audit be combined with a hold point or some quality control activity to avoid duplication of effort?

In order to ensure that particular expertise is available during an audit, it is worthwhile determining whether or not the audit can be timed to coincide with another activity at which specialist personnel from the auditor's organisation will be present. If, for example, a design review is scheduled then the particular engineers will be present: they will be able to examine objective evidence produced by the auditee to determine whether or not it shows that the adequacy of the design output and the efficacy of the design control systems implemented by the auditee. In these circumstances, the audit is likely to be a compliance audit.

I am certainly not proposing that hold points or inspections should replace audits — far from it. One problem associated with such a move is that the quality control activities tend to occur when a task has been completed, which does mean there is a risk that the whole affair will merely serve to confirm that the product has suffered as a result of one or more of the six real causes of quality problems (see Chapter 18). A major purpose of auditing is to forewarn management that such causes do exist and require corrective action BEFORE the product suffers, for this is the best way of ensuring that avoidable costs are indeed prevented. Furthermore, whereas an inspection or other quality control activity can reveal that the product meets requirements, it does not necessarily determine whether the systems can be simplified or whether resources and time are being used ineffeciently.

I disagree with some internationally recognized QA standards which seem to deny that a product inspection for the purpose of process acceptance may count as an audit. The acid test of the efficacy of management systems (which is, after all, the very concern of an audit) is the end product itself (which is the very concern of an inspection). Moreover, the documentary evidence that a management system will generate if it is working well (process sheets, records, etc.) is raw material for the inspector no less than for the auditor. So it makes sense to try to combine auditing with some type of inspection activity if at all possible (on condition that the products being inspected are for one's own company), providing one has first considered the risks associated with the timing of such activities.

If, however, the specialist personnel are to be present for a quality control activity that is unrelated to the objective of the audit in hand, having the best of both worlds is then possible.

Who makes the decisions?

This depends upon the individual company's policies and organizational structure. A small company, for instance, may not have a quality assurance department and, in the absence of a quality assurance manager, the company owner may make the decisions. Some companies adopt a policy of actively involving top management in making the audit decisions as a part of the company's annual plan while other companies delegate the decisions to the quality assurance department or to a quality committee made up of representatives from various departments within the company. Some companies do not make any such decisions at all because they have no auditing system. (This does not necessarily mean that the management is in default for it may well have been decided that a system of audits is not required. Although that decision can be considered to be unwise for the reasons stated throughout this book, the situation is much more dangerous if management has simply failed to face up to whether or not it would benefit the company for audits to be introduced.)

It is essential that management is directly involved in making the audit decisions. The level of management will depend upon the use to which the information obtained from the audit will be put. If, for example, the objective of the audit is to determine whether the company has the capabilities to satisfy the requirements of a new market sector that the company wishes to enter, then the audit report would assist a strategic decision which is, in most companies, the duty of senior executive management, perhaps even the board of directors. That level of management or the board of directors would, therefore, make the audit decisions. Figure 3.1 summarises the external and internal factors affecting strategic decisions and indicates those that are auditable. It can be seen from that figure that audits can provide significantly influential input of great value.

According to the objectives of the audit, some decisions concerning timing, scope etc. can be delegated. For example, if the company has appointed a safety officer, that person can and should be authorised to make the decisions about safety audits. But this does not invalidate the argument that top management or the board should have been the ones to decide in the first place both that such audits will be carried out and that they wish to receive the audit reports. See also Chapter 26.

In the case of external audits, assuming that a quality assurance department exists, the quality assurance manager together with the quality assurance engineer or lead auditor for the contract concerned are generally charged with the decision making, possibly first consulting the purchasing department, the design engineer, the field engineer and others directly involved in the product of interest. The responsibility for the decisions rests with the quality assurance manager, however, and he is also responsible for approving the audit schedule and the manpower allocated to all audits. In the case of internal audits, top management may either make the decisions themselves or delegate them to the quality assurance manager or a quality committee.

When are the decisions taken?

External audits

It is advisable to compile an audit schedule that will list those vendors to be audited. The vendors will be those that are regularly used and those that the procurement department knows will be used in the near future. Such a schedule should be compiled as a minimum on an annual basis and then kept regularly updated. In the case of a particular contract or project, the schedule needs to be formulated at the beginning or, at least, well in advance of procurement activities required to make the product. Audits should integrate with the sub-contract activities as undisruptively as possible, in such a way as to provide the most useful information obtainable. Special care must be taken if the suppliers concerned are to be required to operate under a Just in Time policy given the slim margins for error. The results of pre-award surveys are especially important in helping to determine the frequency, timing and objectives of such audits. Obviously, the decisions can and should be reviewed at a later stage, if fresh developments and problems occur, as is all too likely to in the context of a rapidly changing environment. It should be routine to review audit decisions along with those in other areas when any new situation arises.

Internal audits

The value of drawing up an annual internal management audit plan as part of the corporate annual plan is already recognized in many companies and one may expect an increasing number of organizations to formalize their internal audit planning in this way. The project management should also define its own audit schedule at the outset of a project. The audit can provide valuable guidance to the project manager with regard particularly to the question of whether the resources and time budgeted to each activity will be wisely spent/have been wisely spent/have not been wisely spent. Strangely, many project managers take great care in defining the cost and schedule reports that they want in order to "control" their projects but never ask for a report which will inform them of what they got in return or what they will get in return: that is precisely the information that an audit can provide. Such project audit schedules must be drawn up immediately the project is started, that is to say, at the same time as the project is being organised and planned. In some cases, this might even occur when the company is bidding for a contract.

The same remarks and arguments apply in the case of a product development project stretching from basic research and development through to product introduction.

Ad-hoc audits

Ad hoc decisions to perform audits may still have to be taken occasionally if an unexpected situation develops but this sort of fire-fighting exercise should be the exception, not the rule. There is a severe risk that auditors who possess a troublemaking attitude will use ad-hoc audits as a "catch them out" exercise. (See also page 14.9 in the discussion of clean-ups.)

The role of the board of directors:

The board of directors of any company whatsoever should require an audit to be performed on its behalf at least annually. Such a requirement is totally consistent with the duties and responsibilities vested in it and failure to do so would be most peculiar. Financial figures are totally historical in nature. When the financial accounts reveal that things have gone wrong, the underlying problems may be irreversible unless dramatic surgery, which can substantially affect the shareholders' interests (which the board has a duty to protect), is taken. If a board wishes to protect the future interests of the shareholders properly, it is vital that, in authorizing certain strategic decisions within the company, the board itself is fully informed as to the company's capabilities. The management audit can give that information. In discussing the fact that he specified the performance of audits, A.P. Sloan wrote[4]:

> "...and I do not mean audits in the usual financial sense but one that contemplates a continuous review and appraisal of what is going on throughout the enterprise...This audit function...is of the highest value to the enterprise and its shareholders. I cannot conceive of any board of directors being better informed and thus able to act intelligently on all the changing facts and circumstances than is the board of General Motors".

(Chapter 27 discusses "President's audits").

Gathering the background information

In a company that has set up a quality assurance department, a management audit system and an audit schedule, the information described earlier in this chapter should automatically be circulated to the quality assurance department. In practice, it is surprising how few quality assurance departments actually receive the data they need as a matter of course: it is not uncommon for them to have to ferret out the facts for themselves even after notifying other departments of the information they require. Companies setting up their audit system must arrange for information to be sent directly to the quality assurance department. The major sources of the information will be either the sales or the purchasing department (depending on whether the audit is internal, external, or extrinsic) and the company management.

The alert extrinsic auditor will note the extent to which the quality assurance department receives this information as a matter of course. Failure to keep that department fully involved and informed about the company's business is an indicator of lack of real commitment by the top management. It can signal the existence of a cosmetic quality assurance department.

References:

1. ISO 9001 *Quality systems — Model for quality assurance in design/ development, production, installation and servicing*. Published by the International Organization for Standardization. (ISO).

2. AS 1821 — 1985 *Suppliers' quality systems for design, development, production and installation*. Published by the Standards Association of Australia, Standards House, 80 Arthur Street, North Sydney, N.S.W. Australia.

3. The ISO 9000 series comprises ISO 9000 to ISO 9004 inclusive. See reference 1 above.

4. Sloan Alfred P., *My years with General Motors*, Doubleday & Co. Inc.

4. The Auditee's Organization

Good order is the foundation of all good things.
Edmund Burke.

While visiting a service company in Norway, I came across the following story posted on a wall.

> This is the story of four people:
> EVERYBODY, SOMEBODY, ANYBODY AND NOBODY.
> There was an important job to be done and EVERYBODY was asked to do it.
> EVERYBODY assumed that SOMEBODY would do it.
> ANYBODY could have done it but NOBODY did it.
> SOMEBODY got angry about that because it was EVERYBODY'S job.
> EVERYBODY thought ANYBODY ought to do it, But NOBODY realised EVERYBODY wouldn't do it.
> Finally, ANYBODY blamed EVERYBODY for not helping NOBODY and SOMEBODY wisely concluded that NOBODY is the most helpful person in the company.

If you want a job done make NOBODY responsible!

The purpose of this chapter is to help an auditor analyse the auditee's organizational plans, a task which can be a particularly difficult one for an inexperienced auditor. It helps to remember that all the problems, systems and machines that will be encountered can be divided, analysed, solved and understood. Similarly, all that is necessary is to break down the organization into manageable units and apply simple logic in the analysis. Unless an auditor can accomplish this, there is very little chance that the audit will produce meaningful results.

What has to be done and who will do it?

The product and the corporate strategic decisions concerning the extent to which the product will be designed, manufactured and distributed by the company itself dictate what has to be done and who will do it. A company needs to allocate the responsibility for the performance of each work phase to a person, who might in turn lead a group of people. Even if various phases are to be performed by vendors, there must still be an assigned and defined responsibility somewhere in the company for ensuring that each and every contract phase is properly executed by the vendors concerned.

One job to one person does not necessarily mean that one person need only have one job. Far from it, the essence is simply that each job has been assigned to an individual. In some cases, such as in the auditing of accounts departments or software development projects, it may be necessary for the auditee to ensure that certain positions are kept truly independent i.e. performed by different individuals or departments. In these cases, the auditor will verify that the principle of independence has not been compromised (see also Chapter 24). Independence of duties may have been stipulated in regulations and the auditor will need to ascertain what the particular requirements are as part of the audit preparation process.

The following precepts do not entail or incur excessive bureaucracy. The organization chart, job descriptions and job specifications are the prime components of a corporate quality plan. In not applying careful consideration to each of these, a management is failing in its task to plan the running of the business correctly. Many companies 'organize in' their quality problems rather than organizing to prevent them.

The auditor must review these documents when preparing for an audit so that the extent of actual activities performed at the audit site can be ascertained. This permits better audit planning (see Chapter 9 "Audit preparation"). Accordingly, the auditor will:

a) verify that the various activities which must be accomplished, in order to ensure that the product will be fit for purpose, have been clearly reflected in the organization chart;
b) verify that there is a job description for each position;
c) verify that there is also a job specification for each position;
d) verify that they are all compatible with each other as further described within this chapter.

This analysis is repeated at each level in the organization, depending on the objective and scope of the audit. The last thing to note is the reporting level of the quality assurance manager, if any.

Organization charts

The responsibilities and reporting lines within the auditee's company, division or department can be summarized on an organization chart. It must reflect all of the various work phases and key activities necessary to furnish satisfactory products to the customer and to the community.

The top management decides on the responsibilities and authority to be vested in each key position shown on the organization chart. Frequently these responsibilities and corresponding authority will be contained in job descriptions for the personnel. The auditor should review the organization chart and the associated job descriptions together to ensure that one job is assigned to one individual in such a way that there is no overlap or conflict of duties and to verify that there have been no omissions on the part of the management, which could result in nobody being responsible for a particular job.

The shape of the organization chart

For many years, companies tended to organize themselves on militaristic lines. This led to many hierarchical levels being created, often just to satisfy the egos of individuals rather than to correspond with real trading and operational needs. In large companies, these levels, known as the "chain of command", (the very phrase sums up the attitude), inevitably led to:

—top management gradually becoming out of touch with the real situation on the shop floor, actual product performance and quality, particularly as the company grew in size and range of products;
—industrial dissatisfaction and lack of motivation in the staff;
—internal politics;
—inflexibility to the changing trading circumstances and market needs, brought about by excessive inertia which prevented quick response to those circumstances and needs;
—loss of competitive position and markets.

Many people seemed to ponder over the mysterious successes of small to medium sized companies in comparison to those of large companies, when the reasons were very plain: they have shorter lines of communication which permit top managers and owners really to know both their staff and the day-to-day problems. The modern trend, even in large companies, is, therefore, to keep middle management levels to a minimum. This is often done by creating business centres within a company that are virtually autonomous. The auditor should examine the extent of hierarchical levels carefully to determine whether they are conducive or otherwise to quality achievement (which means profit).

Fig. 4.1 Organisation chart of a large company

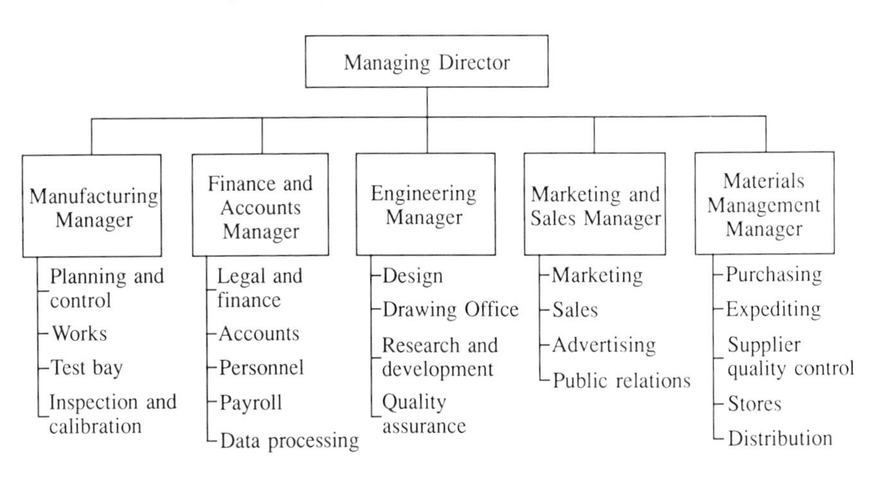

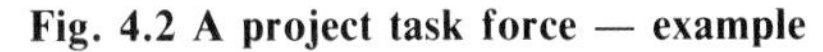

Fig. 4.2 A project task force — example

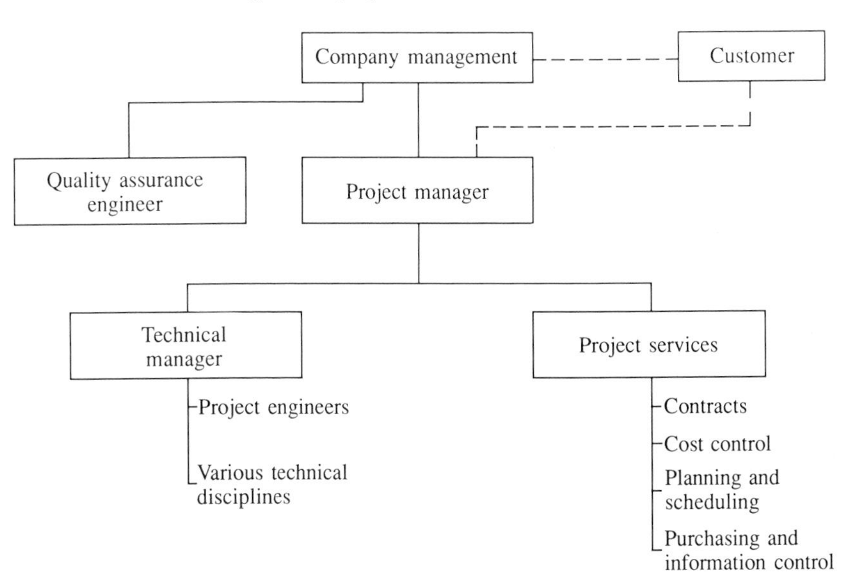

Lack of autonomy can lead to conflicts of interest as the various departments compete for scarce resources or manpower. Where, for example, there are several sales departments, each dealing with individual products, they may all claim the services of a single manufacturing department. As conflicts of schedule develop, jobs get rushed and quality suffers. (Lack of time — one of the six real causes of quality problems.) The organization chart will reflect this possibility. The solutions can be either to provide separate manufacturing facilities/resources within the company or to subcontract.

The span of managerial control

There is a limit to the number of separate and distinct activities that anyone can manage effectively. For many years, it has been recognised that 7 or 8 is, in fact, the maximum. Beyond this, a manager begins to become remote as a result of the inevitable inability to devote adequate time to each one. Decisions can then be of precarious quality caused by this lack of time, combined perhaps with reduced effectiveness through exhaustion or overwork. Some individuals are capable of greater spans of control: most are not.

Implications of the QA manager's reporting level

Figure 4.1 shows the organization of a large company that decided to design, manufacture and service its product but to buy in the various items needed for manufacture and to obtain data processing services from outside. The main functions have been shown on the chart. Within each of the divisions and departments, the auditor will verify the existence of similar charts plotting their own internal organization and reporting levels.

A point to note is that the company in question has decided that the quality assurance manager will report to the engineering manager. This can signify the following:

—that the company does not recognize that a quality programme is essential in every department, that it considers only the saleable product to need attention; accordingly;
—that there is no real company wide quality programme or quality management systems;
—that quality assurance is shown as being of subordinate importance and priority to financial assurance and technical matters, so that;
—the likelihood of the staff believing in, or being committed to, a quality programme is reduced.

In practice, the following often occurs, either of which lead to political squabbles and a difficult working atmosphere if not a state of non-cooperation to the detriment of quality progress:

—the managers on the same senior level resent the subordinate of one of their peers having the authority to require corrective action and, perhaps, to stop work;
—the same managers come to believe that the engineering manager is considered to be superior to them by the managing director.

Figure 4.2 depicts a project task force. Note that there is no quality assurance engineer reporting directly to the project manager. This does not violate the requirements of any internationally recognised quality assurance standard. In fact this style of organization is to be preferred since there is genuine independence for the QA position which reflects the real function which is to provide management with the assurance that its company systems and policies are being properly accomplished on that project. It could indicate the existence of a management exercising the wisdom that the responsibility for quality rests with those who do the job although there is no guarantee of this. The auditor would need to investigate the company's circumstances and results to draw that conclusion.

Fig. 4.3 Extract from a company's organization chart

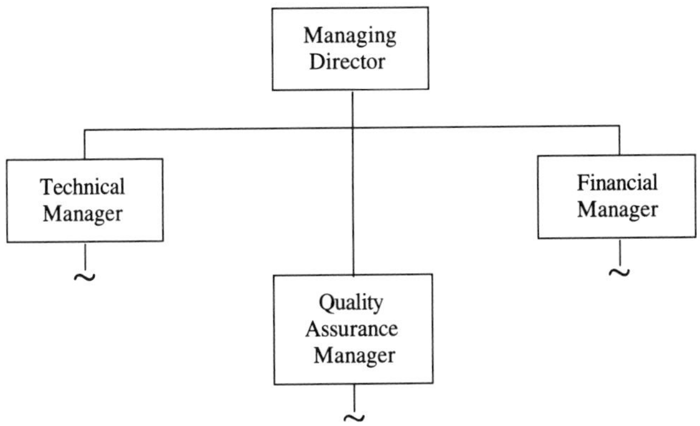

Figure 4.3 shows how a Scandinavian company depicted the organization at the top of the company. The quality assurance manager was drawn at a slightly lower level than the other similar positions. When this was presented to me, I raised the question "Is this box drawn at a lower level because: a) the technical manager and the finance manager are unwilling to consider the quality assurance position to be of equal importance

or b) because the managing director does not consider it to be of such importance?'' The truth was that a) was the case. This led me to wonder who really runs the company: the managing director or his immediate subordinates?

Job descriptions

Associated with each position, there should be a job description. These summarise, as a minimum, the duties, responsibilities and authority of each position also indicating the reporting level.

Authority and responsibilities need to be compatible. Although they should be inseparable, in practice an employee's responsibilities might grossly outweigh the delegated authority. (In this situation, motivation is reduced because the discrepancy is a reliable indicator of management's distrust or undervaluing of its people. Furthermore, it does not assist the development of an individual, ultimately resulting in a political climate which is detrimental to product quality.)

When reviewing each job description, the auditor should verify that each subordinate's job description is consistent with that of his/her superior. This consistency ensures correct planning at each level commensurate with the company's strategic objectives.

Careful scrutiny of the job descriptions, especially the quality assurance manager's, can reveal whether or not there is a genuinely company wide quality improvement programme in place. Very often a QA manager's responsibility and authority stop short at the so called overhead departments within a company. These departments can contribute much towards overall efficiency and cost reduction through quality improvement but few companies grasp the nettle and actually require them to do so.

Job specifications:

Quality achievement ultimately depends on the person assigned to a particular task. Specifying and consequently selecting the correct person is the basis of any sound quality programme. (See also Chapter 5.)

Associated with each job description should be a specification of the level of competence and training necessary if the duties of that position are to be correctly accomplished. A job specification should contain the qualifications, experience, training, special attributes, age (if relevant) which the ideal candidate should possess.

The auditor should look for the existence of job specifications and verify that the personnel assigned meet those requirements.

The inference of titles

Titles can give a clear indication of the level of real interest and commitment by the top management towards quality. When the most senior person in the quality assurance department is referred to as, say, quality assurance controller, supervisor of quality or quality assurance coordinator, there is a clear indication that top management is not fully committed to the supremacy of quality in the company's business. The title should be consistent with the peer positions. When the finance and accounts functions are headed by the "finance director" or engineering is headed by the "technical director" or "engineering manager", the quality assurance position should be similarly headed by an equivalent title, such as director of quality or quality assurance manager, respectively.

Work flow

The work flow will depend to some extent on the scope and nature of the contracts and on whether the company is supplying goods or services. Nevertheless, all contracts and products pass through discrete phases. These are not necessarily chronologically distinct: the purchasing department, for example, may be booking long lead items and materials before the design has been completed but at the same time as the inspection and test personnel may be preparing their test and inspection plan. For a great number of contracts, the phases involved are as shown in Fig. 4.4. In the case of a service contract, such as a design review service, the handover phase will probably follow straight on from design. Some manufacturing service contracts involve only a manufacturing process and, in this case, the design phase may not occur. It is important for the auditor to understand the nature of the contract to gain a clear idea of the phases through which it is likely to pass. The list in Fig. 4.4. by no means exhausts the possibilities so far as phase structure is concerned: the auditor must consider each individual contract afresh.

Once the auditor has determined the phases through which the contract will pass, he can decide which departments should be audited. There may be more than one department actively involved in a particular phase: in the design phase, for instance, there may be a design office, a drawing office and a drawing store, each of which being a discrete department or unit with a distinct task to perform. Again, in the procurement phase, the purchasing department, the goods inwards area, the receiving stores and the receiving inspection department may all be involved. The names of the phases do not reflect all the departments involved at each stage. An example of this in the procurement phase is that an item or service cannot be considered to have been procured until it has been received and found to be completely acceptable and in compliance with the purchase order requirements. This necessitates some degree of inspection and reporting, not just the issue of a purchasing order.

Fig. 4.4 Contract phases — typical

The unit concept

As stated above, before any phase can be considered complete there may be a number of different tasks that have to be performed. Each task can be considered as a unit performing a process (see Fig. 4.5). The unit requires an input and has an output. The output or product may be hardware or software or both: it may be a service. The output differs, however, from the input by virtue of the process performed by the particular task unit. The input is either the output of the preceding unit or a feedback from a downstream unit's output. Together the units make a chain or a network of chains since there may also be units working in parallel with each other. Whatever the arrangement of units, the work flows in one direction through the various phases, the whole chain standing only as strong as the weakest link.

Fig. 4.5 The unit concept

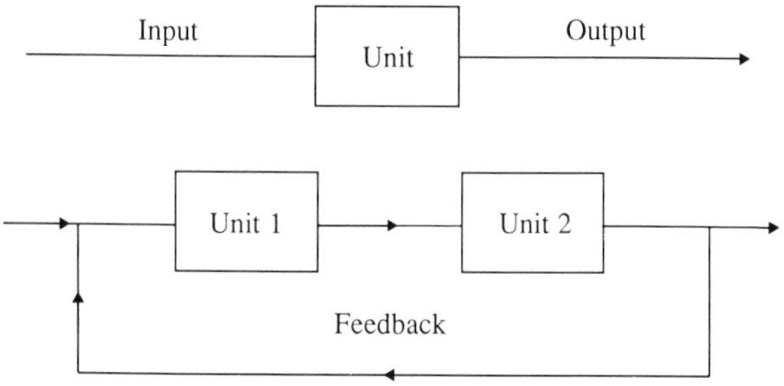

Input
Unit
Output

Unit 1
Unit 2
Feedback

Problems of location and size

Geographic dispersion

Some companies, particularly large ones, have their facilities geographically dispersed, in that different task units are located in different towns, cities, or, in the case of multi-national companies, even in different countries. Sales, design and procurement may be in the same central headquarters, for example; manufacturing, testing and inspection may be carried out in a provincial factory; there may be distribution warehouses in other towns and after sales service units in others yet again.

From an auditing standpoint, geographic dispersion has the following implications:

1. Careful decision making concerning the objectives and scope of the audit will be needed.
2. Especially thorough planning of the audit programme and the composition of the team is required.
3. Some companies have a policy of allocating only a fixed period of time (so many man-days, for example) for the performance of an audit. If this period does not include any allowance for the time spent in travel, a team of experienced auditors will be needed to make the most of the time that will remain for the audit itself.
4. Ideally, all the information required should be obtained on the first visit to each location, to avoid the expense and delay involved in having to return to gather more data later on. The auditor will need to be experienced enough to assess the type and volume of information required, not merely for the audit at that particular location but also for later auditing activities at other sites.
5. Inter-team communication can become a problem. If the audit team is composed of two or three sub-teams, each responsible for auditing at a different location, it may not be possible for the audit team to exchange views by meeting every evening and telephone communications may prove inconvenient and expensive (particularly where a multi-national operation is involved). The outcome may be that the teams lack the information they need to co-ordinate their activities.
6. The audit team must pay attention to the communication systems in operation between the various auditee facilities i.e. the methods by which information is passed. The risks are that quality problems can arise through misunderstandings or vacuums. Geographically dispersed companies commonly rely heavily on electronic data transfer and the audit team will need to audit the quality management systems used for this. This will also include assessing whether or not adequate back-up has been considered

and provided for the event of malfunction, outage or power failure. Companies that operate with minimum inventory and Just in Time (JIT) policies are particularly vulnerable to communication disruptions.

The large industrial or office complex

Sometimes the auditor finds that the facilities he has to investigate are comprised of a vast and sprawling complex. There may be a large office block that contains the engineering department; a building for the sales department; another building housing the research and development group and so on.

This type of layout poses similar problems to those of geographic dispersion. It is important to minimize the amount of walking about that the audit team has to do, not only to cut down on time wastage but also to avoid over fatigue and loss of efficiency. It may make sense to split the audit team into two or three sub-teams, so that each can concentrate on one geographical unit, with a daily meeting being held to discuss progress. It is useful to have a map of the organization's layout drawn up when the audit is being planned, so that the audit team can familiarize themselves with the terrain and avoid tiring and time wasting mistakes.

The small company

The small company poses its own unique problems. Within a small company, it is common to find "multi-functional" people — i.e. people responsible for performing more than one function (an engineer who is also responsible for purchasing, for example). The idea of a unit may, at first sight, appear difficult to apply.

The efficency of this type of company tends to depend particularly heavily on the capabilities of the people involved since channels of information tend to be informal: their ability to keep themselves and others supplied with up-to-date information is also vital. Not everyone possesses the memory or organizational powers to achieve this and small firms often suffer from their lack of formal procedures. The attempt to do without the latter can prove a false economy and, as the following example shows, may put the small firm at a real disadvantage when competing for a large contract (especially in an area such as aerospace or the nuclear industry where a lot of documents and records must be produced).

> One firm was virtually a one many company: the owner was salesman, engineer, chief machinist, welder and draughtsman. The company had a good order book and produced a high quality product. However, it became obvious during a pre-award survey that the company would be unable to cope with the vast amount

of paper-work necessary to handle a contract in accordance with the ASME Boiler and Pressure Vessel Code[1]. To make matters worse, the owner spoke very little English. The solution found was that the customer would prepare and institute all the procedures, instructions, and design calculations necessary for compliance with the ASME code. Fortunately, the quality assurance standards do not preclude the provision of such support.

One of the tasks of the pre-award surveyor should be to assess the work load and capacity of the company's personnel and to report on any support needed to handle the contract. In the above example, it also became obvious that the owner was overworked and was omitting to keep himself fully informed of all the minute details of the potential contract.

Regardless of how small the company is, the precepts of organizational planning and of considering the task elements (see Chapters 5 and 25) for each activity still apply if quality is to be achieved. This means that the auditor takes each task in turn, considering the inputs, outputs and the actual process itself within the limits of the responsibilities and authority which have or should have been assigned to that task. It is important to keep within the confines of one task at a time and to ensure that the auditee does so as well: otherwise the audit becomes chaotic and unsystematic. Such lack of order eventually means that neither party can be sure of all aspects having been covered since the tendency will have been to "jump around".

The time required to audit to a systems depth is not too different in the case of a small company or of a large one: often the same number of activities are involved. Moreover, since small companies are frequently less formalised, there may be more sifting and analysis required of the "quality management systems". Compliance audits can be a different matter, though, because there is more objective evidence to be studied in large companies than is the case in small ones.

References:

1. American Society of Mechanical Engineers Boiler and Pressure Vessel Code is published by the American Society of Mechanical Engineers, 345 East 47th Street, New York, NY 10017, USA.

5. The Four Task Elements

Each morning sees some task begin,
Each evening sees it close;
Something attempted, something done,
Has earned a night's repose
Henry Wadsworth Longfellow.

Introduction

Once the auditor has settled in his own mind the organization of work and the tasks involved in the auditee's enterprise, his next step is to analyse what each task involves so as to establish exactly what he should examine.

Many years ago, when I first became involved in quality assurance and auditing, there were few standards or texts to assist an auditor in his work. The standards did not seem especially lucid and out of necessity I formulated the four task elements and their sub-elements to guide me through auditing and other quality assurance duties. Applying these four elements and sub-elements has enabled me to analyse every work situation I have encountered in developing quality management systems and in auditing, from that of chief executive officers to workshop tasks, service functions and support staff roles, such as accounts receivable and R & D. They have never let me down and the many students from around the world and countlessly diverse industries who have attended my training courses have subsequently had the same experience.

These elements have remained unchanged although in the first edition of this book, which was written in 1978, ''DOCUMENTS'' were considered to be the fourth element whilst in this second edition, that element is dubbed ''INFORMATION'' in order to reflect the increasing dominance of modern information technology and its applications.

In recent years, I have also developed the task element ''ITEM'' so as to create a fifth task element, ''SERVICE'', which is discussed separately in Chapter 25.

Since the first edition, two minor changes have been made to the sub-elements purely for the purposes of clarity. Firstly, whereas I used to consider an item's capability whilst auditing its ''correct type'', I now consider it to be a sub-element in its own right. Secondly, I have renamed the sub-element ''correct generation'' ''correctly checked''.

The four task elements

With the exception of services, every task unit comprises a set of up to four elements, which is necessary for proper performance of the task. The elements are:

THE PERSON — someone to perform or supervise the task;

THE ITEM(S) — something on which to work, such as a component, sub-assembly, raw material, foodstuff, consumable, effluent;

THE EQUIPMENT — the tools and facilities required to perform the task;

INFORMATION — the software and knowledge that are either received or generated by the particular task unit and which is transmitted by means of paper, magnetic, electronic or other methods. Examples of this are specifications, records, computer print-outs, tapes, disks, invoices, labels, stickers, bar codes, drawings, reports, etc.

Each task element has to be audited in order to audit the task unit fully. Fig. 5.1 depicts the four task elements with their sub-elements. (In the case of service activities Fig. 25.1 shows the same four task elements together with the additional task element ‘‘service’’.)

The chain of tasks that comprise a complete quality management system, whose function is to create the finished product or service, is only as strong as its weakest link. Each task element has to be performed correctly if the quality of items or services supplied is to meet the customer, user or community requirements.

The amount that one unit can accomplish also depends on the activities of the units upstream, which supply its input. Similarly, the given unit must satisfy the input demand of other units further downstream. One must remember that the computer maxim ‘‘garbage in, garbage out’’ (GIGO) is applicable to every task. One other important cause of ‘‘garbage out’’ is that the processing unit has processed correct input incorrectly.

The most important of the task elements is THE PERSON. It does not matter how clever the quality management systems are, ultimately they all depend upon human intervention and effort for their success. People are the final determinants of how effective the quality management system will be in practice and therefore of how good the product itself will be. John Stuart Mill rightly observed:

‘‘The worth of a state, in the long run, is the worth of the individuals composing it’’.

Fig. 5.1 The four task elements

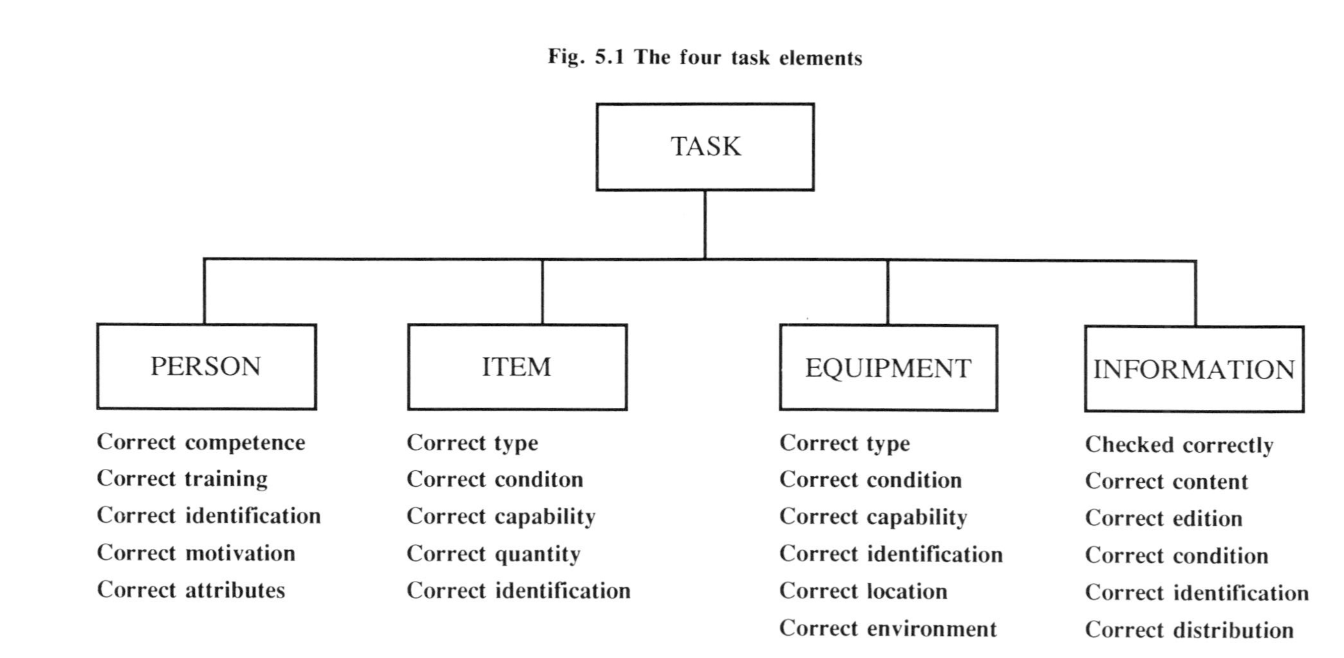

Nonetheless, the auditee should have a system whereby the needs of those work activities being performed, the associated job descriptions and job specifications, are defined so as to assist with the correct selection of individuals for the particular tasks. Job descriptions and job specifications have been discussed in Chapter 4.

THE PERSON

Competence

The person who has to perform a task must be competent to do so. Every task requires a certain degree of experience: some may also call for formal qualifications. No person who falls below the level of competence required should be employed to perform the task in question. In some industries, there may be a need for the individual assigned to a particular task to have completed an examination specifically designed to evaluate the competence level achieved. Registered professional engineers, airline pilots, doctors, drivers of heavy goods vehicles and company accountants are all examples of this type of scheme.

Competence is the *demonstrated* ability of a person to perform a task correctly and completely, right first time. The type of competence that a person will require should be stated in the job specification. Competence is established by means of evaluating the results obtained either by performing the task or by producing a prototype of the product. These are the only worthwhile means of qualifying a person to do any particular job.

The auditor should look for objective evidence to prove that:

- the competence level required for each position is carefully determined;
- the competence level is consistent with the needs of that position (and the product that should result);
- the competence level is consistent with the codes, standards and regulations that apply to the task concerned;
- the person has demonstrated the ability to do that job properly;
- the auditee's management monitors the individual's achievements in order to verify that the requisite competence levels are maintained.

Training

No matter what their ability or experience, people should still receive proper training in performing the tasks assigned to them.

Training and competence are entirely different matters. Some people may undergo extensive training in the skills and knowledge required in a particular task but this does not guarantee that they have learned anything or that they can apply this knowledge such that the product will be made right first time.

The training requirements of an individual need to be defined in terms of:

a) The function and requirements of the company's and the department's product.

> At one supplier of servo-mechanisms, the assembly personnel were trained thoroughly in assembly of the servo-mechanisms. However, the inspectors, who were supposed to inspect the operators' work and to provide guidance on the assembly of products, had not been trained in assembling the servo-mechanisms. As it turned out, they were "trained" by the assembly personnel. Bad habits as well as good ones were learnt.

b) The contribution of the individual to those products.

Training people to understand the contribution that they make to the final product is a good way of obtaining operator commitment, interest in the job and increased motivation.

> A company was experiencing a general and widespread number of quality problems of varying magnitude. The workforce seemed to work reasonably well but did not appear enthusiastic about the work. With the agreement of the management, the entire staff was taken on a visit to see an example of the final product under construction at a customer's premises. Everyone was entertained to lunch, shown a film and models of the finished product and allowed to ask whatever questions they wished. After the return to work, it was remarkable the following week how people at all levels evinced a greater interest in the product by identifying their efforts with it. Quality problems rapidly disappeared.

c) The skills and knowledge required for the actual task.

It is always dangerous to assume that somebody may have the level of basic knowledge that one possesses oneself.

> Some years ago, a friend of mine had been working on a large construction project in a third world country. In order to create as much employment as possible, there was extensive use of local labour. Much of this labour had never seen such a construction site before and was unfamiliar with even the basic tools used. My friend recalled how one day he emerged from his hut to see two labourers with a wheelbarrow that contained concrete. Apparently there was one at the front of the wheelbarrow and one at the back. He gently persuaded them that it would be more convenient to make use of the wheel.

That is a somewhat dramatic example which does, however, have its modern equivalent.

> I was once called to a manufacturer of microelectronic products who was unable to understand why the tiny components were experiencing extensive damage caused by static electricity. Earthing wrist bands for the female operators, conducting work pads, tote pans and the like had all been provided: everything was securely earthed to the bench. However, by standing back from the workplace, one could see that the ladies had cut small rubber mats from some jointing material and placed them under the feet of each work bench. The reason for this was that they did not like the squeaky movement of the benches against the floor. They had effectively insulated the only electrical path to earth able to prevent static damage. Investigation revealed that the ladies had no knowledge either of the problem of static damage or of the importance of maintaining the earth. They each received subsequent training in such matters. The rubber mats were left in place and the benches were correctly earthed.

The nature of the task might be such that it is affected by statutory requirements for specific training, safety and emergency procedures, for example. The auditee must consider the circumstances and ensure knowledge of the regulations applying to the task is provided by means of proper training prior to the individual commencing the functions assigned to him/her.

d) The capability of their department and the company.

> One company became involved in a contract for the supply of pressure containing equipment to the United States. A condition of the contract was that the equipment must be certified according to ASME construction standards. The salesman who negotiated and signed the contract did not consult his quality assurance department to ascertain whether or not the company had or could obtain an ASME certification. With only a few months to go before manufacturing was scheduled to begin, it was realized that obtaining such a certificate was going to pose major problems and create a major expense for the company. The pressure equipment was a standard product line made from a material not recognized by ASME. A complete switch in manufacturing and fabrication methods was required to accommodate such a major change. A complete reappraisal of the design was also necessary and much retraining of the employees involved in welding. The costs were horrendous.The salesman not knowing what signing such a contract would mean to the company or that a requirement

contained in a clause two sentences long, occupying half an inch on one page, would be so significant. Had the salesman been trained in the company capabilities and product, the situation might never have arisen.

e) The department and the company quality management systems.

Many managements seem to suffer from the mistaken belief that this type of knowledge spreads through the company by some sort of osmosis, being absorbed automatically. The process of discovering how wrong this is can be very expensive. In spite of theories about telepathy, I have yet to encounter during an audit any person who possesses the attributes of a "Midwich Cuckoo"!

f) Retraining.

Regular retraining of the person is also necessary whenever the competence level appears to diminish and whenever the job circumstances, such as the technology used, regulatory requirements or the product itself, alter: the auditor should verify the auditee's arrangements on this matter.

g) Training for future assignments and career development.

Organizations must recognize adequately the need to train people not only for today's position but also for the position that management anticipates them holding in the future. Without proper training and preparation for the next position or promotion, there is the ever present likelihood that the Peter Principle will be demonstrated. Every function, from chairman of the board downwards, requires certain skills and knowledge for it to be performed properly and for its product to be right.

In sum, everybody in the company, regardless of their reporting level, needs continual training, retraining and training for tomorrow's circumstances.

Training often fails through the allocation of insufficient resources. Accordingly, the auditor should check that the requisite resources for proper training have been correctly defined and apportioned by top management. Benjamin Franklin shrewdly stated:

"investment in people pays the finest dividends".

Without proper allocation of the resources required for training, a company is failing to invest in its future. No matter how far or how fast technology moves and whatever new fangled pieces of equipment the company may buy, ultimately, people are always required: it is their skill level which will determine how well those technical resources are applied also fixing the return on investment. Sadly, though, training is one of the most neglected areas in most companies. It is one of the six real causes of quality problems, as listed in Chapters 1 and 18.

With these matters in mind, the auditor should look for objective evidence that proves:

— the skill and knowledge requirements for the successful accomplishment of the job are properly defined in its job specification;
— the training requirements of each individual are properly planned, budgeted and completed;
— the training is consistent with the requirements of the codes, standards and regulations that apply to the task and the product;
— the training is consistent with the needs of the product and is effective such that competence can be achieved;
— the auditee's management monitors the individual's development needs and achievements in order to verify that the requisite training programmes are effective.

Identification

Some system of identifying employees is needed because it is essential to be able to tell who has performed each task. There are various methods of identification: the person's name, employee number, initials, a special number and stamp issued to each person or a user name for those using a computer terminal.

Work must be traceable to the person who actually performed it. This is so that when the job is correctly accomplished and the product is fit for purpose, the person responsible may receive due praise and credit for his or her efforts. Likewise, so that when things go wrong, it is easier to determine who has been responsible and then to decide what further training is necessary in order for the person to achieve or regain the requisite competence. In Chapter 1, it was stated that one of the benefits of performing audits is the unbiased assessment of individuals. There is a trend towards the increasing use of audits to assess peoples' performance regularly and to provide appropriate reward and career development.

The auditor should look for objective evidence that:

— means of uniquely identifying the individual assigned to a task are defined and communicated to those who need to know;
— those means are solely used in practice;
— those means are effective such that traceability of items processed, services supplied, equipment handled and information used or created by that individual is possible.

Motivation

Lack of motivation leads directly to poor quality output and tends to raise costs. Hence, it is something to which an auditor should be alert even though it is a matter to which the QA standards do not refer.

Motivation can be affected by factors such as inadequate working conditions, obnoxious superiors, responsibility incompatible with authority, lack of career prospects, inadequate pay. People can become demotivated when they find that in comparable local companies or in other companies within the same industry, the pay levels and conditions are better than their own. When staff find that they are required to use outdated equipment, that other organizations provide better training and staff development programmes or invest in new technology, they can become despondent and disinterested in their job.

An audit should ascertain how such factors are being assessed by the auditee. This could involve dealing with sensitive situations which are further discussed in Chapter 13.

Motivation is not easy to assess but the "vibrations", reactions and body language of the individual being audited can be very telling. An indifferent attitude, avoidance of eye contact, body tension and hostility can all be signs that the motivation of the individual leaves something to be desired. (One must, however, be a little bit wary of over interpreting the meaning behind body language: "He looked at me in a funny way" is hardly the best kind of objective evidence on which to base conclusions and produce a sensible audit report.) Individuals can be very hard to gauge during any audit and experience is the only valuable guide. There is much truth in Charles Dickens' words that people contain "all those subtle essences of humanity which will elude the utmost cunning of algebra".[1]

With the above in mind, the auditor should look for objective evidence that :

— the auditee's management constantly monitors the employment conditions available in the same industry and in local industries;
— work incentives which include career prospects and investment in individuals are not neglected;
— the auditee's management ensures that employees are treated with dignity and respect by their supervisors and others.

Correct attributes

The appropriate attributes will vary from task to task. Good eyesight is an example of an attribute commonly required in manufacturing industry and inspection, particularly nowadays, when microelectronic engineering may involve a product being assembled underneath a microscope. The requirement for "good eyesight" may entail not only accuracy but also good colour vision — the ability to distinguish between different colours of electrical wiring or lamps on a control panel, for example, may be vital. Steady hands may be a necessary attribute for a different task: one would naturally be reluctant to employ a brain surgeon who suffered from delirium tremens. Hearing might be important — a tone deaf piano tuner would be unhelpful to a concert pianist. The needs of the product and the task performed might also require combinations of different attributes, such as eyesight and dexterity (a dentist filling a tooth) or eyesight and taste (a food grader).

Other attributes that may be important can include:

- honesty, for those people who are handling money or other moveable assets (a matter of increasing concern, nowadays, with the advent of modern computerized accounts and stock control systems, which have led to the rise of computer fraud — see Chapter 25);
- integrity, particularly in the case of those people who are performing audits;
- health, where food or pharmaceuticals are being processed or in the case of hospital staff, for example.

> An audit of a food factory revealed that its quality assurance manager found difficulty in understanding why there should be proper health checks and monitoring of staff coming into direct contact with the product to prevent any communicable disease being passed on to customers. His argument "It's never happened so far" sounded hollow. He does not work there any more: management diagnosed that he carried a disease called stupidity, and decided that a humanectomy was the most appropriate corrective action!

Attribute levels, such as eyesight or hearing, might also be stipulated by the regulations that apply to the task. Insurance companies might have restrictions on inadequate attribute levels, such as health factors (heart disease, epilepsy, disabilities) that could affect the risks associated with the task: these need to be considered prior to assigning an individual to the job.

The system for control of most attributes can be adequately assessed by an auditor since so many of them can be tested. The auditor will investigate the stringency of acceptance criteria for those tests as well as the scheduled and actual frequency of those tests being performed. All must be consistent with the needs of the product, process and the industry concerned. Assessing the systems which consider the honesty of employees is an extremely sensitive issue which requires careful handling through appropriate question technique. See Chapter 13 — "Sensitive situations".

With these things in mind, the auditor should look for objective evidence to prove that:

— the attributes required for successful accomplishment of the task are properly defined in a job specification;
— the attributes possessed by the person are consistent with the requirements of the codes, standards and regulations that apply to the task and to the product;
— those attributes are consistent with the needs of the product and enable competence to be achieved;
— the auditee's management monitors the individual's attributes in order to verify that the requisite levels are maintained.

When performing the audit, the auditor should leave the PERSON task element until last. This enables him to ascertain the level of competence, attributes, motivation and training that the equipment, service, items and information require. It is then easier to ascertain whether or not the auditee possesses them. See also the discussion in Chapter 13 — "Useful sequence for questioning".

THE ITEM

The term "Item" is an all-embracing term that may refer to:

— a component, a part, a sub-assembly, raw material, an engineered system or a finished assembly;
— consumables such as the dye penetrant for dye penetrant testing; the filler material and flux used in welding; paint and coatings that are applied to finish or protect a deliverable product, such as a motor vehicle; the chemicals (ingredients, additives, starters) in process baths and chambers that, by virtue of the process, become part of the product delivered to the next work-station, user or customer;
— fluids and liquids that are being processed into a saleable product (for example, milk being processed into cheese; gases being liquified; blood being passed through a dialysis machine; wine being decanted; oil being centrifuged);
— by-products and industrial wastes whose "quality", or lack of it, could affect the company's costs and liability risks (for example, sludges; sewage; radioactive crud; heavy metals — of the non "musical" variety; smoke-stack discharges; toxic liquids, compounds and substances);
— materials used for packaging and protecting the various types of items listed above.

The auditor will first establish the items received at the auditee's workplace and the items to leave the auditee's workplace. For each one, he will consider the sub-elements described below.

Correct type

The correct type of items to be processed and any consumables required must be issued to the person who has to perform the task: clearly, they must be what the designer or specialist has specified. They must be selected in accordance with codes, standards or regulations that apply to the product, process or industry concerned. The type of item selected must also be compatible with the other items with which it will come into contact so that their mutual conditions are not impaired and so that there is no risk to safety.

The auditor will look for objective evidence which proves that:

— the correct type of item(s) is defined for the task to be performed and is communicated to the workplace;
— the type of item(s) is consistent with code, standards, regulations which apply to the task being performed;
— the type of item(s) is consistent with the needs of the task and ultimate product concerned;
— the correct type is issued to the workplace for processing;
— the correct type of item(s) is released from that workplace for subsequent processing or use.

Correct condition

An item must possess certain dimensional and similar physical characteristics, if it is to achieve the correct condition. Other features could include the item's chemical or biological properties such as inertness, acidity or asepticism, for example. Another important aspect of an item's condition is its readiness for the process and consequently matters such as the temperature, homogeneity, clarity, radioactivity etc. need to have been both considered and achieved. Naturally these considerations apply not only to the condition of the item on its arrival at the workplace but also on its departure.

Unless the items are in a condition suitable for processing or for use, money will be wasted. Examples of items in unsuitable condition might be those that are unclean or excessively eroded, corroded, bent, torn, scratched, damaged or otherwise unusable. To ensure that goods stay in a suitable condition, they need to be correctly handled and stored. Handling and storage are matters that are too often neglected in industry. It is not uncommon to find finished ferrous castings left to rust in the rain; expensively machined parts rusted up; chemicals that have gone stale; rubber products, such as seals, that have been allowed to perish; clothing materials or garments that are dirty or stained being supplied to the fashion industry; food packaging that has become damaged or cosmetically impaired so that customer satisfaction and expectation is unfulfilled. The list is endless. The inadequate handling and storing of goods pours money down the drain. Thus one can see that the auditor is verifying that the auditee is protecting his company's (and hence the customer's) costs and assets. Auditors frequently identify inadequate handling and storing practices which provide an opportunity for the reduction of avoidable costs.

One crucial aspect is the safe condition of the item. This requirement applies to incoming items; items that are combined or come into contact with each other; items being sent out for delivery to the customer or user and by-products, such as effluents and discharges, that could affect the community or its environment.

The auditor will look for objective evidence to prove that:

- the correct condition of the item(s) arriving at and leaving from the workplace is fully considered and communicated to the workplace;
- only items that are in the correct condition are issued to the workplace;
- the correct condition of the items arriving at the workplace is protected at the workplace until the items are required;
- the correct condition of the items for delivery to the next process, customer or user, is achieved and protected by that workplace;
- inherent hazards associated with the item(s) are known and controlled;
- hazards that can arise through incorrect processing or by virtue of the process are both known and controlled at that workplace;
- codes, standards and regulations concerning the condition of items are met at all times in that workplace.

Correct capability

There are three aspects of capability that are of importance, these being the basic capability of the raw material used, the functional capability of the item achieved by virtue of its design and inherent safety capability.

Basic capabilities to be considered are those that arise out of the item's chemical, biological and physical attributes. Physical properties (such as melting point, boiling point, tensile strength, impact resistance, conductivity, resistivity, density, viscosity, elasticity, missibility, coefficient of friction, atomic mass etc.) as well as chemical constituency and biological analysis are features that enable the functional requirements for the item to be achieved.

Form and dimensional size, finish and the like endow an item with load bearing, air or other fluid resistance, electrical resistance, capacitance, fatigue and creep resistance, along with other similar functional capabilities. Additional functional requirements such as reliability, maintainability, availability also need to be considered in the case of those items that will become the equipment at another workplace; these are discussed in the section "Equipment — correct capability" (page 5-20).

In order to achieve a safe condition, the basic materials used must possess capabilities which ensure their ability or inability to come safely into contact with, or be mixed with, other items. In the case of effluent, for example, the inherent capabilities such as radioactive half life, virulence or toxicity need to be considered by the auditee in order that the safe condition can be achieved, if necessary by encapsulating the item in specially designed equipment.

The auditor will look for objective evidence to prove that:

— the correct capability of the item(s) arriving at and leaving from the workplace is fully considered and communicated to the workplace;
— only items that have the correct capability are issued to the workplace;
— the correct capability of the items arriving at the workplace is protected at the workplace until needed;
— the correct capability of the items to be delivered to the next process, customer or user, is achieved and protected by that workplace;
— inherent capabilities that can cause hazards are known and controlled;
— codes, standards and regulations concerning the capability of items are met.

Correct quantity

If 50 items are to be processed, the person performing the job must be issued with 50 items. All the items must be in the right place at the right time or — especially in the case of consumables — pressure of production deadlines may tempt people to substitute something that is not suitable. Giving way to this temptation can be a costly, even dangerous, mistake.

The auditor must be alert to the actual quantity of each item issued for it can be a good indication of quality process inadequacies and point to areas of opportunity for improvement. If, for example, when discussing the quantity issued to the operators, the auditor is told "We always give them 3 extra because we know that on average 3 items in 50 won't turn out right. That means we will have the right quantity in the end", the question to be asked is "Since that represents nearly 6% loss of yield what are you doing about trying to improve the process so that you can save this 6%?"

A majority of auditees fail to understand that a few fractions of one per cent, lost at each work stage, accumulate into a substantial failure cost and loss of revenue by the time a satisfactory product has been delivered to the customer.

> Whilst performing a particular pre-award survey, I ascertained that the cumulative effect of all of such extras being absorbed by various processes amounted to some 8% loss. I promptly advised my client to press for an 8% reduction in the contract price since there is no justification in paying for scrap, the costs of which are undoubtedly incorporated in the unit costs. I also advised him to press for a quality programme to ensure that defect free product would be supplied. The contract was worth in excess of $500,000 and my client obtained that 8% reduction. He also got his defect free supplies.

The quantity issued presents an immediate indication of the extent to which people get everything right first time and every time.

The correct volume of supplies is particularly important in some industries, such as the processing of nuclear fuels or the distillation of alcohol, since there are stringent requirements concerning the control and reconciliation of quantities. This is so that compliance with international laws, safety considerations or taxation requirements can be ascertained. Failure to comply with such matters can put a company at risk of loss. Another situation is one where the auditee has to pay a royalty or invoice to a commercial company on the basis of quantities actually used or consumed. The auditor needs to consider the systems and activities of the auditee in meeting his obligations accordingly in order to determine their efficacy.

The auditor will look for objective evidence to prove that:

— the correct quantity of items is specified for the task concerned and communicated to the workplace;
— the correct quantity of items is issued to the workplace;
— the quantity of items used or consumed by the task is known;
— the correct quantity of items is delivered to the next process, user or customer;
— code, standard or regulatory requirements concerning reconciliation of quantities are met.

Correct Identification

All items must be correctly identified either by means of a label on the item itself or its container or by a document accompanying it. A batch number, heat number, works number, contract number or similar systems may be used. In some cases, the identification may need to be unique to each individual item received by or released from the auditee's workplace. It is surprising how much material gets lost or is processed for the wrong contract or product line for want of proper identification.

A major purpose of identification is the need to trace the item to its information, the person who produced the item or the equipment used to produce it. The identification then permits any interested party to investigate further whether or not the item complies with its requirements in respect of type, condition, quantity and so on. In certain industries, such as food, pharmaceuticals or aircraft, where there is a risk to safety if an item does not meet requirements and is thereby unfit for purpose, the need for complete traceability of items is vital. Accordingly, the identification of the item may be constrained by industrial, market or statutory stipulations. Without a proper identification system, a product recall system will be difficult or impossible. It should, therefore, be readily apparent that identification of items is a matter which can affect the company's failure costs and liability position.

For some products, it is also useful for the auditee to develop a system of direct identification either on the item itself or by means of an accompanying document in order to indicate the individual who made it. This has the benefit of linking ownership to the person making the item, which can be a great motivator for quality achievement.

> A manufacturer of computers places a sticker inside the cabinet of completed machines. That sticker states the name of the person who assembled the machine and his home telephone number which the user is invited to call day or night if a problem occurs. Subtle!

The auditor will look for objective evidence to prove that:

— a method for correct identification of items arriving at, used by and leaving from the workplace is defined and communicated to that workplace;
— the method is consistent with the requirements of the codes, standards and regulations that apply to the items used or produced by that workplace;
— items are correctly identified in accordance with that method;
— the method used to identify the items does not impair the correct condition of the item concerned.

THE EQUIPMENT

"Equipment" is a term that embraces:

— machines and process plant that are used directly to process items such as lathes, presses, robotic welders, flexible manufacturing machines, vats and vessels, cracking columns, dialysis units, refineries;

— support facilities such as electrical generators, refrigeration or freezing plant, air conditioning and filtering plant, illumination devices and boiler plant;

— buildings, including factories, warehouses and offices; structures, such as towers, chimneys and exhaust stacks; offices and access facilities, such as roadways, gangways, pathways, stairways, Jacob's ladders etc.;

— hand tools such as spanners, probes, brushes, scalpels; power driven hand tools such as solder irons, electric drills, saws, pneumatic grinders, paint spray guns;

— process utensils such as pans, beakers, strainers, pots;

— consumables and disposables including cleaning papers, swabs, tool bits; reusable fluids and liquids such as cutting oils, cooling water, recycled air or inert gas;

— transportation machines including aircraft, ships, trains, conveyor belts; lifting devices including cranes, fork-lift trucks, elevators and hoists;

— personnel clothing such as uniforms, space suits, diving suits, laboratory coats, surgical gowns, gloves, caps, helmets, visors and masks, boots and shoes;

— administrative aids, such as desks, chairs, filing cabinets; data processing equipment including computers, visual display units, printers, disk drives, CAD facilities;

— communications devices such as modems, telephones, telex and telefax machines, together with their optical and electrical cables;

— instruments and devices used for the measuring and testing of items being processed and manufactured such as ammeters, voltmeters, micrometers, stop watches and clocks, analogue gauges, tensile test machines, charpy test machines, johanssen blocks, ph meters; intermediate devices such as templates and patterns; comparison standards such as colour and texture swatches, samples.

As the reader will no doubt appreciate, all of the above examples of equipment need to be produced before they can be used. When they are being produced by their suppliers or contractors they are ITEMS: once they have been fully commissioned for their operational life at the customer or user workplace, they become EQUIPMENT for it is then that they have become tools to help the customer or user PERSON accomplish the task assigned to him/her.

During its operational life, the equipment will need to be maintained. During maintenance, it is processed as part of a maintenance TASK. When the auditor analyses that task, the equipment being maintained is considered to be the ITEM whilst the tools needed to perform that task are the EQUIPMENT.

The auditor will first establish what equipment needs to be supplied to the auditee's workplace, then determining what equipment will require maintenance. (Even though the equipment may not physically leave the auditee's workplace for maintenance, the auditor will consider that it has been passed over to another TASK UNIT for that purpose. The auditor will analyse that maintenance task separately if it is within the scope and objectives of the audit.) For each piece of equipment, the auditor will then consider the sub-elements described below.

In the case of simple clerical activities, the equipment required may be nothing more than a pen, a desk and a chair upon which to sit. But a filing cabinet may also be required so that documents can be organized, retrieved readily and not mislaid. The auditor will not dwell on such equipment beyond noting that it has been provided, observing, perhaps the general capacity and condition, unless it is to be located in an environment which demands strict cleanliness or decontamination procedures in order to protect the condition of the items being processed.

Correct type

It is essential that the equipment used to perform the process is of the correct type for the purpose concerned. The quality of the item being processed often suffers when substitute or ''make do'' types of equipment are used in an emergency or if the equipment is incompatible with the items with which it comes into contact. In certain industries, the type of equipment and materials used in the item's construction might be restricted by codes, standards and regulations. Even in the absence of such restrictions, the auditee's company or the customer might have its own standards that govern the choice available. Naturally, legal regulations will take precedence.

The auditor will look for objective evidence to prove that:

— the correct type of equipment for the task being performed is defined and is communicated to the workplace;
— the correct type of equipment is issued to the workplace;

— the type of equipment is consistent with code, standards, regulations that apply to the task being performed;
— the type of equipment is consistent with the needs of the task concerned;
— the correct type of equipment is handed over to those responsible for maintaining it or disposing of it.

Correct condition

Aspects of the equipment's "condition" which must be considered are:

maintenance; calibration; cleanliness; handling; security and safety.

The equipment must be in the correct condition to perform the task, being handled in a manner that prevents degradation to itself and to the items and information being processed. The equipment must be marked to indicate its current condition, its maintenance or calibration status and its operability. For machine tools and other equipment, many companies operate either a planned maintenance system or a condition monitoring scheme. Maintenance and calibration of equipment is a service function. All equipment, especially sensitive instruments, gauges or machines, must be handled properly to avoid damage and inaccuracy.

> During one audit, it was noted that the master set of gauges were handled extremely roughly by the calibration department personnel. Upon close examination, the master gauges, a set of Johannsen blocks, were shown to be badly scratched and marked.

Since equipment represents company assets, it is important to protect against pilferage or other forms of loss. One of the advantages of an audit is that the auditor can verify that the equipment which has been issued to a particular auditee is being properly protected and is still in existence.

In certain applications, the equipment may need to be clean in order that damage to or contamination of the item(s) being processed is prevented (in the food or pharmaceutical industries, for example). The auditor must acertain what type of damage is unacceptable prior to investigating the effectiveness of the auditee's controls. Factors such as dirt, liquids, chemicals, microorganisms and detritus may all be unacceptable.

Equipment safety always needs to be considered. Some industries have regulations that relate to specific types of equipment such as aircraft, boiler plant, freezer rooms. These regulations generally cover inherent features that the designer and supplier must incorporate into the equipment as well as operational constraints. The PERSON responsible for the task must be aware of, trained in and competent with regard to these. These operational factors might also include stipulations concerning permissible running hours between periodic maintenance and inspection tasks — the auditee will need some means of knowing when those permissible hours will be exceeded.

The auditor must determine what (if any) regulations, guides, codes and standards apply. In some cases, the auditor may discover that there are no specific regulations or such like for a particular piece of equipment. Nonetheless, in most countries it will be be covered by a national regulation concerning general safety and associated practices such as the "Health and Safety at Work Act". Even if the scope and objectives of the audit do not specifically relate to safety, the auditor still has a civic responsibility to note any unsafe equipment or practice encountered during the audit and to bring this to the attention of the auditee's management.

The auditor will look for objective evidence to prove that:

- the correct condition of the equipment arriving at the workplace is fully considered and communicated to that workplace;
- the correct condition of the equipment arriving at the workplace is protected until the equipment is needed;
- the correct operational condition of the equipment is known at all times by its user and that the equipment is not used in any other state;
- inherent hazards associated with the equipment are known and controlled;
- hazards associated with use and incorrect use of the equipment are known and controlled at the workplace;
- codes, standards and regulations concerning the condition of the equipment are met at all times in that workplace.

Correct capability

The equipment must have been tried out or established as suitable for the task required. New equipment must be shown to be capable of performing the task in hand, which might mean that it has been approved or licensed by a regulatory authority. Sometimes the qualification can be performed by processing the first piece. This is a commercial risk, a gamble that some contracts and some industries do not allow.

The capability of the equipment must be consistent with the task to be performed, with the items or the information to be processed. Thus size, capacity, payload, speed of response, flow rate of delivered fluid, height and reach, range, performance envelope, number of simultaneous users, are all types of capability that may be important. In the case of equipment used for preventing and coping with unsafe situations, its capability to do so, fire pump volume and head, for instance, will be matters for regulatory compliance. In all cases concerning equipment capacity, the auditor needs to determine the appropriate units of performance measurement. In some cases, the auditor may discover that the capacity of the equipment is not being fully utilized. An example of this would be the excessive wastage of space in an office.

> The executives of an American company wished to hire new staff as part of the company expansion programme and thought it would be necessary to build a major extension to its offices. I accompanied one of the executive vice presidents around the offices and demonstrated that the staff were not using the space to best advantage. Result: approximately half million dollars' needless expenditure was avoided.

> A British company decided to introduce computer aided design equipment. The facility performed most impressively at first and the company quickly began to add more terminals for its engineers to use. As the response time started to deteriorate, they eventually came to appreciate that there is a limiting capacity to the machine and its software. An audit revealed that over a six month period the money wasted because high salaried design engineers had to sit idle, while the machine did its best to cope with the workload, exceeded the capital cost of the machine.

In the case of process equipment, its capacity to process the requisite quantity in a given period of time should be ascertained. For example, a conveyor belt which is required to transport 5,000 units per hour when, in fact, it can only deal with 4,650 units per hour will create a bottleneck. The capability of any production line is dictated by the slowest piece of equipment installed within that line.

A variation of this occurs in the case of services relating to the capability to serve the anticipated number of customers at a counter or desk, at a supermarket, bank or fast food shop. The number of tellers, booking agents, sales assistants, clerks and associated equipment required will be dependent on the volume of customers arriving in any given period of time and on the length of time a customer accepts as reasonable to spend in a queue. In designing and specifying such equipment, queueing theory becomes important and the auditor may need to verify that it has been correctly applied and encompasses an assessment of peak load requirements. A feature that can be of particular importance is the capability of the equipment to deal with safety related situations. The width of access passages and escape routes in relation to the authorized number of customers that might be present in an emergency is a case in point. There could well be regulations affecting such matters: the auditor will need to investigate this.

The auditor will look for objective evidence to prove that:

- — the capability of equipment is defined and verified prior to its commissioning and during its service;
- — the capability is consistent with the needs of the task and with the capability of the equipment with which it interfaces;
- — the capability of the equipment has been communicated to the user and is known at all times;
- — the capability of the equipment used by customers in a service situation is consistent with customer expectations and needs;
- — the capability of equipment is consistent with regulations, codes and standards.

In the case of measuring equipment, the capability is determined by means of calibration, range, accuracy and precision being the principle matters of interest. Calibration of equipment must be compatible with the needs of the item being processed as well as the risks associated with the process involved e.g. accuracy and precision of the measuring devices needed to prevent damage to the item or hazards to the people using the equipment that it is helping to control. An additional matter to be considered is that of the regulations applying to the task and its equipment: regulations concerning weights and measures, for example, and quantities sold to the public. The checking of instruments used to control safety related activities, such as aircraft in-flight instruments or boiler pressure gauges is an instance of the same.

The auditor should look for objective evidence to prove that:

- — the calibration of measuring and testing equipment is consistent with the needs of the task and the items or services affected;
- — the calibration is performed in accordance with national codes, standards and regulations;
- — the calibration is performed against known standards;
- — the calibration status of the measuring and test equipment is communicated to the user so as to be known at all times.

Another and vital aspect of equipment capability which needs to be established prior to commissioning and which requires to be continually verified during routine maintenance is its reliability. This has particular implications for equipment which can be safety related such as computers required for air traffic control. The auditor must ascertain that the supporting quality management systems for the maintenance of such equipment are adequate to maintain the correct monitoring and reliability of the equipment. This may also involve ascertaining that adequate back up has been arranged in the event of equipment unavailability. Equipment reliability and back up is a matter of considerable importance for those companies which offer services as their products. Services are dealt with more fully in Chapter 25. Depending on the audit objectives, it may be necessary to check the system used for equipment selection and the methods used to specify its reliability.

The reliability of equipment directly affects its availability which, in turn, affects profit. Unreliable equipment represents a failure cost to the company which must be avoided. The inherent reliability of equipment may be satisfactory when it is new and subsequently deteriorate during its life if the equipment is not properly maintained. However, maintenance itself can take time and cause the equipment to be unavailable in the interim. This represents a further cost, part of which may be avoidable, depending on the maintainability of the equipment. Maintainability of equipment is a particular capability which must be correct and designed in. Equipment maintainability and back up is another matter of considerable importance for those companies which offer services as their products. Depending on the audit objectives, it may be necessary to check both the system used for equipment selection and the methods chosen to specify its maintainability.

Maintainability and reliability are features of equipment that are affected by regulations in some industries. In the air passenger transport business, for example, the reliability of aircraft and constituent parts such as engines is a matter that needs to be demonstrated to the authorities prior to a certificate of airworthiness being issued; in the nuclear power business, the maintainability of equipment in a radioactively "hot" environment has to be quantified and determined to the satisfaction of the regulatory authorities involved.

Both maintainability and reliability are aspects of equipment capability that can render it obsolete as technology advances. Equipment that is still in perfectly good working condition can become a liability if competitors introduce more advanced types which reduce operational costs and thus improve their competitive price edge. In these circumstances, the equipment no longer possesses the correct capability even though its maintainability and reliability have not changed from what was previously acceptable. The auditor has a duty to advise the auditee management accordingly of the risks involved in not replacing the equipment. Those risks present a potential failure cost to the auditee.

The auditor will look for objective evidence to prove that:

— the correct reliability and maintainability of equipment is defined and verified prior to its commissioning and during its operational life;
— the reliability and maintainability are consistent with the needs of the task;
— the reliability and maintainability of the equipment is communicated to the user;

— the reliability and maintainability of the equipment used by customers in a service situation are consistent with customer expectations and needs;
— the reliability and maintainability of equipment comply at all times with regulations, codes and standards revelant to the tasks which the equipment is to perform.

Correct identification

Unless a piece of equipment is self-evidently exactly what it is, it should carry some form of exact identification — a works number, an inventory number or something similar. For example, in a ship's engine room, the machinery is often identified by its location so that when an engineer is told to start the "starboard for'ard generator", he knows exactly which generator is meant.

A major purpose of identification is the need to trace the equipment to its information, the products that it has helped to make, the service it has helped to supply and the people that have used it. The identification permits any interested party to investigate further whether or not the equipment complies with its requirements in respect of condition, type, capability, location etc. In certain industries such as food or pharmaceuticals, where there is a risk to health if the items produced or service supplied do not meet requirements and are therefore unfit for purpose, the need for complete traceability of equipment can be vital. Accordingly, the identification may be constrained by industrial, market, or statutory stipulations. Without a proper identification system, corrective action and further defect prevention would be difficult or impossible. It is therefore clear that identification can assist the company with its product liability prevention activities and, thus, help to avoid failure costs.

Correct identification assists in the management of the company assets and protection of the equipment from loss. It can also be important in the case of equipment that requires specific licensing such as aircraft call signs, motor vehicle registration numbers, pressure vessel tag numbers.

The auditor will look for objective evidence to prove that:

— a method for identifying equipment released for use is developed and communicated to the user;
— the method ensures compliance with the requirements of the codes, standards and regulations that apply to the equipment used and the tasks performed with it;
— equipment is correctly identified in accordance with that method;
— equipment released from the workplace to the next process, user or customer is identified in accordance with that method;
— the method used to identify the equipment does not impair the correct condition of the item concerned.

Correct location

It is part of the planning function to ensure that equipment is in the right place at the right time. There must be no temptation to substitute one piece of equipment for another.

The relative position of different pieces of equipment to each other can affect quality achievement. If, for example, a quenching tank is too far from a furnace, the items may lose too much heat during transfer to the pond and the correct condition after quenching will not be achieved. If an hotel kitchen is too far from the restaurant, the food may have become unacceptably cool by the time it is served to the customer. An illogical or inconvenient layout of equipment leads to excessive handling of items with all the attendant costs and risks of damage. Transportation of items is expensive given the equipment and energy, time, protective packaging, tote pans, pallets etc.; labour and administration required to move the original articles. Major opportunities for cost reduction are often revealed during an audit by attention to such matters. Layout of equipment represents an important aspect of quality planning and when the decisions associated with it are of poor quality, the failure costs can be considerable.

The location of equipment is a matter of regulatory interest in some industries. For example, the authorized operation of a North Sea oil platform is contingent on the operator proving that the platform has been installed precisely where the authorities have approved it. In most countries, the construction of buildings on land is confined to precise coordinates that have been approved by local or national authorities prior to action commencing. In some cases, the location of equipment may be a safety matter governed by regulations such as avoiding the installation of a non-explosion proof electrical apparatus in an explosive environment; keeping cattle or pig pens at a certain distance from food processing areas; avoiding the placement of air intakes for air conditioning equipment near to fume sources.

Another feature is the ergonomic layout of the workplace itself. If the various types of equipment used are inconveniently located in relation to each other and to the person performing the task, the risks of operator fatigue (which can lead to quality problems) and the possibility of industrial injury can occur. Depending on the scope and objectives of the audit, the auditor may wish to pursue the auditee's controls on ergonomic design and layout.

The auditor will look for objective evidence to prove that

— the correct equipment is issued to the correct location where the task is performed so as to be available when needed;
— the relative location of equipment used by consecutive tasks does not impair the correct final condition of the item concerned;
— the location of the equipment does not impair the service performed;

— the layout of equipment used at a workplace presents neither risk to anyone nor difficulty for use;
— codes, standards and regulations that apply to the location of the equipment for the tasks performed with it are met at all times.

Correct environment

The environment in which the work or process is being carried out can affect the quality of the item involved. Environments include office space, chemical baths and tanks, protective and working atmospheres and they must neither contain nor present a "nuisance". A nuisance may include, for example, noise, dust, vibration, static electricity, odours or contaminants. It may be necessary to take special measures to maintain the correct environment: a computer room will, for instance, generally require careful control of the temperature, dust count, pollen count and humidity, all within closely specified limits, records of the conditions achieved being kept for future reference.

The correct environment is, of course, most important in sensitive industries such as food and pharmaceuticals as well as in data processing or in the running of computerised equipment. As a case in point, a dairy factory may require close monitoring of the dirt, detritus and bacterial backgroud levels in order to prevent contamination of the foodstuffs being processed.

Other features of the environment that may need to be controlled can include temperature, ph, pressure, draughts, electro-magnetic fields, static electricity, bacterial count or microorganism levels. Each of these might be too high or too low: some might be unacceptably uneven, stratified temperatures or concentrations of liquids in a processing tank, for example. Lighting levels can present a nuisance: inadequate lighting in a drawing office or for the operator of a microscope can lead to eye strain, fatigue and mistakes; flickering fluorescent lights can lead to headaches and quality problems; neon lights can lead to changes in the appearance of colours used for coding of materials and thus to incorrect selection.

Regulations do govern the control of environments in certain industries where there can be a risk to health or safety. As part of the audit preparation, the auditor must ascertain which ones apply. The audit will then need to verify that the auditee has developed and implemented the systems and practices that will ensure compliance with those applicable regulations.

It is insufficient merely to check the condition of the environment for any nuisances. The audit must verify that the support systems necessary for creating and maintaining the correct environment have been thought through and are being properly implemented.

In a food factory's packing area, butter was fed through a chute onto the wrapping material and weighed. If overweight was measured, the operator removed some butter with his hands and replaced it in the the chute ready for further feeding through. In the event that underweight had been registered, the operator scooped some butter from the chute with his hands and patted it down into the carton. The auditor noticed toilet facilities were available adjacent to the packing area. He visited these and emerged quite concerned because the hand washing facilities available were inadequate.

Inadequate environment can affect the quality of the product drastically. The quality problems are often designed in rather than designed out. As customer expectation and specifications become inexorably more stringent, the result partly of competition offering products of higher specification, environment and equipment that would have sufficed at one time become totally unsuitable for today's and tomorrow's business. Even though it may be in good working order, it is obsolete. This holds particularly true in service industries.

Deregulation of the UK bus industry allowed private companies to compete more with the nationalized bus companies. These private companies sought long distance routes and introduced state of the art buses which featured video films, stewardesses to serve refreshments air conditioning and so on. The nationalized company which had held the monopoly discovered that many customers preferred the equipment of its new found competitors and was thus forced to renew parts of its bus fleet which were probably still serviceable but effectively obsolete. Buses are not cheap acquisitions.

I have visited many food factories whose walls and floors are covered by shiny porcelain tiles. At the time those factories were built, it was genuinely believed that such materials were perfectly adequate to ensure an hygenic environment. However, as knowledge increased, it became recognized that porcelain tiles easily become cracked, that the joints between them are not impervious and that the risk exists of biological or other contaminents building up within cracks and joints. Environmental cleanliness is then difficult to maintain.

It is always a major decision to replace the materials and equipment totally with modern ones. For this reason, prudent management lays aside an amount of money from the profits and allows it to accumulate such that new facilities can be financed. Lack of resources is a real cause of quality problems. Whereas an auditor may feel some sympathy towards the auditee, it does not alter the fact that if the product is suffering, if legislation has changed or the market and external circumstances have evolved such that the environment and equipment is no longer suitable, he has a duty to bring this to the attention of the management and to require corrective action. The auditor is being paid to do just that.

The auditor will verify that:

— the correct environment for performing the task concerned is defined and communicated to the user;
— environmental nuisances are defined and communicated to the user;
— the correct environment is maintained and nuisances are prevented and controlled;
— the environment defined and used does not impair the correct condition of the items contained within it or processed by it;
— the environment defined and used does not impair the service performed within it;
— the environment defined and used does not present a risk to those within it;
— codes, standards and regulations that apply to the environment and to the tasks performed within it are met at all times.

THE INFORMATION

Information is of key importance to human workers, machines and robots. It communicates the results of decisions made by people and of activities performed by machines. There is a fundamental difference between data and information. These have been most succinctly described in the British Standard 3527: PART 1: 1976 in the context of data processing[2] as:

DATA: "A representation of facts, concepts, or instructions in a formalized manner suitable for communication, interpretation, or processing by humans or by **automatic** means".

INFORMATION: "The meaning that a human assigns to **data** by means of conventions used in their presentation".

Clearly from a quality point of view, fitness for purpose depends on ascertaining how a person will interpret and apply data i.e what does the user of data consider to be information. Within this book, however, the term information will be used to cover both information and data. Information to be audited will be related to the task elements and their sub-elements information describing an item's condition, for example, information that records a person's training or competence; information describing the capability of equipment, information detailing the characteristics of a service and so on.

Documents are the most common means of transmitting information. A document is a written or pictorial means of conveying information. It describes, defines, specifies, reports or certifies activities, the requirements for performing activities or the activities' results. Drawings, specifications, procedures, instructions, records, radiographs, computer tapes and disks, purchase orders, process control charts and microfilm are all examples of documents.

Increasingly, however, information is also being communicated by means of visual displays, pulses of light and electronic signals. Whatever means is used, the sub-elements described later still apply.

The auditor will first establish what information needs to be received at the auditee's workplace and then what information will leave the workplace for use by others. There will always be some documents that a unit needs to keep for reference such as industrial standards, codes, agreed procedures, standard formulae: if statistical sampling is one of the unit's tasks, the sampling plans and associated instructions will remain within that unit. The resident documents may have been generated inside or outside the unit. The company expense procedure is frequently a document that is resident in a great number of units throughout a company but which is generated by one unit, perhaps the accounts department. Instructions on the use of equipment, particularly concerning safety features and practices, is a further example of resident information. The auditor should ascertain what is resident and what is not; what is created by that work task and what is not as well as determining the origin of each piece of information that the unit does not itself create.

For each piece of information, the auditor will consider the sub-elements described below.

Correctly checked

Checking is important and must not be abused. The auditor should be alert for "you sign mine — I'll sign yours" arrangements. Often auditees will fail to recognise that a major value of proper information reviews is that the preparer learns from any errors or omissions found. Reviews provide experience and assist in the raising of competence levels. This is an important part of training for the person charged with the responsibility of preparing the information. Failure to take checking seriously is often a cause of repeated mistakes which are costly. Frequently, supervisors are reluctant to verify firmly that their subordinates are capable of producing the right content of information first time around having assumed a level of competence and knowledge that does actually not exist. Such reluctance often stems from embarrassment about checking their subordinates' work or concern about appearing to be unreasonable or distrustful. That attitude does not help the staff to learn, develop and gain confidence: in the long term it is damaging both to the company, the subordinate and the supervisor.

Whereas independent review is valuable, essential in some industries, there should always be a "self check" performed by the preparer. The person performing a task is responsible for the quality of the work produced and should therefore not offer that work for acceptance without having first critically examined for completeness and correctness. It is wrong to waste one's colleagues' and customers' time by presenting unchecked work that contains avoidable mistakes. It is costly too.

A useful type of independent review is to ask the end user, wherever possible, to be involved. The end user determines whether or not the information really is fit for purpose. Accordingly, the auditor should consider whether the involvement of the user is feasible and ask the auditee whether or not it has been obtained. Some contracts or regulations might stipulate the involvement of the customer or a regulatory authority in the review process: the auditor must ascertain if such requirements apply. However, such involvements do not absolve the auditee of the responsibility for checking that the correct content of information has been achieved before its submission to them.

The extensiveness of the review and the degree of independence must be commensurate with the classification of the product and the task to which the information relates. (Classification is discussed in Chapter 3.) The auditor will look for evidence of planning the reviews and checks of information consistent with the classification required. Absence of such planning can prove both unwise and a false economy.

The auditor will look for objective evidence to prove that:

— the information checks are planned;
— the checks are commensurate with the importance and risk associated with the task and product to which the information relates;
— the planned checks include those required by the customer or regulatory body involved with the type of products or tasks to which the information relates;
— the methods of checking to be used are planned;
— the checking methods are commensurate with the importance and risk associated with the task and product to which the information relates;
— the checks are performed as planned;
— those who will perform the checks are provided with all the background information prior to the checks being performed.

Correct content

Information must have the content required both for the unit to perform its task and to enable subsequent units to perform the tasks which they are assigned. Some information a unit receives may be for its own use and some may be for the use of a downstream unit (a workshop traveller, for example, may contain the work instructions for an entire manufacturing sequence that comprises a large number of different units performing different processes): such documentation is passed through and is not necessarily generated by the particular unit.

The content of information must always be based on what the end user really needs as opposed to its creator's opinion of what those needs are. This is certainly true when the information is being created for the purpose of obtaining customer or regulatory approvals. Examples of this include applications for licences; applications for design approvals for safety related equipment; extradition applications. Of course, the content may be prescribed in applicable regulations, codes or standards and the auditor will need to determine what does apply and to verify that the auditee complies with those requirements. The auditor should examine the system to verify that there is a direct feedback of information from user to creator in order that mistakes are avoided or promptly rectified.

Prior to the creation of the information, the task unit will need to be in possession of other information describing the background and what is required. This is further discussed under ''Correct distribution'', see page 5-34.

The content needs to be clear, complete and unambiguous. The essence of information is to communicate something to someone. Completeness can be defined and ascertained but clarity and unambiguity are aspects of style that the information's creator either does or does not possess. That style can be improved but only if the problems are pointed out in the first place. Hence the need for good checking, discussed in the preceding section.

The auditor will look for objective evidence to prove that:

— the correct content of information arriving at and leaving from the workplace is fully considered and communicated to that workplace;
— the content of information is based on the user's needs and is commensurate with the importance and risk associated with the task and product to which the information relates;
— the correct content of information is achieved;
— codes, standards and regulations concerning the content of information are met at all times.

Correct edition

All information that is to be used to perform a task must be of the correct and valid revision. This is not so straightforward as it sounds. There may be a number of revisions that are valid throughout the company but only one of those may be relevant to a particular contract. This type of situation can arise with the ASME code which has addenda or revisions issued every six months. In this case, all the addenda can be valid since a contract is signed against a particular addendum and there may well be subsequent addenda in effect by the time the contract is completed: hence only one revision is correct for the particular contract, but a number of revisions are valid. It is the job of the unit responsible for generating particular information to distribute the correct and valid revisions to the units that require them and to stipulate which revision is correct for the task concerned.

The edition or revision of information must be clearly indicated by some means. An example would be drawings and specifications bearing a title block which contains the revision number or letter: approval certificates, licences and permits might bear start and expiry dates to indicate the period of validity.

Merely verifying that the correct edition is properly identified with that information is, however, insufficient. Upon discovering, for example, that a specification has reached, say, revision 9, pose the question ''Why does it take a minimum of 9 revisions to define the information that the user needs properly?'' Changing the information, checking it and distributing it is very expensive. Excessive revisions can be a good indication that the information has not been fit for purpose (although this is not always the case because sometimes the revisions show the continuing evolution of a product range throughout its saleable life). Often, though, constant revision highlights an area of considerable opportunity for cost reduction, improved efficiency and increased customer satisfaction. Constant revisions signal that the system is poor and there is a serious quality problem which deserves management's closest attention. The vast majority of effort in most companies nowadays relates to the creation, dissemination, absorption and use of information, activities which constitute probably the greatest part of the unit costs. The auditor must always follow up to find out why such profligate waste has occurred. The reasons for so many changes must be unearthed by the auditor.

The auditor will require proof that:

— a method for identifying the correct edition of information arriving at, used by and produced by the workplace is defined and communicated to that workplace;
— all information arriving at, used by or produced by that workplace is identified in accordance with that method;
— only the correct edition of that information is used at or distributed by that workplace;
— codes, standards and regulations concerning the edition of information to be used are met at all times.

Correct condition

Information can be transmitted by several types of medium nowadays and it is the medium that must be kept in good condition. The traditional medium has been documents comprising paper and ink which is susceptible to damage.

Such documents needs to be legible, clean and undamaged and stored and handled in such a way as to keep them in usable condition. One of the reasons why poor photocopies and indecipherable blue prints are so common is partly because in factories or on construction sites, they tend to be mistreated — left exposed to the elements, damaged by rain, sun-faded, covered with dirty fingerprints or torn. Another cause of poor quality documents and one which applies to all industries, is inadequate clarity of reproduction achieved through photocopying.

> At one engineering company, the workshop papers were simply stapled together into a bundle. This was such a size that a vast amount of thumbing through was needed to find any one document. Inevitably, the documents became grubby, torn, jumbled up, and unusable fairly rapidly, an inordinate amount of time having to be spent regularly checking the contents of the documents. The situation had carried on for so long and so many years that it had become accepted as the norm without question. By the simple expedient of changing the size and format of the workshop documents and putting them into a folder for issue to the shop floor, much time and effort were saved.

Where the information is distributed or stored in the form of magnetic media such as computer tapes and disks, this also means that proper protection must be provided to prevent degradation or damage which can be caused by physical abuse, stray electromagnetic radiations, heat, dirt, spilt fluids. Media such as floppy disks are easily damaged by careless handling, such as finger contact with the magnetic surfaces. Staff need to be informed that this type of contact must be avoided.

In some cases, the medium used is film, for example, radiographs, industrial or advertising photographs, micofilm records. Unless the films have been properly processed, there is a risk that the coating will be unstable and will degrade over time. It follows that for archive life applications, the auditee needs a condition monitoring system whereby the state of the files under storage is regularly assessed and compared to a control standard.

Damage and degradation can occur during use, storage or transportation: the above should have drawn the auditor's attention to the need to verify the methods and systems used to protect information and to maintain it in a condition that is fit for purpose at all times. Information creation forms a major part of business expense and product costs nowadays and one can see that there are monetary benefits in protecting the condition of the media on which it is held.

The above describes various means by which information could be lost. Another possibility is loss by theft. Theft can occur when someone steals documents, films, tapes or disks. It can also occur when someone uses electronic transfer: this is discussed in Chapter 24. Prevention of theft means that the auditee must design and implement a security system which covers physical and electronic removal of information. Loss can also occur when the information is destroyed before the statutory time for storage and retention has elapsed. The destruction may be either inadvertent or deliberate but it points to the need for security and a system whereby destruction must be authorized in writing only after a check has been made to ensure that legal or contractual requirements are not being violated.

The auditor will look for objective evidence that:

— the correct condition of information media arriving at and leaving from the workplace is fully considered and communicated to the workplace;
— the correct condition of the information media arriving at the workplace is protected in the workplace at all times;
— the correct condition of information media distributed to the next process, customer or user is completed and protected by that workplace;
— codes, standards and regulations that relate to the retention of information and the condition of its media are met at all times in that workplace.

Correct distribution

Distribution must be based on the finding out of who needs to know what, as opposed to the creator's opinion of who should receive the information. The auditor should ascertain that distributors advise potential users of the type of information that is available. With some products, it may be impossible to find out which users actually need information and some simulation may become necessary. The auditor should check how the distribution needs have been defined and how the organization then verifies that the distribution is in fact correct, such that all those who genuinely need to receive the information have in fact been sent it.

Distribution can be excessive with people who do not really need the information being sent it anyway: distribution can be inadequate with people who need information being unaware that it exists and thus duplicating effort by creating their own version. Basing distribution on actual need is cost effective. Audits can reveal unnecessary and inadequate distribution thereby contributing to savings, which can be considerable.

Information must have passed through the proper official channels before being released for use to any unit. No recipient should accept it without evidence that the correct approvals have been obtained if it does not appear to have been generated according to official practice. Although this is not required by QA standards, it is a simple and highly effective method of ensuring that information is released formally and properly. In addition, the unit responsible for issuing and distributing it should maintain a record or log of its distribution. The distribution list may be included with each copy of the information or it may be kept separately, depending on company practice.

It is also important that the auditee distributes the requisite information to the store or archive in accordance with statutory or contractual requirements. In Britain, for example, a company's financial records must be stored for six years for tax purposes; in the nuclear industry, it is normal for various types of record to be stored over at least the operational lifetime of the nuclear installation to which they refer.

The auditor will require proof that:

- the correct distribution of the information coming to and going from the workplace is defined and communicated to that workplace;
- all information arriving at, used by or produced by that workplace is correctly distributed;
- codes, standards and regulations concerning the distribution of information are met at all times.

Identification

Information must clearly state exactly what it is and to what it relates. Common examples of unidentified documents include design calculations not linked to any particular contract, product range or batch and that are therefore just an impressive looking collection of figures and equations; drawings that do not relate to a product line or a particular contract and purchase orders that contain no details of the contract for which the items have been purchased. Similar problems are found with spreadsheets created on desktop computers: floppy disks that are left unidentified or with indecipherable file names that have not been indexed or created under a formally established identification coding system.

In some circumstances, the identification might be constrained by statutory requirements such as tax codes, social security numbers or other numbers allocated by the local or national government. In such cases, the identifcation system and practices must incorporate those requirements.

The identification that must be available concerns:

a) what the information is (its name);
b) when it was created and which edition it is (see "Correct edition", page 5-31);
c) who created it and who authorised its release (see "Correctly checked", page 5-29);
d) where it belongs (in order to ensure its traceability to the person, services, item, equipment or other information to which or whom it relates).

The auditor will look for proof that:

— a method for correctly identifying the information arriving at, used by and produced by the workplace is defined and communicated to that workplace;
— all information arriving at, used by or produced by that workplace is correctly identified in accordance with that method;
— only correctly identified information is used at or distributed by that workplace;
— codes, standards and regulations concerning the identification of information to be used are met at all times.

References:

1. Charles Dickens, *Hard times.*
2. British Standard 3527: PART 1: 1976. *Glossary of terms used in Data processing: Part 1. Fundamental terms* British Standards Institution, Park Street London W1A 2BS. (Note that standard is the British edition of the ISO standard ISO 2382, Section 01 — 1974 *Data processing vocabulary: Fundamental terms*).

6. Standards for Management Systems

Men acquire a particular quality by constantly acting in a particular way.
Aristotle.

Many contracts now involve one or other of the internationally recognized QA standards and the appearance of the ISO 9000[1] series will result in this particular standard gradually dominating the others. The involvement of QA standards can be either direct, through contract requirements, or by implication, when a company holds out that it complies with those standards when furnishing its products, as in the case of advertising that the company has been successfully assessed against a certain standard. QA standards specify criteria that are essentially no more than good management and present guidelines for formulating a company's management systems. They attempt to communicate various features that the auditee's management systems must incorporate in order to provide an assurance that the contract requirements are being met and that the deliverable goods and services will be of acceptable quality. However, as with all forms of communication, they are open to misinterpretation. As a parody of the old wisdom about communication theory runs: "I know you believe you understand what you think you read. But I am not sure you realize that what you read is not what could be meant." The auditor must consider what the standards REALLY say. If the purpose of the audit is to audit for compliance with the requirements of a particular standard, the auditor has no right to impose his own interpretation of that standard on the auditee.

Although the QA standards share a common aim, as described above, naturally they differ on numerous points of detail and in their phraseology. Some differences are trite: others can be significant. It is possible to get a grip on these differences by studying some of the comparison matrices available. Generating one's own matrix to compare two QA standards is a far more valuable exercise, however, and one that should help to highlight the full implications of the precise language each standard employs.

When studying the criteria contained in the QA standards, the auditor must free his mind of preconceptions and prejudices, particularly those based on practices in use within his own organization. In the ISO 9000 series, for example, one phrase that crops up time and again is "establish and maintain". The auditor must at all costs avoid reading his own experience into this phrase when interpreting the standard. A number of different systems might satisfy the standard's words. Some systems may be cheaper than others and some may appear better than others but seldom will a standard dictate the detail of any specific type of system. All they require is that some particular activity is performed. Two companies with very different systems may satisfy the standards equally well. This fact begins to indicate the risks of relying on assessments performed by third parties who cannot interpret a standard for a particular customer's needs. The more imprecise or weaker the standard, the lower the value of a third party assessment and its resultant certificate. (This is further discussed in Chapter 2.)

When reading the standards, it is also necessary to combine various criteria in order to see what is required for a particular task unit. In relation to training, for example, ISO 9001[2] does not say merely that training of personnel is to be "established and maintained" in one or two departments only: it requires training throughout the company. This is because it refers to personnel "performing specific assigned tasks", an all encompassing phrase. Naturally, in every department of a company, everybody has been assigned certain tasks and therefore one sees that the requirement applies to everyone in the company. When discussing training, the standard also requires "appropriate records" to be maintained. The retention and control of "quality records", as distinct from "records of training", is treated in a separate clause. (Indeed the ISO 9001 is open to interpretation on this point and the definitions contained in ISO 8402[3] provide no adequate clarification of the differences between records and quality records, which in the contractual situation could pose difficulties. Frequently, though, training is considered to be a service and therefore the clause relating to "quality records" might apply but the auditor should approach this with some caution and feel sympathy for the auditee who cannot be blamed for the standard's vagueness.) If, however, the "records of training" are in document form then the ISO 9001 clause which concerns "document control" also applies to them.

An auditor must read the QA standards regularly. It is foolhardy to rely on memory or to assume that one knows them perfectly. It is a good practice to read the applicable standard before performing an audit, during the audit, and every now and then between audits. No auditor should be afraid of referring to the QA standards during an audit. Some auditors seem to think that they will lose face by doing so and appear to feel they ought to be able to quote the various paragraphs verbatim. In fact, the one sure way for an auditor to lose face is to assume that he knows the QA standard concerned and then to find that he has made a mistake.

Apart from the quality assurance standards, the auditor must be aware of the other pertinent criteria that can apply by virtue of the industry in which the auditee is involved or as the result of a specific customer requirement. These might include:

statutes; regulations;
codes of practice;
technical or professional standards; "guidelines".

The auditor must know and understand what the applicable requirements are and carefully take the sum of them. The same illustrative comments described above in relation to ISO 9000 etc. also apply to the consideration of these specific requirements.

Pitfalls in practice

It is easy for an uninitiated auditor to misunderstand what a code, standard or statute says, attempting to impose his own interpretation onto auditees. The ISO 9000 series will suffice to illustrate the main potential pitfalls:

1. Assumptions of consistency

Whereas ISO 9001 requires documents and data to be controlled, data is subsequently excluded from its stipulations for review, approval and change control. Clearly, proper control of data in accordance with the precepts of document control would be a most sensible activity for any organization. Indeed, in an era being ever increasingly referred to as the "information age", a company would be foolish to work strictly in accordance with the standard and ignore the need for full control of data. Failure to control changes in data fully, changes such as those pertaining to financial transactions and records or to safety related calculations could even render a company liable to prosecution. If an auditor is charged with auditing in accordance with that particular standard then this limitation of wording must be borne in mind such that an unfair corrective action request does not ensue.

2. Assumptions of content

ISO 9001 sets no timescale for implementing corrective action. The words "immediate" or "prompt" do not appear in that standard in connection with corrective action. Accordingly, unless otherwise specified by the prime customer, a supplier can take all the time in the world to implement corrective action yet still satisfy the standard. Commercial prudence, however, would dictate otherwise. Recognizing this problem, a satisfactory interpretation with the auditee has to be agreed.

ISO 9001 does not require management reviews to include the assessment of the results of internal audits: it merely notes that it would be a normal practice thereby permitting the abnormal.

It has long been recognized that quality management and quality improvement are primarily concerned with the prevention of quality problems through careful planning, the generally accepted outcome of such efforts being the quality plan: the benefits of such quality plans are well proven. No part of the series mandatorily requires the production of quality plans however. Whereas "NOTES" included in ISO 9001/9002[4] describe quality plans, they do not specifically require them to be produced. They state that "timely consideration needs to be given" — but what does this mean? If the auditee states that he did consider the matter and decided against them, then that is the end of the matter for he has complied with the standard and nothing more can be said.

This has implications in terms of means to verify that quality is being achieved. In brief, both ISO 9001 and 9002 indicate that unless there is a quality plan there is no need to perform final inspection or testing: certainly the requirements about receiving inspection then become so open to abuse as to be positively dangerous in the case of certain products.

3. Failure to cross reference

ISO 9001 requires internal quality audits to be performed. By cross linking with ISO 8402 (which is referenced, thus becoming an integral part of ISO 9001), these audits are to be performed by somebody who is independent of the activity which is being audited. However, there is no requirement whatsoever for them to be performed on a regular or a periodic basis. The ISO 9001 requirement is that they shall be scheduled but there is no indication as to the frequency of scheduling. An auditee needs only to perform such audits once every century to comply with the letter of the standard.

4. Unascertained scope

ISO 9000 series references definitions contained in ISO 8402, which only states what a product MAY be but not what it contractually SHALL be. This is a curious imprecision since the product is the *raison d'etre* of all quality management systems and of the company itself!

I consider a product to be:

an item;
an item's documentation;
a service;
software;
information;
by-products.

The fundamental product of human endeavour, though, is the "DECISION".

The most useful, thorough and comprehensive quality programmes are based on the quality of the decisions taken throughout the enterprise.

There are two ways of considering a product. The first is that a product is merely the end supplies (goods or services) that are deliverable under a contract to a customer: the second is that a product is anything that any person, department or work activity produces and furnishes to any other person be he within the company or outside the company (be he a customer, user or innocent bystander).

If the first meaning is considered to be the case, then the ISO 9000 series is certainly not directing its attention towards a company wide quality programme. If, however, the second meaning were to be taken then the ISO 9000 series becomes more extensive in its application. For the auditor, though, the correct interpretation will arise out of the audit objectives. If an external audit is to be performed, the meaning of "product" will be taken from superior documents that comprise the contract and define its scope; in the case of internal audits, the company policy towards the standard will prevail; in the case of pre-award surveys it will be the auditor company policy towards its suppliers' QA programmes that will influence the matter; in the case of third party assessments, it will be the published terms of reference for the assessment scheme that will prevail.

Another problem is in relation to "documents". Conventionally the term "documents" refers to hard copy or paperwork. However, in an era of information processing through electronic means, the word must necessarily have a different meaning if the standard is to have real relevance in this modern age[4]. Nonetheless, at the time of writing this book, no adequate definition was found in the ISO 9000 series of standards or in the ISO 8402 to which it refers. Accordingly, it is advisable for the auditor's organization to agree with the auditee upon the precise meaning of "documents" so that ill-advised corrective action requests are avoided as well as time consuming arguments. The auditor must ascertain the meaning to be ascribed to "documents" as part of the audit preparation. See also Chapter 5 under "Information".

Sensible compromise not senseless confrontation.

The above illustrates the need for an auditor to prepare properly and to take great care when applying the precepts of any code, standard or regulation. Over the years, there have been fruitless arguments, pointless squabbles and enmities caused by ignorant auditors attempting to interpret the meaning of such documents unilaterally and to dictate the actions which an auditee ought to take. Whenever there is any doubt, the sensible course is for auditor and auditee to agree upon a compromise understanding. This should also be the case for statutory auditors who might have the right to invoke a particular interpretation but do not have the right to abuse their authority and should always recognise that an honest mistake can be made by an auditee. To engage in a battle over an ambiguous, inadequate or imprecise standard is pointless. If the article of contention is a statute or regulation, legal interpretation or case example might be needed. Such potential points of misunderstanding should, however, have been identified and resolved prior to a contract.

> The ASME code[5] has been in existence for many years. ASME wisely recognized that it is impossible to write a standard that will fit all circumstances on all occasions. It therefore developed the "Code Case" system. Whenever two parties disagree on the interpretation of any part of the ASME code, they have the right to appeal directly to the ASME to obtain a ruling on the interpretation of its code. This ruling is decided by a panel of experienced and learned practitioners, their decision then being officially published as a "Code Case" which becomes the interpretation of the ASME Code for future purposes.

In light of the level of interest shown in the ISO 9000 series, perhaps similar "code case panels" should be appointed for specific industries. This development might serve to enhance the series' reputation but a better course of action would, however, be to rewrite it and reissue it.[6]

References:

1. The ISO 9000 series comprises ISO 9000 to ISO 9004 inclusive. See reference 2 below.

2. ISO 9001 *Quality systems — Model for quality assurance in design/ development, production, installation and servicing*. Published by the International Organization for Standardization. (ISO).

3. ISO 8402 *Quality — Vocabulary*. Published by the International Organization for Standardization.

4. Sayle A.J. *The impact of new technology on QA standards*. European Organization for Quality Control (EOQC) Quality Vol XXV111 No. 1. 1984.

5. American Society of Mechanical Engineers Boiler and Pressure Vessel Code is published by the American Society of Mechanical Engineers, 345 East 47th Street, New York, NY 10017, USA.

6. Sayle A.J. *ISO 9000 — progression or regression?* QA News Volume 14 No. 2 February 1988. Published by the Institute of Quality Assurance, 10 Grosvenor Gardens, London SW1W 0DQ.

7. Looking at Departments

Their appearance and their works were as it were
A wheel within a wheel.
Ezekiel, i, 16.

An essential part of the preparation for the audit (see Chapter 9) is to draw up a list of all the departments affected by the objectives of the audit and to select those to be audited. If time is at a premium, a judicious selection of appropriate departments may allow the audit team to form an overall opinion of the state of management systems' implementation throughout an entire organization. If the audit objective is to determine the auditee's ability to comply with a particular QA standard, the auditor must recognise that not all of its clauses will apply to every department and so he must decide which clauses affect which departments.

In analysing the management systems that apply to the work of any department, the auditor has to consider the following questions:

1. What is the function of the department?

In other words what is the department's product? The product might be any combination of the following, as described in Chapters 5 and 25: items; services; information (contained in records, specifications, sales orders, drawings); equipment (for example, after performing maintenance or calibration services) or people (after completion of training services or as a result of providing interview and selection services).

The function might be established in job descriptions, manuals, procedures or work instructions: it might not, however, have been formalised by such devices, merely being understood by mutual agreement with other parts of the organization. See also Chapter 4 "The auditee's organization".

2. Who are the department's "customers"?

Here it is necessary to define the recipient(s) of each of those products. In the case of information, a copy may be distributed to a number of recipients both inside and external to the company. Similarly, an item may be routed to a downstream production unit within the company, to a vendor for further processing or to the final customer. As before, the "customers" might be described in job descriptions, manuals, procedures or work instructions, if these exist.

3. Who are the department's "suppliers"?

This question really has three components since the department may act as its own supplier in some respects whilst also requiring input of personnel, items, services, equipment and information originating either from other departments within the company or from sources outside it. In determining the answers to these questions, once again the auditor will be guided by those job descriptions, procedures et al if they exist. If not, the actual on-site portion of the overall audit will need to allow time to establish the answers.

In defining the department's "suppliers", the following questions are relevant.

(a) What must the department generate itself in order to accomplish its duties? What type of person should perform each task (thinking in terms of competence, training and personal attributes required)? What equipment needs to be used and what environment is necessary? What information must the department prepare for its own use before the task is performed?
(b) What information, services and items does the department need from within the company to peform its function? Which other departments are or should be responsible for supplying the information, services and items? Within a machine shop, for example, the information may include a workshop document package compiled and then issued by the production planning department whilst the items needed may be raw materials received from the store; within an accounts payable department, there will probably be no items but there will be information such as purchase orders, delivery notes, invoices received from a mail room.
(c) What sources outside the company are responsible for providing an input (item or service) to the department prior to its performance of the tasks? These sources may include the supplier, the customer, a regulatory body, an inspection agency and such like. Suppliers are often responsible for supplying items such as those listed in Chapter 5; a customer may have to supply free issue materials, assemblies, or parts. The customer or a regulatory body may require a witness to be present during execution of the task and hence become responsible for supplying that person. The customer may insist on his own equipment being used to accomplish a task and may therefore have to supply measuring gauges or transport.

It is always beneficial — particularly for an inexperienced auditor — to draw up a written analysis of the department's input, output and process in order to arrive at a solution to the question of what quality assurance activities that department has to perform. Producing a written analysis can be a useful

Fig. 7.1

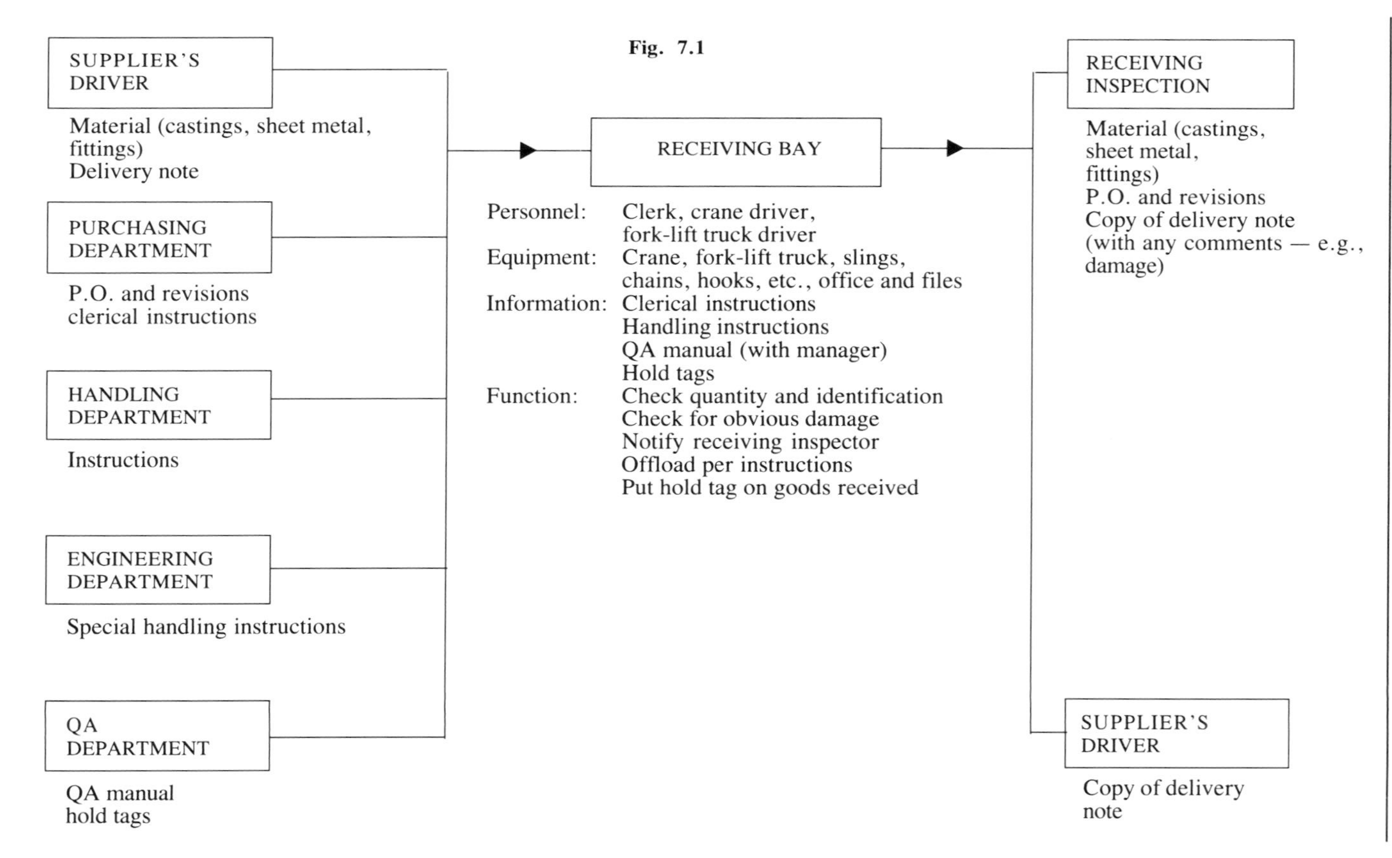
SUPPLIER'S DRIVER
Material (castings, sheet metal, fittings)
Delivery note
PURCHASING DEPARTMENT
P.O. and revisions
clerical instructions
HANDLING DEPARTMENT
Instructions
ENGINEERING DEPARTMENT
Special handling instructions
QA DEPARTMENT
QA manual
hold tags
RECEIVING BAY
Personnel: Clerk, crane driver, fork-lift truck driver
Equipment: Crane, fork-lift truck, slings, chains, hooks, etc., office and files
Information: Clerical instructions
Handling instructions
QA manual (with manager)
Hold tags
Function: Check quantity and identification
Check for obvious damage
Notify receiving inspector
Offload per instructions
Put hold tag on goods received
RECEIVING INSPECTION
Material (castings, sheet metal, fittings)
P.O. and revisions
Copy of delivery note (with any comments — e.g., damage)
SUPPLIER'S DRIVER
Copy of delivery note

exercise, however, and the rest of this chapter is devoted to two simple examples of this type of analysis.

Example 1: A receiving bay

Fig. 7.1 analyses how one company's receiving bay operates. On the input side are items of material received from suppliers and various types of information generated both inside and outside the company. On the output side are items and documents sent to the receiving inspection area and documents for the supplier's driver.

The employees within the receiving bay itself need to have different attributes and experience. The clerk must be numerate and literate; the crane driver and the fork-lift truck driver have to be trained by the work's transportation department so that they know how to lift and sling items as well as how to drive their equipment. The equipment required is regularly maintained, not only to prevent damage to items in case of a drop but also for safety reasons.

From the analysis in Fig 7.1. it is possible to determine which clauses of the applicable QA standard relate to the receiving bay. Fig. 7.3 shows which of the quality assurance criteria of ISO 9001[1], AS 1821[2] and AQAP-1[3] should apply.

Example 2: A receiving inspection area

This is the unit immediately downstream from the receiving bay analysed in Fig. 7.1. Its operations are analysed in Fig. 7.2.

All the items on the input side are the output of the receiving bay. Information in the form of documentary input comes from other departments within the company. On the output side are accepted items (sent to the store) and unaccepted ones (which wait in a holding bay until their fate is decided). Information in the form of documentary output goes to other departments such as quality assurance and engineering.

The receiving inspector within the unit has to have special training in the use of equipment and inspecting techniques. He also needs good eyesight. The inspection area itself needs special equipment, good lighting and an inspection bench.

After completing the analysis shown in Fig. 7.2, the applicable quality assurance or management criteria can be determined by analysing the QA standard invoked for the contract.

It can be seen from Fig. 7.3 that within the receiving bay and receiving inspection area, many of the QA standards' criteria are applicable. Hence, when time is at a premium, it often pays an auditor to concentrate on these areas in order to obtain an indication of the state of management systems'

Fig. 7.2

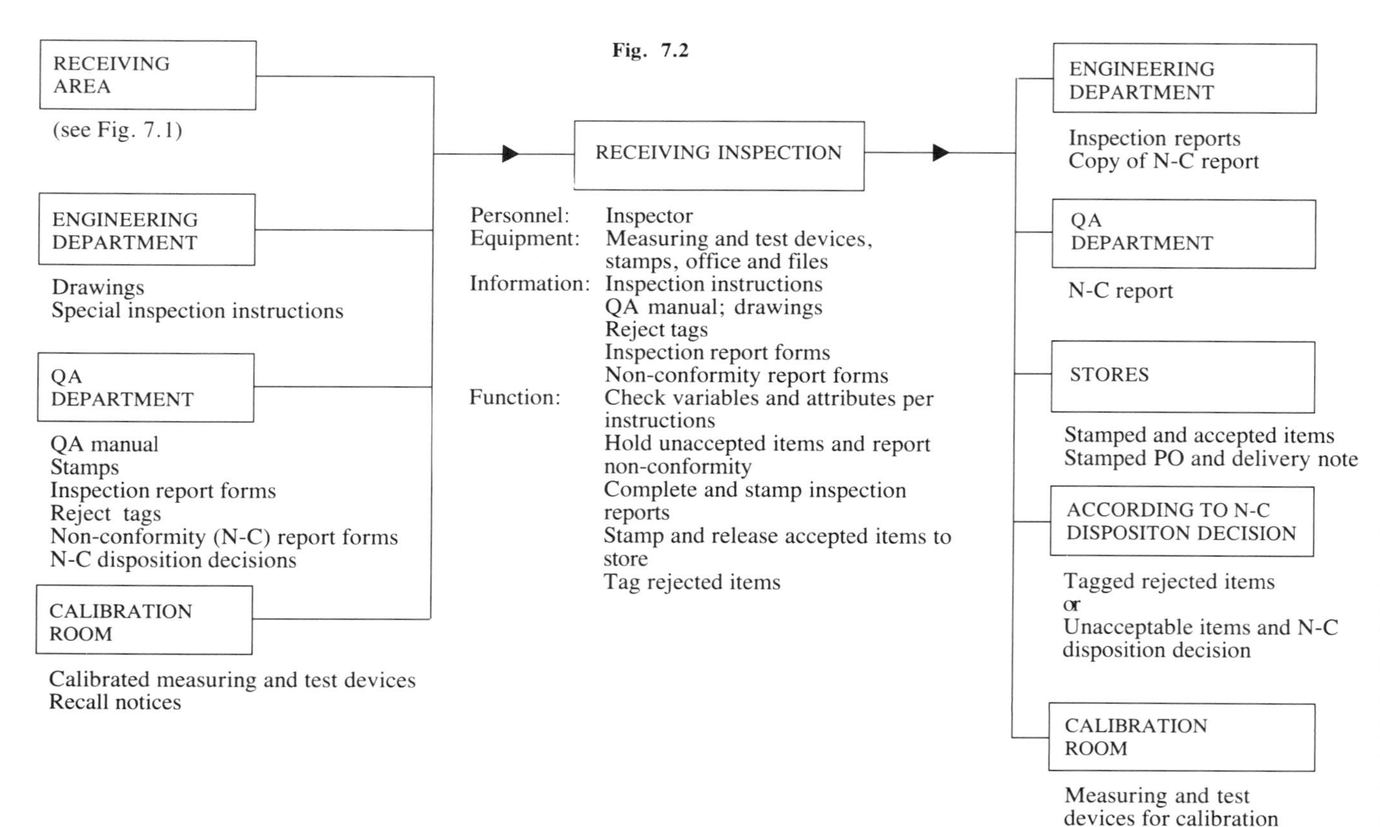
RECEIVING AREA
(see Fig. 7.1)
ENGINEERING DEPARTMENT
Drawings
Special inspection instructions
QA DEPARTMENT
QA manual
Stamps
Inspection report forms
Reject tags
Non-conformity (N-C) report forms
N-C disposition decisions
CALIBRATION ROOM
Calibrated measuring and test devices
Recall notices
RECEIVING INSPECTION
Personnel: Inspector
Equipment: Measuring and test devices, stamps, office and files
Information: Inspection instructions
QA manual; drawings
Reject tags
Inspection report forms
Non-conformity report forms
Function: Check variables and attributes per instructions
Hold unaccepted items and report non-conformity
Complete and stamp inspection reports
Stamp and release accepted items to store
Tag rejected items
ENGINEERING DEPARTMENT
Inspection reports
Copy of N-C report
QA DEPARTMENT
N-C report
STORES
Stamped and accepted items
Stamped PO and delivery note
ACCORDING TO N-C DISPOSITON DECISION
Tagged rejected items
or
Unacceptable items and N-C disposition decision
CALIBRATION ROOM
Measuring and test devices for calibration
Recall notices

implementation throughout the company. It is strange how many companies underrate the importance of these areas, failing to appreciate the value of employing high calibre staff within them. From an auditing standpoint, both the receiving bay and the receiving inspection area can be good barometers to indicate the quality programme of the company.

The kind of analysis set out in Figs. 7.1, 7.2 and 7.3 can be performed for each task unit within a company and the results combined into an overall matrix. Such a matrix can be very useful too in helping a company plan its own internal audits and quality programme. Companies that perform such analyses tend to have better quality management systems which show a better degree of control and provide better assurance that contractual conditions are implemented.

Analysing each department's functions, determining the management systems that it serves and by which it needs to be served is an essential part of the preparation for and conducting of an audit: it is pointless auditing a department unless the auditor knows what he ought to be looking for and hence how much time he can afford to devote to each task. Finally, without such an analysis, there can be no guarantee that a thorough audit of any department has been performed.

Other matters requiring management systems

Other department functions include the proper and efficient use of resources which will be comprised of manpower (persons), equipment needed within that department, as described in Chapter 5 and items that are being processed, since they represent work in progress and cash flow. The sum total of the resources equates to money and the budget for the department concerned.

The auditor will investigate:

—the basis on which the department determines its real budget needs;
—verify that the basis is consistent with the company objectives;
—the management systems employed by the department to monitor its use of resources;
—the system used by the department to analyse the areas of opportunity for resource savings which are not to the detriment of quality achievement.

Over the years, the quality assurance auditors have ignored this aspect of auditing but it is of real importance and is discussed in Chapter 26. The allocation, use and monitoring of resources represent management decisions which can be of quality or can be inadequate. As stated in Chapter 6, the fundamental product is the "decision" and when decisions are of inherently poor quality, failure costs result in the same way as when scrap items are produced.

Fig. 7.3 Department quality assurance criteria

Criteria Description	*ISO 9001 (Para.no)*	*AS-1821 (Para.no)*	*AQAP-1 (Para.no)*	*Receiving Bay*	*Receiving Inspection*
Quality assurance policy/system	4.1/4.2	2.1	201	x	x
Organization	4.1.2	2.2	202	x	x
System review	4.1.3	2.4	203	x	x
Contract review	4.3	2.3	204		
Design control	4.4	2.10	207		
Instructions/ procedures	4.2	2.6	205	x	x
Document control	4.5	2.11	208	x	x
Purchasing control	4.6	2.13	210	x	x
Product identification/ traceability	4.8	2.7	210(c)	x	x
Manufacturing/ process control	4.9	2.14	211		
Customer supplied goods and services	4.7	2.14.3	212	x	x
Receiving checks	4.10.1.1 4.10.1.2	2.13.3	210(c)	x	x
In-process checks	4.10.2	2.14.1 2.14.2	213(a)		
Final product checks	4.10.3	2.14.4	213(b)		
Inspection, measuring and test equipment	4.11	2.12	209		x
Inspection/test/ operating status	4.12	2.16	216	x	x
Product protection, and preservation	4.15	2.18	217	x	x
Non-conformities	4.13	2.15	215	x	x
Corrective action	4.14	2.9	206	x	x
Records	4.16	2.8	205(d)	x	x
Audits	4.17	2.4			
Training	4.18	2.5		x	x
Statistical methods	4.20	2.17	214	x	x

Note: paragraph wording differs between standards; within each standard paragraphs overlap and are open to interpretation.

The proper allocation, use and monitoring of time are also functions of each department. Time is required to perform the various activities such as processing items, creating or reviewing information, providing a service, training people, cleaning or maintaining equipment. It needs to be quantified for each task that is to be performed within the department then allocated and monitored in order that management is continuously aware of progress and problems that may affect it. Since lack of time is a real cause of quality problems (see Chapter 18), time management is an essential part of quality management and is all too frequently ignored by quality management systems: it is certainly ignored by the existing QA standards. Accordingly, the auditor will scrutinise the management systems to

—investigate the basis on which the time budget really required by each task is determined by the department;
—verify that each such basis is consistent with the company objectives;
—verify that the department monitors its use of time;
—check the department analyses the areas of opportunity for time savings which are not to the detriment of quality achievement.

An essential feature in any department is the ability to cope when things go wrong. This means having a non-conformity system ready for immediate use. The auditor must verify that the auditee has prepared for the possible contingencies. However, failures can also provide an area of opportunity if the auditee takes the trouble to analyse the non-conforming situations and determines the real root cause. The cause may lie within the auditee's own department or somewhere else. In the former case, the auditee should have its own corrective action system and, in the latter, the auditee must become an integral part of the company's overall corrective action system. All of the QA standards stipulate requirements for non-conformity and corrective action systems but their individual wording differs to the extent that the effect on an individual department's quality management systems varies. This has been discussed in Chapter 6 "Standards for management systems".

References:

1. ISO 9001 — 1987 *Quality systems — Model for quality assurance in design/development, production, installation and servicing*. Published by the International Organization for Standardization.
2. AS 1821 — 1985 *Suppliers quality systems for design, development, production and installation* Published by the Standards Association of Australia, Standards House, 80 Arthur Street, North Sydney, N.S.W., Australia.
3. AQAP-1 *NATO requirements for an industrial quality control system*. Edition No 3 May 1984 issued by the NATO International Staff — Defence Suport Division.

8. Checklists, Flow charts and Matrices

A great artist can paint a great picture on a small canvas.
Charles Dudley Warner.

The key tool for most audits is the checklist. It is mandatory to use a checklist (or a "procedure") when performing an audit in accordance with the requirements of some industries or standards. In the case of ISO 9001,[1] 9002[2], although there is no requirement for a checklist, internal quality audits must be performed in accordance with "documented procedures", a statement which is open to interpretation. Even in cases where a checklist is not specifically required, it is none the less sensible to generate one in view of the benefits they produce, as described later in this chapter.

Each of the various types of checklist that might be used or encountered has its advantages and drawbacks.

The criteria checklist

This type of checklist is structured in accordance with the management criteria of the regulation, code or standard applicable for the contract or product concerned. As Fig. 8.1 shows, the questions are generally a transposition of the content of a standard's various criteria. In Fig. 8.2, an extract from a checklist of this type is shown.

A criteria checklist can be used for any type of audit (internal or external), for any depth of audit (systems or compliance) and for any scope of audit (full, partial, or follow-up). In each case, the auditor must indicate clearly which departments were audited for which criteria so that someone later reviewing the checklist can draw legitimate conclusions about the extent to which criteria are being implemented throughout the auditee organization.

A criteria type checklist is preferable when auditing against a specific standard, code or regulation. In these circumstances the basic question and the objective of the audit is to determine "Do they or do they not comply with such and such?" The end result must be an unequivocal yes or no statement made by the auditor. Regulations, codes and standards generally comprise various sub set requirements. Thus compliance with a complete standard entails compliance with all of its constituent parts. It is, therefore, advisable for the checklist to separate out the individual topics to be addressed.

Fig. 8.1 Example of criteria checklist question

AQAP-1 Edition 3 Para 208(b)	*Checklist question*
All changes to contractor documentation shall be in writing and processed in a manner which will ensure prompt action at the specified implementation point.	Are all changes to contractor documentation in writing and processed in a manner which will ensure prompt action at the specified implementation point?

Fig. 8.2 Part of a criteria checklist based on the requirements of AQAP-1 Edition 3 Para 210(b)

Checklist question	*Yes*	*No*	*Comments/notes*
b) *Purchasing Data* Does the purchasing document contain a complete and clear description of the materiel and services ordered with adequate direction for ensuring its quality control/inspection? Does the document include as applicable: (1) The type, class, style, grade or other precise identification? (2) The title or other positive identification and applicable issue of specifications, drawings, process requirements or other relevant technical data? (3) The quality control/inspection requirements; eg: the appropriate AQAP or other quality requirements?			

When compiling a criteria type of checklist, it is important to recognize that any particular sentence of a standard can contain a variety of questions. Answering "yes or no" to one particular feature in the sentence does not guarantee that the entire matter has been covered. Accordingly, an alternative way of producing a criteria checklist from that shown in Fig. 8.2 is to break the requirements into greater detail as shown in Fig. 8.3. The structure shown in Fig. 8.2 is only recommended for the well experienced auditor.

Fig. 8.3 Part of a criteria checklist based on the requirements of AQAP-1 Edition 3 Para 210(b)

Checklist question	*Yes*	*No*	*Comments/notes*
b) *Purchasing Data* Does the purchasing document contain a complete description of the materiel ordered? —Is that description clear? —Is there adequate direction for ensuring the materiel's quality control/inspection? Does the purchasing document contain a complete description of the services ordered? —Is that description clear? —Is there adequate direction for ensuring the services' quality control/inspection?			

When preparing the overall checklist, the auditor must remember that the various criteria can apply to various departments. It is for this reason that a matrix of the type shown in Fig. 7.3 should be prepared in order that the auditor does not fail to apply any of the relevant criteria to any relevant part of the organization.

Using the criteria type of checklist requires a tiering of questions. A regulation may, for example, contain many different criteria. One of these might be that the organization shall document and implement a programme that meets the requirements of the regulation. The checklist question concerning implementation can only be answered after all of the others contained within that regulation have been addressed: violation of any one of the criteria clearly means that the answer to whether the auditee has implemented the regulation must be "no".

Figure 8.4 summarizes the advantages and disadvantages of the criteria checklist. It is worth explaining a few of these in more detail here. The notes (D1, A1 and so on) refer back to the figure.

D1. Audits are always performed on a departmental basis. Where more than one department has to satisfy the criteria invoked by a code or standard, it can be very difficult to reflect the true state of affairs on one checklist. The more departments to which the criteria should be applied, the harder the task becomes. It may be necessary to attach explanatory notes to the checklist, and if these should subsequently be detached or mislaid errors of interpretation may be made.

Fig. 8.4 Advantages and disadvantages of criteria checklists

Advantages	*Disadvantages*
A1. Provides ready assessment of compliance with the relevant code, standard or regulation of interest. A2. Focuses auditor's mind on the words of the code/standard etc., and not the auditor's opinion of their meaning. A3. Saves argument with extrinsic auditors about inadequate questions.	D1. Inconvenient when auditing on departmental or individual task basis. D2. Requires experienced, trained auditor to relate requirements to an individual department or work task. D3. Doesn't tell inexperienced auditee what you want.

D2. Before using this type of checklist, the auditor has to be able to analyse the quality assurance needs of each department (see Chapter 7). An inexperienced auditor may be able to do this perfectly adequately but someone with experience should review the analysis to check that nothing has been overlooked. The alternative is to run the risk that some aspects of the code, standard or statute will go unaudited.

A2. Anything that helps the auditor to keep an open mind is of major benefit to any audit.

A3. Some extrinsic auditors are prone to argue about the adequacy of the company's audits unless the checklist produced is responsive to the standards, codes and regulations invoked by the contract. Some QA standards, for example, require that audits be performed "to verify compliance with *all* aspects of the quality assurance programme". If that quality assurance programme is dictated by the QA standard and the checklist reflects the standard (as criteria checklists do), then arguments with the extrinsic auditors should be kept to a minimum. Hence, even though the codes, standards or regulations do not specify any particular type, format or content so far as checklists are concerned, it may foster good relations with customers, regulatory bodies or inspection agencies if one adopts the criteria checklist format.

The departmental checklist

Departmental checklists are structured according to discrete departments and reflect the managerial or operational matters of interest in those departments. This type of checklist can be used for every type, depth and scope of audit. Fig. 8.5 lists the advantages and disadvantages of this type of checklist. An extract from a departmental checklist is shown in Fig. 8.6.

D2. The compiler must not write in questions which reflect his previous experience or preconceived ideas on that type of department's organization.

A2. The auditor retains a set of departmental checklists. When the need arises to carry out a new audit, he can select the checklists which apply to the departments that are to be audited and combine them into an overall checklist for the audit. Each departmental checklist sheet may thus be considered as a building brick and a number of such building bricks can be combined to form the desired new audit checklist.

Fig. 8.5 Advantages and disadvantages of departmental checklists

Advantages	*Disadvantages*
A1. Convenient when auditing on an individual task or departmental basis. A2. Flexible, can be tailored for the company/department being audited by using 'building-brick' sheets. A3. Good for training inexperienced auditors. A4. Tells auditee what you want in a particular area. A5. Useful for partial audits; aids in phased audits and timing in a contract.	D1. Does not provide ready assessment of compliance with the code/standard/regulation of interest. D2. Can reflect preconceived ideas of the auditor who compiled it. D3. Content may be debatable with extrinsic auditors.

A3. An inexperienced auditor often feels uncertain about what to investigate in a particular department. Studying departmental checklists provides useful training and indicates the type of question that could be asked within the department.

A4. This is important when dealing with an auditee who has not previously encountered audits or studied the code or standard in force The auditee is told exactly which departments are of interest to the auditor as well as those

Fig. 8.6 A department checklist used for general purposes

Department/Task	*Result*
Items: a) What items must this task receive to perform its work? Are all those items received? Are they all of the correct type? Are they correctly identified? Are the correct quantities received? Are they all in the correct condition when received? Do they all have the correct capability? b) What items must this task retain to perform its work? Are all those items present? Are they all of the correct type? Are they correctly identified? Are the correct quantities kept? Are they all kept in the correct condition? Do they all have the correct capability? c) What items must this workplace issue? Are all those items issued by the workplace? Are they all of the correct type? Are they correctly identified? Are the correct quantities issued? Are they all issued in the correct condition? Do they have the correct capability? Equipment: a) To work correctly, what equipment does this task require? Is all that equipment present? Is the correct type of equipment at the workplace? Is all equipment at the workplace currently in the correct condition? Is that condition known at all times to the operator? Does all equipment at the workplace currently have the correct capability? Is that capability known at all times to the operator? Is all equipment at the workplace correctly identified? What environmental nuisances must be prevented? Are those nuisances prevented?	
Comments/notes	

Fig. 8.6 A department checklist used for general purposes (cont).

<table>
<tr><th>Department/Task</th><th>Result</th></tr>
<tr><td>Equipment (continued)
b) To work correctly what measuring/test equipment does this task require?

Is all that equipment present?
Is the correct type of that equipment at the workplace?
Is all the equipment at the workplace currently in the correct condition?
Is that condition known at all times to the operator?
Does all equipment at the workplace currently have the correct capability?
Is that capability known at all times to the operator?
Is all equipment at the workplace correctly identified?
What environmental nuisances must be prevented?
Are those nuisances prevented?

Information:
a) What information must this task receive to work properly?

Is all that information received?
Has it all been checked prior to delivery to this workplace?
Is all information received in the correct condition?
Does that information have the correct content?
Is the correct edition of information received by the workplace?
Is all information correctly identified?

b) What information must this task retain to work properly?

Is all that information retained?
Has it all been checked prior to retention at this workplace?
Is all information retained in the correct condition?
Does that information have the correct content?
Is the correct edition of information retained by the workplace?
Is all information correctly identified?

c) What information must this task issue?

Is all that information issued?
Is it all checked prior to issue?
Is all information issued in the correct condition?
Does that information have the correct content?
Is the correct edition of information issued by the workplace?
Is all information correctly identified?</td><td></td></tr>
<tr><td colspan="2">Comments/notes</td></tr>
</table>

Fig. 8.6 A department checklist used for general purposes (cont).

Department/Task	*Result*
Where must that information be issued to? Is that information actually sent to where it is required? Non-conformities and corrective action: Is a non-conformity system defined for this workplace? Is it understood by the operators? Is it used? Is it adequate? Are corrective actions identified as a result of that system? Are they implemented? Are they followed up on to determine their effectiveness? Resources: Is the manpower level required for this task properly defined? Is that manpower level actually allocated to the task? Is there proper monitoring of the actual manpower used? Is the budget required for this task defined? Does that budget allow for space, energy, equipment, items, information, personnel etc. needed for correct accomplishment of the work? Is that budget actually allocated to the task? Is there proper monitoring of the actual budget used? Time: Is the time required to perform the task completely and correctly defined? Is that time actually allocated to the task? Is there proper monitoring of the actual time used? Organization: Has the reporting level for this task been properly defined? Is the actual reporting level the same? Have the task responsibilities been defined? Are the actual responsibilities the same? Have the task functions been defined? Are the actual functions the same? Have the authorities associated with performance of the task been defined? Are the actual authorities the same?	
Comments/notes	

Fig. 8.6 A department checklist used for general purposes (cont).

Department/Task	*Result*
Personnel: Who is involved in this task? Have proper competence levels been defined for this task? Do all persons performing this task have that defined competence? Is that competence consistent with the needs of the task? Has training required for this task been defined? Have all persons performing this task received that training? Is that training consistent with the needs of the task? Is each person uniquely identified to permit work traceability? Is that identification properly maintained? Are demotivators prevented? What attributes are required to perform the task? Does each person possess those attributes? Services: (See Chapter 25) Is the correct type of service being performed? Does the service performed have the correct characteristics? Is the service presented correctly? Is the service correctly identified? Is the service performed completely?	
Comments/notes	

aspects of the departments' work that are of concern to him. This helps the auditee both to inform the appropriate personnel of an impending audit and to prepare for it.

A5. By its very nature, the departmental checklist reflects the scope of the management audit performed. This makes it a particularly valuable aid in assessing the overall implementation of management criteria throughout the auditee organization. At the end of a series of phased audits, for example, it will be readily apparent that all departments have been covered and that the status of criteria implementation throughout the company or a project is known. Furthermore, all interested parties can easily verify that all aspects of criteria implementation as part of the overall quality assurance programme have been verified by the audits.

Companies that do not work to a particular quality management standard or that have special criteria or activities to verify may well find the departmental checklist more suited to their needs than the criteria checklist described earlier.

Fig. 8.7 Advantages and disadvantages of company standard checklists

Advantages	*Disadvantages*
A1. Uniform questions for company audit teams. A2. Train auditors in company requirements. A3. Evidence of consistency for extrinsic auditors. A4. Economy of printing in bulk. A5. Quick review by company personnel.	D1. May not be suitable for all audits. D2. Stereotyped auditors; inflexibility; problems in dealing with different audit objectives.

The company standard checklist

Some companies maintain sets of ready-made checklists (either criteria or departmental) for use during audits. The advantages and disadvantages of these are shown in Fig. 8.7.

The special or custom-built checklist

If the standard company checklists do not fit the circumstances of a particular audit, it may be necessary to generate one specially. The advantages and disadvantages of special checklists are shown in Fig. 8.8.

D2. Familiarity with the layout and content of a checklist encourages fairly rapid review and standard company checklists will be prepared with this in mind. A special checklist may be slower to assimilate because its content and format are unfamiliar to the reviewer.

Fig. 8.8 Advantages and disadvantages of special or custom-built checklists

Advantages	*Disadvantages*
A1. Shows the auditee exactly what the auditor wants. A2. Prepares the auditor well. A3. Good training.	D1. Some extra work involved. D2. Review of checklist is not so convenient.

The usefulness of checklists

Benefits for the auditor

1. A checklist acts as a guide to the person performing the audit.

The word "guide" is important. The checklist must not rigidly dictate exactly what is to be audited. It often happens that, while carrying out an audit, the auditor is put on the scent of a problem and needs to deviate from the checklist in order to assess the depth and significance of that problem with a view to considering what corrective action may be required. So the usefulness of a checklist does not lie in providing an exhaustive list of questions for the auditor to ask during the audit. In fact, a criteria checklist on its own provides no useful questions at all: each question it poses will need to be broken down into each of the task elements that may be applicable to the unit responsible for implementing the criterion concerned.

2. The checklist provides objective evidence that the management audit was performed, that it was performed in accordance with a checklist and that all applicable aspects of the quality assurance programme were verified.

Inevitably, every auditor is himself audited sooner or later (i.e. an extrinsic audit is performed). To retain the checklist on file is important since an audit report alone does not answer all the questions that the extrinsic auditor might need to ask.

3. The checklist is very useful as an *aide memoire.*

An auditor engaged full time on auditing activities will find it very difficult, if not impossible, to retain in his mind the details of every audit. When a question is raised some time after the audit has ended, the checklist will serve as a useful reminder of what happened, what objective evidence was examined, the results and so on.

4. The checklist provides information to the auditor's successors, facilitating continuity of the quality assurance department's work.

When subsequent audits have to be planned, the new auditor will find it useful to be able to refer back to the checklist to get an idea of what was done before, what problems were encountered, what objective evidence was examined and so on. Incomplete records may be a serious embarrassment.

5. The checklist is a very useful place to collect and collate notes during the audit (see Chapter 12).

6. The information the checklist contains helps the auditor to prepare for the exit interview and the audit report (see Chapters 19 and 20).

Benefits for the auditee

1. The checklist reveals the auditor's guidelines and helps the auditee to prepare for the audit.

The checklist must always be forwarded to the auditee before the audit to help him make the proper preparations (see Chapter 9).

2. The checklist helps the auditee train his own staff.

It is quite common for an organization to copy or amend another company's checklist. This interchange of experience and information can be very beneficial. No auditor should take exception to it if the auditee copies the checklist with a view to performing his own audits: this is one level of guarantee that the auditee will audit all relevant aspects of the quality assurance programme for the contract concerned. In the case of an external audit, the supplier might be considered as part of the auditor's own company and one might argue that the auditee is entitled to use the company's information. By studying the checklist, the auditee's staff can familiarize themselves with what is required by the contract, learning exactly which management criteria are applicable to the various departments. Eventually this could improve the auditee's product and, perhaps, lower the price: both developments should benefit the external auditor's company.

3. The checklist provides a useful aide memoire.

The auditee may find it helpful to refer to the checklist later, during the exit interview, when reviewing the audit report or when implementing corrective action, since the checklist contains the information upon which the auditor's conclusions and corrective action requests have been based. With the checklist to assist him, the auditee can explain to the affected departments within his own organization exactly what the audit procedure and conclusions were: he is in a strong position to comply with the auditor's requirements.

4. The checklist provides objective evidence that the system has been independently audited.

A word of warning is called for here. Some organizations claim credit for extrinsic audits in lieu of their own internal ones. Until there is an internationally credible and recognized auditor's qualification scheme, this is dubious practice unless the members of the audit team and the circumstances in which the audit was conducted are both known to be acceptable. Several QA standards have disallowed this use of extrinsic audits either by implication or by edict — ISO 9001 for example, requires that the "supplier shall carry out....internal audits"; AS 1821[3] requires the quality system to be "...audited by the supplier...". Potential customers, too, should be wary about accepting the findings of an unknown audit team as constituting an assurance that the management systems in use are of an adequate standard unless it is the customer's policy to accept certain certifications — such as an applicable ASME certification — as evidence of the state of management systems in lieu of a pre-award survey — see also Chapter 2.

Layout and format of checklists

Some checklists are laid out in a question-and-answer style, the answer being either "yes" or "no". The criteria checklists shown in Figs. 8.2, 8.3 adopt this style. Checklists like this are quick to review since the eye can scan the page and will only stop to consider the significance of "no" answers. This is an example of the application of the "management by exception" principle: if everything has a "yes" answer, all is well and no further investigation is needed. For a large company with numerous audits to perform, such a format has obvious advantages. However, the "yes/no" answer does not allow for the shades of grey that inevitably colour most audits. An untrained auditor, looking for a yes or a no answer can get confused. If, for example, a criterion is applicable to eleven departments and the auditor finds that five of them are a definite yes, five a definite no with one wavering in the balance, it becomes difficult to answer "yes" or "no" without some qualifications.

Another style of checklist is the question-and-results type, an example of which is given in Fig. 8.6, the departmental checklist. With this format, against each question the auditor has to write in his assessment of the situation and any additional remarks. Alternatively, the results may be broken down into "satisfactory", "unsatisfactory" and "not applicable" with space being provided for the reviewer's comments alongside. In the case cited in the preceding paragraph, the auditor would state that five departments were satisfactory, five unsatisfactory and one borderline. It may be hard to review this type of checklist quickly, which can be a disadvantage if a lot of audit reports and checklists have to be handled.

Regardless of its layout and format, the checklist must always provide room for writing notes and for collecting and collating the information upon which the auditor's conclusions have been based. All the examples of checklists in Figs. 8.2, 8.3 and 8.6 allow room for this purpose.

Like any other document, the audit checklist should carry some identification. The front cover, and possibly every page of checklist, should indicate the date of the audit, the auditor and the auditee, so as to avoid the possibility of mistake or misinterpretation later on.

Other checklists and their uses

Checklists provide a very useful tool for a variety of activities other than audits. They constitute evidence that an activity has been accomplished and indicate what was performed as part of that activity. Checklists present an orderly view to any extrinsic auditor and provide useful guidelines to the personnel responsible for performing the activity concerned.

It can be extremely helpful to draw up a checklist for each of the presentations that occur during an audit, exit and entry interviews, for example, and to refer to these lists to make sure that all the relevant points have been covered. Where the exit interview is concerned, a checklist has the additional advantage of making it easier to ensure that the presentation is true and fair. Examples of checklists for the entry interview and the exit interview are shown in Figs. 10.2 and 19.3 respectively.

Flow charts

The QA standards generally give the auditor a choice between using a checklist or using a "procedure" to guide the audit. An exception is CAN3-Z299.1-1985[4] which requires the audits to be performed "....according to audit procedures using checklists which identify the essential characteristics". If we consider a "checklist" to mean a document that describes the matters to be examined then its content and layout can be whatever the auditor desires. In my experience, a most useful layout is the flow chart.

The flow chart is drawn up as part of the audit preparation while reviewing the auditee's description of the quality management system. A flow chart is very useful in analysing the systems that the auditee has allegedly implemented and in determining the various decision points that may have been (or should have been) incorporated. Thus, for example, when an item has been inspected, there is a decision to be taken: is the item acceptable or not? Two routes are open, one of which, in the case of an unacceptable item, leads the auditor to analyse the auditee's non-conformity and corrective

Fig. 8.9 Wizz-Kids Design Services Inc. Flow of Design Documentation

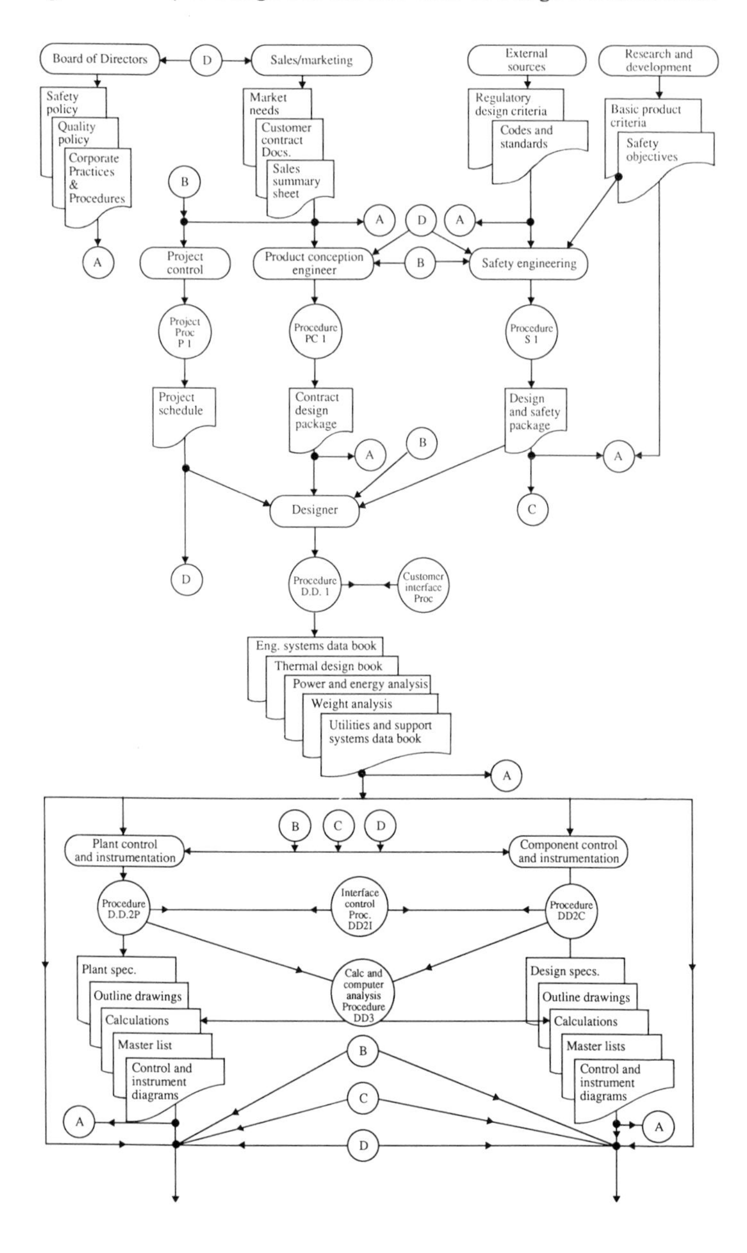

Fig. 8.9 (cont).

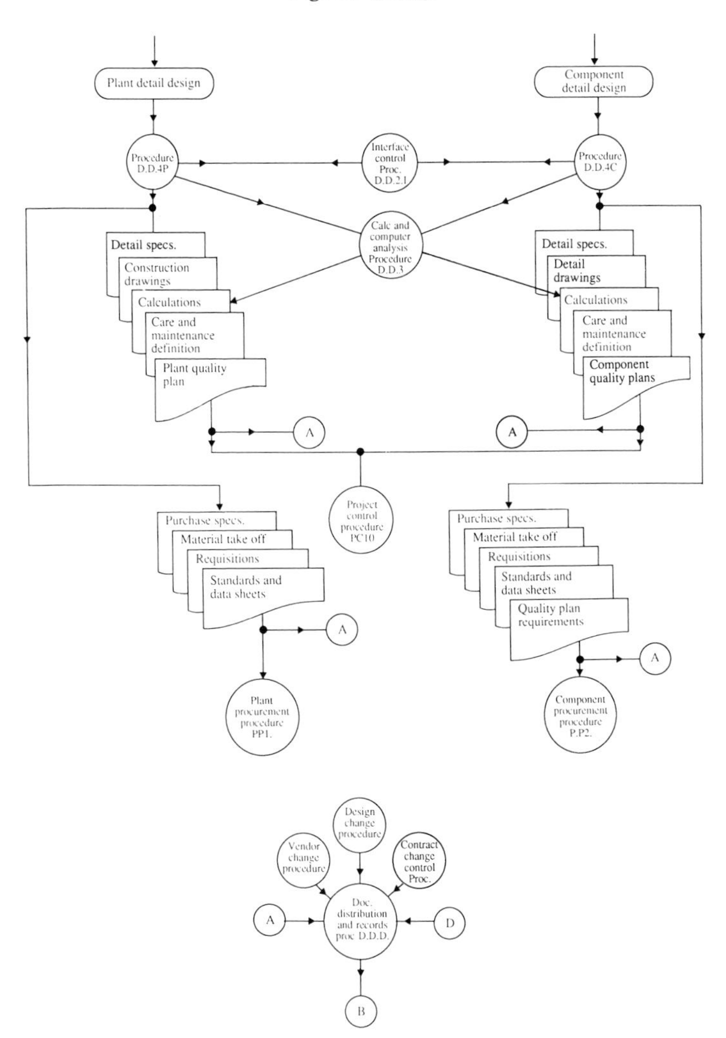
Plant detail design
Component detail design
Procedure D.D.4P
Interface control Proc. D.D.2.1
Procedure D.D.4C
Calc and computer analysis Procedure D.D.3
Detail specs.
Construction drawings
Calculations
Care and maintenance definition
Plant quality plan
Detail specs.
Detail drawings
Calculations
Care and maintenance definition
Component quality plans
A
A
Project control procedure PC10
Purchase specs.
Material take off
Requisitions
Standards and data sheets
A
Plant procurement procedure PP1.
Purchase specs.
Material take off
Requisitions
Standards and data sheets
Quality plan requirements
A
Component procurement procedure P.P2.
Design change procedure
Vendor change procedure
Contract change control Proc.
A
Doc. distribution and records proc D.D.D.
D
B

action system. Absence of such a decision point immediately shows that either there has been an oversight or that the auditee has decided to make this decision at a later stage and take the risk of processing a possibly unacceptable item.

Once the system has been mapped out as a flow chart, this may be used for a compliance audit at a later date.

It can be rather time consuming to draw up a flow chart such as the one depicted in Fig. 8.9 but the exercise can prove highly worthwhile.

The flow chart shown in Figure 8.9 can be marked up as the audit progresses to show those areas which are completely satisfactory and those areas which are not at all. An example of a marked up flow chart is shown in Figure 8.10. The benefit of marking up is that one then has a graphical illustration which depicts at a glance the strengths and the weaknesses within the auditee's systems and which can be presented to auditor and auditee management. It will immediately highlight those matters which require corrective action. This is particularly useful at the exit interview. It is not uncommon to find that managers do not fully understand some of the parlance and terms which auditors may use: the marked up flow charts can be printed onto view foils which facilitate display and discussion. To assist in the promotion of better communication with the auditee, such graphical presentations are without equal.

Flow charts have the considerable advantage over checklists in that they immediately show the logic or the lack of it in the system. An example is provided in Figs. 16.2 and 16.3 and shows how a procedure that, at first sight, may have appeared to be satisfactory did not meet ISO 9001 requirements for Inspection and Test Status.

Flow charting a system enables one to see those areas which present an opportunity for the reduction of resources and time spent and, hence, to spot the opportunities for potential reduction in cost. A flow chart reveals areas which are superfluous to the real need and which could, in fact, be modified. Fig. 8.11 depicts in simplified flow chart form a "before and after" situation in a company and illustrates how resources were saved, throughput time reduced and costs improved as a result.

Task element matrices.

An alternative tool is the matrix laid out on task element basis. An example is shown in Fig. 8.12, These can be produced in blank format, as depicted in Fig. 8.12 and completed specifically for a particular department on the basis of reviewing the documented system description as shown in Figs. 8.13 and 8.14. These have advantages similar to the flow charts in that they can provide a picture of the strengths and weaknesses of audited areas.

Fig. 8.10 Example of a marked up simple flow chart

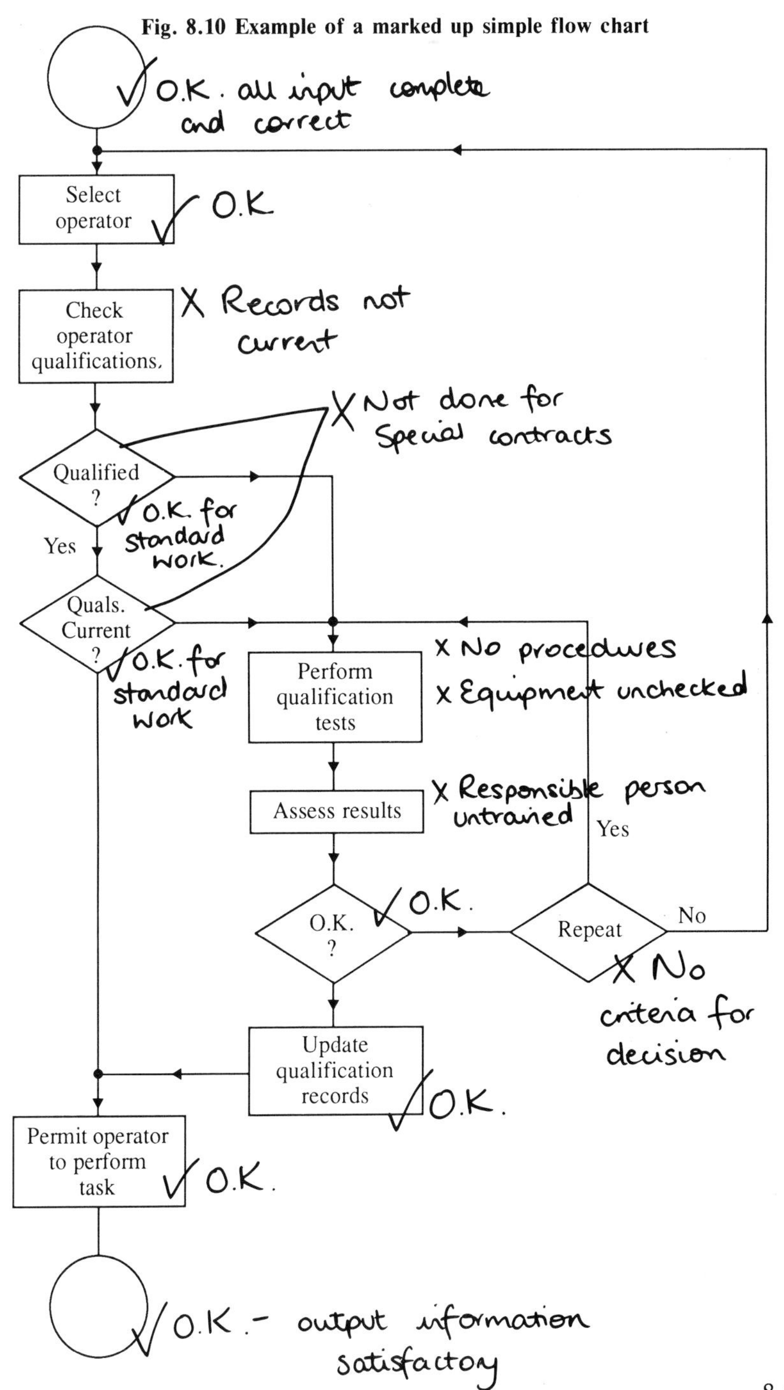

Fig. 8.11 Example of time and resource saving identified by an audit

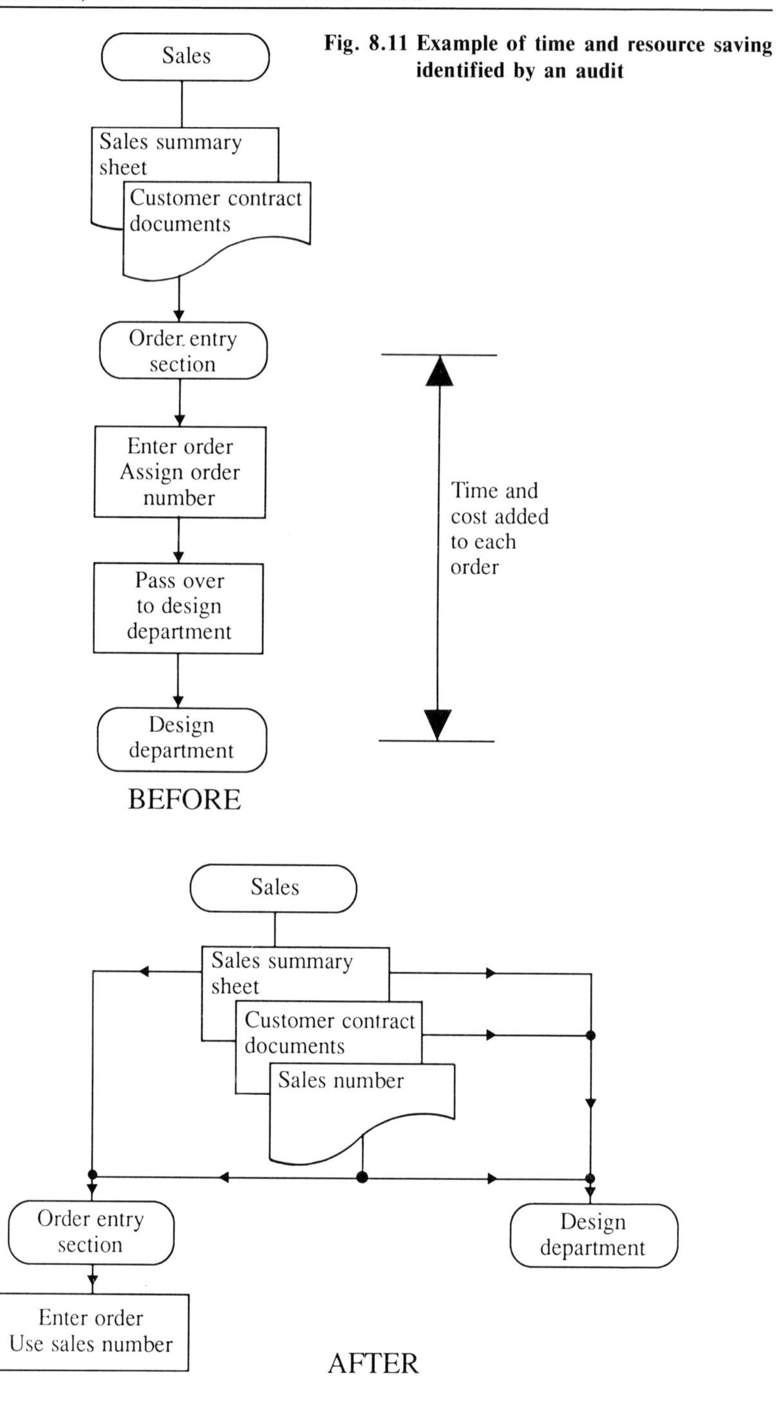

Fig. 8.12 A task element matrix form

TASK AUDITED	Audited By:	Audit Date:	Sheet of
	INPUTS	**OUTPUTS**	**Task Function**
Person *(Description)*			Reports to:
From / to.			Description:
Competence			
Training			
Identification			
Motivation			
Attributes			
Item *(Description)*			**Resources**
From / to.			Defined:
Type			Allocated:
Capability			
Condition			Monitored:
Quantity			
Identification			
Equipment *(Description)*			**Time**
From / to.			Defined:
Type			Allocated:
Condition			Monitored:
Capability			
Identification			
Location			
Environment			
Information *(Description)*			**Non-Conformities**
Checked			System:
Content			Understood:
Edition			Implemented:
Condition			
Identification			
Distribution			
Notes / Comments:			

Fig. 8.13

THE PEELIN PAINT COMPANY Inc.

1.0 Operator qualifications and receipt of items

1.1 All operators shall be pre-approved using the Company Procedure 23 for qualifying and training paint operators.

1.2 Prior to issuing for painting all manufactured items should have been inspected for cleanliness and surface preparation. This inspection should have been recorded on the Works Traveller that accompanies the items. The inspector's signature and date of inspection should have been recorded on the Traveller.

2.0 *Painting*

2.1 The paint shall be thinned for application using a standard lacquer reducer. Proportions to be 1 part paint to 1 part reducer. The paint and reducer shall be issued to the operator by the Stores but the operator shall check the paint's shelf life date and ensure that it has not been exceeded, prior to use.

2.2 Exterior finish paint coat shall be applied to a thickness between 0.75 and 1 mm. using Company colour grey enamel paint. Interior finish paint coat to be applied to a thickness between 0.75 and 1 mm. using white enamel paint no. En-30. All paint shall be applied using the spray guns and the operator shall ensure that the equipment is kept clean at all times. Thickness templates shall be used by the operator to check the wet thickness as painting proceeds.

2.2 The finish paint coat shall be air dried for a minimum of 24 hours prior to releasing the items to the product assembly area. The items shall be left to dry in the drying racks. All thicknesses shall be checked by the operator by means of the Elcometer and shall record and initial the readings on the Works Traveller.

2.3 The Works Traveller shall be kept with the items at all times to maintain their identity. Excess paint shall be returned to the stores.

Doc. no : 86	Description : PAINTING PROCEDURE
Revision no : 2	Sheet 1 of 1
Prepared by : P. Brown	Approved by : T. Jones
Issued by : Design Engineering	Issue date : 14 October 1987

TASK AUDITED PAINTING	Audited By: JOE SMITH				Audit Date: 13th NOV. 1987		Sheet 1 of 1
	INPUTS				OUTPUTS		**Task Function**
Person *(Description)*	OPERATOR						Reports to:
From / to.							Description: Mix paint.
Competence	PROCEDURE 23?						Apply internal and external
Training	PROCEDURE 23?						coats.
Identification							Check thickness and
Motivation							record readings.
Attributes	PROCEDURE 23?						
Item *(Description)*	ALL ITEMS	PAINT	PAINT	REDUCER	PAINTED ITEMS	PAINT	**Resources**
From / to.	INSPECTION	STORES	STORES		PROD. ASSEMBLY		Defined:
Type		GREY ENAMEL	WHITE ENAMEL				Allocated:
Capability							
Condition	CLEAN/ PREP.	SHELF LIFE	SHELF LIFE		DRY 3/4-1 mm COAT		Monitored:
Quantity						EXCESS TO NEEDS	
Identification	WKS TRAVELLER		EN-30				
Equipment *(Description)*	SPRAYGUN	TEMPLATE	ELCO METER	DRYRACKS			**Time**
From / to.							Defined:
Type							Allocated:
Condition	CLEAN						Monitored:
Capability							
Identification							24 hours for drying
Location	All available at workplace						
Environment							
Information *(Description)*	WKS. TRAVELLER	PROCEDURE	PROCEDURE		WKS. TRAVELLER		**Non-Conformities**
Checked	OPERATOR	✓					System:
Content					Input plus thickness readings		Understood:
Edition		2					Implemented:
Condition		legible					
Identification		86	23				
Distribution	FROM INSPECTION	FROM DESIGN ENG.			To Prod. Assembly		

Notes / Comments:
Proportion of paint – reducer = one to one

References:

1. ISO 9001 — 1987 *Quality systems — Model for quality assurance in design/development, production, installation and servicing*. Published by the International Organization for Standardization.
2. ISO 9002 *Quality systems — Model for quality assurance in production and installation*. Published by the International Organization for Standardization (ISO).
3. AS 1821 — 1985 *Suppliers' quality systems for design, development, production and installation*. Published by the Standards Association of Australia, Standards House, 80 Arthur Street, North Sydney, N.S.W., Australia.

9. Audit Preparation

As the proverb says "a good beginning is half the business," and "to have begun well" is praised by all.
Plato.

Preparation is essential to satisfactory audit performance. Unless it is done thoroughly, all the time, effort, and expense of carrying out the audit may be wasted — a situation that is unforgivable should it be allowed to arise. Some organizations, unlucky enough to have experienced only ill-prepared audits, understandably become sceptical about the value of auditing at all. This frustrating and disillusioning experience need not and should not arise if the proper steps are taken before the audit begins. The aim of this chapter is to spell out exactly what these proper steps involve. First of all, however, it is worth saying a little more about the value of good preparation to all parties concerned in the audit.

The benefits of proper preparation

When the auditor is actually at the auditee's site, time is the great enemy. Time usage must be maximized by avoiding any unnecessary activity that could have been accomplished prior to the auditor's arrival at the auditee's premises. The benefits of preparation are severely curtailed when insufficient time is devoted to or allowed for preparation. Management must be made aware of this for it is false economy to deny adequate preparation time.

The over-riding purpose of preparing the ground thoroughly before the audit is to permit the auditor to use the time available to the best possible advantage. Failure in this respect will slow down the proceedings or render the results less valuable. This is obviously undesirable from the auditor's point of view but the auditee will suffer too: the longer the audit drags on, the greater the disruption to ordinary work and the worse the nuisance. As far as the auditee is concerned, any auditor who arrives to carry out an audit without the background information he needs (contract terms, delivery dates, standards and so on) can be regarded as unprofessional and a nuisance.

> On one occasion, I and another representative of my company were scheduled to be observers while a supplier audited a sub-supplier. It became apparent within quarter of an hour of starting the audit that the supplier was completely unprepared. There was no checklist, plan or programme, the contract had not been reviewed, the status of the contract was unknown, as were the delivery dates. My colleague and I, although scheduled as observers, quickly decided to take over the audit. We had already made the necessary preparations (in the course of preparing to act as observers), so we knew the scope of the contract, the delivery dates and the various parameters involved for the deliverable product. It was only because we possessed this background information that we were able to take over and perform a meaningful audit.
>
> The whole experience was illuminating — rather than a two-edged, a three-edged sword principle applied. We were able to see that our own company's departments had performed their functions properly; that the sub-supplier had developed and implemented satisfactory quality management systems and that our supplier had a very weak auditing ability. This last piece of information was passed on to the next of our audit teams to visit the supplier: they made a thorough review of the supplier's audit system, with the expected results. The major part of the problem was simply that the supplier's auditors had performed very few audits, had never been trained and did not realize the importance of proper preparation.

Tactically speaking too, it makes sense to be prepared for an audit. On the auditor's side, it shows that he has done his homework and means business. Members of the auditee's organization are less likely to try to bluff him if he seems to have all the facts and figures at his fingertips. On the auditee's side, good preparation (particularly for an extrinsic audit) can pay off by showing the auditor that the auditee knows what is required of him and takes his obligations seriously.

Audit preparation saves everybody time, money and grief. In some fields, companies are subject to so many audits by customers, regulatory bodies, inspection agencies and consultants that they employ full-time escorts whose sole responsibility is to accompany the various extrinsic audit teams. (The problems of multiple assessment are discussed in Chapter 1.) Ordinary work still has to be done sometime. No auditee is likely to have so much time at his disposal that he feels magnanimous about having it wasted by an inefficient auditor — particularly if the auditee then has to catch up on his own work by doing unpaid overtime.

Fig. 9.1 An audit schedule

HYPER-QUALITY COMPANY LIMITED
1988 Audit Schedule

Issued Nov 1987

Week no.	*Auditee*	*Contract no.*	*Description*	*Product class*	*Audit scope or type*	*Duration (days)/ team size*	*QAE/lead auditor*	*Buyer/engineer*
1								
2	S. C. Rap Metal Products Ltd	1234	Gizmos	1	Full	3/4	BJ/JS	A. Connor/ P. I. Ston
3	Drawing office	1432	Wotnot	1	Internal	1/1	BA/DM	
		1433	Mini-Wotnot	2			BA/DM	
4	Taquee Services Inc.	4321	Computer analysis	1	Partial	2/2	BR/JS	D. C. Flow/ C. P. Yu
5								
6								

Audit schedules

Some companies draw up audit schedules on an annual basis, others on a quarterly one. Audit scheduling is a mandatory requirement of various QA standards, and the statement that audits should be "planned and documented"[1], "scheduled"[2] or that there shall be "quality audit planning"[3] shall be construed as meaning that the audit systems should be laid out as some form of schedule. An audit schedule has two significant benefits:

1. It forewarns people throughout the organization of the audits to be done, of the time allocated for their performance as well as of the personnel, products and contracts involved. This helps people to plan their work schedules, also helping departments to determine their manpower loading.
2. The audit schedule can be produced in extrinsic audits as objective evidence that audits are planned.

In the example shown in Fig. 9.1, we can see the top sheet of a simple management audit schedule. Week numbers are shown on the left-hand side (it is this company's practice to use week numbers rather than calendar dates). The issue date on the top right-hand side tells recipients which revision they hold and whether it is the latest one (it is this company's practice to update the audit schedule every month). The updating period should be whatever best suits the company's purposes and all recipients must be informed of the timescale of this updating period so that they can be assured of having the latest revision.

The audit schedule should indicate all internal and external audits being performed by the company. The column marked "contract number" identifies the contracts that will be audited. The "description" column will help those within the company who are not familiar with the contract number system (perhaps shop-floor staff only know about the Gizmos from S.C. Rap and not about contract 1234, for example).

The company operates a product classification system that reflects the importance of different products. The audit schedule shows the product classification so that people are aware of the products' importance.

The schedule should indicate the scope of each audit, its duration and team size. In Fig. 9.1, three days for four people (twelve man-days in total) have been allocated to perform the S.C. Rap audit. The initials of the quality assurance engineer and the lead auditor are shown to notify these people of their involvement in the particular audit. The names of the buyer and designer are also shown, for the same reason.

Notice that in Fig. 9.1 the external audits are to be performed two weeks apart. This is really the minimum time that should be allowed between external audits, in view of the need for the lead auditor to be able to report on one audit and prepare for the next. Auditing is not the sort of activity one can perform week in, week out. Quite apart from the importance of allowing time for preparation, an overworked employee whose desk is always piled high with a backlog of paper work is not able to work effectively for very long. As a rough guide, the time needed to prepare and to follow up an audit is generally about the same as the time taken actually to perform it.

Audits may be scheduled on a basis of costs, of customer complaints or of customer requirements, according to the company's circumstances (see Chapter 3). The audit schedule may be compiled by the quality assurance manager, by the managing director/president of the company or by a management committee (such as a material review board or similar), depending on company policies and practice.

The audit schedule is distributed to each department concerned The department manager is the usual recipient and it is then his responsibility to notify his staff accordingly. The audit schedule must be kept up-to-date and revised in the light of new developments. Provided that revisions are issued regularly — once a month, for instance — the audit schedule will be an authoritative document upon which departments throughout the company know they can rely. Thus, if a particular manager encounters quality problems with the product being supplied to his department, he can advise the lead auditor that the matter needs to be investigated further if an upcoming audit of the area responsible is shown on the schedule.

Steps in preparing the audit

The sequence of steps required when preparing for an audit is shown in Fig. 9.2. Some of the steps explained below may seem obvious but it is amazing how often some are left out of the audit preparation, with unfortunate results. All are necessary for a thorough preparation.

Step 1. Obtain details of the audit decisions

Chapter 3 contains details of the principle audit decisions that need to be taken before embarking upon the preparation of an audit. The outcome of these decisions must be in their entirety passed over to the lead auditor. The relevant information concerns:

a) the objectives of the management audit;
b) the type, depth and scope of the management audit;
c) when the management audit is needed;
d) the likely impact if the audit is postponed or major problems are uncovered during its course;
e) whether or not the management has decided on particular personnel who must perform the audit;
f) whether or not the audit is to be combined with a hold point or other quality control activity.

It could be that some of this information will finally be decided by the management as a result of the audit preparations described below. Accordingly, some re-iteration is possible.

No audit can be adequately prepared or performed unless the management authorizing the audit clearly states the objectives as described in Chapter 3. Knowledge of the objective is vital because the latter affects the information to be reviewed, the selection of the audit team, the content of the checklist, the amount of time required and the scheduling for performance of the audit.

Fig. 9.2 Sequence of audit preparation steps

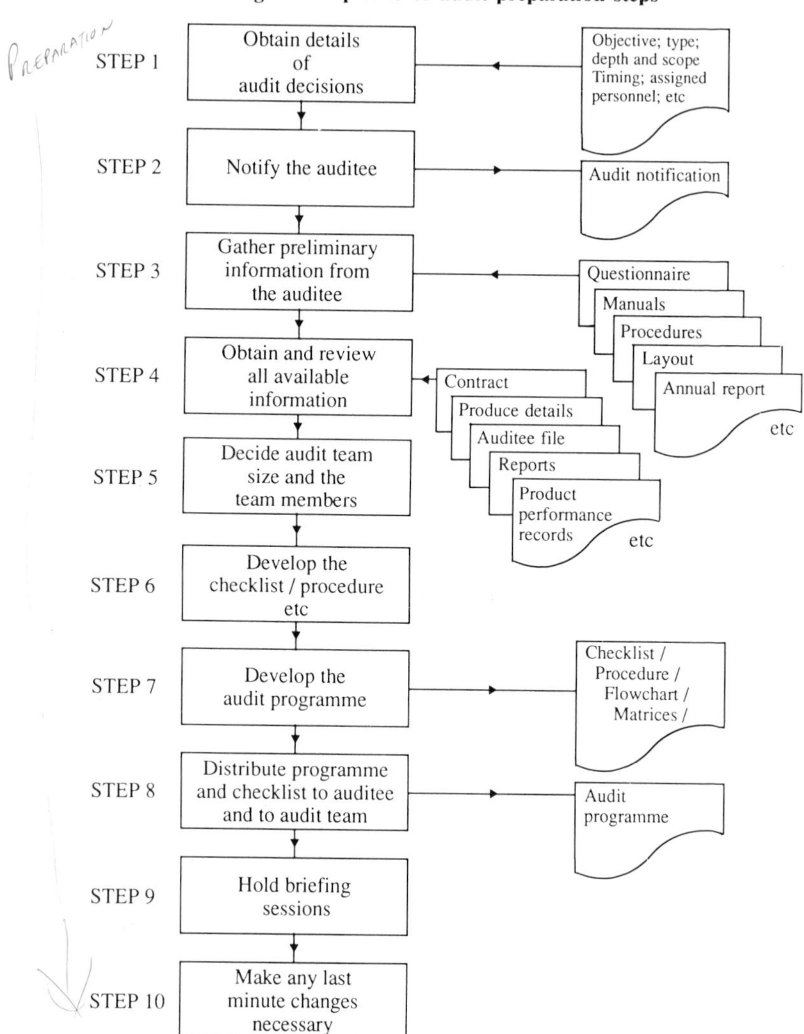

The prime purpose of an audit is to obtain information to assist people to succeed better in their work and to make proper management decisions. It makes little sense to obtain vital information if the decision that it would affect has already been taken. The timing of the audit must depend upon the classification of the auditee's product and upon the importance of the decisions to be taken as a result of the information gained from the audit. Fig. 9.3 depicts a simple project schedule whose audits have been timed so as to be well in advance of new work phases being started. This is so that if the audit discovers any problems with the systems already in operation, management has adequate time to implement corrective action. Trying to backfit essential controls on the job loses time and money. Similarly, the compliance audits are planned to be in advance of completion of those phases so that management will know whether or not the system is being properly implemented and is creating the right results and product.

Fig. 9.3 A simple project schedule showing systems audit points

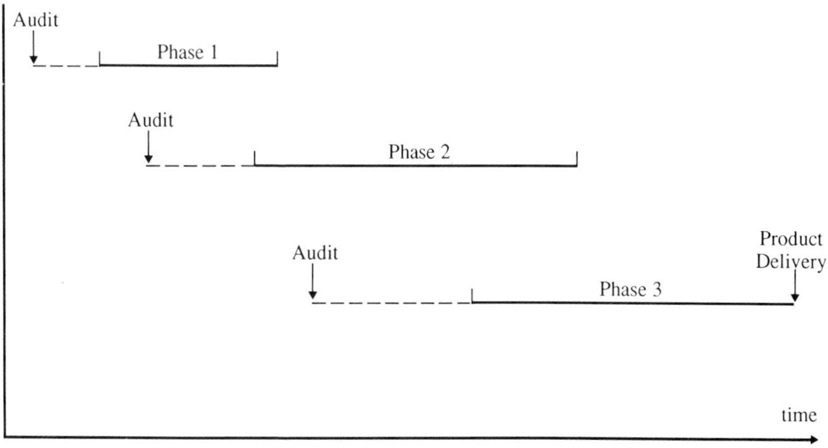

Audit
Phase 1
Audit
Phase 2
Audit
Phase 3
Product Delivery
time

Step 2. Notify the auditee

It is the responsibility of the lead auditor to see that the auditee is notified that an audit is being planned and prepared. The key considerations to bear in mind are listed below.

Timing:

The lead auditor must decide how much advance warning the auditee will need and make sure he gets it. The more warning one can give, the better — the minimum advance notification to be desired is three months. That kind of gap between the advance notice and the audit facilitates the auditee's task of making suitable people available while the audit is under way. The audit schedule should be generated for at least the next six months. In view of the large number of audits and other commitments that an auditee may have to accommodate, giving the maximum forewarning puts an auditor at the head of the queue. Furthermore, when the notification is being given with a view to firming on the audit schedule, a maximum of forewarning for the auditee means a minimum of schedule amendments at a later stage.

Method of notification:

Telephone, telex, telefax, memorandum or letter may be used to notify the auditee. A verbal notification (made at a meeting or on the telephone, for example) should always be followed up with a written confirmation. Some companies have a standard letter (such as the one shown in Fig. 9.4) for the

Fig. 9.4 Audit Notification

HYPER-QUALITY COMPANY LIMITED
Audit notification

To: A. Connor   Date: 1st October 1987
From: J. Smith
Auditee involved: SCRAP METAL PRODUCTS LTD.
Product(s) involved: Gizmos per Purchase Order 1234
Please be advised that we wish to perform an audit 13-15 January 1988
The basis for the audit is requirement of:

- Our contract 87 [X] with Candle Power Corporation
- CAN 3Z299.1 [X]
- Our quality policy [ ]
- Other (specify)

The audit objective(s) is/are to determine the adequacy of systems/verify compliance in meeting the requirements of:

- Our contract [X] # 1234
- CAN 3Z299.1 [X]
- Our quality policy [ ]
- Other (specify)

Documents of particular interest will include the auditee's:

QA manual	X	Procedures	X	Other (specify)

Our audit team will comprise:
To be finalised

The auditee is requested to confirm the above dates as being suitable no later than.
31st October 1988

J. Smith
(Lead Auditor)

lead auditor to complete and forward to the auditee through the appropriate channels. This has the advantage of saving time for the lead auditor and enabling a rapid review on the part of the recipient (purchasing agent, departmental manager and so on).

Information to be supplied:

The auditee should be given as much of the following material as is available.

1. The dates proposed for the audit, which will also indicate the time that the lead auditor anticipates as being required. (This will be further confirmed when the lead auditor has determined the amount of work involved, as discussed below).
2. The basis for the audit, that is to say, on what grounds access to perform an audit is being requested. Such grounds may include a contract requirement (in the case of an external audit) or a requirement of the company's quality assurance programme(in the case of an internal audit).
3. The audit objectives and the documents of prime interest in the audit such as the quality assurance manual, the code or standard invoked by the contract, the procedures or instructions that describe the quality assurance programme required of the auditee.
4. The names of the audit team members if this has been decided. The auditee has to know who to expect and may indeed be acquainted with some of the proposed audit team.
5. A blank questionnaire for providing advance details of the auditee's operation if it is company practice to issue one. The questionnaire might cover points such as the range of products or markets; industrial approvals held; turnover; QA standards, codes and regulations in force plant layout; plant size; number of employees; name of quality assurance manager; process capacities and so on. This information can be useful if the auditing company has no prior knowledge of the auditee's operation. (Those questionnaires apply more in the case of external audits.)

Channel of notification:

The notification must always be sent through the official, formal channels used for the product concerned. What these are will vary from company to company. In some cases, the quality assurance department may be allowed to pass the notification directly to the supplier (in the case of an external audit); in other circumstances, it may have to pass through the purchasing department or the contract manager, depending on company policy. In the case of an internal audit, the notification should be sent by one departmental manager to the other concerned.

One reason for using the official channels is to set an example to other persons and organizations in this respect. Furthermore, new information may have been received by some person in more recent communication with the auditee. It may transpire that the proposed date of the audit would be inappropriate because, according to the latest information, the contract will have been completed a month beforehand. In this case, the lead auditor will have to put forward an alternative date.

Confirmation:

The auditee must be asked either to confirm in writing that the proposed audit dates are suitable or to propose appropriate alternative dates, together with the reasons why the original one was not feasible (one such explanation being, for example, that the auditee would not be able to make persons available during the audit because of holidays or other prior commitments).

Notification and confirmation of the audit dates should take place before the audit schedule is finalized. Changes may have to be made to the schedule in the light of the auditee's response to the notification.

It is just as annoying to arrive at a supplier's to perform an audit only to find that his sales department has not informed the other departments that an audit is to take place, as it is not to be informed by one's own sales department that a customer is arriving to perform an extrinsic audit. The lack of information may not be too serious if all the people concerned are available, but it is common sense and plain good management to keep people informed. The old maxim "Do as you would be done by" is a useful one to apply here. Thus, whoever is responsible for organizing the audit arrangements should also be responsible for keeping the other departments and individuals involved informed of the decisions that have been taken.

> I myself had the experience of not being told until the morning it was due that an audit had to be performed. The QA manager had made all the other arrangements for the audit, omitting just one thing: to tell me that an audit was required and that I was to be the lead auditor.

Step 3. Gather preliminary information from the auditee

Although this section applies mainly to external and extrinsic audits, sometimes the auditee also has to send preliminary information to the lead auditor and audit team before an internal audit too. This is likely to be necessary if the company's departments are geographically dispersed so that information about outlying operations is not readily available at head office. Alternatively, if the company has hired auditors from a consultancy or an outside agency to perform an internal audit, they too may require information about the auditee's facilities in order to plan the proceedings satisfactorily.

The preliminary information the auditor may need includes the following:

1. A completed standard questionnaire, if any was forwarded with the notification (see above).

2. All the material — such as a copy of the quality assurance manual, job descriptions, organization charts, quality plans, procedures and instructions — required for adequate preparation, if this is not already available at the lead auditor's desk.

The copies should preferably be controlled versions, that is, versions which are automatically updated when amended. When preparing for an external audit the lead auditor should check whether or not the contract requires a controlled copy to be submitted. If the contract does not contain such a requirement, the auditee is perfectly entitled to issue uncontrolled copies.

3. A layout of the facilities.

This helps the lead auditor to assess the physical size and spread of the departments that are to be audited. (For the auditing problems that physical size can cause, see page 4.11) Sometimes a layout of the facilities is provided by the auditee's company as an appendix to the quality assurance manual.

4. A copy of the company's annual report or other profile material.

Although this information is more frequently of use in the preparation of external audits, it may also be of use in the case of internal audits of company business centres or divisions that the lead auditor has not encountered before. Such material often contains photographs of the facilities and the equipment in use. This can give the audit team valuable clues as to the auditee's policy regarding replacement and maintenance of equipment, housekeeping and other facilities but they should take these pictures with a small pinch of salt. The photos might also depict new equipment which the lead auditor can see will require the presence of a specialist as part of the audit team.

> One company had a most impressive profile book containing glossy pictures of a very orderly looking department. When the audit team later walked through that same department, they could hardly recognize it: the housekeeping was atrocious. When the audit team discussed the housekeeping with the particular department manager, the latter effused at length about the impracticality and impossibility of having everything shipshape and shining. One member of the audit team quietly said to that manager "We know you can do it. Here's your photograph of it." When the picture was placed before him the manager went rather red and then claimed that the photograph was taken before his time. Patently true but his statement did tend to compound his sins!

5. Names of the official contacts who will be available during the audit such as the department/divisional manager, quality assurance manager, contracts administrator or the salesman concerned.
6. The normal working hours of the various departments to be audited. This is important information since it can affect plans for travel and for the carrying out of the audit, particularly when the working hours in different parts of the organization are not the same. In an hotel, for example, the conference department might work different hours from the catering department or the housekeeping department; similarly, the reservations department of an airline might work different hours to the maintenance crews.

In the case of a foreign auditee, it may also be prudent to enquire about possible clashes with the anticipated dates for the audit caused by national holidays.

> I was asked to audit an American company in Los Angeles and discovered that the start date proposed would be impossible because it coincided with the anniversary of George Washington's birthday, which is an American national holiday.

Step 4. Obtain and review all available information

The lead auditor must review all the information listed below when preparing for the audit. After the team has been selected and obtained (see step 5 below), the individual auditors may not each need to review all the details but the more each one can review, the better. The lead auditor should decide exactly what information each individual is to review as part of the audit preparation. The list below applies to both internal and external audits. (In the case of an extrinsic audit, when a company's lead auditor may be assigned to act as escort for the extrinsic audit team, the same information should be reviewed, since it will be relevant to the extrinsic audit team's terms of reference.)

Information to be reviewed includes:

1. Contract and specifications, standards and codes invoked therein, details of the contract performance schedule and any milestone payments.

The milestone payments may be conditional upon satisfactory audit findings. This could well be the the case where a pre-award survey team has required that special contract clauses and safeguards be included, coupled to a milestone payment. In these circumstances, the audit team must be aware that, upon completion of the audit, the chief buyer (in the case of an external audit) or perhaps the sales manager (in the case of an extrinsic or an internal audit) will ask the audit team whether the milestone payment can be either claimed or made.

2. If available, the quality assurance manual, procedures and instructions describing both the quality management systems and methods of implementation.

In some cases, this information may not be available. Some external auditees insist that copies of the documents will be made available only at their own premises, on the grounds that they contain proprietary information which is not for release to external organizations. This possibility should have been clarified before contract signature and the auditor's organization should be aware of when and how access to such information for review purposes will be provided. It is extremely difficult to prepare for an audit without reviewing this information and, should it be unavailable, the time allocated to carrying out the audit may need to be extended to allow for the team's reviewing of it at the auditee's premises. If the information is forwarded to the auditor before the audit, it must be reviewed and any apparent or potential deficiencies noted.

When reviewing quality assurance manuals and similar documents, one should make allowances for any possible language barrier, given that the auditee's mother tongue might not be the same as the auditor's. It would be unfair and unreasonable to assume that simply because the wording or grammar is poor, the quality management systems are automatically deficient. They may indeed be deficient but it is the task of the auditor to verify that fact during the audit and not to prejudge the issue. Furthermore, it is good practice to advise the auditee of the correct phrasing if any inaccuracies or obscurities have been noted. (If language problems are apparent from this information, it could herald the need to allow for language barrier difficulties during the audit: possible courses of action are described later in this chapter.) The other side of the coin is that it is not safe to assume that because the documents appear to be satisfactory in every respect, the systems are implemented and efficacious.

The lead auditor should check whether those documents have been reviewed previously within his department or company, determining what deficiencies, if any, were noted by the reviewer. This does not mean that a previous review by another person(s) excuses the lead auditor and audit team from carrying out their own review. This is not only because may the earlier review may have been incorrect but because the omission of such a review would, in any case, be an abrogation of the responsibility of the whole audit team to perform the audit properly, ultimately being able to present a true and fair view of the auditee's systems and their implementation.

3. The auditee file.

This will contain information about the auditee, copies of previous audit reports, survey reports, reports of non-conformities and problem histories, maybe even an auditee rating. It may be especially useful to know about areas previously found to be deficient and about recommendations previously made. In the case of an external audit, it is important to know of special safeguards required by a pre-award survey for inclusion in contracts with the supplier as well as to know the names of personnel who have been associated with (who should, therefore, be familiar with) the supplier.

4. The information sent by the auditee.

This will enable the audit team to plan how to overcome problems created by geographic dispersion or by a large complex, also permitting them to work out the sequence in which the various departments should be audited. Other profile material can yield useful information, raise questions that need to be resolved during the audit or indicate the need for particular expertise within the audit team.

5. Inspection and field reports.

It is a grave and all too common error to neglect these reports, which should be on file somewhere. The inspection and field personnel are in a unique position to assess the true quality and fitness for purpose of the product being supplied. The files may contain plaintive reports about recurring deficiencies, reports that have not been acted upon or that have required previous action. In any case, the files will indicate to the audit team areas that should be examined, with a view to preventing repetition of the deficiencies.

6. The corrective action request file (if one is kept).

It is advisable to maintain such a file and it should be kept at the quality assurance manager's desk, so that he can review it periodically to determine if any issues are still open and require action to be taken accordingly. This procedure gives a bite to the corrective action system both for suppliers and for internal departments. The file may reveal some trends in deficiencies. The audit team should select some closed-out corrective action requests in order to verify that the auditee is taking continued corrective action. It is not necessary to devote a great deal of time to this side of the audit but it is good practice to show the auditee that corrective action should not be considered a one-time exercise or expedient.

7. Product performance records, warranty claims.

These can provide useful guidance on the actual performance of the auditee's product when in service, namely, whether or not it really is fit for purpose, also detailing manifestations of problems that the auditee should have addressed or should be addressing.

All the information listed in 1-7 above should be available within the quality assurance department since it is essential for the satisfactory execution of quality assurance duties.

8. Other useful sources of information to be tapped.

There are many other sources outside the quality assurance department which can provide useful information for the preparation of an audit.

a) In-house sources

Various departments within the auditor's own organization can provide useful background information about the auditee, the work or contract's status and any problems to be anticipated. Various departments, for example, may have difficulty in obtaining from the auditee the information required for review purposes or have experienced problems with its content.

> During the preparation of one particular external audit, a design engineer complained that an inordinate amount of time was being spent correcting the design calculations submitted by a particular supplier. These contained not only misinterpretations of the industrial standards applicable for the contract but also mathematical errors. The audit team suspected that, although the calculations submitted carried a signature alleging that they had been reviewed, they had in reality been signed without having been reviewed at all. This was verified during the audit and brought to the supplier's attention.

Other personnel may have various concerns regarding the quality of the specifications, other documents or items being provided by the auditee to them.

The purchasing department (in the case of an external audit) should always be consulted and asked about their experience of the auditee's past performance, about the buyer's understanding of the present status of the contract (which may not agree with the actual status encountered during the audit) and about any contracts that are being considered for award to the supplier concerned. If future contracts are under consideration, which may have different requirements from those at present, the audit team could state that any incapabilities exposed by the audit will not be acceptable during any subsequent contracts, this statement forming a necessary part of the audit report. The buyer should be asked about any imminent milestone payments or any other points of concern. It is important, for example, to know if the buyer is having problems obtaining the information, that the supplier is required to submit for the approval either of the auditor's organization or of the auditor's customer.

The customer service and product support staff (particularly those out "in the field") should be consulted if the audit affects items or services with which they have been or are involved. These are the people who see the true picture of the quality of the product supplied to the customer. They stand first in the firing line when irate customers complain of deficiencies: it can be a chilling and unpleasant experience. They may know of problems with products being obtained from a supplier or from the auditor's own organization; there may be deficiencies or inadequacies in the documentation; equipment might not have the requisite capability of providing customer satisfaction; the supplier's personnel in the field may be inadequately trained and perform badly. Whatever the case, these customer service and product support people are quick to appreciate any help from an audit if it will make their lives easier, as frequently it can.

> Prior to the performance of some major work at a customer's premises, a partial audit was planned and executed. The audit was performed at a time that permitted adequate opportunity to correct any deficiencies encountered. Some quite serious inadequacies were discovered and put right before the work commenced. When the actual work did begin, it was behind schedule by several weeks. However, as a result of the audit a number of improvements were made that affected management systems, equipment and documentation: eventually everything was completed several weeks ahead of schedule.

The document control area (if one exists within the auditor's organization) can provide document numbers and revisions received. A selection of documents' numbers must be taken on the audit in order to verify that the correct versions are being used in the execution of the contract, and, if the auditee is responsible for submitting documents for approval, that the latest documents have indeed been submitted for review.

b) External sources

In the case of an external audit, the company may have some consortium or joint venture partners who have agreed to exchange audit reports. Recent reports may provide useful information or alert the audit team to a potential problem. The auditor's company may be a contributor to a scheme in operation within its own industry which pools external audit reports: perhaps, information is available from that source. Even so, the company may still perform additional research of its own on the supplier of interest.

c) Reconnaissance visits

Occasionally, it may be decided that the lead auditor should visit the auditee before the actual audit. Such a decision would depend upon the company's policy, the location of the auditee the costs involved (related to the size of the contract), the nature of the item or service involved in the contract and the status of the work. The purpose of this type of visit would be to obtain information to assist in planning the audit, an assessment, perhaps, of the size of the auditee's facilities and the sequence in which the various departments and task units should be tackled. Discussion of previous visits to the supplier's facilities by other persons within the auditor's company may also produce useful information: the lead auditor should not neglect this possibility.

d) Telecommunication

A telephone call, telex or telefax communication with the auditee can sometimes provide the extra information that the audit team requires to prepare for the audit.

It should by now be apparent that there is no shortage of information available if the audit team and lead auditor care to look. The only excuse for failure to collect it is in the undesirable situation whereby management requires the audit to be performed at such short notice that preparation is absolutely impossible.

Step 5. Decide the audit team size and the team members

Although this decision should be the responsibility of the lead auditor, it is often dictated by others such as the quality assurance manager. It is my contention both that the lead auditor, who will, after all, be held responsible for the satisfactory execution of the audit, should have the authority to require the participation of such personnel as he considers necessary and that it is the duty of the auditor's management to do everything possible to make those persons available. The lead auditor's decision on team size and membership can be broken down into five stages.

1. Decide how much work is involved.

This depends upon the audit objectives; information received and reviewed; the type, depth and scope of the audit; the experience of the auditor(s); the number of contracts involved; geographic dispersion and plant layout; as well as the departments and processes to be audited.

2. Decide who is needed.

As stated above, the management must do its best to make available the people required by the lead auditor. It is a false economy to take so few people that the audit cannot be satisfactorily completed. The team may consist of a permanent full-time auditor plus a member of the quality assurance department and a quality controller for the contracts concerned. It makes sense to include the last two people because if problems arise, they will be held responsible for verifying that corrective action has been satisfactorily accomplished. Thorough familiarity with the auditee's systems and any problems that require resolution can do a great deal to help the quality controller to carry out his duties. This holds true for internal audits as well as for external ones.

In deciding who should make up the audit team, the lead auditor will naturally be constrained by company policy and the costs involved.

Use of specialists:

There is a mistaken belief that if somebody understands the principles and techniques of auditing, he or she could audit any type of operation. An auditor must never lose sight of the product: it is the very thing for which the quality management systems are created. In order to assess whether or not these systems are suitably stringent, it is essential that the auditor completely understands the product, the industry and their needs. Nobody can be an expert in everything. Different activities have different products. Few people are fully experienced in the product of every department in a commercial organization. To ensure that the audit is properly conducted, in preparing for the audit, the lead auditor will decide which areas will require particular expertise and will structure the audit team so as to contain the necessary specialists. It might not be essential for an individual specialist to be present throughout the entire audit: a specialist need only attend for that period of time in which his or her particular knowledge will be brought to bear.

One type of specialist that might be necessary is the interpreter. Knowing that the auditee's mother tongue is a foreign language, the lead auditor must choose from the following options:

1. to include in the audit team one or more auditors who are proficient in the auditee's mother tongue;

2. to obtain a member of the auditor organization's personnel who is proficient in that language to act as an interpreter;

3. to hire an interpreter for the duration of the audit.

If none of the above is possible or if management will not permit the hiring of a translator, there exists one final option:

4. to rely on the integrity of the auditee organization to provide bona fide translations for the auditor.

In the event of option 4, the lead auditor should impress on his management the potential limitations both on the audit an on the veracity of the results. Working in a foreign language may also dictate the need for extra auditing time to secure the requisite amount of objective evidence and coverage.

Audits are not cheap exercises. Considering the benefits that can result from them, it is foolhardy for any management not to support the lead auditor's request for experts. The apposite question must always be "who must go?" not "who can we spare?"

Whereas it is generally impossible for an individual to audit everything effectively without expert assistance, it is possible for a competent lead auditor to lead the audit of any type of organization. Such a person understands the principle audit matters that need to be covered: they include the task elements described in Chapters 5 and 25. To give an example: in any department a lead auditor will know that the content of information must be correct but he may not be able to judge the correctness of the content. It is at this point that the specialist will be asked to advise the lead auditor on the correctness of the information's content. Similarly, the lead auditor may be unable to decide whether or not equipment has the right capability for a particular operation — again, a specialist can be asked to advise.

3. Check on the availability of the potential team members.

The ideal team from the lead auditor's point of view may be uavailable because of holidays, sickness or prior commitments (such as other audits, business trips or meetings).

4. If sub-teams are to be used, the lead auditor must decide on the team leaders.

In making this decision, he will take into account the experience of the individuals involved because each sub-team leader must have the experience and training to be able to lead those in his sub-team satisfactorily.

5. Notify the actual team members accordingly.

Step 6. Develop the checklist

It is the responsibility of the lead auditor to decide upon the format and content of the checklist and to generate tht checklist accordingly (see Chapter 8).

When the lead auditor has decided on the type of specialists that may be required to help perform the audit and once management has agreed to make them available, they should be required to assist the lead auditor in ensuring that important matters have been covered in the checklist.

Fig. 9.5 An audit programme

HYPER-QUALITY COMPANY LIMITED

AUDIT PROGRAMME
Audit of S.C. Rap Metal Products
Audit Programme

Dates: 13-15 January 1988
Location: Stonehenge, England
Purchase order: 1234 Product: Gizmos

Audit team:				
	Team A.	J. Smith	Lead auditor	H-QCL
		G. Thomson	Auditor	H-QCL
		D. Bailey	Observer	Candle Power Corp.
	Team B.	B. Jones	Team leader	H-QCL
		P. Davidson	Auditor	H-QCL
		R. Robertson	Observer	Candle Power Corp.

Audit basis: BGPV QA Spec. ABC 123 Revision 4; S.C. Rap QA manual.

Departments to be audited:

Team A	Team B
Contracts	Receiving
Design	Receiving inspection
Drawing office	Stores
Document control	Production planning & control
Quality assurance	Machine bay No. 1
Purchasing	Special coatings
Records	Heat treatment
Calibration laboratory	Inspection and test
Warranty and product support	Packaging and despatch

Wednesday 13 January 1988

0900 Arrive at S.C. Rap facilities, Stonehenge
0915 Entry Interview; Brief description of organization and contract status by S.C. Rap personnel.
0945 Audit commences: Team A Contracts, design, drawing office.
Team B Receiving, receiving inspection, stores.
1600 Completion of first day's activities.
Evening Team conference.

Thursday 14 January 1988

0900 Reconvene at S.C. Rap facilities to continue audit:
Team A Purchasing, warranty and product support, quality assurance
Team B Heat treatment, special coatings, inspection and test
1600 Completion of second day's activities.
Evening Team conference.

Friday 15 January 1988

0900 Reconvene at S.C. Rap facilities to continue audit:
Team A Document control, records, calibration laboratory.
Team B Machine Bay 1, packaging and despatch, production planning and control.
1600 Completion of third day's activities.
Evening Team conference.

Monday 18 January 1988

0900 Exit interview, presentation of audit findings to S.C Rap management.
1030 Depart.

Step 7. Develop the programme

An example of a programme is shown (without the checklist) in Fig. 9.5. While developing the programme, the lead auditor should:

1. Decide the amount of time required for the audit.

Audits fail to deliver their full potential results when inadequate time budget is allocated for their performance. Time shortage represents a false economy.

Fig. 9.6 depicts the time benefit obtained during an audit. There is an initial period during which the benefit being obtained is low. As audit time increases, so does the quantity of objective evidence seen by an auditor. The more objective evidence obtained, the greater the benefit arising from the audit. Eventually, a point of diminishing returns is reached beyond which the expenditure of extra time merely reveals "more of the same" type of objective evidence.

Fig. 9.6 Audit benefit-time curve

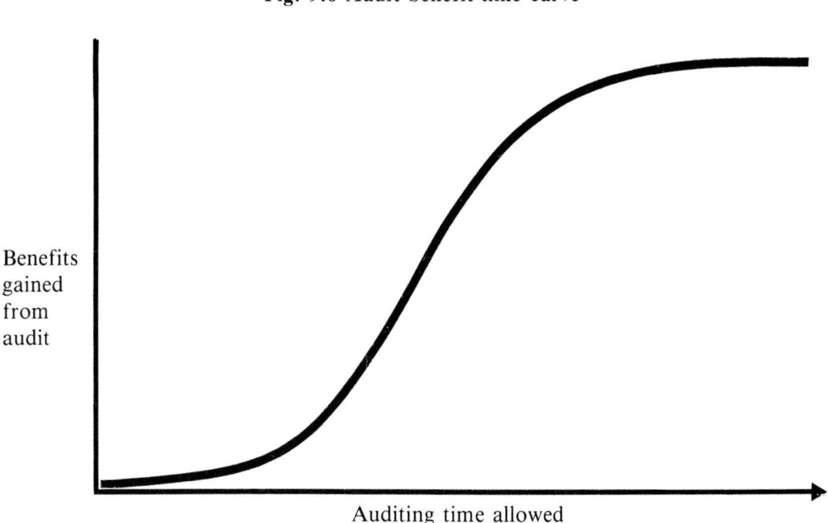

Since the early 1980s, the North Sea oil industry has taken quality assurance more seriously than ever. As a result, large numbers of audits have been performed. However, many of these audits

> have been allocated a totally inadequate time budget, the vast majority being allowed little more than a couple of days in which to audit an entire company fully. I am of the opinion that the North Sea industry has not received the benefits commensurate with the vast amount of money and manpower expended, principally because a prime objective of these audits seems to have been to accumulate documentary evidence that "somebody went there," as opposed to examining the auditee's quality management systems critically and determining which can be simplified as well as how to save on resources, time and cost. If more time had been devoted to the audits, the benefits would have been considerably greater.
>
> Frequently, the above has reached absurd proportions. I recall an encounter with an acquaintance one day. From a brief conversation, I ascertained that he was assigned to audit a complete company in the morning, have lunch, drive 30 miles and then audit another company in the afternoon.

The time needed for audit performance depends mainly on the following factors, which the lead auditor should determine when formulating his audit schedule:

—the depth of audit (system, compliance);

—the objectives (such as the follow-up of corrective action requests or the introduction of a Just-in-Time philosophy. The importance of the decisions taken by management as a result of the audit must also be considered);

—the number of different work activities or departments to be audited;

—the typical amount (sample size) of objective evidence that the auditor might wish to see in order to obtain a certain confidence that a true and fair view has been obtained;

—the availability of specialists and whether or not sub-teams will be used;

—the speed or experience of the individual auditors. Every auditor develops his or her own methods and question technique. This has a considerable effect on the speed with which the auditor can cover any particular area;

—the size of the auditee's facilities and whether there is any geographic dispersion between principal activities to be audited. If the latter is the case, then the lead auditor needs to allow time for travelling between them. (See Chapter 4.)

Example:

A supplier has to be audited.
The number of key activities to be audited is 18.
The lead auditor estimates that, on average, each department will require approximately 2.5 hours to audit.
Knowing that the auditee works a 7.5 hour day, the lead auditor wants the audit team to work a 7 hour day in the auditee's premises.
Thus, the total time required for the audit is:

$$\frac{2.5 \times 18}{7} = 6 \text{ man-days (approx)}$$

However, the lead auditor's management says that the audit must be completed within 3 days, Therefore the total number of sub-teams must be 2. The end result can be seen in the programme shown in Fig. 9.5.

2. Fit in with the normal working hours and allow at least half an hour in the morning for the auditee's people to open mail, allocate work to their departments, start up machines, sign letters and so on.

This half hour's grace makes it less likely that proceedings will be interrupted by the auditee's staff requesting decisions on routine or urgent problems. It also permits the auditee to make it known that he does not wish to be disturbed during the course of the audit unless absolutely necessary.

3. Never plan a late afternoon finish if there is a major local event on.

It is sometimes unavoidable that in order to complete auditing in a particular area, the audit team's work extends slightly beyond the auditee's normal working hours and, hence, the auditee's personnel go home later than usual. If some special event like an important football game, a parent/teacher meeting, a carnival or a parade, makes it particularly likely that staff will want to get away from work on time, it is only reasonable and human to try to avoid a late finish that would cause inconvenience and possible undue annoyance to the auditee's personnel.

4. Allocate the work.

The lead auditor will have decided what can be done, given the actual manpower and time available, and will have listed the departments that are to be audited accordingly. It may be necessary to select departments so as to get the best "feel" in the time available for the auditee's management systems and their efficacy (see Chapter 7). If auditing a manufacturer the lead auditor may decide to have one team audit all activities in the works while another team audits the offices (the software, namely). This sort of hardware/software split is shown in the example of an audit programme given in Fig. 9.5. If auditing a service organization the lead auditor may decide on a foreground/background split — see Chapter 25.

Step 8. Distribute the programme to the auditee and to the audit team

1. Prepare at least two copies of the checklist and programme for the auditee, in the case of an external audit. For an internal audit, a single copy should suffice.
2. Attach a copy of the checklist to each copy of the programme.
3. Prepare one copy of the checklist and programme for each member of the audit team, that is, one copy for each of the auditors and one for each of the observers who may be participating.

When forwarding the programme to the auditee, the lead auditor should try to adhere to the following rules:

—always use the official, formal channels (see earlier section on notifying the auditee).
—try to ensure that the programme will arrive at the auditee's facilities at least two weeks in advance of the audit.

This gives the auditee's people a chance to assimilate the programme and to contact the auditor if they foresee any difficulties. Make some allowance for postal delays where the auditee is located abroad. While compiling the programme, the lead auditor should have in mind a target deadline for forwarding the programme to the auditee.

3. Never forward untidy or illegible documents.

Scruffy documents create a bad impression and can make it difficult for the auditee to understand fully what the audit team wants. The result may be delays or difficulties during the audit.

4. State which of the auditee's key personnel should attend the exit interview.

It is desirable that the auditee's senior managers should be forewarned that their attendance at the exit interview would be appreciated. The more senior a person is in a company, the more valuable his time may be and the more important it is to forewarn him.

In the case of an external audit, the auditee's senior management is generally interested in learning of any problems that the customer has encountered and, therefore, makes every effort to attend the exit interview. There is something seriously wrong with a company if its senior management is not interested in its customer's impression of its management systems, facilities and products or in his assessment of whether the contract conditions are being met or not.

> At the beginning of one audit, the auditee's quality assurance manager informed the audit team that the company's vice president would not be available to attend the exit interview because he was away attending a meeting in another city for the entire week. Later that morning, while the team were busy auditing in a department, a secretary came running up to the department's manager to give him a message that the vice president wanted to see him immediately in his office. The lead auditor turned to the department manager and said "While you're with him, would you please remind him that the exit interview is on Friday and that we will be pleased to see him there?" The quality assurance manager's face wore an expression of acute embarrassment. The moral of the story is that if you are going out of town, make sure everybody knows that you are out of town, and then remember to be out of town!

Step 9. Hold briefing sessions

The importance of holding a briefing session depends upon many factors, among them company policy, the audit team members' experience and abilities, the scope of the contract, auditee history, the extent and complexity of the audit, personal relations with the auditee, participation of third parties (consortium partners performing joint audits, inspection agencies, customers, other observers) and the geographic dispersion of the audit team members. Sometimes the relationships between customer and supplier or — in the case of an internal audit — between the quality assurance department and the auditee's department are such that it is simple common sense to forewarn the members of the audit team of potential friction. This must not be taken to mean that they should turn a blind eye to any deficiencies, merely that they should be alert to possibly sensitive areas and adjust their conduct accordingly.

> Prior to one particular audit, it was necessary to inform the audit team that another contract with the supplier concerned had reached the stage at which the companies' attornies were exchanging letters. Although the dispute had not spread to the contract with which the audit was concerned, the team was advised that any discussion of the contentious contract might be prejudicial both to audit execution and to the company and should therefore be avoided.

Sometimes, when a customer, a regulatory body or an inspection agency is participating as an observer, it is advisable to hold a briefing session so that everybody understands exactly what their duties are in the execution of the audit. This will also show the observers that the auditor's company takes its audits very seriously.

When using specialists, one must make sure that they are aware of the need to keep their feet on the ground. They must not let matters of idle curiosity allow them to lose touch with the real needs of the audit.

If not all the team are able to attend the briefing (perhaps because of geographic dispersion), those unable to attend should be informed of what happened during the session. It may be possible for the audit team to meet for a briefing session during the evening before an audit, once they have all arrived.

Special attention has to paid to the ''new auditor'', as described later in this chapter.

Step 10. Make any last minute changes necessary

Occasionally the audit programme may need to be altered in the light of input received from the auditee, from the customer, from work or contract progress or from the briefing session. Any substantial changes must, of course, be communicated to all concerned, namely, the auditee, the audit team and the departments affected within the auditor's company. It may be necessary to indicate the changes at the entry interview meeting (see Chapter 10). In more serious cases, the audit may have to be postponed but this course should only be adopted if no other alternative presents itself.

Work out what to take

No job can be performed properly without the right tools: an audit is no exception. The following items are typical of the things that it is useful to have on hand for the performance of the audit.

1. Contract(s), specifications and standards. If the contract is very bulky, a photocopy of the relevant pages will suffice. The quality assurance programmes, specifications or standards are always of a convenient size to tuck into a briefcase.
2. The audit programme and checklist (it is surprising how many auditors forget them). These may already contain certain mark-ups, such as QA manual references and other memoranda, that the auditor will want during the audit.
3. A selection of document numbers that are applicable for the product and activities concerned as well as a note of their revision status.
4. The copy of the QA manual, procedures, instructions etc., that were reviewed as part of the audit preparation. It cannot be assumed that the revisions reviewed are in fact those that are implemented.
5. Personal checklists and vade mecum. Many auditors find it useful to take along a notebook in which to jot down abbreviated details of findings and experiences during an audit.

6. Entry interview and exit interview attendance forms. This is rather gilding the lily but I make a point of taking a blank form for each meeting to serve as a reminder that an attendance list should be generated.
7. Corrective Action Request blank forms. If corrective actions should be required as a result of the audit findings, they will have to be written up and presented at the exit interview. A supply of blank forms is therefore necessary.
8. A tape recorder and blank tapes. A tape recording of the exit interview is a useful way of informing those who could not attend of what was said. It also helps the auditor to check the actual phrases used at the exit interview which can save time when compiling the audit report and prevent arguments about who said what in sensitive situations. A small pocket recorder is the easiest machine to use for this purpose.

Preparing a new auditor

There is always a first audit for every auditor. In some cases it can be a nerve-wracking affair because the auditor is not certain of his duties or what he should be looking for. The lead auditor can prepare his new colleague by in following ways.

1. Give the auditor a departmental checklist (see Chapter 8) and ask him to mark in the clause numbers of the codes, standards or regulations concerned against each question. An alternative is to give him a criteria checklist and ask him to mark in the departments involved.
2. Ask him to review the auditee's quality assurance manual against the audit checklist to suggest areas to which particular attention should be paid.
3. Ask him to mark up his checklist against the quality assurance manual, showing paragraph numbers, exhibit numbers and other references to the quality documents.
4. Review his marked-up checklist and explain any errors *before* getting to the auditee's premises.

The fourth point is of critical importance: it tells the lead auditor whether the new recruit understands the aims of the audit, is aware of the contract requirements and can interpret the QA standards. From this the lead auditor can infer whether or not the new auditor will need special guidance during the audit. The review must be performed before reaching the auditee's premises so as to spare the auditor the embarrassment of exposing any misconceptions publicly. This precaution will also protect the entire audit team from losing face with the auditee, as they may if the auditee feels that the team is composed of people who do not know what they are doing.

References:

1. ISO 9001 — 1987 *Quality systems — Model for quality assurance in design/development, production, installation and servicing*. Published by the International Organization for Standardization.

2. API Spec. Q1, First edition, January 1, 1985, *API specification for quality programs*. Published by the American Petroleum Institute, Production Department, 211 N. Ervay, Suite 1700, Dallas TX 75201-3688.

3. CAN3-Z299.1 — 1985 *Quality assurance program — Category 1*. Published by Canadian Standards Association, 178 Rexdale Boulevard, Rexdale (Toronto), Ontario, Canada M9W 1R3.

10. The Entry Interview

Speak thy purpose out;
I love not mystery or doubt.
Walter Scott.

Upon arrival at the auditee's premises, a meeting between the auditee and the audit team takes place. This meeting is sometimes called the entry interview.

Attendees

Fig. 10.1 shows those who, ideally speaking, should attend the entry interview. In the case of an audit that is proceeding at two locations, the lead auditor can only be available at one of them so the sub-team leader conducts the entry interview at the other. Similarly, the auditee will be unable to have certain of the personnel indicated on the table present at both locations. In this situation, the auditee usually makes arrangements for

Fig. 10.1 Entry interview attendees

	AUDITOR ORGANIZATION	AUDITEE ORGANIZATION	
		Internal audit	*External audit*
MUST	All auditors who will audit that location Team leader/lead auditor and observers for that location	Manager of area to be audited and/or area supervisor	QA manager, contract engineer, contract administrator
OPTIONAL	Specialist(s)		Managing director, engineering manager, production manager, sales manager

appropriate personnel to be present at each location. In the case of an external audit, for example, the quality assurance manager may be present at the location where the lead auditor is conducting an entry interview whilst his senior QA representative is in attendance at the second location. Some suppliers require that the senior management be present at the entry interview to meet an external audit team, to give it a warm welcome and assimilate what will be happening during the audit. It should also be noted that certain attendees in my chart are purely optional. Their attendance will depend on the needs of the audit, company policy or perhaps simply on them happening (or not happening) to be at the auditee's premises at the time of the entry interview.

Explaining the role of observers

During the proceedings, the lead auditor or team leader must make clear to the auditee that an observer is an observer, a guest rather than a participant as of right (unless the contract or regulations specifically states otherwise). This is particularly important when the auditor's customer is attending as observer. The auditee then knows that all comments and questions coming from the observers will be directed to him through the audit team. Observers should act in the manner expected of guests and the audit team should not be afraid to remind an observer of his role. However, if the customer is performing an extrinsic audit as of right, then the customer is running the audit and is responsible for taking such actions as are necessary to obtain the information required (provided that those actions are within the contractual limits).

> At one external audit, the audit team's customer was to be represented by an inspector who, it had been agreed, would act as an observer. That inspector's superior (the QA manager) arrived and stated that he would also be an observer during the audit. Relationships between the audit team's customer and the supplier being audited were extremely strained because of that QA manager, who had previously caused many unnecessary problems for both the audit team's company and for the supplier by acting beyond the limitations of the contract. Knowing that the individual's intent was to cause trouble, the lead auditor immediately refused to have him as a participant during the audit. When the QA manager refused to leave, the lead auditor stated that unless he did so, the audit would be postponed and no observers from the customer's organization would be allowed. The gentleman concerned was finally removed from the premises. The audit then proceeded smoothly and satisfactorily.
>
> The lead auditor knew the prime contract conditions, was acting within his company's rights and received the full support of the supplier and his own management.

Allaying fears

If this is the first time a company has audited a particular auditee, the latter possibly being unfamiliar with the mode of procedure, it is wise to explain the methods and the purpose of the audit exactly in order to put people's minds at ease. It may be that the only meaning of the word "audit" previously encountered by the auditee is in the context of the financial auditing of books.

> One company had been extremely unenthusiastic about providing access for audits to be performed by their customer and had put forward reasons for postponing the audit several times. An ultimatum was finally issued to the effect that the audit must take place by a certain date and, reluctantly, the company was forced to agree. When they arrived at the auditee's premises, the audit team were told that the managing director would be completely unavailable for the week because he had suddenly been taken ill: arrayed in front of the audit team were nearly thirty individuals from varying levels of management of the company. Also present was the financial director. It very quickly became apparent that the auditee believed the audit to be some kind of meeting leading up to an apocalypse for the company's management. When the lead auditor explained the purpose of the audit, the expressions of relief visible on everybody's faces were most memorable. The next day, the managing director appeared to have made a miraculous recovery from his illness and was back at work.

It must be remembered that an audit can make some people so nervous that they go sick rather than face it. This not necessarily indicates that they have something to hide — they may simply be so concerned about getting things right that they "worry themselves to death" in case the audit should reveal some minor deficiencies which would reflect adversely upon themselves. The entry interview can do much to assuage these feelings and fears. Fig. 10.2 shows a checklist that summarizes the proceedings.

Duration

Unless there are some particularly contentious points that must be clarified during the entry interview, half an hour or thereabouts should be quite adequate to cover the proceedings described in Fig. 10.2.

Attendance list

At the entry interview, especially one held before an external audit, the audit team must always initiate an attendance list, which all present should be requested to sign. If, during an extrinsic audit, the audit team does not initiate an attendance list, the auditee should do so. The entry interview is an official, formal meeting that could have contractual implications should points of contention later arise as a result of the audit. It is therefore advisable to record exactly who was present to represent the various parties involved.

Fig. 10.2 Proceedings for entry interview

Lead auditor/team leader	*Auditee*
	1. Introduce personnel (more applicable for external audit).
2. Distribute attendance list. Introduce audit team. Explain each individual's function in the audit and contract (more applicable for external audit).	
3. Explain purpose of audit, the basis and programme.	
	4. Explain contract/work/product status.
5. Ask for a knowledgeable escort for each team (more applicable for external audits).	
6. Ask for confirmation that information submitted is latest version. If not, assess why latest not submitted.	
7. Ask for a meeting room to be reserved for the team's use, if necessary (more applicable for external audits).	
8. Confirm working hours, lunch break and tea break times. A quick lunch, please (more applicable for external audits).	
9. Fix a time for each day's summary meeting with auditee.	
10. State the tentative time for the exit interview and which members of auditee's management should attend, if possible.	
	11. Question time.
12. Ensure all present have signed attendance list.	

The entry interview is the first occasion for the audit team to encounter the auditee: much useful information can be gleaned from it. Note should be taken of who speaks on behalf of the auditee since this may well reflect the real power structure within the auditee's company or department. This informal organization (which may be miles away from the formal structure laid down in the QA manual) may be of crucial importance in determining what actually gets done within the company: anything that helps to indicate that company mode of operation will be very valuable to the audit team. The informal methods of working may or may not be efficacious for the contract. The audit team will have to try to determine exactly what really happens and decide whether or not this is satisfactory. Quite frequently, it is at this stage that the first indications emerge of lack of top management commitment to quality. Seemingly innocent remarks of the type listed in page 12-10 can provide the clues.

The entry interview may also produce other valuable impressions — who seems to know what, how the various departments interact and so on. The conduct of the auditee's representatives can provide hints as to what tactics the audit team should adopt when dealing with particular individuals or departments. It is not uncommon for the entry interview to be a platform at which some people want to "make it clear from the start that this audit team will see what I say they'll see".

The audit team (and especially the lead auditor) must make it clear from the outset that they have a job to do. This can be achieved quite politely although the team must be prepared to be firm if necessary. Provided they act within the limitations of the contract, the audit team should have no problems in the case of an external audit. For internal audits, the firm's quality management policy and the audit objectives state the limitations of the audit team's authority.

Escorts

The lead auditor must tell the auditee who, ideally, should act as an escort. It is unwise to become overloaded with too many escorts (one really is enough). The escort should be knowledgeable about the management systems operating within the various areas to be audited. He should also have sufficient status to ensure that the auditee's personnel give the maximum co-operation while the audit is going on.

> During one audit, it was decided that the quality assurance manager and quality assurance engineer would accompany the audit team. At some point, it was noted that the audit ensemble had swelled to 12 people: the team leader, an auditor and an

observer, two escorts, the contract manager (who had caught up with the audit "to see how things were going"), the supervisor of the particular department being audited, one operator who was actually being audited, the patrol inspector at that particular location, the shop labourer (who had stopped sweeping to listen and try to help with what was going on), and two other bodies who had simply appeared from somewhere. The audit had reached a contentious point, with everybody trying to help by explaining to everybody else what should and should not happen as well as what had probably occurred. Absolute pandemonium ensued. Order was restored when the lead auditor asked the escorts to request that everybody not directly concerned leave.

11. Audit Methods

Knowledge advances by steps, and not by leaps.
Thomas Macauley.

With increasing experience, each auditor will develop his or her own method of performing an audit. A common trait in inexperienced auditors is the absence of a structured approach to auditing individual tasks and hence the entire auditee activities: they appear to believe that if they keep asking questions as inspiration occurs, then, when they cannot think up any more, everything must have been covered.

The vain hope that, by their running around at random, the job will get done, is busy-ness as opposed to business and does not provide any degree of assurance that all necessary matters have been treated.

THE AUDITOR MUST DEVELOP A SYSTEMATIC WAY OF WORKING.

The following method is suggested since it has provided me with pleasing results over the years. Fig. 11.1 lists seven distinct and sequential steps which constitute a gradually increasing depth of investigation. These seven steps are applied at each level in the auditee's operation, that is, across the entire company, across complete divisions and departments as well as in individual task units. The objective evidence to be collected is discussed in Chapter 12 "Information Collection".

Fig. 11.1 Audit sequence

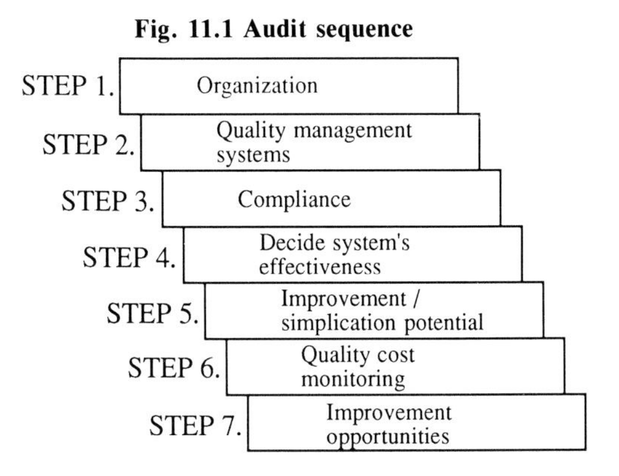

STEP 1: Organization.

The starting point must always be to investigate the auditee's organization plans. Organization planning is the first stepping stone on the path which leads to quality achievement: without this foundation, quality problems and chaos will result. The auditor has to assess whether or not the organization has been properly conceived in relation to the basic needs of the product and industry.

Fig. 11.2 shows those matters which the auditor must bear in mind. The very first is the vital question "What is the product?" The auditor must:

NEVER LOSE SIGHT OF THE PRODUCT.

It is the needs of the product, the importance of the product (classification) and strategic decisions that will prescribe the organizational needs of the auditee. The type of objective evidence to be sought is listed. In assessing the auditee's organizational proposals, the auditor will review the information indicated in Fig. 11.2, keeping in mind the principle concerns shown. The good auditor will never read his own opinion into what a statute, regulation or standard says. Thus, when considering the auditee's organizational plans for compliance with such documents, one must always work to the letter and retain an open mind. See Chapter 4 for a discussion of organizational matters.

STEP 2: The quality management system.

Once the status of the auditee's organizational plans has been established, the auditor then examines the auditee's quality management systems. Fig. 11.2 lists the objective evidence that the auditor will peruse to determine whether or not the auditee's proposals for those systems are satisfactory. The auditor will continue to be aware of the matters raised in Step 1 as well as of the precise words of the statute/regulation/code or standard which applies. The existence of a reliable planned audit trail, between the various task elements and interfacing work activities, traceable back to the customer, regulatory body or other pertinent requirements must be verified.

The examination of the auditee's organization and system proposals should have been completed as part of the preparation of the audit particularly as those proposals are generally contained in documentation. Upon arrival at site, to maximize time usage, the auditor will merely investigate those matters revealed by the preparation to require clarification.

Depending on the audit's objective, the auditor may also wish to investigate the system for allocating resources and time to each task. As has been stated in Chapter 1, lack of time and lack of resources are real causes of quality problems. Time and resource management are inseparable and essential components of quality management: see also Chapters 7, 18 and 26.

Fig. 11.2. Audit sequence showing matters of concern and typical objective evidence

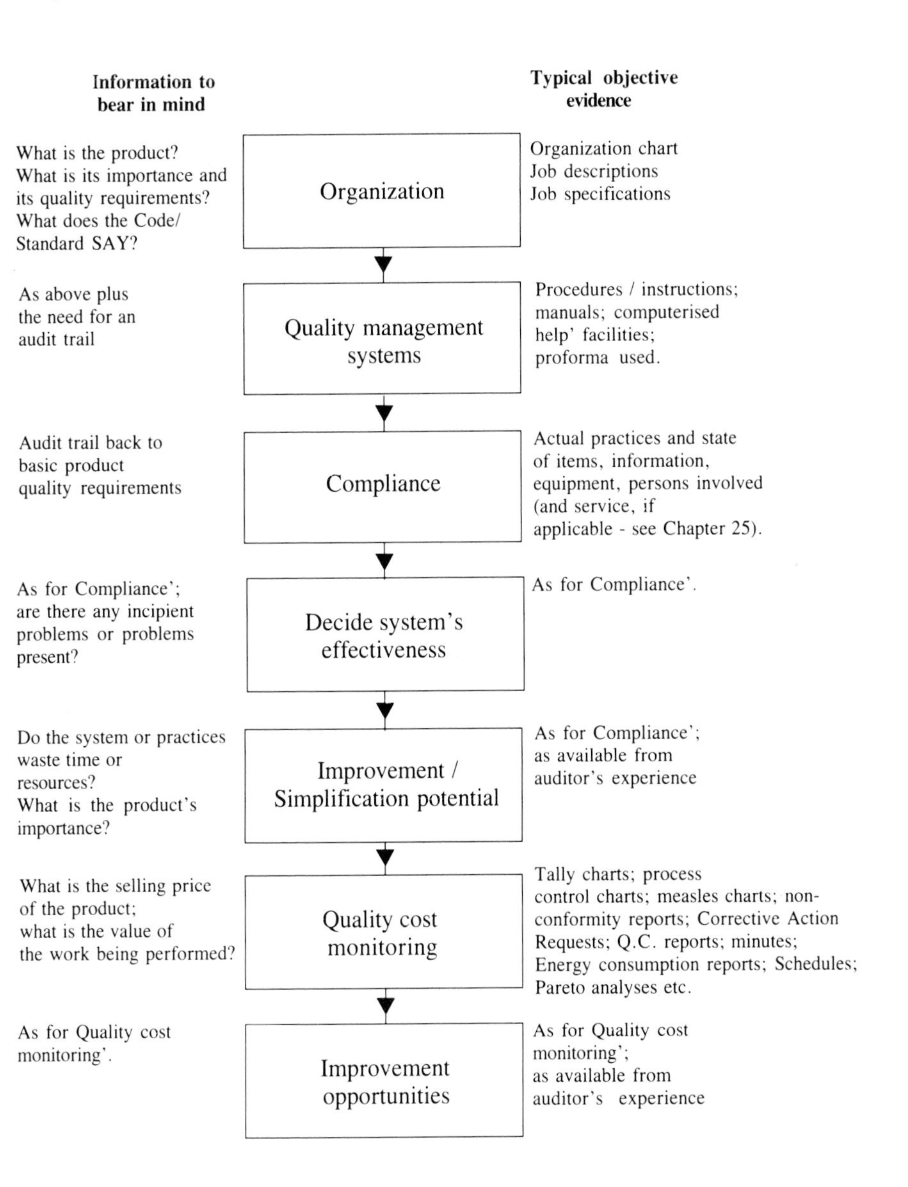

STEP 3: Compliance.

Having assessed the organization and system, the next step is to investigate the extent of compliance with them. Compliance audits are only possible once work has actually started except when the auditee, either because of the sensitivity of the product or for staff training purposes, decides to have a dummy run or to produce a prototype of the final product. In some industries and for some products, this may be neither possible nor practical. By going through the task elements at each particular workplace systematically, the auditor will examine objective evidence furnished as a result of the various tasks being performed. While checking compliance, the auditor must follow the audit trail already assessed in STEP 2, above.

STEP 4: Deciding on the system's effectiveness.

The objective evidence obtained in step 3 enables the auditor to decide whether or not the system and practices are effective. Fig. 11.2 shows the principle matters to be kept in mind: these remain directly related to the product. The product requirements and the audit trail should not have been violated. Evidence of either present or incipient problems must be noted.

Quality management systems can appear to be impressive on paper but the litmus test of a system's effectiveness is the product to emanate from its application.

STEP 5: Improvement or simplification potential.

The possibility for improving or simplifying systems or processes must now be considered. Audits must be of a constructive nature and the auditor has a duty to be helpful at all times. It is all too easy to tear systems apart but offering constructive criticism for improvement requires true professional competence. The proficient auditor has a duty to help the auditee and to provide advice. ''Improvements or simplification[s]'' which would be unwise given the classification of the product must not be proposed. (It is worth repeating that the product comes first: never lose sight of the product.) The essential question is: on the basis of the objective evidence studied, do the implemented systems appear to waste time or resources?

Flow charts are of great assistance in answering that question. Specialists may be able to offer some advice concerning new techniques or equipment that are available to help reduce costs, save time and resources whilst maintaining or improving product quality.'

It is very important to try to help the auditee at every opportunity. As stated in pages 1-8, 1-9 the auditee is investing in the audit. Resentment and hostility towards management audits develop when auditees do not perceive much real benefit from their investment. Incompetent auditors tend to be nit-pickers, destructive critics who thrive on confrontation. By offering advice and constructive help to the auditee, the auditor will help to reduce barriers of resistance substantially, creating a spirit of co-operation which is of benefit to both auditee and auditor alike. See also Chapter 14.

STEP 6: Quality cost monitoring.

The next step is to investigate the auditee's methods of quality cost monitoring given that a quality cost system is an essential part of a corrective action system. The auditor will examine the data capture methods, the non-conformity and corrective action systems and an example of the information created by them.

Quality costs do not need to be quantified in monetary terms: monetary equivalents, such as percentage yields, errors per document, tally counts, rework hours, downtime figures, grade to rework ratios and the like will suffice. The essence is to ascertain whether or not management really is aware of the costs of producing the product in each area. The absence of a quality cost system for the areas assigned to him means that a manager is not managing, that those areas are out of control. The quality cost data captured provides the manager with the opportunity to improve efficiency and outgoing quality levels. Without this information, opportunity is lost and ultimately the business is at risk or, in the case of the civil service, taxpayers' money is at risk. As Harold Geneen rightly states:

> "the drudgery of the numbers will make you free . . . The numbers are there to reflect how well or how poorly your business is doing".[1]

Naturally, the quality cost systems should not cost more to operate than the potential benefits which can accrue. The auditor should not look for unreasonably complex and costly methods of capturing such data. The data might exist in tally charts, process control sheets, non-conformity report forms, corrective action requests, quality circle reports or minutes of meetings — whatever. Each of these provides feedback which identifies opportunity.

STEP 7: Improvement opportunities.

Provided that there is a system for quality cost data capture, the results of its operation should be reviewed to identify trends or potential opportunities for improvement. The competent auditor might be able to bring extra experience to bear, interpreting the auditee's data in a different way from that of the auditee, potentially giving rise to opportunity. Even if a formal system does not exist, the auditor should consider carefully the objective evidence of the auditee's quality management systems and level of accomplishments to try to identify areas that could constitute an opportunity for the saving of resources and time. Clearly, such improvement would need to improve quality or, at least, not compromise it.

Following the system

There are various paths that the auditor may take through the departments and units involved in a quality management system, as the work passes through the various contract or product phases (see Fig. 11.3). Each of the following three methods has its advantages and disadvantages (see Fig. 11.4).

Trace forward

In the trace forward method, for a full audit, the auditor starts auditing within research and development or sales, selects the product or order(s) of interest and follows it (or them) through the various departments and units associated with the phases of the contract through to the despatch/shipping department (or whatever the department from which the product is handed over to the customer is called). In the service industry, an example might be in auditing an hotel's quality management systems by following the path encountered by a guest from reservations, porterage and reception through to check-out and departure.

Trace back

This method works in the opposite direction to the trace forward method. For a full audit, the auditor retraces the steps involved in completing the chosen contract right back to the sales department. Trace back is particularly useful when auditing services: in the case of a fast food store, for example, the auditor might start at the point of consumption, work back through point of sale, food preparation and back towards, say, receipt of foodstuffs in the store. Thus the delivered product and service results are seen first and their "geneology" established: any illegitimates can then be readily identified and banished from the family!

Random department

Here, the auditor visits all the departments or units that are of interest in whatever order he chooses. With this approach, the auditor has to be especially careful not to miss a unit or department that is of interest.

Fig. 11.3 Trace forward and trace back audit methods

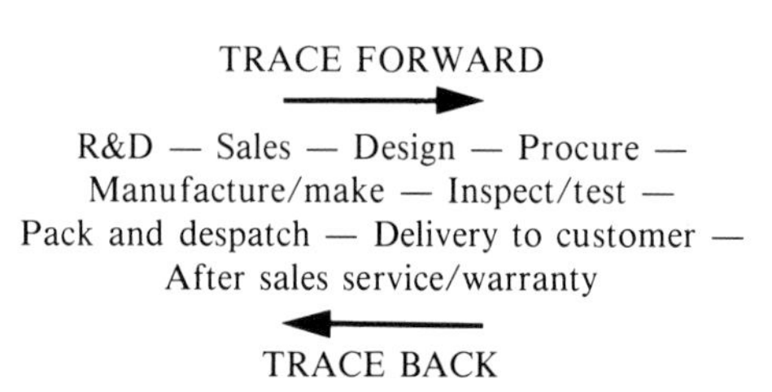

Fig. 11.4 Audit methods: advantages and disadvantages

	Advantages	*Disadvantages*
Trace forward	Shows logical system through the company. Easy for training. Aids pre-planning of arrival times in departments. Deficiencies at front end found more quickly (these can have greater cost impact).	Logical flow broken if people unavailable for short period. Not so flexible. Not practical for partial audits, since traceback is also required.
Trace back	Can start in any department and hence is suitable for partial audits. Easy for training. Aids pre-planning of arrival times in departments. Results (objective evidence) of department's work seen prior to arrival.	Logical flow broken if people unavailable for short period. Not so flexible. Front-end software not seen until the end: time shortage at front end needs to be avoided.
Random department	Very flexible; minimizes disruption. Not upset if people unavailable. Gives broad picture fairly quickly. Good for pre-award surveys if time is short. Good for partial audits.	Requires experienced auditor. Can mean avid note taking.

It is important to remember two points when a particular contract is selected for the performance of a *full* audit.

1. In order to see the whole contract, it is necessary to select one that is *completed*. In the case of an external audit, this is probably not the auditor's contract and the audit may run into proprietary information problems or Official Secrets Act limitations which are imposed on the auditee and hence on the auditor. In the case of an internal audit, the selection of a completed contract, due for hand-over to the customer, may also present difficulties: it may be difficult, because of financial considerations or internal politics, to persuade management to institute corrective action at such a late stage, even if deficiencies have been discovered which affect the quality of the product. That is a matter of top management support and attitude which the auditor may be unable to alter.

2. When carrying out a full audit, the auditor tends to get to know the particular product or contract intimately and the explanations given by the auditee acquire unique nuances for him. This "feel" for the contract can speed up the proceedings and reduce the amount of note taking required.

In the light of the foregoing, it is, therefore, quite common for a phased audit to be planned in order to monitor the progress of an individual project or contract.

Obtaining objective evidence

There are three principle methods of obtaining objective evidence. They are by:

a) examination of objective evidence such as documents, reports, computer print outs, VDU displays, item numbers, equipment details, as described in Chapter 12 "Information Collection".

b) observation of performance. The auditor requests the auditee to demonstrate how the work is performed at a given workplace.

c) re-performance of the task. This can be useful in the case of, say, design calculations. A specialist member of the audit team can quickly re-check calculations to see if the same or similar results are obtained.

> While auditing a mechanical equipment design area, I decided to re-check certain stress analyses quickly since my original specialism is mechanical engineering design. A number of errors which could have affected the safety of the components concerned were found. These were corrected. However, the real problem was that since the calculations bore evidence of review and approval, I could not have much confidence in the quality of the review and approval work. This led to a whole series of different questions being raised.
>
> Similarly, while auditing a hygiene laboratory at a food factory, I asked a chemist on my audit team to re-check some culture plates, to compare his results with the laboratory's. That chemist possessed that area of expertise: I did not.

An approval signature on a document provides no guarantee that the work was properly checked. In order to gain confidence that the signatory's work has value, a spot check is necessary.

Spot checks

The auditor must have spot checks carried out on items that have allegedly been inspected or tested. It is essential that he should select the items for spot checks himself — this makes it impossible for the auditee to "fix" the spot checks in advance by choosing specially prepared items.

Documentation must be spot checked for availability and compliance with requirements of the quality management systems, particularly when a pre-award survey is being performed (subject to the limitations discussed in Chapter 2).

The auditor must remember that for compliance audits, whatever is selected is probably only a *sample* of all the items/documents that are available. Hence, even at the best of times, the auditor is only spot checking. The auditor may wish to have some level of confidence of unearthing any significant quality problem by following a statistical sampling plan (such as MIL-STD-105D[2]), when choosing which items or documents to check. To follow such a plan may involve checking a large number of documents or items and, in my experience, a relatively small number of spot checks is sufficient to reveal a major problem such as management system deficiency.

The auditor must try to assess the true magnitude of any problem he encounters and avoid making an issue out of trivial deficiencies, human errors or isolated mistakes. Depending on the audit objectives and the criticality of the decisions that will be taken as a result of its completion, it may be reasonable to select, say, six or ten of a particular type of item or document and to leave the checking there, provided that absolutely no defects are found within the sample. If, however, the sample shows up one or more deficiencies, then the auditor must either spot check further items or documents or ask the auditee to purge the files or items to discover the true extent of the problem. The justification for this practice is as follows. If out of the sample, no deficiencies are found, then there is a system present, working, and known to the personnel concerned. If one deficiency is found, then the system, rather than simply not being implemented, may be in a period of gestation (having just been introduced) or may need to be further instilled into the personnel affected. If further spot checking reveals that the deficient document or item from the first sample is the only one, then the problem is more likely to be human error (that is, an isolated occurrence). (For further discussion of this topic see Chapter 17.)

The need for re-inspection or re-testing depends on the product or contract status and on whether a hold point has been integrated with the audit. Combining the audit with a hold point can have tremendous value (as discussed in Chapter 3). The acid test of the quality management systems is that the product is fit for purpose and complies with the contractual and legal requirements involved. This means that the product is both what the customer wants and what society, through legislation, requires it to be. The hold point results in a decision that the product is acceptable or unacceptable in its present form. The decision that the product is unacceptable in its present form does not necessarily mean that it is scrap — it may be possible to render it acceptable by further investigation, suitable efficacious reworking or repairing.

Places to look

When ascertaining the storage conditions of items or when checking for uncontrolled items such as consumable materials and other essential material, the auditor must conduct a thorough search, looking behind and underneath things, boxes, tables, shelves and so on. He may find, in work areas, that material which should be of controlled issue is not recalled to the appropriate storage area after use, when an excess amount has been issued or when some remains after the work is completed.

> In one company, it was the rule that consumable materials were not to be retained in the work areas. However, the auditor noticed, when standing back from the area, that some of these materials had been placed on the top of an air duct that ran above the work places.

The auditor should not be shy: he should feel free to ask the auditee to open a few cupboards to check for uncontrolled material, superseded documents or instruments not within the auditee's calibration system.

> In one company, the work areas were thought to be completely clean and the audit party was about to leave when the lead auditor happened to open a cupboard within a restricted welding area. Inside, there were several different types of uncontrolled material. The company concerned had never thought to conduct a periodic examination of their personnel's lockers.

If it is decided that the lockers should be periodically examined for uncontrolled items and superseded documents, it may be advisable to perform such an examination in the presence of the union representatives, who do generally understand the need for a periodic examination and are most co-operative. It is well known that some folk in manufacturing industries like to collect pieces of material for performing home jobs (weld rods for making gates or repairing motor vehicles, for example). Knowing this, it is better to tell the work force that the company would prefer to let them take home a few electrodes to repair their motor vehicles rather than have them try to hide material in their lockers with the result that the company loses business or has unfavourable findings during extrinsic audits.

It is a mistake only to work in "two directions": all that is overhead might not be well either.

> Following maintenance activities at a food factory, loose nuts, bolts and other miscellaneous detritus were left in precarious positions on the top of silos, pipework and ducts. That filth, which could easily drop into the prime product was only visible by climbing the access ladders provided in the factory.

The auditor must open up boxes: sometimes boxes or containers do not contain what the label claims they do.

> During one audit, a team leader discovered a large number of opened containers containing critical consumables. He explained to the auditee that these containers should be removed from the working area and destroyed after use in order to prevent the excess consumables getting into the wrong boxes. The auditee's department manager asserted vehemently that such a situation could not occur within his department. At that moment, the second member of the audit team produced several boxes, each of which contained the wrong material. The manager immediately ordered a purge of the area and all incorrect material and containers were removed and destroyed. The auditors later returned to the area and verified that the action had been completed. Trust and verify!

References:

1. Geneen, Harold (with Alvin Moscow), *Managing*, Avon Books, 1984, New York.
2. Military Standard Mil-Std-105D, *Sampling Procedures and Tables for Inspection by Attributes,* 1963. Government Printing Office, Washington, D.C., USA.

12. Information Collection

Now what I want is, Facts. Facts alone are wanted in life.
Charles Dickens.

Many auditors are unsure about what information to gather and how to collect and collate it. The two precepts below are guiding principles.

— Never trust your own memory: so much information has to be collected during an audit that it is doubtful whether even a chess grand master could carry it all in his head. Write down the information as the audit progresses.

— Do not clutter up your mind with trivia. Keep only the essential information in your head: store the detail in written form.

Use of the checklist, flowchart or task element matrix

Whichever of these aids is used, it should contain plenty of space for the auditor to note down the various types of objective evidence seen. Facts gathered during a management audit must be noted down. This has the following advantages:

1. it keeps the notes and doodles together;
2. it reduces the risk of losing the notes (jottings on the back of cigarette packets, bus tickets and odd scraps of paper do rather tend to get lost and are difficult to file at a later date);
3. if the information is written in against the appropriate checklist question, it is there to refresh the mind later on.

The quantity of objective evidence to collect

Some auditors agonize over the quantity of objective evidence to be obtained i.e. the sample size. A statistical sampling plan is helpful when selecting, say, examples of documents for scrutiny (MIL — STD — 105D[1] is often suitable): large samples needed to create the desired confidence level in the system, however, will incur considerable time expenditure which may not have allocated in the audit preparation. Sampling tables are only of real value during compliance audits. For systems audits, used to decide whether to commence an activity or not, there may not actually be any objective evidence of compliance available.

What to record

If a matrix of the type shown in Fig. 8.12 is used, then the type of information to be recorded becomes self evident for it relates to the task elements and their sub-elements (see Chapters 5 and 25), as indicated below.

1. The key person(s) interviewed.

The auditor will probably meet quite a number of auditee personnel and it may be hard to remember every name. Should corrective action be required in a particular area, it is a sensible move to record which representative of that area was present when particular problems were discussed and corrective action, perhaps, agreed. It is not necessary to take the name of absolutely everybody interviewed. Generally, that of the area supervisor, or perhaps just the escort, should suffice.

2. Document numbers and revisions, the place where those documents were found along with a description of the document type (process specification, order, drawing, inspection record, etc.): similarly for computer program or data listings, details of disks, tapes and the like should be recorded as well as information concerning access to them at the workplace being audited.

The purpose of recording these details is to enable the auditor to verify at another location that the issuer and the recipient are using the same information.

3. Equipment numbers or other identification details.

These details must be taken so that the auditor can check on the calibration and maintenance status of instruments and equipment used for process control or product acceptance purposes and so that he can check that other equipment — such as overhead cranes, processing chambers (chemical baths, heat treatment furnaces, vacuum chambers, for example) — are maintained, their condition remaining in accordance with process requirements. If the records of calibration and maintenance are maintained within the same area as that in which the instruments or equipment are found, the auditor need only make a special note of the equipment identification numbers if discrepancies arise (in which case, the severity of the discrepancies should be recorded).

4. Item identification.

Items might be identified by part number, heat number, batch number, contract number/name or such like. The identification may be on the item, on a document (possibly a bar code) accompanying the item, on the container that contains the item or on the shelf upon which the item is resting.

5. A selection of the document/information/equipment recipients as specified on the distribution lists.

It is not usually necessary to check all recipients, particularly in the case of a lengthy distribution list. If, for example, there is a total of five recipients, it may be sufficient to verify that, say, three of those five have received the correct revision of the document, the information, or the equipment concerned.

6. Identification of personnel.

The identification may be the person's name, works/employee number, initials or a unique stamp issued to the that person. The auditor will verify that the stamps in the person's possession are the ones issued to him and that their condition is not such as will damage the items which are stamped (some metal stamps, for example, have sharp edges or are damaged in such a way as to create stress raising notches or electrolytic cells on the item).

The auditor must verify that the training and qualification records are traceable to the person concerned and, in the case of stamps, that the person has his own stamp, no-one else's.

> At one manufacturer's premises one person had a stamp with the number 6 on it. When turned upside-down, the stamp could be mistaken for a 9. With a mischievous twinkle in his eye, the person whispered in the auditor's ear: "If the job is good, it's a 6, — if it's bad, it's a 9". The possibility of mistaken identity was quietly eliminated by withdrawing the 9 stamp.

In the case of people using computers, check that passwords are unique and maintained securely. Some programs automatically maintain a log of those people who have gained access to the program, also recording the time of access and whether any updates were changed, detailing the nature of the change if any has occurred. This permits ready traceability of work to an individual. Similar remarks apply to the use of magnetic pass cards for gaining access to secure work areas or offices.

7. The appropriate revision and paragraph number of references in the QA manual/procedure/instructions etc.

These details should in any case have been marked into the checklist as part of the off-site preparations for the audit. Differences between that which was available for audit preparation and that which is actually being implemented, are to be noted. If some aspect of an activity is found to be in a state of non-compliance with documented requirements, it is essential to accompany any request for corrective action on the auditee's part with a reference to the paragraph(s) concerned.

8. The condition of the environment.

The auditor should make a special note of any poor conditions, bad housekeeping and nuisance levels. These may not only cause damage or impair the quality of the product: they may also result in personnel fatigue, which leads to lack of concentration or poor performance, thus, affecting the job adversely. This is especially true in the case of people using word processors and computer terminals which require lengthy periods spent gazing at a visual display unit.

In recent years, the phenomenon known as the "sick building" has been recognized to cause poor quality work and excessive staff fatigue. The sick building phenomenon is common in modern open plan offices which rely upon air conditioning systems of doubtful effectiveness.

9. Flow charts, system doodles and scribbles.

Often, during the course of the audit, in order to understand or explain the management system, the auditor or auditee may make a sketch or doodle to indicate how the system works, how documents are routed, how particular problems are solved. These should not be thrown away: they are often very useful for reference at a later stage.

Mental notes

Information about many points not apparently directly related to management systems can prove relevant because of their effect on the quality of work produced. All the points below may fall into this category.

1. The employee's workload.

When people have too much to do, they may become physically and mentally fatigued and there is a consequent risk that they will try to cut corners and fail to implement the system correctly. The result is poor output.

In some cases, overwork can lead to eyestrain — an obvious cause of substandard output. Most people need good vision to do their jobs.

> At one company, an inspector had the task of examining mass-produced printed circuit boards for visual defects. In the middle of the afternoon, the auditor noticed that after looking briefly

> at each circuit board, the inspector tended to rub his eyes for a moment. This prompted the auditor to question the true quality of the inspected work and to enquire whether the auditee regularly checked the eyesight of his inspectors. A re-examination of that day's boards revealed that inspection errors had increased throughout the day.

The employees workload may also be such that there is the risk of folk rushing the job "to get it out the door" or "to keep up with schedule". This inevitably leads to quality problems one day. An equally serious possibility is that an unsafe product is made or that unsafe practices emerge. (In the air transport industry, this problem is well recognized, a fact which explains the limitations on the number of hours that airline pilots can legally be allowed to work before relief.) See Chapter 18 under "Lack of time".

2. People's reactions and the human climate.

Do the work force seem involved in their work, keen to produce high quality products? Some individuals may feel little interest in their job, the management systems and quality assurance in general. The cause may be lack of motivation, lack of discipline or lack of respect for the quality assurance department itself.

3. Do the employees seem to know their jobs and are they organized?

4. Employee attitudes.

Some people take the view that "near enough will do". These people tend to make decisions that are beyond their competence, without resorting to the proper authority. This may result either in a product which becomes unsuitable for use at a later stage or in delays, caused by the need to rework. See Chapter 18, under the discussion "Lack of discipline".

5. Does the place look orderly and is the housekeeping satisfactory?

Once he is on the spot, the auditor can often form a rapid judgement as to whether or not it would be desirable to take a thorough look at the housekeeping system in operation at a particular location. There is an old saying that one can judge a workman by the way he wears his overalls. It frequently happens that if a place looks orderly, few deficiencies, if any, are to be found there. A disorderly work place where desks are piled high with documents collecting dust and littered with unwashed coffee mugs, where filing cabinets support kettles and teapots, where product samples lie around gathering dust and rust, where the cracked window pane is patched up with peeling drafting tape, heralds the sort of chaos that is, in my experience, often a sign that the people are not over-proud or over-conscientious about the quality of the work they produce.

The personal filing system, which only one person can understand, may well be found in this setting, with the inevitable result that documents are frequently mislaid.

Disorder indicates lack of organization and lack of discipline.

6. Does the supervisor/manager want to answer all the questions?

The auditor wants to interview the person who actually performs the work, not the supervisor or manager. However, some supervisors and managers want to answer all the questions, either in the fear that their subordinates will commit an error which will reflect adversely on themselves or because they feel it is their right and responsibility to speak up since they know what is going on. In this situation, the auditor must make it clear to the supervisor or manager that the ''worker'' should be the one to answer the questions, explaining that this is because the purpose of the audit is to see what is actually being done and to verify that the management systems are being implemented. He must make it clear that it is of benefit both to the auditor and to the auditee's management to allow the ''worker'' to give the answers.

7. Do the people interviewed *really* not speak English?

Some auditees try to play the language game (see page 15-8). This type of attitude reflects a lack of concern for the auditor's organization and may indicate fundamental attitude problems or a dislike of quality assurance in general.

8. Does the auditee try to bluff his way out of a tight corner?

The auditor must make it clear that he is not fooled by bluff, indeed, that bluffing is likely to have an adverse effect on the audit report. An auditee who is honest enough to admit to uncertainty on some points, promising to try to find answers later, deserves full marks for co-operation and concern for the management systems and product involved. However, the auditor must bear the auditee's promise in mind and ask for the answer at a later stage of the audit. See also page 15-8 ''Amnesia''.

9. Do the people *know* the QA manual or associated procedure? Do they know where to find these documents? Do the people *know* what is in the contract/specification/code?

If employees have trouble locating relevant passages when they need to refer to the manual or other information, this may well be a sign that they look at these documents rarely, if ever. Where this happens, it is not uncommon to find that what the person believes the document to contain and what it actually contains are totally different.

10. Do the employees act promptly when some deficiency or other problem comes to light?

Prompt attention is generally a sign of a genuine desire to please the customer and/or to mitigate the potential reaction of their own management. This can indicate problems with motivation or with top management support for quality (or lack of it) being reflected in the work force attitudes.

11. The general condition of the equipment (lifting slings, machine tools, buildings, broken palates, stockyard and the like).

This is very similar to 4 above. An auditor may, for example, find that a couple of items of equipment are in poor condition while similar equipment elsewhere is generally satisfactory. In these circumstances, an isolated rather than a general problem exists. The general state of the equipment can provide an impression of the management's equipment replacement and investment policy.

12. Access space.

> A manufacturer of air conditioning equipment won an order to supply a complete module that would be used to control the accommodation environment on an oil platform. The module was duly erected in the company's workshops. However, on completion, it was found that nobody had considered the need to get it out of the workshop for shipment. Two stark choices presented themselves: either to demolish the whole of one side of the workshop building or to dismantle the module totally, ship it to site, re-erect it, replacing all the cabling that would have to be scrapped as a result and incurring a penalty charge for the late installation of the re-built module. The latter was chosen.

> A company won a similar order to the one described above. Recognizing that there was insufficient floor area within its buildings, it considered that the product could be successfully erected immediately outside its workshop, in the open. To "protect from the weather" a scaffold covered with tarpaulins was erected over the work area. A seasonal storm ripped the tarpaulins off and a deluge of rain ruined a substantial amount of electronic equipment. The company accepted that it had been unwise and replaced the damaged parts. However, when the product was ready for shipment it was discovered that it was wider than the company's access road. Enquiries established that there was no crane capable of lifting the whole thing over the top of the company's buildings. It was dismantled and re-built. These

> potential problems had been brought to the management's attention in an audit report. The company's owner had, however, chosen to ignore the warnings, dismissing them with the statement "We know what we are doing." Perhaps he knows a little more now.

Poor layout and inadequate access are common causes of quality problems which generally have their roots in a lack of the resources required to do the job properly. In service industries, for example, it is common to find pure clutter in the behind-the-scenes activities that the paying customer should never see.

13. Are the requisite stickers on the parts? Are the job cards with the parts? Are drawings covered with "red ink"?

By comparing the picture the company presents of the external auditor's contract with what seems to be the general state of affairs in other areas, the auditor can sometimes arrive at a conclusion as to whether or not the auditee has "cleaned up" (see page 14-9) before the audit. There is nothing wrong with cleaning up in this way but after the audit, problems can arise when the situation reverts to a more normal state. It makes sense, therefore, to note how well things are being done in areas unrelated to the particular contract or product of interest. Extensive use of red ink mark-ups is often a good pointer to quality management systems that are inadequate and partially replaced by fire-fighting expedients.

14. The informal organization.

Companies that embark on a quality assurance programme generally appoint a quality assurance manager and allege in their quality manuals that all kinds of vital authorities are vested in the position. In reality, this is no guarantee that the person is considered to be of the same importance in the company as, say, the financial director, marketing manager or other such appointments. Carefully noting the location of offices, style of furniture, company cars and other facilities made available to the quality assurance manager can be quite revealing.

> During an audit of a company based in the north of England, I had occasion to visit the quality assurance manager's office. It was located at the farthest corner of the works; the office furniture was literally falling to pieces and the only chair available for his visitors had no back, this having broken away some years previously. The place was grimly decorated and was situated immediately outside was the company garbage tip on which the kitchen waste from the work's canteen was deposited. My visit

occurred during the height of summer, the refuse tip stank and was infested with flies and vermin. The place was most unpleasant. The main office block, however, was comprised of an attractive modern building which housed not only senior management but most of the middle management as well. Having established that the quality assurance manager was the only one not to be given a decent office, I asked the managing director why and received the reply that "Because he has to deal with the product, it is the most appropriate location for him to be convenient for the work." To this, I immediately enquired why, if that was the case, the production manager and works managers' offices were not similarly located since there was adequate space for them. I received no reply.

If the company believes that financial assurance is important for company survival, then why does it not show similar belief in quality assurance? The latter is the sine qua non for the former. Whereas the quality assurance department is powerful in theory, it is often other departments who really rule the roost.

At one company, an audit team found that the receiving inspectors were releasing critical material to production despite the fact that the quality assurance manual forbade this. When questioned, the inspector replied "It's more than my life's worth — if production tell us to release, then that's the end of it."

In one large company, an audit team found that the purchasing department controlled the operation to such an extent that the quality assurance manager had to give up his office to a buyer (the latter supposedly having to carry on such complex and confidential monetary negotiations that a closed door office was necessary). The quality assurance department received very little support or co-operation from the members of the purchasing department and this state of affairs was, unfortunately, endorsed by the senior management. It was not unknown for a buyer to waive the quality requirements for a contract: in some cases, where essential safety-related equipment was being purchased, the buyer had even waived the requirement for submission of a quality assurance manual.

15. The REAL practice.

Whilst visiting a major computer manufacturer, I was invited to go into the "clean room". Cap, gown, boots and mask were provided, to be put on prior to entering. Upon entering, a relatively low positive air pressure was noticeable as a draft gently blew through the entry door — the wrong way. Once inside the room, an unofficial entry door to the area was discovered. It was open virtually all the time and provided the real main point of entry and exit for people wandering in and out, not always correctly dressed.

During a visit to a food processing plant, the works manager offered to take me into the processing areas and escort me around them. As he arose from his desk, he automatically picked up his cigarettes and lighter and put them in his pocket. Smoking is not permitted within the food processing areas.

A friend of mine was auditing a supplier of steel stock. Whilst in the records department, he noted that a clerk was faking a certificate by altering the material properties stated on it. The clerk smiled and quickly tried to ease my friend's concern by saying "Don't worry Jimmy, it's not for your job!"

16. Indicators of lack of top support.

The auditor should be alert to the words and phrases employed by the managers and supervisors at all levels in the company. They can indicate the real feeling towards a quality programme and the true degree of understanding of the importance of quality. To cite a few examples:

— "of course quality is important but it does cost a lot of money";
— "it causes a paper monster";
— "naturally we have a quality programme; we've done inspection for years";
— "we work to QA standards only when the customer specifies it";
— "a quality programme? OK, if you are prepared to pay for it";
— "we were forced into it by our customers";
— "if it were our choice, we would use our commercial systems";
— "can you tell us where we could buy a quality manual?";
— "of course we have a quality assurance programme — we appointed a QA manager".

Collect the information as you go

Throughout the audit, the auditor should watch, look and listen. It is especially important to listen to explanations of how the system works because these may vary from department to department. The auditor can often obtain answers to some of the checklist questions without even having to ask, purely by paying attention to what goes on around him throughout the audit. The simple act of walking through the premises, for example, can give the auditor a picture of the equipment, the conditions, the housekeeping and overall orderliness of the work place as well as of the general atmosphere.

One auditor noted that when he entered each of the workshops or stores, a fork-lift truck horn would sound twice and when he left it would sound once. It soon became quite apparent to the auditor that the fork-lift truck drivers were warning everybody within the workshop that management representatives were about. The industrial relations within that particular company were very poor.

References:

1. Military Standard Mil-Std-105D, *Sampling Procedures and Tables for Inspection by Attributes,* 1963. Government Printing Office, Washington, D.C., USA.

13. Question Technique

Questions are never indiscreet. Answers sometimes are.
Oscar Wilde.

Naturally, every auditor develops his own style and technique of questioning which evolve with experience and are worked out on the basis of past successes and failures. The latter are bound to occur at some point, particularly when the auditor is relatively new to his task and liable to errors of both commission and omission. Past experiences like this can be turned to advantage if only the auditor is willing to learn from them. For this reason, the auditor should always try to devote a few minutes to a post mortem shortly after the audit is over. As the old saying goes: it is a bad man who never made a mistake and a worse man who never profited from one.

Inexperienced auditors naturally tend to rely heavily on the checklist, unaware, perhaps, that no checklist asks *all* the questions which are necessary to arrive at the truth. They may also feel unsure about how to pose questions correctly. I hope this chapter will be particularly useful in suggesting ways in which they can overcome their initial difficulties.

Six friends

The beginning of Rudyard Kipling's poem "The Elephant Child" goes as follows:

> "I keep six honest serving men
> (they taught me all I knew).
> Their names are What and Why and When
> and How and Where and Who".

These six words — how, what, why, when, where and who — are six friends for the auditor and must figure in all the auditor's questions. When used properly, the six friends *force a response*. Asking "Do you have a copy of your company price list?", for instance, may elicit the answer "yes" but this is to ask only half a question since the auditor has still to verify the existence of the price list by a further enquiry. A more detailed question ("Where do you keep your copy of the company price list") forces a more specific answer (“in the filing cabinet”). This answer tells the auditor three things:

1. the auditee knows that he should have the price list;
2. the auditee alleges that he has received the price list;
3. the price list is allegedly protected (in the filing cabinet).

An even more valuable question for the auditor to ask might be “Who provides you with your copy of the price list?” An answer such as “I receive my copy direct from the sales manager” tells the auditor the following:

1. the auditee knows that he should have the price list;
2. the auditee, if the answer is correct, knows where the price list actually comes from (this may be at variance with the QA manual, quality management system, procedure or whatever).

If the auditee’s answer is at variance with the system/QA manual/procedure, the auditor knows that one or both of the following is true: either

1. the auditee does not know the system or
2. the system, as implemented, does not tally with the system as documented.

Questions framed in a judicious manner (encompassing the six friends) can yield much verifiable information within a short space of time. Remembering that time is the enemy of the auditor, one must never ask two questions when one good one is enough.

The seventh friend (the crunch question)

This is the simple request, “Show me”. Properly used, it will enable the auditor to verify the auditee’s response to the kind of question described above. The auditor in the example above might ask “May I see the price list?” or “Could you please show me the price list?” The answer has to be “yes” or “no”, either the auditee has the price list or he does not, either it is either in the filing cabinet or it is not.

The prime purpose of an audit is to verify that a system has or has not been developed, documented and implemented: verification cannot be achieved unless at some point the auditor poses a “Show me” question. An audit is conducted by examination of objective evidence: if objective evidence has not been requested, it cannot be examined and therefore an audit is not being performed.

The unit concept

The auditor must relate the six friends to the unit concept relevant to the task being audited. He needs to ask how/what/when/where/why/who in relation to the input, the output, and the task or process being performed, finally verifying with the crunch question “Show me”.
For example:

"from where do you receive information?" is related to the input side of the unit.
"where do you keep information you require?" is related to the information residing at the workplace.
"to where do you forward the information? " is related to the output of the unit.

The answers to all these questions are important in helping the auditor determine how well the unit understands its role as part of the chain of units involved in the product, project or contract being audited. In the case of a trace-back method of auditing, the auditor may want to ask where the work output goes and then work back to ascertain the source of the input.

It is always vital to request "Show me what you do/where you put that/how you do that, please" when checking at the compliance level. (See Chapter 11, "Audit Methods"). The auditor then watches, quietly noting whether or not the methods are at variance with the system description and/or contract requirements. If the auditor notes some variation between procedure and practice, he must then ask "Why do you do it that way?"

It is of great value in auditing to keep the unit concept clear in one's mind, to split the work into input, process and output and to ask questions on each of these individually and in turn.

The hypothetical question

In some cases — particularly during a pre-award survey, where there tends to be little objective evidence available — it can be useful to ask questions of the "What if..." or "Let us suppose..." variety. The answers often expose the depth of understanding of the systems in operation as well as the amount of thought invested in creating them.

> I once had to perform a pre-award survey on a company about which I was told "they are a very new company and have brand new premises." Upon arrival at the supplier's location, I discovered that this was an understatement. The facilities consisted of a huge workshop which contained nothing but an overhead gantry crane, a few offices, a telephone line, a typewriter and a desktop copier. Fortunately, the company had written its QA manual. There had to be quite a bit of "What if-ing" and "Let us suppose-ing" during the pre-award survey. In this case the "What ifs" were designed to elicit whether the parent company's practices (which were known to my company) were known to this subsidiary and were likely to be implemented.

The best way to use the hypothetical question is in conjunction with one of the six friends. An example might be "Let us suppose that the documents you receive do not show the correct approval signatures on them what would you do (or who would you notify)?" After the auditee has made some reply to the first question, the auditor might then ask "Can you please show me the instruction to that effect?"

An example is often a useful means to help the auditee understand the auditor's line of thought. Without one, the line of questioning may seem obscure or far-fetched. Sometimes an example suggests itself naturally, if for instance, the auditor has encountered a problem at another location that he would not wish to see repeated in the unit being audited. Using this type of example may at least alert the auditee to the possibility of some problem arising and may spur him on to take preventive action.

It is unwise to lose sight of reality by overdoing the "what if": it can make the auditor appear rather foolish.

"I don't understand..."

If the auditee's explanation or response is either unclear or unsatisfactory, the auditor should not be afraid to say: "I'm sorry but I don't quite understand. Could you explain that again please?" Some people are reluctant to ask for an explanation or an answer to be repeated for fear of appearing dimwitted. The auditor must put aside this fear. He must *always* continue questioning until he understands the answer and is satisfied that the truth has been obtained. He should, for example, always ask "Can you show me another example please, I think I'm beginning to understand but I want to be sure". An auditee is very seldom unwilling to repeat or to rephrase an explanation or answer for the auditor.

Systematic questioning

The auditor must develop his questions in a logical sequence, not jump about between disconnected topics. As a rule, the questions should follow the sequence of work in the unit being audited. ("OK, you've done this, this, this then how/where/when/why/who...?")

It is good practice for the auditor to voice his understanding of how the system works, so that the auditee can correct any misconceptions. For instance, the auditor may say "OK, so you do this, then this, and then...", and the auditee may interrupt with "No. We actually do this, this, this, then that, and then....". Acting in this manner helps the auditor to keep an open mind about the situation and places him in a stronger position later on to say "But when I told you of my understanding of the way that unit works, you did not correct me at that time. Why not?"

The silent question

Silence can be extremely powerful because some people find it uncomfortable and to break it they volunteer something they "shouldn't". When the auditor looks at the auditee, saying nothing, the latter may feel that a response is expected of him, and because he is not sure quite what the response should be, he may say more than he otherwise would. This type of question often produces information of use to the auditor.

Non-questions

The auditor must avoid falling into the habit of asking the auditee a question and then answering it himself. He might just as well not ask a question at all as do this. Furthermore, he may well supply an incorrect answer, which the auditee may be reluctant to put right. The erroneous assumption may not be exposed until much later on (when the auditee will say, at last, "We never told you that", or "*You* said that, we didn't"), whilst the auditor's misconception may have put his investigation off course in the meantime. This is simply not conducting the audit properly.

The obvious or "dumb" question

The auditor should never be afraid to ask a question, even if the answer seems so obvious that it is scarcely worth asking. The obvious question may turn out to be the very one that the auditee is dreading because some glaring deficiency is about to be revealed. The obvious question may seem very similar to the non-question ("It's ridiculous to ask that, even a fool would....."). Ask the "dumb" question and then hear a pin drop!

The unasked question

In the course of examining the objective evidence, the auditor will find that some questions are answered before they have been asked. In such cases, he should answer the unasked questions out loud ("OK, I see on this specification the correct signatures, the acceptance criteria and the references to the company standards"). The auditor is not asking the auditee to point out what is under his very nose: he is informing the auditee that he is noting the content of the objective evidence. Analysing the evidence aloud like this helps the auditor to follow the system and the auditee to follow the auditor's line of thought. It also informs all concerned that the auditor knows what he is looking for, that he is not missing anything and that he is thorough. It may be that the auditee has included various details in one set of documents purely by accident, and that they will not be found in another set of documents in another area: from the auditor's words, the auditee now knows that deficiencies will be found in the other area. This often happens when the auditee is in the process of developing and implementing the quality systems i.e. during the period of gestation.

Inverse questions

One often encounters auditees who are resentful of being either audited or subject to the strictures of a quality management system. In order to deflect attention from their desire to work their own way regardless of others, they may claim that the systems restrict their creativeness (a common plea of designers, software engineers, computer programmers) or could reduce their operational scope to the detriment of the company (salesmen often claim, for example, that the paperwork and formality of involving line staff could prevent a sales order being obtained). When auditing such people, I have found it useful to pander to their ego initially by starting my questions as follows:

"Can you please tell me if you are getting all the co-operation that you feel you need to do your job?" This is not what the auditee expects and the response might be:—

"I'm not sure what you mean."

The auditor continues, "Well, are you receiving all of the latest information that you need?"

Auditee: "I think so."

Auditor: "You don't sound too sure. What exactly would you like to have?"

The auditee now perceives that someone has finally realized his position at the centre of the universe, relaxes and starts to specify his utopian requirements.

The auditor will then ask who might be able to provide that information: the auditee will express his state of knowledge about the organizational interfaces and how the system works. The auditor will then ask for examples of exactly what "they" are currently providing for the illustrious auditee. There is generally a shortfall, so the auditor asks:

"How have you told them of what you need?"

The auditee is forced to present objective evidence of his requests or to admit that there has been no communication. In the latter case, the auditor will suggest that direct contact is made by the auditee with those interfaces in order to get the information. "They clearly do not understand the vital nature of your position, perhaps you should go and see them yourself to explain precisely what you need."

That inverse questioning of asking a peacock if he/she is getting all the co-operation it needs, rather than asking for elaboration on how they are a "slave to the system", breaks the barriers down.

The auditor will use similar questions to ascertain the items, equipment, training and so on that the auditee feels he requires, and then uses similar questions to determine whether other people have informed the auditee of their needs of him. If not, one will then suggest that he makes direct contact with the downstream interfaces. In the event that the auditee feels resentment about helping others to do their jobs, by going to them to ascertain their needs, a picture of an unfair attitude can be presented. Generally, however, the auditee is intelligent enough to realise what has happened and will become more co-operative.

Comparison questions

This type of question, much used in compliance audits, compares the content of the information, such as the work instructions, with actual practice. It is posed *after* the other questions have been asked and actual practice established. Apart from establishing how well the people know the contents of the information, the use of the comparison question is to determine the desirability of an amendment to that information in cases where the words do not reflect actual practice, *provided* that the actual practice is in accordance with customer, product or legal requirements ("I see that you operate in such a such manner but the work instruction says this, this, this. Since your method of operation is in compliance with the contract, I suggest that you amend the instruction to reflect actual practice"). Obviously, if the practice is at variance with the instructions and any of those requirements, then this may warrant a formal request for corrective action. This is more fully discussed in Chapter 17.

The comparison question is of particular use when auditing foreign companies that do not speak the auditor's mother tongue and have difficulty finding the right wording to use in their documents. Here, the auditor should explain why the word or phrase is wrong and suggest a suitable alternative that would describe actual practice more accurately. In some cases, it may transpire that the auditee has misunderstood the particular requirements because of imperfect understanding of the language used. It is the auditor's duty to correct such misunderstandings without making a big issue out of them.

A useful sequence for questioning

Questions should be related to the actual work flow. When auditing the compliance aspects of any particular task, a useful sequence is:

1. organizational questions concerning the function of the task and responsibilities of the person;
2. questions concerning each of the task elements (see Chapters 5 and 25), taken in turn. The order in which they are taken is irrelevant although questions concerning the "Person" sub elements are often best left until last because at that point the auditor will have obtained a better understanding of the competence, training and attribute requirements that the task. In the case of a trace forward method, the questions concerning inputs are posed first, followed by questions concerning the outputs;
3. comparison questions;
4. hypothetical questions.

A simple example of question technique

Auditor: "What is your function and how do you know what your duties are?"

The auditee will describe the product(s) of his efforts and the associated responsibilities. The auditor will take appropriate notes.

Auditor: "To be able to make that product what materials and other items must you receive?"

The auditee will describe the various items (viz. materials, assemblies, sub-assemblies, components) that are needed. The auditor will record these on his checklist.

Auditor: "Please tell me where each item comes from."

The auditee describes the upstream interfacing departments/ functions. The auditor notes this detail to help build a picture of the system.

Auditor: "Let's take each item in turn. Please show me some examples of each."

The auditor then investigates the sub elements applicable to each of those items in turn, noting the identities of the samples taken and the results obtained, including discrepancies, as the audit proceeds.

Auditor: ''Would you please tell me, what equipment do you use to do your job?''

The auditee will describe that equipment. The auditor will make a list of all pieces of equipment that are necessary, ascertaining which upstream interfacing departments issue or maintain each piece. The sub elements applicable will then be investigated for each piece of equipment in turn, the auditor noting equipment identities and his findings, both good and bad, for each.

The auditor then continues by ascertaining what environmental nuisances must be avoided: he details them and records the fact of their existence or otherwise.

Auditor: ''In order to do this work, what information do you require?''

The auditee will provide a detailed list of the documents and other information that is necessary. Once again, the auditor will note the answers in a list, ask for examples, make his own selection, investigate the sub elements applicable to each and record the results, good and bad, in the checklist.

Auditor: ''Please tell me from where each one is issued to you.''

The auditee will provide that detail and the auditor will record it, thus further building up a picture of the system interfaces upstream of the workplace currently under scrutiny.

Auditor: ''Would you please show me how you actually process one of these items?''

The auditee will then proceed to perform his or her job. The auditor will note the methods that are used, any deviations from the documented system and the attributes of the person (problems with dexterity and similar), not interrupting the auditee until the particular task is finished.

Auditor: ''How do you identify that the product and information were produced by you?''

The auditee will state the method used and the auditor will verify the efficacy of this, making appropriate notes.

At this point, the auditor will raise any questions that may have arisen from the methods actually used on the job and check that the activity actually performed matches with the job descriptions. It is important not to attack the auditee. Accordingly, the auditor may say

Auditor: ''I note your methods are not the same as described in the procedure/work instruction, why do you do it that way?

The auditor will satisfy himself with the answers and then proceed to ask similar questions concerning the four elements, related this time to the output. For example:

Auditor: "Where do you send these items when they are finished?"

The auditee will provide a list and the auditor will make a note of this information concerning downstream interfaces.

Auditor: "In what condition are you required to forward them?"

The auditee will describe the items' conditions along with any packaging and preservation that is required. The auditor will investigate the accuracy and efficacy of those requirements, taking notes of examples of objective evidence and the results obtained from that investigation.

Auditor: "What information do you also produce upon completion of the job and where do you send it?"

The auditee will describe the information and documents that are created and the distribution of each.

The auditor will note the distribution stated by the auditee and will check to see that there is no break in the audit trail.

The auditor will do likewise for equipment that requires maintenance or calibration. According to the circumstances, the auditor might then investigate the condition in which the information and equipment are required to be, when despatched from the auditee's workplace, in the same manner as described above for the items. He will then proceed in similar fashion to "what if" questions such as.

Auditor: "What if any of the items/equipment/information you receive are incorrect, what do you do/who do you notify?"

The consistency of such actions will be checked against the responsibilities in the job descriptions.

According to the level of person being audited and the audit objectives, the auditor might now proceed along similar lines with questions concerning time and resource allocation and management. Having seen actual practice and the needs of the task the auditor will now investigate the PERSON sub-elements.

Auditor: "With what training have you been provided?"

The auditee will describe the training (if any) that has been received. The auditor will note this information, obtain objective evidence and do likewise for attributes such as eyesight checks. When finished at the workplace the auditor will thank the person for his or her co-operation.

Presentation of questions

Always direct the questions to the person who *performs* the task being audited, *not* to that person's superior. If the latter tries to answer all the questions personally, the auditor must politely put a stop to the interventions.

The auditor must never talk down to anyone. Any auditor who acts as if he knows it all and is superior to the auditee is unlikely to get the auditee's full co-operation. Such a state of affairs makes it much harder to obtain valuable information and results. It is a worthwhile exercise to "talk the man's language" (but not bad language). An operative may not understand much about the finer points of the quality assurance programme or statutory requirement, but he will understand about the things with which he has to deal every day. The auditor should try to phrase his questions with this in mind, incorporating, for instance, some concrete examples relating to matters with which the operative will be thoroughly familiar.

Always speak clearly and carefully — this is a basic principle of effective communication. If the auditee cannot hear what the auditor is saying, he will find it very difficult to produce a useful answer. He may well end up answering a different question altogether. If the auditee seems not to have heard or understood the question, repeat it, rephrasing it if possible. As a corollary to this, the auditor should look at the auditee, not to the side or at his own feet when talking. In a busy, noisy environment, failure to look at the person to whom you are talking can render you inaudible. Apart from that, the auditee's facial reactions and body language can be valuable guides to the veracity or otherwise of the responses made.

Sensitive situations

Certain matters of a sensitive nature might need to be raised during an audit. An example of this would be auditee's checks on the honesty of personnel who are assigned to tasks where such an attribute is vital.

For internal audits such situations are best handled by, say, the quality assurance manager auditing the personnel manager on a one-to-one basis. This would mean that other internal auditors need not concern themselves about such a sensitive matter. Obviously, in these circumstances, confidentiality is especially vital and thus dictates the need for the audit to be performed by a senior member of management, such as the quality assurance manager himself.

On external audits, the matter is even more delicate because the auditee may consider the auditor to be prying into matters which should not be any of his concern. The external auditor has to act diplomatically to avoid raising hostility. A useful ploy is to present a realistic scenario to the auditee.

The auditor might, for example, postulate that his own organization, in providing the auditee with free issue material, is naturally concerned about security and might then gently ask how pilferage would be prevented. Alternatively, the auditor may stress that certain data which will be provided to the auditee is of a highly confidential nature and must only be brought to the attention of selected trusted employees. From this position, the auditor can raise the matter of the security screening of those people who may be involved. Naturally, the scenario that the auditor describes has to be realistic and based on actual need. The auditor must avoid areas which will not be directly related to his legitimate prime concerns.

Personnel security checks are becoming increasingly common as the number of businesses providing services to customers, such as banks and insurance companies has grown. Where companies are offering design services to customers that issue them with confidential data, security is naturally important. Companies offering data processing services where monetary transactions are being handled also necessitate the investigation of such sensitive matters. Another field in which security is of concern is national defence.

Always give praise when it is due

Finally, give credit where credit is due. A compliment ("nice job", "orderly office", "efficient operation"), sincerely given, goes a long way towards eliciting an auditee's co-operation. Naturally, this should not be overdone to the point where the auditor sounds sycophantic. The essence of any quality programme is to ensure that work is done correctly. When evidence proves that this is so, the auditee deserves some expression of appreciation. After all, when things are not so good, that type of news is quickly relayed back but the opposite is not always the case in working life.

Personal demeanour

The auditor should not only look interested in the auditee's work and responses — he must *be* interested as well. Genuine interest is more likely to enlist the auditee's full co-operation, particularly in the case of people engaged in mundane tasks. On an internal audit, the auditor is more likely to elicit constructive suggestions for improvements from the operatives if they know that he is interested enough to follow their suggestions through: this is good for motivation.

At all times, the auditor must be courteous and helpful. When asking to see objective evidence, he must say "please" ("Could you show me the records, please?"). Another point of good manners is not to look distrustful of people or to regard their responses with suspicion. The auditor should not adopt an air appropriate to dealing with a back street garage.

Always apologize for unduly interrupting people ("I just want to ask a few quick questions, please"). If the auditor has to return to an area to obtain more or fresh information and finds the auditee engaged in other activities, such as a meeting, he should not assume he is entitled to break in without some justification or apology. It is unreasonable to interrupt people's coffee or tea breaks. It is good practice to note the time of such breaks and to suggest that the audit team removes itself from the workplace then for a cup of tea or coffee. If it proves impossible to avoid interrupting the break, always apologize ("I'm sorry to interrupt you, but can you please show me...?") If the auditor is known to be reasonable and courteous, people are more likely to co-operate and say "No trouble at all".

It should virtually go without saying that the auditor should both be and appear to be impartial and unemotional in his dealings with the auditee (an audit is supposed to deal with verifiable facts, not emotions, after all). Having said that, no auditor should be afraid to relax and appear human. Many auditees are nervous of audits, especially if previous audits have turned out to be quasi-witch hunts and finger-pointing exercises. Try to put the auditee at ease by taking a seat or suggesting a cup of coffee, perhaps. Break the ice by mentioning the weather, the football team, a picture, a pin-up on the wall or such like. An occasional quip can help.

Unavailable information

Sometimes the information that an auditor wants is not available when he requests it. This does not necessarily mean that something is wrong either with the system or with its implementation. The auditor should not waste time, he should simply say "OK, could you find out for me, please, and let me know the answer?" This gives the auditee an opportunity to look for the answer or to perform a purge of the area concerned in order to get to the true facts of the situation.

Gathering opinions at grass roots level

It is most enlightening to ask the people for their blunt opinion about the quality programme and the systems, their uses, benefits and impact on day-to-day tasks, as well as for any changes that they may care to suggest. Most folk are delighted to get the opportunity to speak out and what they say may be illuminating not just for the auditor but for the auditee's management as well. It is not uncommon for constructive and cost-effective criticism concerning the implementation of the management systems within the company to be produced. These suggestions should be given serious consideration. In the case of an internal audit, it is a good practice for the audit team to inform people of the outcome of their suggestions and to give the reasons why any were discarded. It encourages employees at all levels to feel involved in the quality programme if they are given proof that their opinions are considered important. This is good for motivation, for morale and for industrial relations. Furthermore, if suggestions made at grass roots level are implemented, the people will have a vested interest in making them work.

The constructive approach

It is a cardinal sin for an auditor to produce destructive criticism of an auditee's systems. The auditor who justifies his existence by fault finding and the number of Corrective Action Requests he issues is never welcome — from an audit of this kind, the auditee gains nothing. Constructive criticism, by contrast, can benefit everyone and an auditor who is known to produce useful suggestions will enlist the co-operation of management easily. He will find his work goes more smoothly too: people will be more willing to talk frankly to him and will waste less time covering up, if they know he is not simply interested in finding fault. Always remember that the auditor is meant to be

FACT FINDING NOT FAULT FINDING.

So, the golden rule for the auditor is to be constructive at all times. When a deficiency has been found, the auditor must always suggest examples of corrective action that would satisfy his organization ("As corrective action, you could consider these alternatives...."). This gives the auditee a choice between a number of courses, any of which would satisfy the auditor. This is obviously a much more sensible approach for the auditor to take than to require corrective action without specifying what form it should take, then rejecting the auditee's proposals at a later date. The last method wastes time, is annoying to everyone concerned and is also indicative of crass bad manners.

If the auditor can perceive a way of improving the auditee's system, he should tell the auditee about it, tactfully. He might say:

"Have you ever tried or considered...........?"
"Would it be better to...?"
"Although you meet the requirements of the product/code/standard etc., how about...?"

Constructive suggestions may help the auditee to improve the efficiency of his operation, possibly enabling him to reduce costs. This could lead to lower prices for the auditor's company (in the case of an external audit) or to greater competitiveness (in the case of an internal audit).

So, the auditor's organization has as much to gain as the auditee by approaching the audit in a constructive fashion.

Two-edged swords

It is not uncommon for the auditor to find that his own organization has been the root cause of a problem discovered during an external or an internal audit. If the responsible person from the auditor's organization is present during the audit, then the auditor must question him right there and then.

Audits are two-edged swords. The auditor sees not only what the auditee is doing but also the results of work performed in his own organization. Answers to all of the following questions and more may come to light:

— has the auditee been provided with the correct information?
— does the information show evidence of the correct reviews and approvals?
— has the auditor's organization's management system been bypassed?
— have the auditor's customer's requirements been properly incorporated into the information provided to the auditee?

The auditor must never assume that his own organization is perfect. He must demonstrate to the auditee that he is open-minded and determined to get to the truth, whatever this may be, and that he is prepared to question members of his own organization. People are more responsive to individuals who are known to be unbiased and fair in their dealings with all.

The auditor's stature

If the auditor discovers that he has been wrong in his assumptions or conclusions, it is best to admit it to the auditee and to apologize. This may happen, for example, if fresh evidence throws a new light on earlier findings. In these circumstances, the auditor must say something like, "Well, in the light of this evidence, it appears that my earlier conclusions were wrong. I'm sorry for that misunderstanding and pleased that you showed me this new information." Someone who is big enough to admit to being wrong, and apologize for his mistakes shows his fair-mindedness and maturity. Such an attitude elicits co-operation and respect from the auditee.

14. The Auditor's Conduct

"And how did little Tim behave?" asked Mrs. Cratchit.
......."As good as gold," said Bob.
Charles Dickens.

Auditing conduct and question technique frequently overlap. Indeed, it may be difficult to make a clear distinction between question technique, auditing methods and auditing conduct. I shall include under the heading "conduct" means that the auditor may choose to adopt in order to achieve the audit's objectives. Hence conduct includes many more forms of behaviour than simply questioning technique.

Projecting the right image

One of the most valuable things for the auditor to do is to try to project an appropriate image of himself and his company to the auditee's organization. The first five precepts listed below are all important in this respect.

1. Look the part.

As a representative of his company, the auditor should dress so as to reflect credit on his organization. A smart, tidy appearance creates a favourable impression on the auditee and also boosts the auditor's confidence in himself.

2. Remain calm and courteous.

The auditor sets an example to others by his own conduct during the audit. If he allows himself to become flustered and emotional or to engage in heated arguments, the proceedings are likely to go downhill fast. By remaining calm and polite in all circumstances, he gives himself the best chance of obtaining useful results from the management audit.

3. Be punctual.

A punctual auditor gives the impression that he means business. A chronic late arriver irritates everyone and also wastes valuable time.

4. Be precise.

Loosely phrased questions or requests can cause a lot of confusion. The auditor should consciously strive to convey exactly what he intends in all his communications with the auditee. Failure to do so wastes time.

5. Be prepared.

An auditor who has made proper preparations in advance (see Chapter 9) gets off to a flying start. He has no need to waste people's time ascertaining details he should have checked in advance and he earns the auditee's respect by knowing what he is doing. An ill-prepared auditor will find it much harder to enlist the full co-operation of the auditee.

Conducting the proceedings properly

Many of the items under this heading read rather like moral prescriptions. However, tactically as well as ethically, it is always good to adhere to them. By adopting the right approach, the auditor will avoid making mountains out of molehills and in doing so will smooth his own path.

6. Keep a sense of proportion.

The auditor should not make it his business to ferret out examples of human error. These will invariably turn up if you dig deep enough in any organization since everyone (even an auditor) makes an occasional mistake. This evidence of human fallibility should be of far less interest and concern to the auditor than evidence of a real deficiency in the management systems. If the evidence suggests that general control in an area is satisfactory, the auditor should accept this and move on to a new area, not linger in the hope of digging up a few faults. The magnitude and significance of a deficiency is the vital issue: to pursue unimportant errors indefatigably is to waste time and effort and to risk alienating the auditee as well. Remember a prime objective is to obtain a TRUE AND FAIR VIEW.

7. Make allowances.

If some deficiency is detected and human error is the cause, the auditor should always try to put the error in perspective. He should, for example, consider what pressures the auditee was under at the time the mistake happened — poor working conditions, fatigue, domestic difficulties, personal troubles and so on. Even the most diligent folk can make mistakes when the pressure on them grows too great. It may be that the auditor can do something to improve the situation discreetly without having to issue a formal request for corrective action. By so doing, he may be able to foster a good working relationship with the auditee's staff and enable the rest of the audit to run smoothly.

8. Be honest.

An auditor should never try to cover up for his own organization. If the latter is to blame for a deficiency, he should admit this. Similarly, he should not try to conceal his own ignorance or uncertainty on any points raised by the auditee nor should he try to gloss over his past mistakes. If he ignores this advice and the subterfuge subsequently comes to light, it can have a very detrimental effect on the course of the audit.

9. Be human.

Some auditees still view the auditor as something of a bogeyman. If the auditor can manage to break the ice somehow — with a joke, possibly — he may help the auditee to relax and get things moving. If a difficult situation arises — one involving a deficiency on the auditee's part, for example — the auditor should try to defuse it. He might truthfully say, for instance, that he has come across the same mistake made by other organizations in the past. The proceedings can be held up if emotions get too high or personnel become over-anxious.

10. Be determined, decisive and direct.

It is always a good idea for the auditor to display his determination to get the business of the audit conducted efficiently and promptly. The auditee must not be allowed to think he can get away with presenting incomplete information or delaying the proceedings unnecessarily. When sufficient evidence has been collected and sifted, the auditor should not hesitate to come to a conclusion on the basis of it and he should then convey his decision directly to the auditee. Once there is enough evidence to form the basis of a sound judgement, there is no point in going over and over the same ground or in watering down conclusions.

11. Get on with the job.

The auditor should avoid spending a lot of time in unnecessary or irrelevant conversations. Here, again, he can set an example to the auditee and demonstrate his resolve to get the business of the audit conducted as efficiently as possible.

12. Be fair.

The auditor should be fair in the way he approaches the different departments he audits, not go to one especially prepared to find fault. Personal dislikes or prejudices must not be allowed to influence his investigations. If he shows a bias, the auditor will lose the auditee's confidence.

13. Be independent.

The auditor, not the auditee, should be the one to make decisions as to what will be examined (bearing in mind the constraints mentioned on page 11-7).

If he allows the auditee to choose what he is going to see, the auditor may well end up being led by the nose.

14. Use your powers of deduction.

Sometimes the auditor will run up against a brick wall in his pursuit of information — this is often the case, for example, if the person he needs to see is temporarily unavailable. In this situation, it is worth trying to deduce the missing information by examining the evidence in units upstream or downstream of the unit concerned. An auditor may be able to reach some conclusions as to the unit's performance by examining units downstream of it or units which it supplies with feedback. By auditing upstream, he may be able to deduce with what information the unit is supplied. The interaction between units means that an auditor may have a fairly good idea that a deficiency exists long before he actually arrives to audit the unit in question. If, for example, goods of the wrong quality are being received, the auditor may suspect that the purchase orders are incorrect because the purchasing department is omitting certain key quality requirements. By auditing units upstream of purchasing, the auditor can determine whether the information purchasing receives is reflected in the purchase orders (the auditor will have examined copies of purchase orders in the receiving area). If there are any variances between the quality requirements conveyed to the purchasing department and those involved in the contract, the auditor can conclude that there is a problem within the purchasing department without even visiting it.

15. Know who's who.

An auditor should master not merely the names but the positions and interrelationships of the auditee's personnel. If he does not do this, embarrassing mistakes may occur.

> One external auditor was discussing a number of deficiencies with Mr. A. A further meeting had to be arranged for the following morning in order to continue the discussions. At the next day's meeting a Mr. B entered the discussions. His knowledge was not as extensive as Mr. A's, a point which the auditor commented on to Mr. A. Unfortunately B was, instead of A's subordinate, his superior.

16. One swallow does not make a summer.

If the auditor finds a couple of deficiencies in the area being audited, he has two alternatives. One is to recommend a purge of the area in order to get to the truth, assess the true magnitude of the problem and put the deficiencies into correct perspective. The second alternative is to perform the purge himself, if time permits and if he doubts the auditee's good intentions.

It makes sense to give the auditee an opportunity to perform the purge himself unless the auditor feels that he cannot be relied upon to do so properly.

> During an external audit of a supplier's design department, a few incorrect design calculations were found. A purge of the contract calculations was recommended and was performed by the auditee. The latter requested that all work be stopped in order to give the design department an opportunity to correct the deficiencies that had turned up in other calculations and to assess the impact on the contract itself. In this case, the auditee took the initiative, acted responsibly, and demonstrated his desire to get things right to the satisfaction of his own company and of the customer. The root cause of the problem turned out to be one particular design engineer involved in the contract concerned. The senior engineer, who was responsible for reviewing and approving the calculations, was quietly reprimanded for signing the design calculations without reviewing them. It became clear that an important factor contributing to the problem was the excessive workload of the design department, which was understaffed.

The point to remember is that it is in the auditee's own best interests to ascertain the extent of any problem which arises and to instigate prompt and effective corrective action. Failure to do so may lead to far more serious problems at a later stage and to incurring the displeasure of senior management in the auditee's organization. The basic instinct of self-preservation can generally be relied upon to make the auditee take the purge seriously. In the few cases where the auditee does play down the problem in public, knowing very well that it is more extensive than he says, he will generally go away quietly to rectify the situation at the earliest opportunity. The result is usually the same in the end and it is the result which counts.

> During one internal audit, three out of a sample of ten non-conformity reports were found to have a common deficiency. A purge of a further 100 documents revealed one further case of the deficiency and nothing more. The nature of the deficiency was found to be inconsequential — the non-conformity reports were used for statistical purposes and as a record — so a formal request for corrective action was not issued.

17. Discuss any problem immediately, on the spot.

Doing this saves the auditor any arguments later on, when people's memories have grown hazy, and allows him to clarify the problem and to collect fresh evidence relating to it. If the discussion reaches an impasse, the auditor should not get involved in an argument. He should agree to differ from the auditee and refer the problem to a higher echelon of the auditee's management. Another advantage of discussing a problem on the spot is that it helps the auditee understand the nature of the auditor's doubts and may suggest suitable corrective action. Even if this cannot be determined, it is a great help for all concerned to have the problem clear in their minds before the exit interview (see Chapter 19). Moreover, the operative concerned may be able to suggest effective corrective measures and, since he would not normally be present at the exit interview, this on-the-spot discussion may give him his only opportunity to make his voice heard. Whether his suggestion is the one finally implemented or not is less important than showing that his ideas are considered of value.

18. Be prepared to return to an area, if necessary, to obtain fresh evidence or to reassess the activity in the light of fresh evidence supplied by the auditee.

Willingness to go back and re-audit an area shows that the auditor has an open mind and helps him enlist the co-operation of the auditee's staff.

> During one audit, it was found that certain documents were not being processed as the available quality procedure prescribed. It was not possible to determine the reason for the variance between procedure and practice because the man responsible was temporarily inaccessible. It transpired during a discussion with the quality assurance manager that the procedure had been changed without the person concerned being given a copy of the new version. In order to determine whether there had been compliance with the correct effectivity point, the audit team returned to the area concerned, looked at the evidence again and found that the person responsible had, in fact, complied with the verbal instructions received. The problem was not caused by a failure to comply with procedure but rather by failure to issue the correct revision of the procedure to the person involved.

19. Be aware of union relationships.

The auditor should be aware of whether or not the area being audited comes under the "jurisdiction" of a trade union. If so, he should ask for a shop steward to accompany the audit team around the area concerned. This prevents operatives complaining to their trade union and, possibly, exacerbating a delicate situation, if one already exists. It is particularly important to have a union representative present if there is to be a locker purge (i.e. if the operatives' lockers are to be opened and examined for superseded documents or uncontrolled materials). As audits have now become more commonplace, those representatives and the employees tend to understand the reasons for such activities and are generally unconcerned.

20. It is vital for the audit team members to conduct a private conference amongst themselves.

In the case of an external audit, the meeting generally takes place in the evening, perhaps in the motel or hotel at which the audit team is staying. Each auditor must remember that his colleagues do not communicate by telepathy. The information that has been obtained during the day's proceedings must be exchanged and analysed.

The meeting is so important because it enables the team to review their progress and, if necessary, reassign tasks. Some members may be ahead of schedule, others may have encountered problems and had to spend more time in particular areas than was originally anticipated. In this case, those who are ahead of schedule can take on auditing some of the departments previously assigned to other team members.

It often works well to hold the progress meeting after the audit team have had a chance to take a shower or a bath to refresh themselves and to read through any documents provided by the auditee during the day (such as procedures relevant to the areas to be audited next day or something similar).

The audit team must be sure to exchange the information that they require for the following day (document numbers, people's names/identification mechanisms, details of equipment seen and so on). They should also discuss the occurrence of general problems which are found to be cropping up across a number of the auditee's departments. It is usually possible to classify the defects discovered into the category of one of the task elements (see Chapters 5 and 25) and the requirements of that task element. Deficiencies discovered in a number of departments, for example, might be traced back to lack of training in the various quality management systems or to poor methods of handling. It is important to categorize the defects in preparation for presentation at the exit interview.

21. Know thy time.

Time is the enemy of the auditor. The auditor must be aware of the overall progress of the audit so as to avoid wasting precious hours on trivia. It is better to spend time auditing the more crucial areas, investigating those few vital problems rather than the trivial many. The audit team must, however, not allow the schedule to dictate to them if they feel that the problems encountered warrant deeper investigation. A word of warning, though: in certain countries (such as Switzerland) people will expect the audit team to make an appointment for meetings and to arrive strictly on time. If the decision is made to depart from the original schedule, the audit team must inform the auditee and request that information be passed on to the departments which might be affected by a late or early arrival. In any case, this practice is simply a matter of courtesy in any country. If the audit team feels it is necessary (in the light of discoveries already made) to spend more time than planned on the audit, then they should notify their own organization of the situation, explaining why they think more time will be needed.

22. Dispense with unnecessary escorts.

The auditor must have only the escorts that he wants *and* needs in the area being audited (see page 10-5). If he finds he is collecting too many followers, he should ask them to disperse. They will simply obstruct and slow down the proceedings whilst their presence raises the cost of the audit quite unnecessarily. Whether the management audit is internal or external, such increased costs will damage the competitiveness of the auditor's own organization in the long term and will reduce or eliminate the cost benefit of performing management audits.

23. At the end of each day, let the auditee's representatives have a brief summary of what has been happening (without commitment, if final evidence has still to be obtained).

This summary is a courtesy measure that is always appreciated by the auditee. It also rules out the need to make embarrassing revelations at the exit interview and in the audit report by forewarning those involved of the nature of any deficiencies encountered. There is nothing creditable in saving the deficiencies for the exit interview with a view to gloating over people's surprise and embarrassment.

It may turn out that the auditee is well aware of the problem and has already instituted corrective action. In this case, the auditor must verify that corrective action is under way and that it has been documented and approved by the appropriate authority. He must also determine whether or not the auditee's proposals appear to be efficacious. If they are, then the auditor should not report the deficiency as a Corrective Action Request issued by his organization.

If the auditee is unaware of the problem, the forewarning provided by each day's brief summary meeting permits the auditee to communicate to the appropriate level of management that certain findings have been made and to consider what corrective action could be proposed at the exit interview. The senior management, who will be present at the exit interview, will appreciate the forewarning and the chance to formulate their own proposals for correction action. If the auditor has a good idea of the sort of corrective action which would be considered acceptable by his company, it is constructive for him to pass the information on to the auditee at this point (see Chapter 17).

Sometimes the senior management present at the brief summary meeting will appreciate a private discussion with the auditors or lead auditor — an example of this would be if they may have sensitive information of which they feel the audit team should be aware but which is not for general dissemination.

> During one audit, I was called to the auditee's managing director's office for a private discussion. He asked me bluntly whether or not I thought that the company's quality assurance manager was suitable for the position he held. I answered honestly that I felt the QA manager was unsuitable since he lacked the requisite knowledge and the personality to obtain the introduction of the quality assurance programme into the company. The managing director stated that this was similar to his own opinion and that the QA manager was to be replaced within a couple of months although the news had yet to be broken to the QA manager himself.

Confidences of this kind must not be betrayed: the details must not be included in the audit report which will be disseminated throughout both the auditee's and the auditor's company. One must bear in mind that they are hearsay as opposed to factual objective evidence. Nonetheless they are confidences and must remain so which means that they must not be loosely disseminated throughout the auditor's organization or anywhere else.

24. Keep an eye open for obvious "clean up" jobs.

One reason for forewarning an auditee of an audit is to give him a chance to put his house in order to some extent. It is perfectly natural that he should do this and it should give the auditor more cause for concern if the auditee makes no effort to clear up a messy operation before the audit begins. The school of thought that advocates an unannounced audit as a means of catching the auditee out will, I hope, soon fall into disrepute since it is based on a totally misconceived notion of the purpose of auditing. Certain QA standards, such as API Q1[1], do require "unscheduled audits" to be performed whilst some companies performing third party assessments for the purpose of registering a company's compliance with a particular QA standard stipulate that they shall be provided with access for unannounced assessments. I regard such requirements to be unhelpful and negative: such behaviour by assessors is disgraceful and amateurish for it denotes the actions of a troublemaker, not a professional person.

There is normally no need to worry about the clean-ups that the auditee carries out before the audit team arrive. Clean-ups rarely solve major problems. A major problem is generally of a magnitude that is equivalent to implementing a new QA programme. Such implementation is always a lengthy process and it is doubtful whether any auditee would be able to solve a major problem between the time of notification of an audit and the arrival of the audit team. A false clean-up is a good thing to spot, however, because it indicates the probable normal state of affairs is. If the latter looks unsatisfactory, a pertinent remark would be quite in order.

> The receiving and storage area of company was of corrugated steel construction and in a poor state of repair. The lower parts of the steel sheets had corroded to such extent that draughts and moisture were entering whilst the walls were damp with condensation. During the audit, however, it was noticed that the metal storage racks had neatly typed labels taped on to them describing the contents of the shelf. The adhesive properties of that type of tape quickly deteriorate in a moist environment and so the auditor knew that these labels were, at the most, two or three days old. In parts of the stores, a number of the labels had already fallen off. Although areas of the shelves had been dusted, the items themselves had not. It was apparent that a false clean-up had been attempted. The QA manager shook his head and said "Well, it was worth a try".

A clean-up shows that the auditee *is* concerned about the outcome of the audit. The audit team is not on a fault-finding exercise, and if a clean-up achieves the right results, why worry? Obviously, if the clean-up has not achieved the right result, then the auditor will, in any event, note the deficiencies.

25. Remember Murphy's Law!

It is uncanny how an auditor finds the one superseded document still in use when all others have been withdrawn, the isolated human error in many situations. Murphy has been called the patron saint of auditors. Since the auditor is generally sampling he cannot hope to see every document, item or person involved in the quality system.

> During one audit, it was found that all the work areas were clear of uncontrolled materials. The auditee had, immediately prior to the audit, been around the various areas and attempted a purge of all uncontrolled material. This was a daily occurrence in the shop concerned. In spite of this, when the audit team arrived in the area where its contract work was about to start, a pile of uncontrolled material was found in a cupboard.

The auditor could be guided by Murphy and, upon finding a deficiency that may indicate a possible problem, require a purge. However, if on the basis of a limited sample the auditor finds all to be satisfactory, he could leave it at that. The reader can decide for himself, on the basis of past experience, how wise this last course would be.

26. Good guy — bad guy approach.

Some auditors believe a good method is to have two people on a team, one of whom adopts the "tough guy" approach while the other adopts a "soft guy" image. The idea is that the auditee's personnel will start to talk more of how things actually are. This method is unprofessional and betrays an attitude more befitting the thug than a professional auditor. It cannot be condoned and must be avoided. An audit is not to be regarded as an opportunity for confrontation. Such an approach benefits nobody. The good guy — bad guy approach does not alter the objective evidence available for perusal, a fundamental point to be made since audit results are not to be based on matters of opinion derived from fear — it is objective evidence that is needed.

References:

1. API Spec. Q1, First edition, January 1, 1985, *API specification for quality programs*. Published by the American Petroleum Institute, Production Department, 211 N. Ervay, Suite 1700, Dallas TX 75201-3688.

15. The Auditee's Conduct

Cunning is the dark sanctuary of incapacity.
Lord Chesterfield.

In the same way as there are right and wrong ways for an auditor to conduct the audit, an auditee can have a right and a wrong approach to the audit. Some nefarious tactics are still occasionally used by some auditees or their personnel although this is growing rarer as audits become more commonplace. Some of the commonest tactics are listed below to help an inexperienced auditor recognize the symptoms. Of course, some auditees may display the relevant behaviour quite innocently, so the auditor should be discreet in concluding that the auditee is deliberately being obstructive.

There are 12 main tactics which obstructive auditees adopt. I call them the "Dirty Dozen". They are listed in Fig. 15.1 together with a summary of how to deal with each one. Various manifestations of each of these are now discussed.

Time wasters

1. The waffler.

This individual can speak at length, says nothing, and never answers a question concisely. Politicians indulge in such tactics. It wastes time and achieves nothing.

2. The "dog and pony" show.

This is a rather apt American expression for a lengthy presentation, generally during the entry interview, accompanied by impressive charts, slides, company film or video and exhibits. The content of the presentation may or may not be of use to the auditor. Even if it is, the auditor has to verify what has been said during the presentation, by the examination of objective evidence and thus, as the dog and pony show presentation is of no value to him, he should politely call a halt to the proceedings.

3. The long lunch (or steak lunch).

The external auditor is generally the recipient of this tactic, particularly in countries such as France or Italy where food is almost a religion. Instead of being allowed to take a quick lunch in the canteen, the auditor is faced with a four course meal, an aperitif, plenty of wine, and maybe a liqueur afterwards. This not only wastes time but also makes it difficult to concentrate during the afternoon.

There is a variation on this ploy, whereby the auditee tells the auditor: "We know a delightful little restaurant just a short drive from here, where we would really like to take you because the food is excellent." At lunchtime, there is a wait of five or ten minutes while the cars arrive, the short distance eventually turns out to be a thirty minute drive, the actual lunch takes two hours to consume, and a further thirty minutes is spent driving back to the auditee's location.

The auditor should obviously try to avoid offending the auditee when refusing the long lunch but he should none the less remain firm. It should also not be forgotten that in some companies the business lunch is looked upon as a perk for the auditee's people, who seldom get the chance to eat out on the company and who look forward to it.

4. The late arrival.

The audit can be delayed if personnel arrive late for work or for their appointments.

> At one audit, the quality assurance manager, who was the escort, arrived 45 minutes late each morning and delayed the audit team as a consequence. The lead auditor soon rectified matters by announcing on the third day that he was extending the audit to make up for the time lost due to late starts and such like. The next day the QA manager was early.

5. The long way round.

Although it would be normal practice to use a short cut through a building to get from A to B, during the audit the escorts may use a circuitous route. This is a rather foolish tactic: the auditor will soon get his bearings and recognize when the long way round is being taken. The auditor should suggest, for example, "Would it not be quicker if we cut through the stock yard?"

6. The forgotten document.

One of the escorts "forgets" essential documents. Upon arriving at the area to be audited, he says: "Oh dear me! I've left the documents in my office, I'll have to go back and fetch them".

> During one audit, the lead auditor noted that an escort did this twice. The company was of the large complex type and it was a

> full 15 minute walk from one end to the other. The third time that the audit team was starting out from the escort's office, the lead auditor noticed a particular document, which would be required later on, left lying on the escort's desk. He placed it in his bag. Sure enough, upon arriving at the destination, the escort smiled and apologized for having lost the document. The smile soon disappeared when the lead auditor produced it, saying "Don't worry, I picked it up for you".

7. Interruptions.

It is the easiest thing in the world for an escort or manager to demand "No interruptions until we're finished". An endless queue of visitors who drag the escort away for a few minutes at a time, phone calls demanding immediate attention and so on all waste time.

8. The "clean room".

With this tactic, everybody has to spend five or ten minutes putting on caps/gown/boots and signing the log sheet before entering the room because the escort says "It's a strict rule, you know". However, upon entering, the auditor notes that one or two of the operatives are not acquainted with the "strict" rules, and that visitors who come in afterwards have not been obliged to follow the same "strict" procedures.

> On one occasion, an audit team had to get dressed in cap, gown and boots to examine the clean area. The quality assurance manager entered the area to see how the audit was progressing. he was wearing neither cap, nor gown, nor boots.

A variant of this is the trip to the medical department to collect safety spectacles, when it subsequently becomes plain that no one in the works wears safety spectacles and that other visitor is obliged to wear them either. (I am not, however, suggesting that safety spectacles are unnecessary — rather that the auditee should have them ready).

9. Lack of preparedness.

If the personnel are not forewarned by their management, the people whom the auditors need to see may be unavailable.

> A department manager complained bitterly to an audit team that nobody had informed him that an audit was to take place and that he was rather busy. To his credit, he quickly re-scheduled his work, made alternative arrangements and escorted the audit team while they audited his department. As it transpired, it was a most impressive area, under good control, and one where no deficiencies were found by the audit team. That company is in Switzerland, where people appreciate and expect an appointment to be made.

It is a good practice for the auditor to tell the escorts as the audit progresses roughly when he expects that they will arrive in the next areas and what will be done later that day. This helps preclude the possibility of people not being forewarned.

Fig. 15.1 The 'Dirty Dozen' and how to deal with them.

Tactic	*How to handle*
Time wasting	Tell the auditee you will extend the audit if progress is unsatisfactory.
The 'Cook's tour'	If it has no value, stick to your audit programme.
Provocation	Remain calm and polite
Fixed ballot	Refuse and select your own sample of objective evidence
Special case	Take extensive notes and wait till the auditee gets himself confused.
Trial of Strength	Be prepared for audit; know your facts; be firm.
Insincerity	Ignore it.
Pity	Show polite sympathy and then get on with the job.
Absentees	Call for the deputy, manager to explain the area; audit inputs and outputs to determine efficacy.
Amnesia	Go back and get it yourself.
Language barrier	Have a translator on team or advise your management of the risks in advance.
Bribes	Refuse them, report it and stop dealing with that auditee.

The "Cook's tour"

During the entry interview, the auditor may be presented with an audit programme constructed by the auditee. If the programme does not meet his own requirements, the auditor should politely convey to the auditee both the fact that it is not acceptable and the reason why. He should then state what he wants to audit, when he wants to go there, and who else should be present. The auditor should take care because in some companies and countries people expect adherence to a plan or procedure. This is why the auditor should supply an audit programme (see Chapter 9) prior to the audit so that the auditee can distribute it to departments concerned. Unless this is supplied, the auditee is bound to try to make his own arrangements or plans.

Provocation

According to this, happily rare, tactic, the auditee tries to make the auditor annoyed and argumentative so that the audit can be stopped.

> On one occasion, an auditor was becoming so angry and argumentative that the conversation was beginning to deteriorate to the level of personalities. The auditee knew that this particular auditor could be easily aroused. The lead auditor spotted the situation and quickly stepped in to prevent the auditee's QA manager from halting the audit by calming things down and asking the auditor to be quiet.
>
> On another occasion, an auditor and auditee comprised an Israeli and an Arab. (I will not reveal which was which). As the lead auditor, I found that a considerable amount of diplomacy was needed to prevent a replay of the Six Day War.

The fixed ballot or loaded dice

The auditee may try to select the contract/item/operator/document for the auditor to see. This can be similar to the "Cook's tour", described above. As Chapter 14 points out, the auditor must always select the objective evidence that is to be audited.

The special case

When a problem arises, the auditee's response is always "Ah yes, but this is a special case because...." This may well be true if the auditor is auditing a contract that is not his own. However, unless the auditor is firm, every contract/document/item becomes a special case. The auditor should politely ask the auditee exactly how many quality management systems and variations thereof are in effect and how the auditee manages to control the situation. In these circumstances, the auditee sometimes becomes so confused about the "special case" that from department to department the explanations about "special cases" start to conflict with one another.

The trial of strength

The auditee, at some point, tries to test the auditor's resilience, knowledge or firmness. If the auditor fails this test, the auditee loses respect for him and the auditor may as well pack up and go home. Control of the whole audit is at stake.

Insincerity

The auditee indulges in flattery, sycophancy and false admiration of the auditor which is designed firstly to make the auditor think more of himself and less of the audit and also to convince the auditor that the auditee's people are "nice" and very friendly. Variants of this are the unctuous look or the "kill him with kindness" attitude that some auditees adopt.

> A senior manager in an auditee's company had been oozing humility, compliments and false admiration throughout an audit; they became increasingly obsequious as problems were revealed. At the exit interview, I confirmed that certain matters had been found to be deficient and that I intended to issue some Corrective Action Requests. At this point, the tone changed and the manager concerned said unprintable words to the effect "How can you be such a horrible person when I've been so nice to you?"!

The auditor must not become affected by false admiration and must concentrate on the job in hand. The best way to handle insincerity is to be polite but ignore it.

Pleas for pity

Here, the auditee tries to make the auditor feel sorry for him so that the auditor will ease up or disregard his findings, either out of sympathy or the fear of having somebody commit suicide during the audit. The auditee may claim that he is unwell today, that he was sick last night, that the doctor said he really should not come into work at all (being a hero). Alternatively he may play the geriatric ("When you get to my age...."). The auditor should offer polite sympathy but refuse to be diverted from his investigation or discouraged from reporting his findings faithfully.

> Whilst auditing one company, the quality assurance manager started to tell me a heart-rending story concerning the state of his health and how he had made a special effort to come into work that day. Strangely, at the outset of the audit, he had seemed perfectly cheerful and the tragic decline seemed to increase in direct proportion to revelations of deficient practices. I listened with sympathy and stated "I really appreciate the special efforts that you have made in order to be here today. As a result, I would like to feel certain that I have done an especially thorough job so that you do not feel your sacrifice was wasted".

The absentee or indispensable man

The auditee claims that the man who has the key/knowledge/book, whatever, is not available or away today. This may or may not be true. Of course, some people try to make themselves indispensable by refusing to pass on their knowledge to others.

> At one manufacturing company, the production controller, who was really running the whole works, refused to write anything down and kept all his information in his head. His fear was that if he wrote the information down, he would become dispensable to the company and could find himself out of a job.

> An audit revealed that an engineer had not adequately specified a product that was to be purchased. Although at the time the original purchase order was placed, an adequate specification appeared to be available, essential details to guide the vendor had neither been adequately included nor subsequently confirmed in writing. The investigations showed that the engineer in question lived in fear of losing his job because, in the straightened circumstances of his particular industry, redundancies were common. He tried, therefore, to make himself indispensible.

These are human problems that can only be solved on a case-by-case basis. So far as the auditor is concerned, he must make it clear that the situation is unacceptable. Except in a genuine emergency, the people needed should always be made available during the audit. If they are absent, then the escorts or QA staff ought to have provided themselves with sufficient knowledge to enable the audit to proceed. If all else fails, the auditor may just have to try to deduce the effectiveness of the absentee by assessing the evidence available from other areas (see page 14-9).

When the auditee claims that somebody is indispensable, the auditor must ascertain who is the allegedly indispensable person's supervisor or manager. Then he must request that the latter comes to the workplace to explain how the area works and to show objective evidence of what is being done. Since any supervisor or manager is responsible for the quality management systems in that area, that person must be familiar with them. Or must he?

Amnesia

When this tactic is employed, the auditor has continually to chivy the auditee for the information that he has asked to be provided before the end of the audit. The auditee who acts in such a way may be hoping that the auditor will forget that the information was ever requested. The auditor must make it clear that he will continue the audit until the information is forthcoming.

If information is constantly not made available, the options are:

a) to obtain the information immediately from wherever it has allegedly gone or whoever may be using it;

b) to return to the area responsible for providing that information immediately on completion of the current aspects of the audit;

c) to return to that same workplace upon completion of the entire audit and prior to the exit interview whilst making it clear that if this will entail an extension to the time required for the audit, so be it.

Language barrier

The options available for dealing with a genuine language barrier have been described in page 9-18 "Audit Preparation".

If, however, he is playing games, the auditee exploits the language barrier by claiming not to speak the auditor's mother tongue. Unless the auditor speaks the auditee's language, this can create a problem and waste time. The auditee's aim may be to claim to misunderstand the explanation, questions and information discussed or examined during the audit. It is a quasi-political tactic.

> An auditor encountered an individual and asked if that person spoke English. The response was "Nein". The audit proceeded in the auditee's language. However, at one point, the auditor noted that in the person's open valise was an English copy of *The Day of the Jackal* by Frederick Forsyth. At the end of the discussion, the auditor remarked in English to the auditee that he hoped he would enjoy *The Day Of The Jackal*, since it was a good book that would help him to improve his English. The auditee looked surprised and embarrassed for a moment, then laughed. When the auditor next spoke to that particular individual, it was amazing how much English had been learnt.

Sometimes an auditor may find it useful to play the language game himself but for a different reason. The private chats and asides between auditee's personnel can be enlightening and help him to assess whether or not the auditee is acting in good faith.

> A design engineer was being most unco-operative with an audit team. The QA manager spoke quietly to the design engineer and the auditor was able to mentally translate that the manager had said: "Why do we have to drag every piece of information out of your nose?" The design engineer went fairly pale at being reproved by a senior manager. The auditor knew immediately that they were about to make better progress. They did.

The bribe

The auditor may encounter this distasteful practice when the contract is large or of critical value to the auditee. It may occur during the pre-award survey or during the external audit. Fortunately it is comparatively rare.

> During a pre-award survey a potential supplier was so desperate to win the contract that a substantial bribe was offered in private to the lead assessor. The latter did not know how to manage this situation. After returning to his company, he consulted with a

senior manager who promptly telexed the potential supplier stating "We note your revised offer to be as per original less the discount offered to our lead assessor during the pre-award survey". The contract was, naturally, offered to an alternative source.

The right tactics

Having looked at the tactics the auditee may adopt to hinder the auditor, it is necessary to mention those he should adopt to help him. These tactics will be the reverse of those just listed. Naturally, it is important to keep a sense of proportion here as elsewhere. I am not suggesting that the auditee should starve the audit team, deny them tea or coffee or give incomplete/terse answers to questions.

The auditee's escorts must be alert for the incipient use of the wrong tactics by the departments or units being audited. It should be remembered that an extrinsic audit provides, or should provide, an independent, unbiased appraisal of the auditee's practices, equipment, policies and so on. As such it is good "free" consultancy. An extrinsic auditor who is experienced, trained, constructive and helpful can be of great benefit to the auditee.

All too frequently, the extrinsic auditor is the only person who can elicit action and improvements in the management and quality systems from the auditee management. This is because the extrinsic auditor has that all important lever: the customer's requirement/opinion or the regulatory body's endorsement/approval of the auditee's practices or product. This amounts to money and potential loss or gain of business for the auditee. It is commonly called "customer pressure" and, judiciously used, it can solve some apparently intractable problems.

A QA department had struggled for a number of years with a workshop manager over the introduction of a material control system that would be up to modern QA standards. The spur for action came from my threat (as extrinsic auditor) to refuse to accept a complex product that had been fabricated for my company. My justification was that there was no evidence available to prove exactly what materials had been used in the welding process or to indicate the qualifications of the welders nor were there any test results to show whether or not the welds were satisfactory. To the workshop manager's credit, the situation was rectified in a very short space of time and a solution was found to analyse the materials that had been used in the fabrication of this complex structure.

Desperation

In difficult circumstances, the most punctilious of auditees can be driven to adopt desperate measures for dealing with an audit team.

> A friend of mine related an incident that occurred when his company was being audited. He had been the quality assurance manager for over twenty years and ran a tight ship, so tight, in fact, that an extrinsic audit team were becoming increasingly frustrated, unpleasant and a general nuisance. Recognizing that they had to justify their existence, the QA manager waited till the team had departed one evening and then went along to a department that was to be audited the following day. He instructed the foreman to remove a couple of calibration stickers on some measuring equipment and to scatter some spare material under the work benches. The audit team glowed with pure delight when they found this "disgraceful set of affairs". Two Corrective Action Requests were issued on the spot to my friend, who acted as if suitably chastened. The audit team then announced that the audit was complete. Immediately after the team left that "filthy area", the foreman replaced the stickers and threw out the loose material.

I leave the reader to decide whether my friend's action was right or wrong.

16. Quality Management Systems

A fail safe system fails by failing to fail safe.
John Gall.

Codes, standards and regulations always state requirements that an auditee must meet but it is rare for them to stipulate specific methods. ISO 9000 series[1] of quality assurance standards, for example, contains phrases such as "establish and maintain", "plan, establish, document and assign", "arrange for" and AS 1821 — 1985[2] uses similar phrases. NS 5801[3] frequently asks that "A system shall be established which ensures..." whilst AQAP-13[4] says, inter alia, "provisions shall be made for. . ."

The responsibility for compliance with a standard clearly rests with the auditee, as does the freedom of choice in the methods to be be adopted, unless an authority or the customer has intervened and imposed its own interpretation on an auditee, either by contract or by code/regulation. Assuming that no such intervention has occurred that freedom of choice does not rest with the auditor: he retains only the freedom of choice as to the audit method to be used and has the right neither to impose any particular system on the auditee nor require changes to a system that meets the standard, simply because he does not like it. In all cases, however, compliance with a standard has to be demonstrated, which means that objective evidence must be created by the auditee and presented to the auditor for consideration.

It is one thing to establish a system, quite another to maintain it. Maintaining a system entails knowing how well it is performing and obtaining feedback on its results. Feedback involves the provision of information, often in the form of documents. Documents are objective evidence and it is objective evidence that the auditor is looking for. Objective evidence is required to prove both that some activity has been "established and maintained" and that management has "ensured". Feedback systems and their associated documents will gain increased prominence and attention in years to come as product liability legislation becomes more stringent (particularly with the concept of "strict liability"). As Greville Janner states[5]: "Every court knows that memory is an unreliable guide to the truth. Documents — notes, memoranda, diary entries, letters, contracts and the like — made at the time are far more likely to reveal the truth."

Types of system

There are two types of system that can be implemented as part of a quality programme: an open system or a closed-loop one. Only the closed-loop type of system provides feedback of the results obtained when an activity has been performed. If there is a closed loop model then the system is capable of being maintained and the system will "ensure that" an activity will yield the desired results (eventually, but perhaps not on a first time basis).

Fig. 16.1 Open and closed-loop systems

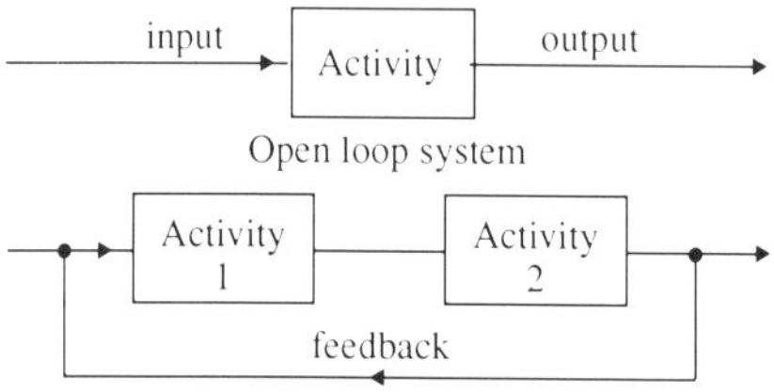

input
Activity
output
Open loop system
Activity 1
Activity 2
feedback
Closed-loop system

Open system (Fig. 16.1):

Here, there exists an input, a task being performed and an output from that task. Assuming that the task is correctly performed, the input controls the output. If both input and process are correct, the output will be correct. If the input is incorrect and the processing correct, then the output will be incorrect. Correct input and incorrect process will also yield an incorrect output. And, of course, incorrect input and process will also produce incorrect output. Unless, however, the task process receives information that states "Your output is wrong", it will carry on wasting time and money in yielding an incorrect output. Regardless of how well the system is set up initially, there is no guarantee that it will maintain itself and consistently yield the right results without intervention. This is the risk all open systems run. They are unreliable.

Closed loop system (Fig. 16.1):

This is an open system that has been provided with a feedback loop (engineering examples include overspeed governors on engines). Once feedback has been provided to a unit to the effect that its output is incorrect, it is then possible to analyse the root cause of the problem, apply corrective action and maintain the desired results. The root cause must necessarily be either that the input is incorrect or that the task process itself is being performed incorrectly, or a combination of both, just as for the open loop system.

The input and the task process can themselves be analysed into the task elements (see Chapters 5 and 25) in order to determine which individual elements or combination of elements are resulting in the unit's output being incorrect. This is the principle of trouble shooting.

Tools for analysing systems

Information is easier to assimilate if it is presented in a visual form such as a diagram or flow chart. These illustrations can make explicit the logical connections between different parts of the system and, by presenting the auditor's line of thought graphically, they can save a lot of unnecessary misunderstandings. It may be particularly useful to present the frequency of occurrence of trouble spots in a system or their magnitude by means of a diagram such as a pie chart or histogram, while flow charts and family trees can express in different ways a system's internal logic and can help to pinpoint possible origins of problems. Fig. 16.3 is an example of a flow chart analysis of a system, that at a first quick reading of its procedure, as reproduced in Fig. 16.2, appeared to be reasonable: the flow chart reveals a different picture that proves non-compliance with ISO 9001[6], AS 1821.

If the auditor finds it necessary to draw a picture in order to analyse the auditee's system, he should attach it to the audit checklist for future reference because it will help to refresh his mind at a later date (see Chapter 12).

What requires a system?

Each of the task elements — the person, the items produced, the service supplied, the information and the equipment — requires its own feedback system. The flow chart in Fig. 8.10, relating to control over the selection of an operator performing a task, was matched by other charts relating to the items being processed, the information and the equipment. In the case of a service a similar chart would have been produced.

The quality management system must be designed to serve the needs of the task being investigated: that task may in turn serve another or the same quality management system.

Systemantics

John Gall's book *Systemantics*[7] contains a number of valuable precepts for the auditor to bear in mind. They include the following.

1. Always be wary of systems that are allegedly "fail safe". The example shown in Fig 16.2 was presented to me on such a basis. As John Gall states, "a fail safe system fails by failing to fail safe".

2. When considering corrective action, the auditor should *always* recommend simple systems, preferably by building on the strengths already available in the auditee's existing systems. (An example is described in page 17-9, whereby existing systems were enhanced to control CAD tapes, disks and

Fig. 16.2 Example of a procedure for analysis during an audit.

INDICATION OF INSPECTION STATUS

Applicability and objectives
This procedure applies to the requirements for indication of inspection status on items in the various stages of production. Its main objectives are to ensure that production stages are applied in a logical and systematic manner and that progress beyond one inspection stage does not occur until satisfactory inspection has taken place.

Inspection marking system
A colour band code shall be applied at each inspection stage.

A "Yellow" band shall be marked on each item that is to be prepared for processing. The colour band shall be approximately 10 mm wide. The inspector shall place his initials and the date inspected next to the yellow band.

A "Blue" band, of similar dimensions to above and adjacent to the yellow one shall indicate acceptance of the preparation and that the process may proceed. The inspector shall place his initials and the date inspected next to the blue band.

A "White" band, of similar dimensions to above and adjacent to the blue and yellow bands, shall indicate that the process has been performed correctly, is visually acceptable and has passed the necessary quality tests. The inspector shall place his initials and the date inspected next to the white band.

A "Red" band, of similar dimensions to above and adjacent to the yellow and blue bands, shall indicate that either, the process has not been performed correctly, is not visually acceptable or has not passed the necessary quality tests. The inspector shall place his initials and the date inspected next to the red band.

No further work shall be conducted on the affected item(s) until all unsatisfactory areas have been determined and the correct repair procedures determined.

The colour band status code shall be commenced from the "yellow" step and followed until a satisfactory process has been performed. All repairs shall be recorded on a "non-conformity" report and processed as required by Chapter 17 of the Quality Procedures Manual.

Fig. 16.3 Flowchart of colour code system described in Fig. 16.2

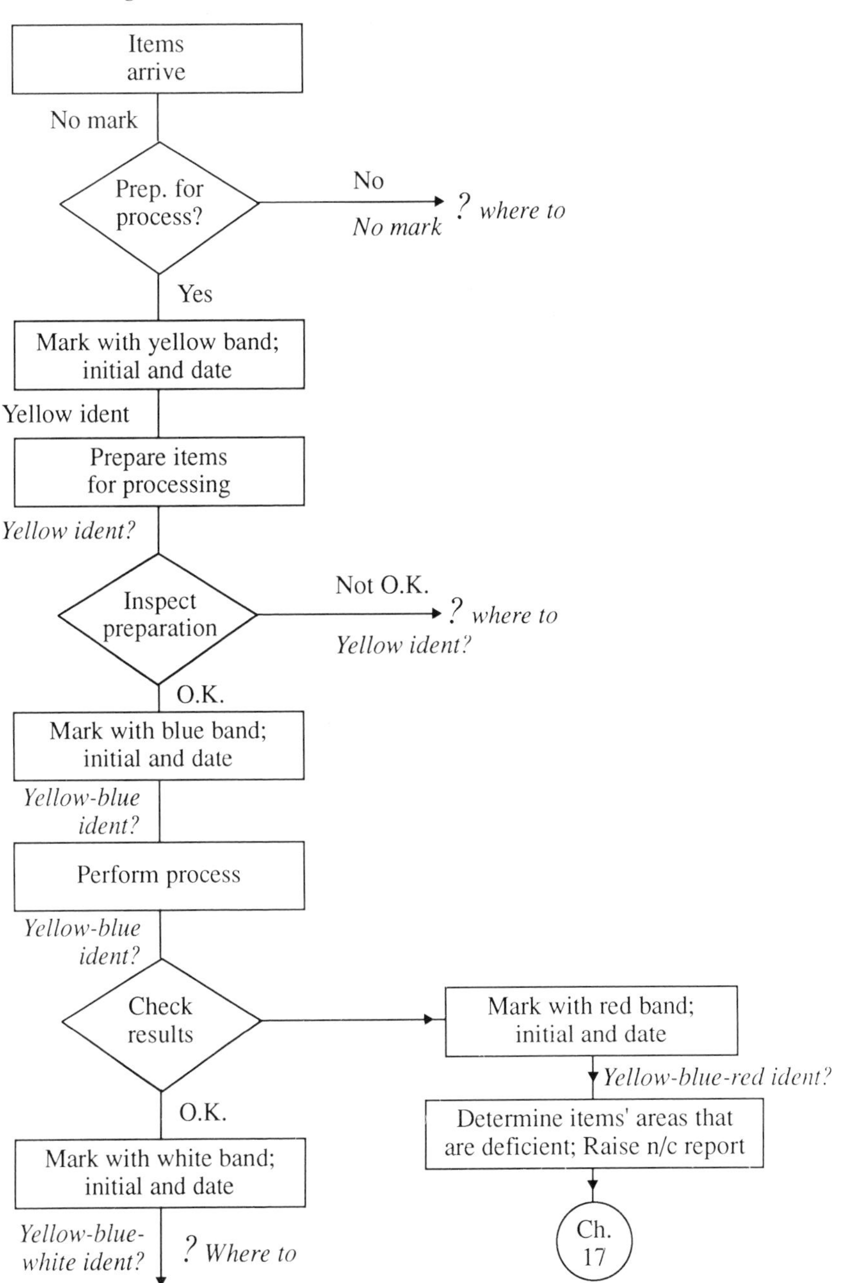

changes made to them). If one finds that a simple system has been implemented and works, that system must be respected and not tampered with. As John Gall says, "The systems that work best are the simple ones. Simple systems cost least in time, money and grief".

Analysing a system

When performing a systems audit the auditor should:

— determine the objectives of the system (i.e. the product and its associated requirements);
— determine where those objectives originate;
— look at the final task involved and determine which of the task elements apply there;
— review the organization plans and procedures to determine where each of those elements originates;
— repeat those steps progressively back to the origin for each of those task elements. (Note that there will be supporting elements identified at each task and that the auditor should keep to the main track of the principle task element being traced before going on to look at others).

When performing a compliance audit on a system the auditor should:

— repeat the actions detailed above for the systems audit;
— check at the final task involved that those requirements are being achieved; (This is similar to an inspection but it merely ascertains that the system can work and that the auditee has the *capability* to supply product to certain requirements. Note that ISO 9001, 9002[8], 9003[9] are concerned with a supplier's "capability" which is of limited value in a quality assurance world.)
— then trace through to determine if each task involved in the system operates as the system requires. (This provides objective evidence of the *reliability* of the system since the various weaknesses in application are identified together with facts concerning their frequency. Quality professionals are concerned with the system's reliability as opposed to its capability.)

References:

1. The ISO 9000 series comprises ISO 9000 to ISO 9004 inclusive. See also references 6, 8, 9 below

2. AS 1821 — 1985 *Suppliers quality systems for design, development, production and installation* Published by the Standards Association of Australia, Standards House, 80 Arthur Street, North Sydney, N.S.W., Australia.

3. NS 5801 *Requirements for the contractor's quality assurance. Quality assurance system*, 1981. Published by Norsk Verkstedsindustris Standardiseringssentral (NVS), Haakon VII's gate, Oslo, Norway.

4. AQAP-13 *NATO Software Quality Control System Requirements*. Issued by the NATO International Staff — Defence Suport Division.

5. Janner, Greville, *Product Liability*, 1979 Business Books Ltd.

6. ISO 9001 — 1987 *Quality systems — Model for quality assurance in design/development, production, installation and servicing*. Published by the International Organization for Standardization.

7. Gall, John, *Systemantics*, Pocket Books, Gulf & Western Corporation, 1230 Avenue of the Americas, New York, NY 10020, USA, 1978.

8. ISO 9002 — 1987 *Quality systems — Model for quality assurance in production and installation*. Published by the International Organization for Standardization (ISO).

9. ISO 9003 — 1987 *Quality systems — Model for quality assurance in final inspection and test*. Published by the International Organization for Standardization (ISO).

17. The Corrective Action Decision

And now remains
That we find the cause of this effect;
Or, rather say, the cause of this defect,
For this effect defective comes by cause.
William Shakespeare (Hamlet)

After collecting all the evidence needed, the auditor's next move must be to analyse it, with a view to deciding:

1. whether or not corrective action should be taken;
2. whether or not a formal request for corrective action is warranted;
3. what this corrective action might be;
4. what the underlying root cause of the deficiency discovered really is.

The decision to require formal corrective action is not one the auditor should take lightly or without consideration of all the factors involved. This chapter outlines factors that he should have in mind when the moment comes to make such decisions.

Chapter 11 described an audit method and a suggested sequence to be followed by an auditor. Obviously there are occasions when any one of the seven steps shown in Fig. 11.2 may be found to be deficient. The auditor then has to decide whether corrective action is necessary. Fig. 17.1 enlarges on Fig. 11.2 and each of the seven steps is now discussed.

STEP 1. The auditor should have ascertained the organization proposals within each department. Any problems encountered with the auditee's proposals for the structure and planning of his organization could be most serious. Where there is no organization, there can be either overlap or conflict of duties or unallocated responsibilities: everything is left vague. Upon encountering a potential problem, therefore, the auditor should follow the path described in Fig. 17.2. Within that diagram, any aspect of organizational problems in any single department cannot be regarded as a trivial affair and should warrant the issuing of a Corrective Action Request (CAR) unless the auditee is aware of the problem and his proposed solutions are satisfactory to the auditor. Lack of organization reduces the reliability of the quality management systems.

STEP 2. If the auditor finds problems with the quality management systems proposed by the auditee either for any department or in general, such problems usually constitute a situation which will warrant the issuing of a CAR. Provided, however, that the auditee can prove his awareness of the system problem and can satisfy the auditor by furnishing proof and efficacious proposals for redressing the situation, a CAR will not be issued, as shown in Fig. 17.2. The potential reliability of the system depends on how well it has been conceived.

Fig. 17.1 Audit sequence and corrective action decision

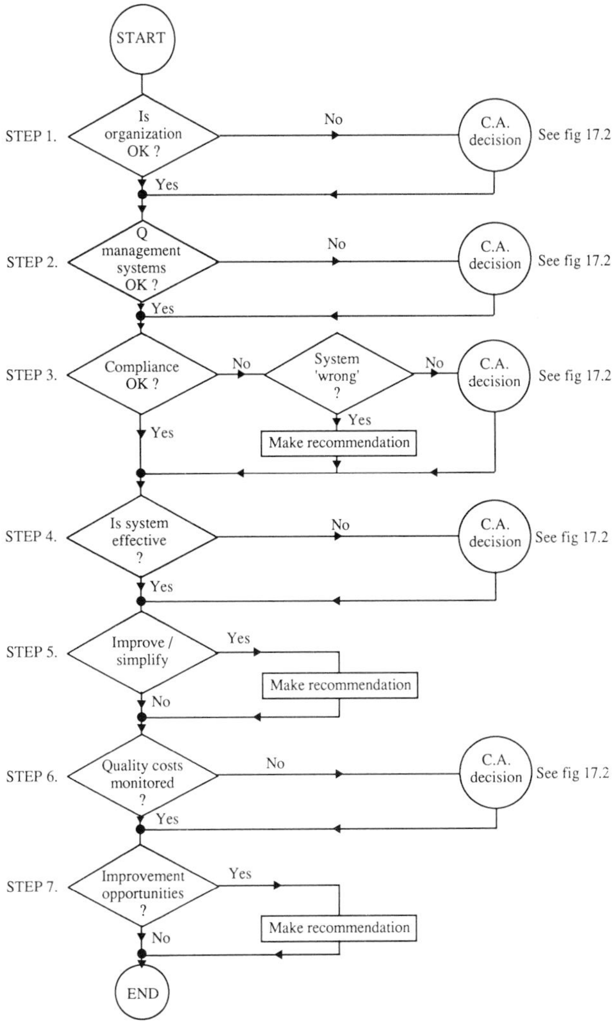

STEP 3. The auditor must not immediately rush ahead with the issuing of a CAR if non-compliance with the quality management system has been found. The auditee's personnel might have found the planned and documented "system" to be inadequate when implemented. They may have found alternative and better ways of doing the job while still achieving the right results.

Recollect what the product's needs really are. Provided that the product as required is not suffering, the implemented system is efficacious even though it has not been documented properly. In such circumstances, the auditor should merely recommend that the auditee documents the system that is actually being implemented. At this juncture, inform the auditee that, in not having accurately documented the actual practice, he is "selling himself short". (This is one particular area where some auditors would disagree with my advice but I take the view that it is the result that matters. Even though many quality assurance standards do require that a system be documented and implemented, my personal view is that the implementation is far more important than the documentation.) I consider it to be negative to issue a CAR to people who are merely doing what is required although they happen not to have recorded the exact details of how they do it. My experience is that when an auditee sees that he is receiving due credit for doing the right thing, the recommendation is acted upon and the auditor is perceived as being fair-minded. Receiving a CAR is a poor reward for diligent employees who, by their actions, have demonstrated their reliability for taking care of the product. No matter how well a system has been designed, its reliability is totally dependent on the reliability of the people entrusted with its use. Reliability to supply product that meets requirements is of greater importance than capability to do so since it is reliability of practice which provides real quality assurance.

If, however, the objective evidence shows that the product is suffering and is not being furnished in accordance with requirements, then the auditor must go through the corrective action decision sequence as described in Fig. 17.2.

STEP 4. A most critical decision is to determine whether or not the system is effective. This is done on the basis of collecting and collating sufficient objective evidence. If that evidence indicates that the system is not effective, the auditor should follow the sequence described in Fig. 17.2.

STEP 5. As stated in page 11-4, the auditor must be constructive and helpful at all times. Accordingly, the auditor has to consider whether the objective evidence and the analysis of the system show that there is room for improving or simplifying the system. The auditee may be achieving the right results i.e. a product that is fit for purpose and made right first time but the analysis of the system may nonetheless show that the methods used are inefficient in that they waste time or resources. The auditor's suggestions for improving or simplifying the system *are not* the subject of a Corrective Action Request. The auditee is, after all, achieving the right result — so, make a recommendation.

Poor auditors do not take the trouble to perform this essential step in the audit sequence. They seem to regard audits as being witch-hunts or finger pointing exercises, which they are not. A pertinent recommendation provides the auditee with a stimulus to thought that often leads to even better ideas for improvement. Many organizations tend to believe that the status quo cannot be improved but the mere challenge and demonstration that there could be room for improvement frequently makes folk think harder and arrive at even better suggestions. Obviously, every improvement benefits both auditee and auditor.

The best auditors all have one thing in common: they have personally defined, designed and commissioned quality management systems as opposed merely to being observers of other peoples' efforts. This enables them to understand fully the thought processes and difficulties encountered.

STEP 6. As stated in Chapter 11, quality cost systems are an essential part of a corrective action system and of management control. They measure a main quality management system's reliability and highlight areas of opportunity . If such data capture mechanisms do not exist, one can hardly believe that useful corrective action systems can be obtained. Under these circumstances, the auditor should follow the decision sequence shown in Fig. 17.2.

STEP 7. Provided that the auditee has a system for capturing performance data, the auditor should peruse its results. It may be possible to interpret the data in an alternative way to the auditee. This may also stimulate the auditee's thoughts towards improvement and extra effort. Such circumstances justify a verbal recommendation as distinct from a formal Corrective Action Request.

The corrective action decision

Fig. 17.2 illustrates a sequence of decisions and actions to be taken.

Note 1:
Upon finding a deficiency, the auditor must either perform a purge of the area or, preferably, request the auditee to do this himself (see page 14-5). The object of the purge is to assess the frequency with which that particular type of deficiency occurs i.e. to assess the *true* scope and magnitude of the problem. The results of the purge will enable the auditor to decide whether the deficiency is an isolated or a frequent error, his decision needing to be based on a sample of sufficient size to permit confidence in his conclusions.

a) Isolated errors:

A common cause of isolated errors is found in simple human fallibility, due to somebody having an "off-day". I do not believe in issuing a formal request for corrective action in such circumstances, provided tht some means can be found to have the deficiency quickly and quietly corrected on the spot. If, for example, one or two items are found which carry no means of identifying their acceptance status but the auditor is aware that the normal methods are in use elsewhere, he should ask for the items to be reappraised and correctly identified there and then (e.g. with a hold tag, or an appropriate signature on a document). If this sort of corrective action is taken, I act as if the auditee has just performed an internal audit and corrected the deficiency. In my view — and not all auditors would agree with me — it is the result that matters. My approach does have the advantage that when it is necessary to issue a Corrective Action Request, the auditee will be aware that this is not done unfairly.

Fig. 17.2 Corrective action decisions

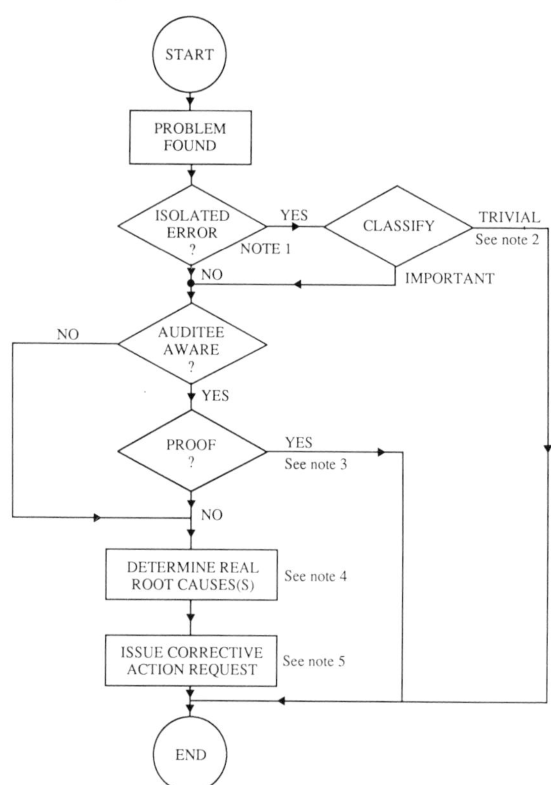

b) Frequent errors:

Frequent errors occur as a result of one or more of the six real causes of quality problems, discussed later in this chapter. They also occur during the gestation period of introducing a quality management system.

It is not my practice to issue a formal request for corrective action in the case of a gestation period problem or in the isolated instance of a new employee, who has not yet fully settled into the activity concerned, making a small error. Learning curve problems still occur when a system has been documented, even, perhaps, partly implemented, if an individual concerned in the activity of interest requires further training in that activity. In these circumstances, it is only fair and reasonable to give the auditee a chance to put his own house in order.

Note 2:
Some problems may be found as a "one off". The auditor must keep in mind the nature of the product and decide whether the particular problem can be considered either important or trivial. For example:

— An auditor selects and reviews 25 purchase orders and discovers one which does not show evidence of revision status. The objective evidence clearly indicates that there is a system in practice, the system is effectively implemented but an isolated human error has occurred. At this point, the auditor will require that the purchase order is corrected on the spot and re-issued.
— An auditor reviews 25 purchase orders and finds that 3 are concerned with the procurement of safety related items. One of these three has not referenced the correct statute. Since safety is involved, the auditor should trace through the system and determine why such an omission was made, issuing a Corrective Action Request to cure the real root cause of such a problem so as to prevent recurrence (that is unless the auditee is already aware of the problem etc., as shown in the remainder of Fig. 17.2).

A crucial aspect of classifying deficiencies is not only the functional importance of the product but also the frequency with which that type of problem has been encountered throughout the entire auditee organization. For example:

— An auditor discovers that 2 invoice clerks out of 15 have not been properly trained in the detailed work methods required in their department; in the purchasing department the auditor finds that 1 buyer in 10 is not properly trained in the methods used in that department; in the field support department the auditor discovers that 2 new recruits out of a total staff of 20 have not been trained in the methods to be used within that department; in the sales department the auditor discovers that 1 salesman in 12 has not been trained in the methods to be used in that department. Further investigation reveals that all of those inadequately trained people have recently joined the company. Such circumstances will lead the auditor to diagnose an error that is widespread throughout the company and to follow the remaining parts of the flow chart in Fig. 17.2.

To categorize the type of error and to determine whether a single incident constitutes a trivial or serious problem in terms of product fitness for purpose, the auditor will rely on the advice of specialists in the team. If such specialists are not present, the auditor should seek advice from his own organization as to the significance of his finding.

Note 3:
In determining whether or not the auditee already knows of the problem, the auditor should seek objective evidence demonstrating not only total awareness but also the action being taken. The latter must be directed at curing the real root cause of the problem as distinct from the symptoms. Acceptable objective evidence includes Corrective Action Requests, memoranda, minutes of meetings, internal audit reports, investigation reports.

If that action does not appear efficacious, it must be properly and fully discussed with the auditee. It may become necessary for the auditor to trace back through the system and determine the real root cause (or causes) so that a Corrective Action Request can then be issued.

Note 4:
To discover the real root cause of the problem, the auditor must trace through the system. There can be several contributory factors and circumstances (i.e. causes) that create an inadequate situation. When the real root cause has been unearthed, the true extent of the problem, must be established. This will then enable the auditor to determine the necessity or otherwise of stopping the work. (Stopping the work in progress is further discussed later in this chapter, together with the factors involved in such a decision.)

Note 5:
CARs are only formally delivered during the exit interview after the auditee has been given every opportunity to correct the real root cause of the problem.

Corrective action prior to the exit interview

As pointed out in page 14-8, the auditor should let the auditee know about his findings promptly to give him the chance to take efficacious corrective action before the exit interview (if possible). This course of action has many advantages, as detailed below.

1. It saves the auditee's face.

Since senior management is likely to be present at the exit interview, it may cause someone considerable embarrassment to have adverse findings disclosed there. Most people are extremely thankful to be given the chance to put their house in order discreetly even if they are initially hostile to the auditor's criticism.

2. It gives the auditee the chance to display a genuine concern to improve matters.

Underlying the concern may be either a genuine respect for quality or little more than the instinct of self-preservation. The people who are the real problem are those who evince no desire at all to put things right.

3. It is good human relations.

Giving the auditee the opportunity to correct the situation shows reasonableness, fairmindedness and humanity — the kind of qualities that will make it easier for the auditor to gain the confidence of those with whom he must deal.

4. It saves a re-audit or follow-up, therefore saving time and money.

5. IT IS THE RESULT THAT MATTERS.

Pre-empting a formal Corrective Action Request should bring about the desired result more quickly than if the auditor insists rigidly on formality. If, for some reason, effective corrective action has not been carried out by the time of the exit interview, the deficiency will then be reported and figure in the audit report as a formal corrective action request.

Being constructive

After finding a deficiency, the auditor must always suggest corrective action that would satisfy his organization as being efficacious if implemented. The simpler the corrective action, the better, particularly if it builds on existing strengths. The following examples should illustrate this point.

> An audit of a design department revealed that the engineers kept their own magnetic tapes and disks which contained the results of their computer aided design efforts. As they used each others tapes and similar material at will, the procedure resulted in there being no record of the effective version of any particular design. The auditor suggested that the tapes and disks should be retained

within the drawing store (suitably protected from damage) and that a log-out/log-in book be operated by the store. The design manager would separately authorize (in writing) the issuing of the software; he would also authorize all changes required, using the existing document change control system. The plotter was removed to the drawing store to be operated in there by the registry people so that proper numbering, recording and distribution of changes could be effected in accordance with existing practice. Thus maximum use was made of existing systems and virtually no cost was incurred.

A company was experiencing low yield with its products that were heat processed by passing them over a heated plate. The status quo had never been challenged since the company assumed that the low yield was a fact of life. An audit revealed that the heated plate gradually became covered by drips from the product and that these drips would burn on and build up until heat transfer to the product was impaired. Occasionally the product would knock off a piece of the burnt filth. The required process temperature was thus not being consistently achieved. Simply by issuing the operators with a scraper to clean the plate, the problem was overcome and yield was improved to over 98% from its previous best, which the supervisor estimated at around 66%. The underlying problem was found to be a lack of training of operators and supervisors in the process involved, the equipment used and the need for cleanliness. It took only a few minutes to inform them of this need and a simple sign sombrely stating: "KEEP THE PLATE CLEAN AT ALL TIMES" was mounted on the machine.

During one audit it was found that quite inadequate steps were taken to quarantine items whose status was either indeterminate or unaccepted. It was decided that a quarantine area should be built. The auditee was concerned about the cost of building a new room or structure and about the lack of space within the works and the manufacturing complex. The auditor explained that the quarantine area did not need to be elaborate. He proposed that the apprentices cut up and weld together some angle steel sections, cover it with chicken wire or chain link fencing, make a simple door in the same manner and put a padlock on it: the padlock key should be held by a suitable member of the quality department. This structure was completed within a day and the apprentices had a lot of fun making it. It cost next to nothing but it achieved the desired effect.

In each of the three examples above, corrective action was taken prior to the exit interview and none of the deficiencies was reported formally in detail (either at the exit interview or in the audit report).

While discussing the deficiencies with the auditee, the auditor should refrain from dramatizing or exaggerating the situation. A missing ''hold'' sticker very rarely portends an imminent apocalypse. It should, however, be made clear exactly why the deficiency is considered a deficiency. This is especially important with an auditee who is not used to audits, quality assurance or the particular product or contract requirements involved. It is the auditee who will have to implement corrective action and he can hardly be expected to do this efficiently and quickly unless he understands precisely why the situation demands it.

> Visiting the receiving inspection area of a medium sized company, an auditor asked ''What do you do with the goods until you receive all the certificates you have requested from the supplier?'' The supervisor immediately responded ''We know what you are leading up to — we don't have a quarantine store as yet but the management has authorized expenditure of $12,000 on the building of one''. The auditor asked ''Why are you building a quarantine store?'' The reply was that the company believed that this was necessary in order to comply with its national QA standard. Knowing that standard well, the auditor stated ''That is not necessary, a simple hold tag system and an area identified by painted lines marked on the floor, for example, would comply with that standard''. A discussion followed for a few moments until the supervisor was convinced that the auditor was perfectly correct. The company had wanted to do the right thing but had been advised by a ''consultant'' that only a building resembling Fort Knox would suffice.

Always remember that cheap, quick, simple but efficacious corrective action is more likely to be acted upon promptly by the auditee, particularly if it sounds ridiculously easy to implement.

Is corrective action really required?

In some circumstances, the auditor may decide to dispense with corrective action entirely — if, for example, the area in which the deficiency turned up was one through which the contract of interest had already passed. Provided evidence shows that the requisite system had previously been functioning properly, the auditor may decide he can safely let the matter rest.

In performing a compliance audit of a supplier, an auditor discovered that the date when calibration was due for a considerable number of gauges in an inspection and testing area had expired. Examination of the works travellers proved that at the time the product had passed through the particular area, the expiry dates had not been exceeded. The auditor decided not to issue a CAR since he was satisfied that the product could not have suffered and would not be affected because it would not pass through that particular area again. The auditee felt rather foolish at having allowed the calibration periods to overrun. A good calibration system was available, if only it had been implemented. Apparently, however, there had been a changeover in staff: the previous calibration room superintendent had retired and a much younger man had taken over and was still settling in. A recommendation was sufficient in this case.

The Corrective Action Request form (CAR form)

A CAR form concisely presents the finding, the justification or reason for stating the finding as well as the corrective action proposed, undertaken and verified to have been efficaciously implemented (see Figs. 17.3 and 17.4). It provides objective evidence of follow-up and close-out of corrective actions and is standardized to permit swift review by the auditor's organization. When an organization is performing vast numbers of audits, a standard form saves much time and money.

The lead auditor should write the CARs that he intends to present to the auditee at the exit interview. They should be prepared on the eve of the exit interview to allow for any fresh evidence disclosed during the audit. This procedure avoids holding up the audit and minimizes distractions.

There are some points to note about Fig. 17.3., which are detailed below.

Issued to: Within this box, the auditor identifies the person or organization found to be responsible for the root cause of the non-conformity. This is determined by tracing back through the system from the point at which the problem has manifested itself.

No: The CAR form is allocated a unique number (top right-hand corner).

Non-conformity at variance with: (The justification reference). This particular box on the form is extremely important. If one cannot clearly state what aspect of code, standard, regulation, instruction, procedure or other requirement the auditee has violated, then the Corrective Action Request is unjustified. This in turn indicates that the auditor acted improperly. The

Fig. 17.3 A corrective action request form (CAR)

<table>
<tr><td colspan="6">HYPER-QUALITY COMPANY LIMITED</td></tr>
<tr><td colspan="6">CORRECTIVE ACTION REQUEST</td></tr>
<tr><td colspan="2">Issued to:</td><td colspan="2">Issued by:</td><td colspan="2">No:

Date issued:</td></tr>
<tr><td colspan="6">Non-conformity description</td></tr>
<tr><td colspan="3">Auditee concurrence
with non-conformity description

Signed: Position:

Date:</td><td colspan="3">Non-conformity at variance with:</td></tr>
<tr><td colspan="6">Recommendation(s) for corrective action</td></tr>
<tr><td colspan="6">Corrective action commitment

Date for completion of CA: Signed: Position:

Date:</td></tr>
<tr><td colspan="6">Follow-up and close-out action

The corrective action is verified as
efficacious and this CAR is now closed out. Signed:
Position:
Date:</td></tr>
</table>

Fig. 17.4 A corrective action request form (CAR)

<table>
<tr><td colspan="3">HYPER-QUALITY COMPANY LIMITED</td></tr>
<tr><td colspan="3">CORRECTIVE ACTION REQUEST</td></tr>
<tr><td>Issued to:
S.C. RAP METAL PRODUCTS LTD.</td><td>Issued by:
H-QC LTD.</td><td>No:
SCR/88/1/01
Date issued:
15th Jan. 88</td></tr>
<tr><td colspan="3">Non-conformity description
Stored consumables have deteriorated and are unusable. J. Smith</td></tr>
<tr><td colspan="2">Auditee concurrence with non-conformity description
Signed: Position:
Date:</td><td>Non-conformity at variance with:
CAN 3 Z299.1
PARA 3.5.12 (b)</td></tr>
<tr><td colspan="3">Recommendation(s) for corrective action
Document and implement a system for recording and monitoring of shelf life of stored items. Train staff in importance of shelf life control and in the use of the procedure. Verify proper implementation during internal audit.</td></tr>
<tr><td colspan="3">Corrective action commitment

Date for completion of CA: Signed: Position:
Date:</td></tr>
<tr><td colspan="3">Follow-up and close-out action

The corrective action is verified as efficacious and this CAR is now closed out. Signed:
Position:
Date:</td></tr>
</table>

justification reference is is also vital because the auditee will need to explain to his personnel, who must implement corrective action, exactly why and where they have deviated from required practice.

Auditee concurrence: This box is completed by the auditee to acknowledge that the CAR is fully justified. A signature does not commit the auditee to a particular course of corrective action, it merely signifies that the auditee has decided to commmit his organization to corrective action in the specified areas. Inclusion of such a box on a form helps to forestall misunderstandings concerning whether or not the CAR was accepted by the auditee. Providing the auditor has worked on the basis of facts, i.e. objective evidence, it is unlikely that any auditee will refuse to acknowledge the truth of the situation.

Recommendation(s) for corrective action: As stated on page 17-8 the auditor must always make some recommendation concerning the type of corrective action that will satisfy his organization. I hold the view that if an auditor cannot suggest how to solve a problem, he should not be auditing.

There are always two parts to a recommendation. They are:

a) the action which the auditee should take in order to cure the problem and prevent its recurrence; and,
b) the action that the auditee should take in order to verify constantly that a) continues to be implemented.

Many auditees are unsure of the action to be taken so as to prevent quality problems. This is particularly true in the case of companies which are relatively new to the concepts of quality assurance. It is not very helpful for an auditor to walk away from the situation by telling the auditee "That's your problem. It's up to you to solve it and I'm not going to tell you how". Some external auditors hide behind directives, allegedly issued by their own legal departments, that they should offer no advice at all. A judicious disclaimer for such advice should be sufficient and would, generally, be understood by the auditee. In the case of internal audits, however, any reasons why an auditor should not give advice to colleagues on how to cure quality problems remain a mystery. Even in the case of external audits, such behaviour shows an attitude that is not conducive to the building of good teams. A customer needs its suppliers just as much as suppliers need their customers. A helpful relationship is far better than a destructive one.

I have seen some CAR forms that state "corrective action required". They are not helpful. The benefit of making a recommendation is that the auditee can consider the auditor's suggestions and may be able to find something even better. "corrective action required" can have a constricting effect on useful dialogue.

Corrective action commitment: This space is reserved for the auditee to state precisely the corrective action to which he is prepared to commit himself to. This commitment is designated and signed by one of the people responsible. Note that the auditee has to commit himself to a final date for completion of corrective action.

Follow-up and close-out action: This space will be completed by the auditor's organization to indicate the type of follow-up and close-out action that will be required in the light of the auditee's commitment. There is a space for the auditor to attest that the corrective action has been verified as efficacious. Until this attestation is made, the Corrective Action Request is not considered to be closed out and corrective action is not recorded as having been successfully implemented.

Fig. 17.4 shows how a form such as Fig. 17.3 might be completed and issued to an auditee at the exit interview.

Cure the deficiency or cure the cause?

The answer is simple: CURE BOTH

There is a significant difference between the Non-Conformity Report (NCR) and the Corrective Action Request (two documents commonly used in a quality assurance programme). The former is directed at rectifying a situation and deciding what to do with a particular product that has been found to be defective. The decision may be: re-think the product; re-write; re-define; re-draw; re-compile; re-program; re-do; re-work; repair; use-as-is; scrap; return to supplier. NCR's do not ask "Why did this situation occur?" The Corrective Action Request on the other hand directly addresses that question and proposes a solution to the underlying cause in order to prevent its repetition. When producing a Corrective Action Request, the auditor's recommendations must be directed at curing the real root cause.

Curing the deficiency is a short-term solution. It helps set the ball in motion again but it is really a fire fighting exercise. The prime purpose of corrective action is to root out the cause of the deficiencies. Such extirpation is the long-term cure since it aims to prevent any recurrence of the deficiency: it is fire prevention as opposed to fire fighting. Curing the real root cause of quality problems increases the reliability of the quality management systems which in turn reduces the likelihood of failure costs. Only by attacking the root cause of the problem will it be possible to achieve real cost reductions that will benefit both auditor and auditee.

One question that must always occur to an auditor is "How is it that I find these deficiencies and the auditee doesn't?" In the case of an external audit, this should lead the auditor to examine the supplier's internal audit system and the training, ability and experience of his audit personnel. The auditee will have to continue to verify that corrective action is being implemented and for this he will have to rely on his own internal audit system. Similar remarks apply when an internal audit has been conducted: the department or unit should be performing its own audits and the auditor should question the effectiveness of these.

The six real causes

The auditor must think each problem through, and analyse the system(s) as well as the checks and balances involved. A deficiency may turn out to have multiple root causes — both lack of system and manpower, for example. The root causes are

1. Lack of organization: measures have not been taken to plan activities or to assign responsibilities and methods for properly accomplishing them.
2. Lack of training of the personnel: thorough training or retraining, as described in Chapter 5 has not been accomplished
3. Lack of discipline: individuals do not follow the systems and methods required to achieve quality.
4. Lack of resources: "spoiling the ship for a ha'p'orth of tar" (or "trying to make a silk purse from a sow's ear"); inadequate or incorrect finance for the work that has to be done; insufficient manpower allocated to do the job.
5. Lack of time: rushing or being forced to rush the job, too much pressure of work, overwork or inadequate manpower.
6. Lack of top management support (the most common cause).

Each of these are further discussed in Chapter 18.

Example:

The following example illustrates the point about a deficiency having more than one root cause. The auditor involved had to analyse the ways in which the departments were interacting in order to get to the problem's roots.

> During one audit, the audit team found a number of castings in the machine shop that did not contain the requisite stamp indicating the foundry heat number. This number should have been stamped on to each casting so that it could be traced to the material analysis report and the characteristics and properties of its material ascertained. The auditor proceeded to amass information with a view to finding the underlying causes of this problem.

The machine shop was staffed by a machine shop foreman, machinists and patrol inspectors. The auditor asked "Why have the patrol inspectors not noticed this problem? Do they check for the heat number or not?" It was discovered both that the patrol inspectors had not been told that the castings were required to have a heat number stamped on them and that they were unaware of why the heat number was required and why it was so important. The patrol inspectors were therefore in no position to prevent work and money being wasted in machining articles which could not be traced back to the requisite material certificate.

The auditor elicited the information that the castings were released from the stores and went on to discover that in the stores, there was no record of the castings' heat number. Moreover the stores had no facilities for storing by heat number because they had never been told that this was necessary. As fresh batches of castings were received they were stored according to type. Examination revealed, that the batches had become mixed.

As a next step, the auditor went to the receiving inspection department (the trace-back method of auditing) and discovered that the receiving inspectors did not check either for a heat number or for a material certificate from the supplier's foundry. The reason given was that the practice of making such a check had been discontinued because it took six to eight weeks to get a certificate. The auditor asked "Why do you release the items to stores, and hence to production, without a material certificate?" The answer was that the production department forced the issue.

Upon checking a number of purchase orders, the auditor noted that these did not always ask for a heat number to be stamped on each casting from each batch: only certain parts asked for the heat number. The auditor then verified that the purchasing department accurately transcribed on to the purchase orders the requirements passed on to them by the engineering department via a material requisition. The auditor naturally began to wonder why the engineering department did not always ask for a heat number to be stamped on each item from each batch. So he put that question to the engineering department. He was told that the requirement was omitted on "non-critical" items. The auditor then asked "Which items are "critical", which are "non-critical" and where is there a list to be found stating which are which?" There was no list in existence: each engineer had his own interpretation, in borderline cases, of what constituted a "critical" or ''non-critical'' item. Moreover, the auditor found that prior to releasing the material requisitions to the purchasing department, nobody in the engineering department reviewed and approved them for correct content and requirements. As a result of one deficiency — lack of a heat number stamped on the castings — a number of questions had arisen in the auditor's mind.

1. Why did the inspectors in the machine shop not look for the heat number? Answer: The QA personnel did not train them to look for the number or even tell them that it was necessary.
2. Why were items released by the receiving inspection department? Answer: The production department forced the issue, the problem being that the QA department lacked authority.
3. How would a receiving inspector know, in any case, which was a critical and which a non-critical item? Answer: There were no such means available because the engineering department had not made a list and had, therefore, issued one to their own department or to the receiving inspection department.
4. What happens if the material is incorrect? Answer: (a) six to eight weeks of production would be at jeopardy because it took six to eight weeks for the material certificates to arrive (this was equivalent to a considerable amount of cash); and (b) the answer given by production was ''It's never happened yet''. The auditor's immediate retort was ''How do you know it's never happened yet if the material certificates aren't checked?'' There was no reply.
5. The auditor decided to check some of the material certificates received. Out of 25 certificates, he found three critical components with the wrong analysis/properties. This naturally led to his next question ''Where are these parts now?'' Answer: ''We don't know.''
6. ''Why does it take six to eight weeks for a material certificate to be received?'' Answer: The laboratory that analyses and tests the castings is so successful that it has an over-full order book.
7. Last question: ''Why couldn't the auditee have discovered this state of affairs for himself?'' Result: After looking at the audit system and interviewing some of the internal auditors, it was clear that the audit system was inadequate and the auditors untrained.

The corrective actions recommended included the following:

1. Train the patrol inspectors and receiving inspectors to check for heat number of critical items. Provide a written instruction to this effect.
2. Provide an instruction that no critical material will be released by receiving inspection until the material certificate is available, has been checked by the quality assurance department and found to be satisfactory.

3. The engineering department must generate a list of critical and non-critical components, this list being distributed to all engineers and to the quality assurance department (to whom the inspectors reported directly).
4. Document and implement a system to ensure material traceability for critical items throughout manufacture.
5. Provide an instruction to the engineering department that all material requisitions are to be checked for correct content prior to release and that the purchasing department is to reject a material requisition which does not contain evidence that such a check has been performed.
6. Increase the frequency of internal audits and provide audit training for the quality assurance personnel responsible for performing such activities.

The auditor also recommended the auditee to look for an alternative (possibly duplicate) source of laboratory testing so that they could get the results of tests on the supplier's product more quickly. Finally, the auditor confronted the top management of the company to ask whether or not, in the light of the gravity of the findings and of the fact that the production department had overruled the quality assurance department, the statement of authority at the beginning of the quality assurance manualand signed by the managing director, had the full endorsement of top management or whether the action taken by the production department was actually endorsed by top management.

It is worth noting as a postscript how many departments and organizations contributed to the problem discovered in the machine shop: the machine shop itself, stores, the receiving inspection department, the receiving department, the supplier's laboratory, the purchasing department, the engineering department and the quality assurance one. Production and top management were also critically involved and contributed in no small manner to the problem.

Consider the side effects

Upon discovering the real root cause of the problem, the auditor should also find out what other areas have suffered, could suffer or are presently suffering. An example of this could be an auditor discovering a problem in the way that a particular customer's accounts have been processed. The root cause is found to be an inadequate system for reconciliation. Further investigation shows that several thousand customers' accounts have all been processed by the same inadequate system. Clearly this constitutes a serious situation which has enormous cost implications to the company.

The potential cost of failure to tackle a quality problem has many aspects. The auditor's company, the auditee, the customer and the community may all suffer eventually.

In practice, very few companies accept contracts that contain clauses for consequential damages liability. The liability is usually limited to replacement of the item concerned. In an extreme case, it tends to be the insurance underwriter and hence the community, who bears the cost of defective items (although legislation on product liability is rapidly changing this situation). Whoever ends up picking up the bill for actual damage caused by deficient output, the deficiencies inevitably mean that time and money are wasted.

Limitations on the auditor's authority

A situation can be so serious that the auditor considers it necessary to stop work. Regrettably, the authority to do so may not have been vested in him. Similarly, there are occassions when an auditor is not allowed to issue a Corrective Action Request. The auditor must be aware of the delegated limitations and act accordingly. This topic is discussed in Chapter 20.

Pre-award surveys and Corrective Action Requests.

As discussed in Chapter 2, because there is no contractual relationship between auditee and auditor, the latter has no right to issue a Corrective Action Request during a pre-award survey. However, the auditor can make a statement such as:

> ''In the event that my company decides to award this contract to you, we will require corrective action for the following.'' (The auditor will outline the corrective actions required). ''Satisfactory completion of that corrective action will be made a condition of payment at the first contract milestone.''

The auditor's organization will then incorporate the requirements for corrective action into the contractual terms and conditions. Knowing the implications, the auditee then has the choice to accept or to decline the contract offered by his potential customer.

Third party assessments and Corrective Action Requests

The assessor has the duty to issue Corrective Action Requests to auditees who are seeking a certificate of qualification against a quality assurance standard, code, regulation or statute but who do not meet the latters' requirements fully. It should be part of a professional assessing authority's working procedure to ensure that this is done. It is not, however, necessary for a CAR form to be used although they are rather convenient vehicles of communication. The assessor could include the CAR details as shown in Fig. 17.4 in the text of his report, but this practice has drawbacks and I do not recommend it.

Naturally, no certificate of qualification must be issued unless and until all CAR's are verified as closed-out: in any case, only rogues and incompetents would do such a thing. Their certificate would be a falsehood that misrepresents the assessed company's practices and pours discredit on professional assessment schemes.

Stop work decisions

The decision to stop work pending the implementation of corrective action is one no auditor should take lightly. He must be prepared to do so, however, if he judges that the situation demands this course of action. The key factors involved in a stop work decision include these

1. Safety or legal implications. Whenever safety or legal requirements are being compromised, the auditor must promptly request stop work and seek the full support of his own management. In the event that management chooses not to support the stop work decision, it is vital that the auditor places his recommendations on the record in order to demonstrate that he acted in a responsible manner and discharged his duty of care.
2. Financial considerations. Where substantial risk of loss can be incurred by allowing the situation to continue unresolved, the auditor should advise his management and seek support for stop work. Whenever money is at risk, most managements are supportive of any saving action.
3. Work status and delivery date. Where the auditor ascertains that a major milestone, such as delivery of product to the customer, is scheduled to occur before satisfactory corrective action could be taken, stop work must be required and management support obtained.

Before requiring stop work, the auditor should carefully assess the scope of the stop work necessary. Naturally as much useful work as possible should be allowed to continue and only those matters which are genuinely unacceptable and require stop work should be considered.

In deciding on stop work, determine the type of corrective action that should be taken in order that work could be restarted. When advising management of the reasons behind a stop work decision, give all the facts including the recommended corrective action, the likely costs, the financial and legal implications, the time necessary to implement satisfactory corrective action and the true scope of the stop work required.

I strongly recommend that an auditor informs his own organization of his intention to call for a halt in work, explaining why he believes he is justified in doing so. He should do this before the exit interview so that he can ascertain to what extent his organization will support him. There is nothing worse for an auditor than to ask that work be stopped, pending implementation of suitable corrective action, only to find that senior management of the auditing organization have overruled the decision (perhaps for internal political reasons) and left him out on a limb. When this happens, it becomes all too obvious to the auditee that the auditor has, in reality, no backing from his organization at all. Sometimes the auditor's own customer/inspection agency may be able to exert the necessary pressure to support the auditor. Such pressure and support must be discreetly sought, if necessary. Regardless of whether the auditor's management declares its support for the auditor or not, if the latter feels that stop work is necessary, particularly in circumstances involving health or safety, he should put the matter and his reasons on the record on his return to his office.

> Whilst running my audit training course, on one particular occasion, a couple of the trainees expressed concern that, in putting things on the record when management has refused to back them, they might be putting their jobs at risk. I advised them that if they cannot have the courage of their convictions, they should not be auditing.

Presenting a CAR to management

The auditee's management will need to have the following information before they take any action.

1. An evaluation of the significance of the problem and the need for its eradication.
2. The total cost saving from curing the cause and preventing a recurrence of the effects (this may or may not be in monetary terms — management is generally quite capable of working out the financial implications of a statement such as "Sixteen per cent of your deliveries are damaged because of inadequate handling"; "One fifth of your invoices do not get payed promptly because of inaccurate customer discount calculations"; "One meal in eight is sent back from the restaurant because it has been improperly cooked or is not what the customer ordered").
3. The reasons why a cosmetic or fire fighting exercise is of no use.
4. How (and at what cost) the proposed cure will extirpate the problem.

Remember the following empirical relationship:

Saving — Expenditure = Corporate Action, Speed and Help (CASH).

In the final analysis, it all comes down to money: if there is no monetary incentive, very few managements are motivated to do anything. The auditor should, therefore, not waste his time requiring corrective action for a trivial problem. The money involved in corrective action may be seen in terms of either a current loss or a future potential loss. In the case of an extrinsic audit, for example, the auditee's management may be aware that the customer's auditor may recommend, in extreme cases, that the auditee's company be removed from the qualified supplier's list, with consequent loss of business. Another potential monetary loss might be that caused by future action under product liability legislation — and this will be an increasingly important factor as the awards in the courts rise in value.

The Corrective Action Request log

The auditor's organization should always maintain a log of the CARs that have been issued. The advantages of this are that the log provides a quick guide to the status of CARs, summarizes the auditee's performance and constitutes objective evidence as to the status of follow-up and close-out of corrective action: it can, therefore, be presented to any interested third party. This log should be kept by the quality assurance manager at his desk. The knowledge that the manager is periodically reviewing the status of CARs spurs the quality assurance staff on to ensure that they follow up and close out corrective actions. Moreover the log provides feedback to the auditors and gives a certain bite to the CAR system.

18. Typical quality problems and their real causes

Sometimes we may learn more from a man's errors than from his virtues.
Henry Wadsworth Longfellow.

Throughout this book, many examples of quality problems and actions taken to prevent or cure them have been given. Within the following pages, a further selection of typical problems that the auditor may encounter is presented. As should be apparent, not every problem constitutes a true deficiency. One of the recurring themes of this book is the need for the auditor to be aware of what the codes, standards, regulations etc. really require. Sometimes the wording of the relevant document is open to more than one interpretation — phrases like ''shall establish'', ''ensure that'', ''arrange for'' can each be satisfied by a number of very different systems and the auditor must never assume that only his preferred type of system is acceptable. An open mind is a valuable asset when auditing.

The following examples are grouped under four headings corresponding to the task elements discussed in Chapter 5. One extra category is included, namely, matters concerning the auditee's practices for dealing with corrective action and his non-conformity handling system. Unless otherwise indicated, the examples mentioned apply in internal as well as external audits.

Information

Problems, or apparent problems concerned with information and its control are various and are detailed below.

a) *Correctly checked*

— No objective evidence that the information has been reviewed is available on it.

Objective evidence may be available in the form of a letter or a memorandum rather than as a signature *on* the document. This is quite satisfactory and should not count as a deficiency. Where information is contained on computer tapes and disks, an original signature on the software is, in any case, impossible. Alternative means such as memoranda or review reports are essential.

— A readiness review of an information package is not performed.

This requirement is not directly imposed by QA standards. However, in the case of contracts that take several years to complete, it is advisable that the information packages collated during the execution of the contract be given a review prior to release. This is so because, in most organizations, the staff change continually and many fail to hand over a job properly to their successors. Hence there may be some unresolved matters of which the successor is unaware.

> While performing an audit at a construction site, it was noted that the package of documents issued to the construction personnel contained a number of specifications that did not bear the requisite customer approvals: in some cases the documents had even been disapproved. Somehow, these documents had never been rewritten. Upon investigation, it was found that the personnel responsible for collecting the document package together had changed several times during the course of the contract concerned, which had been running for four or five years. The corrective action required fell into two parts: the correct and approved documents had to be obtained and issued to the site whilst an instruction had to be given that all packages of documents should be reviewed for completeness and readiness before being issued to the site.

This type of problem can be overcome by instituting a handover system and maintaining a record summarizing both the total contents required in a package and the status of review of each constituent part.

— There is no mechanism for obtaining the customer's review/approval of information/corrective action proposed by the supplier.

Before laying the blame at the auditee's door, the external auditor must make sure that the contract *has* asked for such a mechanism. If not, and should the auditor feel such a mechanism to be needed, corrective action may be required in the auditor's own organization after the audit is over.

— The quality assurance department does not review information or changes to it.

Few QA standards impose this obligation on the QA department, and, in my view, it should not be the QA department's role to carry out information reviews.

— Information is reviewed after it has been released for use.

The auditor should make a note both of the date when information was prepared and of that when it was reviewed and approved: "preliminary" issues may sometimes prove still to be in use when the product is about to be delivered to the customer. Note that some QA standards only imply, rather than state explicitly, that a review is necessary prior to release. The auditor should check that the standard states a particular point at which information must be reviewed. A case in point is ISO 9001-1987[1] which requires design input requirements to be "reviewed by the supplier for adequacy" but *does not specify* that the supplier must perform such a review *prior* to the design activity being performed, even though one can readily appreciate the desirability of so doing. Similar remarks can be made of AS-1821[2] and many others. If the auditor discovers that the auditee only checks design input for adequacy when checking the design output, as many organizations do, he is in no position to issue a corrective action request, merely a recommendation.

— Documents have been signed as reviewed without being reviewed properly.

If the code or standard concerned asks for a review of documents, it may only specify an *independent* review, which, provided that the reviewer is competent, does not necessarily rule out the "You sign mine, I'll sign yours" agreement that flourishes in some departments. Standards seldom state that the person who reviews the documents has to be the superior of the person who prepared it, as some auditors erroneously assume.

— "Minor changes do not need to be authorized."

The auditor should beware that this phrase — which some auditees write into their procedures — does not become stretched to the point of covering every eventuality. Most standards preclude it (CAN3-Z299.1-85[3], ISO 9001, for instance). Many auditees use mark-ups to indicate changes and QA standards recognize this to be the case: AS-1821 or ISO 9001, for example, do not preclude the use of mark-ups to documents already issued whilst CAN3-Z299.1-85 permits marking-up provided that it is done "according to established procedures" as, indeed, does AQAP-1[4].

— The final "hold" point does not require that the information, such as a record package, is checked for contract compliance before release.

The customer may well be purchasing not only physical items but also the information and records associated with them. In this case, one cannot be certain that the contract has been fulfilled unless that information is checked prior to release. This is an implied requirement of most QA standards and is, in any case, simple common sense. Every company should perform this check, particularly bearing the product liability point of view in mind.

b) *Correct content*

— The content of instructions is not appropriate to the circumstances.

The phrase "appropriate to the circumstances", which figures in some QA standards, is obviously open to interpretation and the auditor must take care to consider each case scrupulously on its own merits. If he feels extra information ought to be included, a recommendation to this effect must be made. A formal Corrective Action Request may be unwarranted.

Similarly, an expression such as "the effective implementation of documented quality system procedures"[1] leaves the content of those procedures completely unspecified.

— Rework and repair procedures do not explain the method of dismantling and re-assembly in order to prevent further damage to non-conforming assemblies being processed.

This is a particularly common complaint in the case of encapsulated or hermetically sealed components. Again, it must be remembered that instructions should be "appropriate to the circumstances". If there is a requirement that "procedures have to be "acceptable to the quality assurance representative", this is a prescription that the auditor (who may be the customer's quality assurance representative) should never abuse by adopting an unnecessarily rigid attitude.

— The qualified suppliers' list does not include suppliers of services.

The better QA standards require objective evidence (not necessarily a list) that all suppliers of items *and* services have been *evaluated* and selected somehow. While it is common practice for companies to keep a list of suppliers found to be acceptable for the supply of particular goods, the names of suppliers of services are often not included. The term "services" covers design, special processes, financial audit, training, transportation, catering, cleaning, maintenance, calibration, waste disposal, vermin control, inspection, test, computing, installation — in fact, anything that affects the product (as stated in Chapter 6) and that the auditee subcontracts to an outside source; it also covers those services discussed in Chapter 25.

— Forgeries.

The era of photocopiers and correction fluid has allowed the unscrupulous to fake certificates and records. The auditor must not hesitate to ask for originals or certified copies of originals.

c) *Correct edition*

— Effectivity dates/locations for changes are not stipulated.

Some standards (such as MIL-Q-9858A[5], AQAP-1) require such a stipulation whilst others (such as AS-1821) only imply that it is necessary. The auditor must check the applicable codes, standards, regulations for the wording involved. This is particularly important in the case of an internal audit because the company may be working to two or three different sets of requirements, each for a different customer. This can be confusing for the auditee's own staff, as well as for the auditor.

— Changes are made by means of "attachments".

QA standards do not preclude this practice but a lot of stapled or pinned attachments to the prime document are annoying and confusing for the user as well as being liable to be lost or disregarded. The auditor should use his discretion: if the practice appears to be causing quality problems, he should recommend that attachments are not used.

— "Superseded" copies of documents found to be still in use.

Caution is needed here: the "superseded" copy may be perfectly acceptable for continued use. A standard product may, for example, still be being produced as a previous "model" that has been sold to a current customer. One classic example is the ASME Boiler and Pressure Vessel Code addenda, issued every six months. The auditor must check the particular requirements for the contract being audited.

d) *Correct condition*

— Information is illegible or damaged.

Some examples of these problems have been described in Chapter 5.

e) *Correct distribution*

— There is no acknowledging of receipt of changed information.

QA standards tend not to require the recipient of information to provide a receipt to its issuer but they do require that *documents* are distributed and used at the location where the particular activity is to be performed. Hence some auditors ask the issuer of a document, "How can you be sure that the documents have arrived there?" The acknowledgement receipt method was developed by some auditees in response to this problem but there are other methods by which the auditee can make sure that the documents have arrived at their destination.

— The quality management system, as described in the QA manual or procedures, has been bypassed.

The auditor should assess whether or not bypassing the system is significant before he issues a formal Corrective Action Request. If bypassing the system achieves the same result as required by the code, standard etc., then the auditor should simply recommend that the written procedure is changed. *Never knock initiative:* it is a precious commodity in short supply. If the auditee has found a quicker, better system to use then both his own organization and the auditor's may reap cost benefits. This has been further developed in Chapter 17.

An auditor discovered that a sales department issued contract documents directly to the line departments. The auditee's procedure required that, upon receipt of an order, all contract documents be routed through a small unit that would allocate a unique number to the contract. That unit had become progressively overloaded to the extent that a backlog of two months' work had accumulated, which obviously meant that time available for contract completion was being lost. In order to save time and get things going, salesmen had decided to phone the unit, have a number allocated, mark it onto the documents and then distribute these to the line departments themselves. Although the sales department was acting in a manner that conflicted with the official procedure, the end result was exactly the same as if they had not done so. The auditor recommended that the procedure be updated to reflect the actual practice.

— Updating of information is difficult or impossible because the current location of the original document, as issued, is not accurately known.

I once asked an auditee how he would find the documents issued on a particular job if, say, one of them had been revised. The company, which was geographically dispersed, had a computer that monitored the progress of every contract and all the information applicable in a number of locations. The auditee alleged that within two or three seconds he could locate any individual document in use and obtain a report of every location at which the document currently was to be found. He also offered to trace every contract and department that had been affected by any particular revision of that document as well as those "superseded" versions that could still be effective for past customers who were still using the products they had bought from the company. He proved his claims. Not all companies are as well organized and punctilious.

> At another company, a "document control centre" was asked a similar question to the above. The answer was "We'll phone around to see if we can find it." The next question posed was, "What do you do if you don't find it?" The response provided was "Then it's lost, so why worry?"

Tracing and retrieving information that is contained in computer files requires controls such as those described in Chapter 24.

— Information retrieval is not performed.

Most QA standards do not require retrieval of information, their only stipulation being that the use of superseded *documents* must be prevented. It may not be essential for superseded copies of documents to be returned to the issuing department for destruction — indeed, in certain cases this would be neither possible nor reasonable. Purchase orders, issued to a supplier, for instance, are irretrievable because they have certain legal implications concerning a contract as signed and agreed between supplier and customer: the supplier is unlikely to hand over such contractual documents.

> A company ran a number of tape controlled machines. Each particular item had its own tape. When the item was changed a new tape was issued to the machine operators but an audit revealed that they did not destroy the old ones or return them to the design office, which produced and distributed the tapes. Investigation showed that superseded versions of the items were regularly being produced and then mixed with existing stock. There was no way of telling which tape was which or to which model any individual item in the store belonged.

— Document exchange control is not centralized.

Some auditors assume that all document changing functions should be centrally controlled but in fact QA standards generally do not specify centralization. For software, a library can be essential (see Chapter 24).

— The results of pre-award surveys or external audits are not fed back to line departments.

> During an audit of a geographically dispersed company, it was found that the works' quality assurance department was auditing and performing pre-award surveys of the suppliers of welding electrodes. At head office, it was found that the welding department engineers were specifying certain manufacturers' electrodes but had no knowledge of the pre-award surveys and audits being performed by the works QA department, let alone

> of the results. Some suppliers whom the works' QA department had found to be unsatisfactory were still being called out in the specifications from head office.

Similar examples could be quoted for many other types of information that an individual department possesses but does not distribute, with the result that people make errors out of ignorance or "re-invent the wheel". Knowledge of who-does-what, which is derived from good organization, can help to forestall these occurrences.

f) *Correct identification*

— "What is it?"

Creating information is a costly process and it is surprising just how much is not fully identified in order that folk know to what it relates. Common examples include calculations that are merely a jumble of impressive looking figures; print-outs of work, performed on desktop computers, that have no title or identification number; floppy disks that are unidentified; test records that do not specify a particular customer order.

The requirements (or lack of them) for specific identification of information in many QA standards leave much to be desired and the auditor should tread warily here.

Equipment

a) *Correct type*

— No objective evidence is available to show that the equipment has been qualified.

Remember that it may be practical to qualify the equipment on the job or by analysing a first piece, made using the equipment, and which is for ultimate supply to the customer. Some codes and standards do not preclude this practice and the contract may well permit it.

b) *Correct condition*

— No planned maintenance records of plant and equipment are available.

The auditor should check to see that plant, such as cranes, is regularly maintained. Apart from such maintenance being, in most countries, a legal requirement to prevent accidents, most codes and standards generally imply that such control is necessary.

> An auditor was arguing at length with an auditee that the cranes, slings and handling equipment should be monitored, inspected and tested. The auditee disagreed and had no sooner finished

making his point when the telephone rang to announce that a very expensive item had just been dropped and irreparably damaged. The auditee rapidly lost his "it couldn't happen here" attitude of five seconds earlier.

A supplier who was confronted by one of his customers with the need to check out lifting equipment, refused to admit the necessity for doing so. During a previous contract with the same customer, a safety-related structure weighing about 100 tons had been dropped. Although the customer's representatives had witnessed the actual drop, the supplier's representatives were adamant that it had never happened and never could have. A very interesting attitude towards quality...

— Items become damaged because of inadequate hand tools.

Hand tools should be maintained because they can directly affect the quality of the work. Examples of this fact include wire strippers and crimpers used for electrical assembly or installation work; surgical instruments; dirty ladles, spatulas and the like used for preparing food. Many people pay quite close attention to capital plant and high value equipment but fail to consider the correct condition of such relatively small or low value articles: these are rather taken for granted and become abused, misused and damaged. In extreme cases, hand tools can deteriorate to the point that they become dangerous in themselves.

— The working condition of process equipment is inadequate.

The working condition of equipment is not only affected by its maintenance but also by the way in which it is controlled during operation. It is not uncommon to discover inadequate process controls on temperature, flow rates, feed rates, pressures, voltage, amperage, power levels, rotational speeds etc.; no reference standards for acceptable work; no guidance on the process conditions or no monitoring of the actual process conditions.

— The maintenance frequency is not based on the usage rate and the frequency is excessive.

QA standards cannot state what is a "suitable" frequency for maintenance activities, such as calibration. In many companies, various pieces of equipment that are subject to calibration are only used infrequently. If possible, the auditee should consider calibrating his acceptance equipment on the basis of actual usage. This can be a real cost saver. The frequency of maintenance activities can be assisted by the use of process control charts containing the usual decision points based on known process capabilities. Standards do tend to use words such as "periodic" which are open to interpretation and abuse.

> At one company that considered its engineering products to be of high precision, it was found that the inspection and acceptance equipment was only infrequently calibrated. Some gauges had not been calibrated for as long as nine to twelve years. There was no means of positive recall and the internal audit system had never challenged the veracity of the inspection and acceptance equipment.

It is not uncommon to find that acceptance and inspection equipment is not traceable to a national standard despite the fact that QA standards ask for traceability to such standards. Occasionally, there may be some debate as to what constitutes a national standard.

> An auditee once informed me that his calibration equipment was traceable to a national standard. On looking at the documentary evidence brought forward to support this claim. I noted that the document was issued by a private company. After some considerable discussion, the man responsible for calibration had to admit that, although in his country this particular company was considered as a high authority on calibration, it was necessary that they be requested to attest that their own gauges were traceable to that country's national standards. Considerable difficulty was experienced in eliciting an attestation from that particular company, who were most upset by the request. No company should assume that its foreign customers are intimately acquainted with the company's supplier's national calibration system.

That incident was one of several identical ones I experienced whilst performing a series of audits during a visit to the UK some years ago. Subsequent visits revealed that the gauge suppliers had changed their certificate to include a statement to the effect that they also certified that the devices used to calibrate a customer's gauges were themselves of known accuracy, traceable to UK national standards. In spite of the fact that the auditees proudly displayed approval certificates from the British Ministry of Defence and others, apparently no one had ever queried the lack of audit trail to national standards before.

> At another company, the veracity of its master gauges was questioned. The reply given was "But they are XYZ company's gauges". I explained that this did not necessarily mean that the gauges were correct and, after some considerable discussion, it was agreed that XYZ company should provide an attestation that the master gauges supplied were traceable to a national standard also stating the accuracy and precision of the gauges supplied to their customer. The gauges in question had been purchased seven

years previously and it transpired that no certificate of attestation was available. At my insistence, the gauges were sent away for calibration. The auditee was considerably embarrassed when the results came through.

A company had assumed for many years that its inspection equipment was accurate enough for its needs. Since there was neither a calibration system nor any master gauges, none of it was traceable to national standards. The company entered into a multi-million dollar contract which invoked AQAP-4[6] and, contrary to my advice, took little action towards calibrating its equipment, building 26 high value items of machinery for its customer. Inevitably, the company was audited, with the predictable results, which led to the purchase of master gauges and to the introduction of a calibration system. To determine the correctness of the completed machines, every one had to be dismantled and, when the rechecking was performed, each was found to contain major components that were unacceptably outside the engineer's requirements. The affected components were replaced and the machines were re-assembled and re-tested for performance whilst the records reviewed and corrected to record the identities of the replaced parts. It cost a small fortune, many times the originally anticipated profit.

Audits regularly reveal that although the process equipment is maintained at prescribed intervals, the maintenance equipment used to check it is itself of unknown accuracy or precision. Another frequent occurrence is to find that, although an auditee has a calibration system for ensuring the accuracy, precision and so on of his inspection and test gauges, the actual tools used for production are not included in that system.

A company introduced a well thought out calibration system for the inspection and test equipment. The management were genuinely puzzled when they found that this did not reduce the defect level of work coming from its production machinery.

Another company purchased an expensive machine centre to improve production efficiency but decided to use it also to check out its inspection gauges. The managers were unable to understand why this was undesirable. Things finally came to a head when it was found that the gradual drift in accuracy of that machine centre was such that customers were complaining that the spares did not fit the products supplied some time before. The inspection records had naturally shown that the machine was maintaining its accuracy whilst the "well known problem of inspection gauge drift" in the company had been overcome by adjusting the gauges when they were checked against the machine centre!

c) *Correct capability and identification* are discussed in Chapter 5.

d) *Correct location*

— Substitute equipment is used.

Failure to provide the right equipment to the right location at the right time may tempt people to use alternative equipment more readily to hand. Substitute equipment may or may not be equivalent to that specified for the process. Under pressure to produce results or meet deadlines, people often gamble on substituting equipment which they think or claim to be equivalent to that required. Such equivalence must be verified prior to use.

f) *Correct environment*

— Processes that involve chemical or biological baths have neither clean baths nor control of contaminants, stratification, sedimentation, solution strength, temperature, pH value and the like.

Examples of processes that can be affected by one or more of these problems are cleaning, pickling, etching, plating, developing of film, dip coating, sterilizing. These processes can be monitored easily by simple control charts but frequently are not.

Most QA standards require that the environment be suitable for the process. Even though they do not define "environment", I have always considered it to include the biological, chemical or other fluids into which the items are completely immersed during processing. Shortcomings which crop up with persistent regularity include silt in the bottom of the baths; unmonitored solution strength; uncalibrated or unmaintained temperature control equipment; inadequately maintained pH monitoring equipment; no instructions provided to inform people how and when to add the solutions, how to mix solutions and how to test for the required strength, temperature etc. It is also common to find that, in certain continuous processing baths, make-up chemicals are introduced from only one side of the bath during processing and are inadequately mixed, with the result that part of the batch being processed is subject to excessive solution strengths.

Similarly, a vacuum is an environment in which a process is performed, and must be regarded as such by the auditor. One often encounters gauges that are out of calibration or are damaged; seals that are not maintained; the absence of any alarm to warn of high pressure.

— Cleanliness of work areas and storage is inadequate.

In the electronic industry, small circuits are very sensitive to dust and many other substances that can damage them.

> An auditor noted that one company kept a large number of ready-made printed circuit boards within the stores. These boards were then assembled into modules for particular applications. The stores were unclean and the printed circuit boards were covered in dust. It not only took much time and money to try to clean these printed circuit boards but the success rate of cleaning was poor. In effect, money was being thrown down the drain. The auditor recommended that the stores be kept cleaner, with a suitable kind of atmosphere control, and that the printed circuit boards be protected in non-static polythene bags or something suitable.

Vermin control is important in various industries such as food production, catering, pharmaceutical and health care.

> In checking the efficacy of vermin control in a food storage warehouse, I became well satisfied both that rat poison was used in the form of pellets being put out and that these were effective. The problem was that I found several decomposing rat cadavers in obvious places.

> At a similar store, the frequency of checking the pellet trays was clearly inadequate: ancient cobwebs were to be found woven across the empty trays. Strangely, though, the auditee's records showed a weekly check of the trays and constant replenishment of the pellets.

— The "clean" room is not clean.

The auditor should look for positive air pressure supply, a dust count, humidity control, handling access and nuisance control/prevention. The nuisances that occur in the clean room vary according to the product involved and might include static electricity, vibration, fumes, odours, draught, personal cosmetics or similar substances. In pharmaceutical and health industries, cleanliness also entails the provision of aseptic conditions. The auditor must determine what constitutes a nuisance for the particular contract concerned, see page 5-26.

> Upon entering one "clean" room, the auditor noticed that one of its walls did not extend up to the building roof. The auditeee explained that this was open to allow the overhead crane to enter and leave. Behind the wall in question was a workshop which was anything but clean: sparks and dust were being generated by

grinding work and these were entering the clean room. A film of dust was everywhere.

A company manufacturing visual display units was experiencing substantial defects with the external coating applied to the tubes. Although the tubes were carefully cleaned prior to the coating being applied in a clean room, dust and detritus still settled on the tubes and became encapsulated in the coating, with unacceptable results. The tube surface was prepared in an antechamber which was part of the clean room. An audit revealed that, after the cleaning operation, the tubes passed along a slow moving conveyor to the coating station above which was the air delivery tube. This air supply maintained positive air pressure to the clean room. Surrounding the air outlet were streaks of black filth which indicated that the air supply was unclean. The filters had not been changed for years. Examination of the ducting showed that, although changing the filters would be a relatively small task, the ducts downstream of the filters were thick with filth and cleaning them would be a major undertaking.

Audits are not exercises performed at a desk or by looking at pieces of paper- the auditor has to be prepared to get his hands dirty, especially in "clean" rooms!

Items

a) *Correct type*

— Item design does not preclude incorrect assembly.

The auditor should look for one-way connectors, plugs, dowls and so on. This is particularly important for valve installation in pipework systems. Again, it is not an explicit requiement of QA standards but it is a matter of common sense, especially to reduce product liability risks.

— Incorrect type of item issued.

The auditor should ascertain how the auditee ensures that only correct materials or versions of items are issued for processing. Issuing incorrect types of material is not only risky but also wasteful because the work may have to be redone. Waste is contrary to the objectives of a quality programme. Amazingly ISO 9001-1987 permits this practice (as did the superseded BS 5750-1979) "for urgent purposes" provided that the auditee can immediately recall and replace the items "in the event of non-conformance". There are many situations when the pressure of production could result in unsafe types of item being released innocently — "Take heart, widow Smith, we replaced the items as soon as your husband's accident proved them to be the wrong type. Incidentally, we would appreciate a copy of the death certificate to support our corrective action files".

b) *Correct condition*

— Items are found to be in poor condition as a result of poor storage, handling or shipping.

Some companies have adopted the excellent practice of performing inspections (often referred to as "product audits") to assess the condition of their items is after shipping and when they reach the ultimate customer.

— Handling and stacking arrangements for delicate items are inadequate.

> An auditor found that completed items were simply thrown into a box and were handled roughly within the stores. They were being damaged as a result. It was decided to improve the stacking arrangements so that the individual items did not come into contact with each other after completion. This move saved a considerable amount of money.

— Packing of the finished product which does not protect its quality.

> During one audit of a truly clean room, it was noted that the pristine, clean assemblies, that were ready for despatch, were packed into a wooden box full of straw. After such packing, it was found that the straw had covered the items in dust. They had to be re-cleaned.

— No provision is made for clean and protected storage at the site.

> At a construction site, it was noted that cleaned pipework was stored out in the open, with no protection whatsoever. Many items were covered in rust and filth.

— Inadequate control of shelf life of stored perishable items.

The need to control shelf life is one of the implicit requirements of QA standards that may be open to debate. It is wise to have a first-in-first-out rota in the stores and to maintain a list showing the date when items were received, the date of their manufacture and the extent of their useful life. Typical items that can deteriorate are rubber products, resins, insulations, foodstuffs, paints and coatings, photographic film and process chemicals. The auditor must ascertain the requirements of the particular QA standards and contract. Most auditees quickly appreciate the fact that deteriorated stored items do not enhance product quality, readily accepting the need for a shelf life control system once this is suggested. Purchasing on a Just in Time basis can help to alleviate this problem but can prove uneconomic for small deliveries of consumables.

— Suppliers of particular categories of item are not audited.

Some auditees make the quite unjustified assumption that the items purchased from a big name company must be good and that the company need not be audited. In fact, even huge multinationals can periodically experience quality and safety problems with the items that they supply. Not all QA standards require external audits to be performed and the auditor is advised to check this point.

c) *Correct capability and correct quantity*

These have been discussed in Chapter 5.

d) *Correct identification*

— Items bear no name or objective evidence of their identification to permit traceability.

Not all items need to be marked for traceability, so the auditor must ascertain this point before deciding whether or not the lack of identification is a true deficiency. The classification (or criticality) of the item should provide the key to determining whether or not complete traceability is required for every individual piece. Classification is mentioned in Chapter 3.

— Items are marked incorrectly or inadequately to show their acceptance status.

This is the second type of identification that QA standards require. External auditors must, however, avoid assuming that their own company's systems are the only acceptable ones.

Persons

a) *Correct competence*

This has been explored on in Chapter 5.

b) *Correct training*

— The person is not suitably trained or indoctrinated to perform his or her task.

The auditor must attend to the exact wording of the regulations, codes and standards concerned since this area can prove to be contentious. The words "suitable", "training" and "indoctrination" are all open to differing interpretations and do not necessarily call for formal classroom training or written tests. Often people invoke "grandfather" clauses, which are so flexible as to allow much abuse and licence.

It is essential that, apart from understanding the designated task for which he is responsible, the employee knows and understands the company's systems, capabilities and product, as these all affect his task.

> One company found itself in almost insurmountable difficulties because a salesman signed a contract that invoked a particular type of industrial standard and quality system with which that company and its product were incapable of complying without major changes of administrative procedure as well as fundamental design and material changes.

Salesmen are particularly liable to this sort of error: their desire to clinch a particular sale or to meet their sales target can make them overlook some of the implications of the deal. It is essential for them to be fully aware of their company's true capabilities. in terms of product and system, and to understand exactly how the product has been designed and is manufactured.

An audit revealed that the auditee's inspection personnel, who were not taught how one particular product of the company was assembled, were the very people responsible for verifying that the assembly had been carried out correctly. In reality the operatives knew more about the product and assembly than the inspectors did.

— Auditors (i.e. internal auditors) do not seem to find the deficiencies that the external auditor has.

It is a common fault among companies to tell a person "Tomorrow you are an auditor, my son". Untrained auditors waste time and money both for their own organization and for the auditee (see Chapter 1). If the external auditor finds a number of deficiencies, the competence, training and experience of the internal auditors needs to be re-assessed.

— Objective evidence is not available to attest to training/certification/competence of the personnel.

This problem occurs regularly. The auditee should develop a system of employees' files, which should be kept from the moment of hiring and constantly updated to reflect new skills, training and the state of attributes such as eyesight. Whereas QA standards can be vague about the content of those records, certain industries' regulations are not. The auditor must ascertain the precise requirements.

c) *Correct motivation*

This has been discussed in Chapter 5.

d) *Correct attributes*

— Eyesight is not tested.

Even though QA standards do not state that eyesight (or other personal attributes required in producing items) must be checked, it is a matter of common sense that this should be so Some industries' regulations require this to be done.

> It was found that a particular inspector's eyesight had deteriorated to such an extent that he was virtually blind: he certainly could not read the indications on the measuring equipment accurately. The inspector was an old man who was afraid of losing his job and becoming unemployed. Nobody had questioned him because he had been performing inspection of years but there had been a number of customer complaints about the quality of items being released.

> At the entry interview for one audit, I explained that a particular area of concern would be eyesight checks for both accuracy and colour. I mentioned the problem of the virually blind inspector to which I referred above. The QA manager found the story incredible: he could not believe that any company would fail to notice such a situation. The company was manufacturing an electrical product which contained a good deal of coloured wiring. In addition, the calibration system in use relied on colour coding of the instruments to indicate the calibration status. That evening, the QA manager was dining out on the story of a blind inspector. When he had finished, I asked: "Do you know that one of your inspectors is colour blind?" The QA manager was so surprised that he dropped his knife and fork onto his plate. It was, in fact, his chief inspector who was colour blind.

> One company engaged a new inspector to examine pressure containing components by means of dye penetrant techniques. Almost immediately, the production department started to complain about the poor quality of items released after inspection (a rather curious complaint considering that it was the production department who had made them). It was found that the new inspector's acuity was so bad that he could not discern the small indications within the dye penetrant developer. When asked about his eyesight, the man grew very angry but he eventually agreed to go to the company's medical department for an eye check. He returned most apologetic and stated that he had not realized that his eyesight had deteriorated to such an extent.

> A company engaged a manager reputed to possess special expertise which would help to revolutionize its methods. Since his work entailed careful deliberation about what to do, he was given his own office rather than a desk in an open plan area, so that he would not be disturbed. After lunch each day, he could be seen through the glass partition that separated him from the main office, reclining in his chair apparently deep in thought with an eye staring transfixedly at the ceiling. Knowing the importance of his mission, nobody wished to disturb him. This state of affairs went on for some months until the company discovered the staring eye to be made of glass and the expert fast asleep. The quality manager wrily remarked that all experts should be included in the eyesight checks.

These examples show how common it is for eyesight to be neglected, both by operatives and by companies. Regular checks should be made for acuity and colour vision. In the case of products that are assembled underneath the microscope (as an increasing number are nowadays) or microsurgery it is particularly important to have regular checks on personal eyesight, which dictates the ultimate quality of the product.

Similar remarks can be made about other personal attributes (such as dexterity) that are necessary and which affect quality.

— Personnel who do not comply with the document's requirements.

This may be no bad thing, in which case the auditor should not stifle initiative. The people who actually have to perform the job quite often proclaim the document/procedure/manual to be rubbish. If this turns out to be the case, the auditor must take a look at the feedback system, the internal audit system and the people who generated the "rubbish". Provided that the results required by the contract, the QA standard or management policy are being achieved, the best course is to change the document so that it reflects the actual practice and this is what the auditor should recommend. A recommendation is usually adequate because the people responsible generally recognize the need for their documents to reflect actual practice: few people like to admit to being out of touch with what actually happens within their own organization or to allow documentary evidence to that effect to exist after the situation has been drawn to their attention. A formal request for corrective action to change the document would be unfair. The real cause of the problem (in most cases, lack of a feedback system) is what could warrant a formal request for corrective action.

Corrective action and non-conformities

— The conclusion "use-as-is" is excessively exercised.

QA standards do not preclude excessive exercise of this conclusion. Even so, the auditor should look for the underlying reason why "use-as-is" figures so prominently behind the non-conformities discovered.

— Tolerances are widened.

Again, QA standards do not rule this out, but freedom must not turn into licence. The auditor must investigate the matter further: there may be a perfectionist designer who has never learnt (or never been told) what the company's capabilities really are and who invokes excessively tight tolerances that are expensive to meet. However, should tolerances be widened, the effect on interfacing items, overall function and fitness for purpose must be assessed by the auditee. The auditor must verify that this is written into the design change control system, for it is often overlooked.

— The corrective action file is not retained by management.

The auditor must remember that the standards do not ask for such a file to be maintained (let alone say who should keep it). What the standards *do* require is that corrective action be reported to an *appropriate* level of management. Just what level is "appropriate" tends to be a hotly disputed issue, and the auditor must keep an open mind on the subject. However, it is a very healthy sign when top management maintains such a file or gets involved with it, since this adds an edge to the corrective action system. Management's failure to do so can herald a lack of top management support for quality.

— Either management does not ask for a breakdown of bad quality costs or there is *no* breakdown of the costs.

Only certain QA standards (Mil-Q-9859A, for example) require a "quality cost" system but, again, it is healthy if management takes the initiative. ISO 9001 makes no mention of this matter.

— Corrective action responses from sub-suppliers or internal departments are either not prompt or are not expedited.

Different QA standards dictate different rules for implementing corrective action. ISO 9001 expresses no particular time frame, nor does AQAP-1; CAN3-Z299.1-85 requires the auditee to do things "promptly" (which, to my mind, is the responsible thing to do). Once more, it is essential for the auditor to be thoroughly familiar with the codes and standards used on the audit.

REAL CAUSES OF QUALITY PROBLEMS

Many years ago, as a result of having performed a lot of audits, I detected a recurring pattern of six underlying causes of quality problems that have constantly needed to be addressed through Corrective Action Requests. They are:

1. lack of organisation;
2. lack of training;
3. lack of discipline;
4. lack of resources;
5. lack of time;
6. lack of top management support.

1. Lack of organization

Lack of organization divided into the three particular components of:

a) undetermined responsibilities and authorities;
b) undefined management systems;
c) inadequate communications.

a) undetermined responsibilities and authorities:

This has been discussed more fully in Chapter 4. ''Organization''. The purpose of organization is to determine what jobs must be done in order to achieve customer satisfaction, by furnishing a product that is fit for purpose. The fundamental tasks of organizing are to decide who is going to do what; to determine what level of responsibility and authority will be required for each position and to select carefully the people with the requisite competence and abilities to discharge the duties allocated to them.

When auditing, one might find that the company structure has not been defined; that job descriptions have been inadequately conceived and lead to conflicting responsibilities and an overlap of duties; that delegated duties are inconsistent with the manager's assigned responsibilities.

b) undefined management systems:

The management systems should prescribe the methods and means of communication between the various departments and individuals so as to form a complete and continuous chain. It is not uncommon to find in a company that is embarking on a quality programme that the management systems have not been thoroughly thought through and are ad hoc. Management systems are required regardless of the company's size. All managers are duty bound to decide how these departments want their departments' work to be executed and how they are to interface with other parts of the company and with organizations outside it — regardless of the level of formality that is appropriate. Written procedures are meant to help explain the methods and provide a training vehicle for the staff.

Sometimes an auditee genuinely believes that he has created a good quality management system. Careful analysis during an audit only reveals that it is "circular" in nature and is therefore useless. For example:

> During an audit of a chemical laboratory. I enquired of its manager "How do you calibrate your pH meter?" The laboratory manager replied "We check the pH meter against buffer solutions." I asked "Where do you get these buffer solutions from?" To this he replied "We make them up ourselves." I then enquired "How do you make these solutions?" The response was "In accordance with the Government authority's approved procedures". These were checked out for correct revision, validity etc. The next question I posed was "When you have made up these standard buffer solutions how do you check them?" To this the laboratory manager replied "Using the pH meter"!

c) inadequate communications:

Methods of communication have to be thought through in terms of who needs the information that the company or any given department produces. Recipients of information may be either within the organization or outside of it: communication problems can arise from any one of the following.

Language barriers: Special care must be exercised when the information user's mother tongue is a foreign language.

> Apparently, one of the contributing factors to the DC10 air crash outside of Paris was that the instructions written on the fuselage for closing the rear cargo door were in English on a Turkish airline's plane that was being serviced at Paris. It appears that the airport employee who attempted to shut the cargo door was unable to do so because he could not understand the instructions provided.

Certain communications must be in the language that will permit the recipient to understand, otherwise product liability risks can ensue.

Attitudes such as "We won't talk to them"; "they never help us; they think they are so clever, let them find out for themselves" confound good communications. No system will prevent this sort of behaviour for ever and the only remedy is to develop a responsible attitude as part of the corporate quality culture. The example set by management is crucial for, when staff detect that their manager is feuding with another department, they naturally take sides and join in.

Attitudes such as "We didn't know what they wanted"; "we didn't know they had it" can each presage unhelpfulness, pure laziness or absence of team spririt, none of which builds up the right corporate quality culture. A must not only be encouraged to tell B of his requirements from B's particular department: A must also be encouraged to inform B of services or items which A could provide to help B.

2. Lack of training

This has been more fully discussed in pages 18-16/17 and in Chapter 5.

There is little point in carefully avoiding the problems described above under "Lack of organization" if the people in the company are not trained in the systems and methods that are to be used or if they are not told with whom they are to interface. Many companies spend a lot of money in producing a quality assurance manual and distributing it. If, however, the users have not been trained in its contents all that expenditure is pure waste.

3. Lack of discipline

Regardless of how carefully thought through the systems may be and how much training has been provided, people are the real determinants of how well things turn out. Their self-discipline and attitude towards the job is of prime importance. The discipline can be affected, however, by a number of factors, principally:

a) the example set by supervisors and managers;
b) company wide quality campaigns/culture;
c) personal attributes;
d) inflexible systems;
e) de-motivating environments.

a) The example set by supervisors and managers:

A major cause of staff not following the systems and methods as intended, arises from bad examples set by their supervisors and managers. There is little point in spending much time and money in carefully devising the systems and procedures that are to be followed if one knows that the manager will waive them in order to get a product out of the door in time to the customer. It is a constant temptation. Every organization knows that urgent circumstances inevitably arise at sometime or other, so when the systems and methods are devised, they must also cater for those urgent situations. Failure to have considered that set of trading circumstances and operational conditions indicates either a lack of forethought or pure stupidity.

Waiving the systems sends a clear signal to the staff that compliance does not really matter, that the systems are not sacrosanct. From that point on, the work descends into chaos and ad hoc practices. Nobody knows how the department will operate, how it is meant to operate, what its needs are and what its budget needs to be in order to achieve the duties assigned to it. Moreover, staffing levels cannot be accurately defined, nor can people's performance be assessed since there is no yardstick for measurement. It is therefore vital that people in managerial and supervisory positions set an example by following the systems that have been designated for use within the department, improving them whenever possible or necessary.

b) Company wide quality campaigns and culture:

Unless a quality campaign extends company wide to include all line and staff activities, there is a considerable risk that the line departments will become disenchanted.

> In recent years, I have met numerous people in line functions who no longer care about the company quality campaign, which they rightly perceive as unfair. Common criticisms take the form of "They keep pressing us to take care of quality but our pay packets still contain errors/the sales force continue to send us incomplete information too late/those in the office still churn out the same rubbish to us and nobody tells *them* to do a better job".

These demotivators and frictions build up preventing effective team work and healthy attitudes. The auditor should ascertain the extent of the quality campaign or QA programme and take note of simmering resentment such as that described above.

c) Personal attributes:

Some people stubbornly refuse to follow the agreed methods or systems, insistent on working their own way. Such attitudes must not be tolerated. In the case of a company involved in the furnishing of safety related products, anybody who does not follow the necessary systems which are known to ensure a safe product must be stopped, unless their own methods do not jeopardise safety. Even in this case, they should be encouraged to consider further the impact of their methods on colleagues before continuing with them. In persistent cases, this could ultimately necessitate firing the miscreant from the company. For those people whose work is not safety related, it is incumbent upon their peers and their supervisors to point out that, by not following the department and company methods, they might be causing difficulties and problems for their colleagues in other areas, a consequence which would be both unreasonable and unfair. It cannot be tolerated for long because those diligent employees who are doing their best will view as unfair the fact that somebody else is allowed to "get away with it". Gradually, they start to say "well why should I bother?". This ultimately leads to chaos and work being completed either incorrectly or indifferently.

A frequently offered defence is a claim that the systems etc. are of no use. The counter action is to impress on those people that they have a responsibility to make a suggestion as to what would be satisfactory. One encounters many people who are quite adept at criticizing or tearing apart someone else's ideas but there are relatively few who have the ability genuinely to think a problem through or to take a blank piece of paper and specify exactly how a department or organization ought to operate.

d) Inflexible systems:

Quality management systems should not be designed so as to be inflexible. People are employed principally because they possess a brain and are able to think. They are employed for the experience and skill that they can bring to the job and for the day-to-day decision making capability that they have. Regardless of their position in the organization, everyone makes decisions. When systems are too inflexible, they remove the great motivating freedoms to innovate and make decisions. People begin to want to "beat the system" and find a way round it as a form of protest.

I contend that many quality assurance practitioners have much to answer for. By constantly seeking to make procedures ever more detailed and inflexible to cover all circumstances and contingencies that could possibly arise in the workplace, they have helped to demotivate staff. Why is it that managers have been justifiably critical of quality assurance auditors over many years? Simply because whenever there has been a quality problem, instead of trying to uncover the root cause and curing the problem, the response has been to impose another piece of paper, adding further bureaucracy to the workplace. Not very helpful. Certain activities do need to be planned in fine detail, this being the case especially in high value, high risk and safety related situations such as in the operating of a nuclear power station or in flying of an aircraft. Even in these situations, however, there comes a time when one needs to rely on people's ability to think quickly under difficult circumstances.

The probability that a procedure will be read is at most inversely proportional to the square of its thickness. The auditor must ensure by his approach and attitude that he does not become counter-productive towards quality by promoting inflexible systems, explained in tomes full of procedures.

e) Motivation:

The above reveals that a central cause of lack of discipline is also a lack of motivation. It is important that any demotivator that can occur is prevented and extirpated. Motivation has been discussed in Chapter 5.

4. Lack of resources

Lack of resources can be caused either by pure wastage or by their inadequate estimation and allocation to areas where they are really needed. The allocation of resources needs to be properly planned and it is my contention that an essential part of the management audit is to investigate the basis on which resources are determined and allocated. (Resources audits are discussed in Chapter 26.)

As stated previously, it is not possible to determine where the available resources really are required unless the company has first of all organized itself thoroughly and thereby defined the systems needed for the product that it intends to sell. Only by getting organized, can one define the resources required in each of the various departments. The enterprise as a whole requires a management system which ensures that resources are properly estimated, allocated and monitored in every department. The auditor must look for proof that such a system exists, has been communicated throughout the organization, is implemented and is effective. Furthermore, every department, cost centre, division, project etc. must constantly look for ways by which resources can be saved although not to the detriment of quality since that would represent a false economy. Managers must also ensure that none of the following, which can starve individual areas of essential resources, is allowed to occur:

a) over-complex management systems;
b) irresponsible attitudes;
c) unrealistic estimates;
d) uneven allocation;
e) inadequate re-investment;
f) failure to modernize.

a) Over-complex management systems:

Problems can occur because an over-complex system eats up valuable resources. The systems must be economic. Too few quality management auditors analyse the systems to see whether or not they use the resources properly. When a system is too complex, it wastes manpower and budget which could be put to better effect in other areas. Auditors should be on their guard, watchful for any signs of this development. Many of the real breakthroughs and benefits that occur in quality programmes happen by identifying this form of waste.

b) Irresponsible attitudes:

People can have a most peculiar attitude towards resources. No matter how much is allocated to them, they always want more. It is a kind of Parkinson's Law[7] in that the individuals and departments concerned will always manage to devour whatever resources are allocated to them completely. It is well known for example, that people in governmental organizations are loath to return unused resources for fear that their following year's budget will be cut accordingly. Hence, resources are always used up according to the allocation made. This is an unfortunate type of attitude and is one that is difficult to break down. Effective teamwork requires everybody to realise that excess resources should be returned for use in another area to greater effect. Everyone must appreciate that this will improve quality elsewhere in the organization and fund real solutions to problems, thus benefitting everyone.

c) Unrealistic estimates:

It is not uncommon to find that bids and tenders or product development plans are based on totally unrealistic figures. People can be over optimistic from the most well meaning point of view. (Over the years, I have found this to be particularly true of software supply projects — see also Chapter 24). This has the result that, in order to complete a job on time, something has to give and part of the job is rushed. It is a totally false economy and there are many examples that have been reported which bear testimony to this.

d) Uneven allocation:

The actual allocation of resources can be most unfair. I have come across many instances of uneven allocation based on either bad planning or pure favouritism. Often, one particular department or manager receives an over-generous share of the resources either because his face fits, because he makes such a fuss that his management want to keep him quiet or because the superior allocating the resources happens to have a particular affection for the work being carried out in that particular department. Uneven allocation means that someone somewhere else is having to make do and is often cutting corners and encountering avoidable problems in his own department as a result. On several occasions, I have experienced favoured managers gloating over the difficulties of their fellow managerial colleagues. All of this leads to strains in the team and is a great demotivator. It sets up pointless rivalries in which people are more concerned about being "one up" on other departments than with getting down to business, solving the company's problems and maturely working together as a team.

e) Inadequate re-investment:

Business is generally cyclic and every company experiences good and bad profit years. Prudent management will use the years of strong profit to re-invest in the company's future development. History can show many examples of industries that failed to do so with the inevitable result that traumatic restructuring and rationalization becomes necessary in the lean years or as the product range becomes effete.

Today's quality problems are the direct result of inadequate management decisions of the past. Securing future quality achievement means that the company must re-invest in new skills, new technigues, new equipment and new products. A company wide quality programme must extend into the strategic decisions made by the board of directors, encompassing re-investment decisions. The average auditor will not have much opportunity to investigate this aspect of a company's quality programme, but the president's audit can and must. (See Chapter 27).

It is unwise for one year's resource allocation to be based on the needs previous year because product lines and market strictures change and are in a constant state of flux. To slash the following year's budget simply because the resources allocated for the previous year were not required in their entirety can be unrealistic for the same reasons. Remembering that business circumstances can alter, the successful manager who, without impairing quality, has saved on resources allocated in the previous year should not be hamstrung for next year's needs which may be totally different. The performance of that department could deteriorate and quality problems result from having to "make do".

f) Failure to modernize:

There comes a point when equipment which may still be perfectly serviceable is a liability to the company because of new technology and developments. By not replacing the equipment, a company can find itself disadvantaged, especially if one's competitors have already modernized. Failure to modernize means increased costs which are, to my mind, failure costs just as much as those incurred by the company's production of defective items. It all ends up in the unit price or reduced profits. New equipment might not only incur reduced running costs by virtue of its greater efficiency but might also be able to work to higher specifications. This has also been discussed in Chapter 5 under "Equipment".

I firmly believe that an essential part of a quality programme is the constant search for improved methods and potential applications for new technology throughout the organization. One finds many instances of people continuing to work in old fashioned ways when, for example, an inexpensive desktop computer could perhaps reduce their workload and allow them to work more accurately and productively.

Resources can be wasted not only because new equipment, techniques or new technology is not used but also because the investment is not understood. Frequently companies are found to have acquired new equipment which is lying idle or used ineffectively.

> In one American company, a very sophisticated machine tool which cost approximately $1 million lay idle for nearly 18 months because people did not understand how to use it. Many excuses were proffered such as "We didn't have the right tooling";

> "We're waiting for the machine to be finally installed and commissioned". An audit revealed the real reason was that the machinists were apprehensive about using new technology.
>
> A service company spent $25,000 on a desktop publishing system which lay virtually idle for nearly a year because the staff did not learn to use it. They had pestered the management for that equipment but when it arrived, they avoided proper training. It was used for minutes of meetings and simple one page lists that could easily have been produced on a typewriter. But the laser printer did at least make those lists and minutes look pretty and the management was thus fooled into thinking that the investment had been worthwhile.

Instances such as the above can occur when people either lack training in the type of new technology that is available or when they also lack the time to learn how to use the technology properly.

> A number of years ago, a company purchased a numerically controlled machine tool which worked from holorith cards. One day, whilst rushing to start the machine working, the operator accidentally dropped the box of cards. Quite innocently and quickly he gathered them up from the workshop floor and stuffed them all back into the box: he had no idea that the card sequence was critical. When the machine started it totally ruined a valuable piece of material. The holorith cards had been programmed to move the machine head to the next position on the basis of the previous position of the head as opposed to moving relative to a fixed datum. What had not been appreciated was that if the card became mixed up the machine tool head would move a wrong position. Investigation revealed that there had been insufficient investment in the training of people and inadequate time allocated for people to learn how to use and program that machine tool properly.

Resources need to be carefully planned on the basis of the company's trading strategy. As part of the plan, the acquisition of resources needs to be carefully thought through and proper capital appropriation needs to be plotted, not just in respect of purchasing the new equipment or techniques but also in terms of training the people who will have to use it.

5. Lack of time

Time is a type of resource that I single out because of the prevalence of quality problems derived from inadequate control of it. Quality problems result when people are forced to rush their job. I consider time management to be an essential part of quality management, indeed, a prerequisite for a successful quality assurance programme, and, accordingly, I have over many years directed auditors' attention to the necessity of asking questions as to how the auditee's time is managed. The answers generally reveal opportunities for improvement and cost reduction. Lack of time is the quality management version of the saying "Marry in haste, repent at leisure!" Despite its critical effect on quality, to the best of my knowledge, none of internationally recognized QA standards even mention proper management of time. It is a shameful omission.

Every enterprise requires a management system which ensures that time is properly estimated, allocated and monitored in every department. The auditor must look for proof that such a system exists, has been communicated throughout the organization, is implemented and is effective. Every department, division, project etc. must constantly search for ways which time can be saved but not by sacrificing quality, for that also would represent a false economy. Managers must also ensure that none of the following, which can deprive individual areas of essential time, occur:

a) over-complex systems;
b) irresponsible attitudes;
c) unrealistic commitments;
d) selfishness;
e) excessive workload.

a) Over-complex systems:

Systems that are too complex can waste time, in that needless activities, bureaucracy and checks eat into the time budget allowed for a job. Wherever possible, one must strive either to eliminate needless tasks or to design the system such that essential tasks are performed in parallel to the greatest extent possible. Fig. 8.11 shows how a complex system wasted time through pointless activities.

b) Irresponsible attitudes:

Some people will use as much time to do their job as is allocated to them. It is Parkinson's Law in that the work will always expand to fill the time available. However, excessive time allocated to one person often means that somebody else has been denied the time he needs to do a good job.

c) Unrealistic commitments:

Sales orders: It is quite common to find bids and tenders that are totally unrealistic about the time required to effect proper delivery to the customer. Salesmen can be overzealous in the commitments they make on behalf of the company. Promising unrealistic delivery dates introduces the risks that corners are cut, incomplete or unsatisfactory products are delivered and that the customer becomes annoyed. It not only costs a lot of money to rectify the problem at the customers' premises but there is the real risk that further business will be lost and the company's reputation for quality will be damaged. A salesperson might consider that he has done a good job in reaching or exceeding his targets but, if that achievement means that he has committed the company to a trading loss, nobody benefits.

But the sales staff also require help and it is equally vital that the company sets up its systems and organizes itself in such a way that it can provide its salesforce with realistic and meaningful delivery times for presentation to the customer.

New products: In a similar way, development plans for new products can be unrealistic and over optimistic. Sometimes design and development staff are coerced into making rash promises by the pressure exerted from top management.

Production deadlines: Production people can also be unwise in predicting release dates for products, especially new lines. Unforeseen hitches can easily arise: they tend to do so even more frequently when time pressure is exerted irresponsibly. Inadequate involvement of the production people in the design and development work will lead directly to that — such a phenomenon occurs with monotonous regularity.

A common problem encountered in the service sectors is that of support staff (who service or install new equipment required for supplying the service to the customer) underestimating the time required to get everything into proper workup order. There is a particular tendency for this to happen when they are not involved in the design of the service itself. See also Chapter 25.

Clearly, to ensure that there is a responsible allocation, planning and commitment of time, people should work together as a team. The auditor can check how the various commitments are made and who is involved.

d) Selfishness:

Fig. 3.2 depicts a typical bar chart representation for the various phases that work might go through in a company. The people working at the front end of any set of activities, project or contract have a duty to ensure that they prevent any slippage of time as far as possible. What tends to happen is that the front-end activities view the total time available for the complete project and say "Well, if we lose a few days, the other departments will pick it up, so let's not worry". A cancer develops as the subsequent phases reason "It was handed over to us late and we still want our rightful amount of time to do our job" and then they too exceed their time budget a little, further reasoning that if the previous department can do so why can't they? Eventually, the poor souls at the end of the line are pressurized to meet the delivery dates and commitments that were originally made to the customer, having their time allocation slashed in the process. Although they do the best they can, they look for shortcuts, overlooking or waiving an essential quality check, for example. The product is shipped, the customer complains and more money is wasted. It is shortsighted and unfair to steal time allocated for a colleague's work.

In recent years, there has been a trend towards "fast-track" projects. That rather seductive name has persuaded many managers into taking unwise shortcuts only to discover that they have incurred excessive long term costs. These can have a great effect on the lifetime costing of the product obtained from the co-called "fast track" project. Several managers have confided to me that they regret not having tempered their "fast track" enthusiasm with better decisions. Trying to avoid important tasks can be a case of throwing the quality baby out with the bathwater.

e) Excessive workload:

Another cause of lack of time is, of course, the excessive workload of certain individuals. Whenever the burden of work is too great, due care and attention to tasks in hand is reduced as people strive to get work finished. The familiar results, previously mentioned, then occur. The prime cause of excessive workload, however, is a lack of manpower resource which has already been discussed.

6. Lack of top management support

a) Attitude/motivation:

A majority of managers regard "quality" as being rather mundane topic not worthy of discussion: it's not a "sexy" subject. It is treated in an assumptive manner, i.e. managers assume that the quality of their work is good and that anybody who does not agree is automatically an uninformed critic and an adversary.

Corporate attitudes emanates from the board of directors who show their priorities towards quality not only by the direct interest they take in it but also by the way in which they constuct their board, by the type of expertise which they admit to their ranks. There is generally an imbalance at the top of companies: too many economists, accountants, legal advisors and the like, few of whom tend to know much about the product, what constitutes its quality, how quality is achieved in any department and, thus, what the business's quality needs really are. This is not to say that they are inherently bad or irresponsible by nature: far from it. The problem is that they lack the training and appreciation both of quality management techniques and of the importance of quality.

The problem becomes particularly acute when the balance of the top management's and the board of director's expertise is wrong. Overdoing the financial, economic and legal representation at either of those levels is unwise. After all, how many people does a company actually need to obtain financial advice? Surely no more than it needs the people who are there individually to provide the specific technical and product advice which is, in any case, the core of the company's business. A company earns nothing when its products cannot compete in quality terms. If a board of directors wants financial assurance, should it not also want quality assurance in its ranks?

The balance of expertise at the top of the company is not a subject in which the regular auditor can easily involve himself: it is a topic that the president's audit can and must address. See Chapter 27.

Top managements tend to look for the quick and easy fix. Some have foolishly believed that all of their problems will be solved if the company obtains an accreditation to one of the QA standards such as ISO 9001. Life is not that easy and those standards do not provide the answers that will be found through constant attention by management to quality throughout the company at all times.

Believing that the only involvement necessary from top management is to sign policies, promote slogans and shake hands is wrong. They must become directly involved and remain so.

b) Management education:

It is only in relatively recent years that business schools have begun to realize the necessity of teaching executives and managers both the importance of quality and means of achieving it. It is futile to learn sophisticated ways of calculating profit and budget if in the final analysis there is no money being earned. The curriculum of business schools has until recently been totally out of balance. They have failed to stress that customers will not buy rubbish and that the prime task of the manager is to concentrate on achieving quality if he wishes to secure the desired cash flow, market share, growth rate and so on. Fancy ways of calculating cash flow and profit projections are useless if the product does not sell or if the failure costs are not prevented by means of assiduous application of the quality management techniques. A business plan that does not state how quality and hence profit will be achieved is a worthless piece of paper and a pipe dream on which no responsible financier, banker or pension fund should waste its time.

c) Time management:

Many top managements would genuinely like to get more involved in the quality aspects of the business but find they do not have the time. This can occur through inefficient use of their time or as a result of staff cutbacks.

> I have come across a number of problems resulting from the recession years of the 1970s and early 1980s, when managers had to reduce staff so far that they were forced to perform subordinates' tasks themselves. Although they appreciated where and why quality problems were occurring, they no longer had the time to cure the problems or to manage their departments properly. This then established a vicious circle as things became progressively worse.

Frequently, however, the managers' lack of time arises from constant fire fighting in their attempts to mitigate the effects of quality problems. Another self-defeating circle.

d) Cancer of complacency:

Too many managers use the argument "We've been in business for the last three generations/50 years/(or whatever) and the customers come back because we have a fine reputation for quality." Their "experience" leads them to believe that customers will always be there and that their reputation for quality will always support them regardless of future market conditions. History is filled with examples of companies who felt that their previous successes were strong enough to withstand the future. In the UK, in particular, there has been an almost unending trail of sick companies seeking governmental financial support when they have found themselves unable to compete in the world markets. So long as top management and owners believe that their early reputation will carry them through, new competitors will smile inscrutably and ultimately put them out of business.

It is foolhardy to assume that the customer will be prepared to fund inefficiency, outdated technology and waste. They won't.

The real reason behind the stock market crash of October 1987 was simply that American managements had assumed for years that their fellow countrymen would continue to buy whatever American industry produced. Oriental and European producers were perceived by ordinary Americans as providing better quality and so the balance of trade deficit soared. A healthy trade balance would have reduced the US federal budget deficit and hence its effects. The crash of 1987 provides a superlative example of the effects of competitors winning customers from complacent managements who disregarded the importance of quality. None of the major business magazines, newspapers, politicians or television discussion programmes recognized this.

References:

1. ISO 9001 — 1987 *Quality systems — Model for quality assurance in design/development, production, installation and servicing*. Published by the International Organization for Standardization.

2. AS 1821 — 1985 *Suppliers quality systems for design, development, production and installation*. Published by the Standards Association of Australia, Standards House, 80 Arthur Street, North Sydney, N.S.W., Australia.

3. CAN3-Z299.1 — 1985 *Quality assurance program — Category 1*. Published by Canadian Standards Association, 178 Rexdale Boulevard, Rexdale (Toronto), Ontario, Canada M9W 1R3.

4. AQAP-1 *NATO requirements for an industrial quality control system*. Edition No 3 May 1984 issued by the NATO International Staff — Defence Suport Division.

5. Military Specification Mil-Q-9858A *Quality program requirements* 1963. Government Printing Office, Washington, D.C., USA.

6. AQAP-4 *NATO Inspection System Requirements for Industry*, edition No. 2 June 1976 issued by the NATO International Staff — Defence Suport Division.

7. Parkinson, C. Northcote, *Parkinson's Law*, Penguin, Harmondsworth, 1965.

19. The Exit Interview

"The time has come," the Walrus said,
"To talk of many things;"
Lewis Carroll.

The findings and conclusions of the audit team are presented to the auditee in summary form at a meeting attended by both the entire audit team and the auditee's key representatives. This meeting is known by such names as exit meeting, exit critique, close-out meeting, summary meeting and so on. In the case of an external or extrinsic audit, the exit interview must be regarded as a contractual or as a statutory meeting, according to the identity of the auditor's organization. Similarly, during a third party assessment, the exit interview can be regarded as a quasi-contractual meeting because the assessing body is acting on behalf of unknown future customers. It always takes place after all the investigative and analytical work of the audit has been completed. The exit interview is extremely important and the auditor should prepare for it thoroughly so that the proceedings may be properly conducted. The purpose of this chapter is to suggest a framework and format to help the auditor with this task.

Attendees

Fig. 19.1 shows the attendees for the exit interview. In one section are the people who must attend, in the other section are those who may wish to attend or whose attendance may be desirable but not essential. The level of auditee management in attendance should be at least one level higher than the highest level of activity management to have been audited. Fig. 19.2 depicts this.

As was stated in Chapter 1, a prime objective of a management audit is to obtain information for use by management. It is clearly essential for the auditee's management to be present at the exit interview since at this meeting the audit team produces its conclusions as to the effectiveness of various departments audited in complying with the company's contractual and legal obligations or with other matters that form the audit objectives. The audit team will also disclose its assessment of the status of the management policies and procedures implemented in the area(s) audited, of the status of equipment, of the competence of personnel or of whatever related to the objectives of the audit. This information should be of prime concern to management and it would be foolish to dismiss the opportunity to be present when it is made public. This is particularly true in the case of external audits. it would be a strange company that was not interested in its customer's conclusions as to whether or not the company was meeting its contractual obligations, even stronger if the audit was conducted by a regulatory body concerned with statutory compliance. As more and more organizations of every sort come to appreciate the value of audits, the presence of senior management at the exit interview will become increasingly a matter of course.

Fig. 19.1 Exit interview attendees

	AUDITOR ORGANIZATION	AUDITEE ORGANIZATION	
		Internal audit	*External audit*
MUST	All auditors, team leaders and the lead auditor	Managers of areas audited and/or area supervisor, QA manager.	QA manager, escorts, contract engineer, contract administrator, other management* and its immediate superior[1].
OPTIONAL	Observers; Auditor management representative; Specialist(s)		

*i.e. management of areas audited.
[1]see fig. 19.2

Among the attendees at the exit interview for an external audit, the presence of the QA manager's superior is of particular importance. The QA manager (assuming such an appointment has been made) generally bears the responsibility for the efficacy of the company's quality management systems (which should include those management systems implemented in order to achieve legal as well as contractual compliance) and it is essential for the QA manager's superior to be aware of the extrinsic auditor's judgement of the effectiveness of that manager's department. If that superior's time is so precious that he cannot be present himself, it is good practice for him to nominate someone (not the QA manager) to be his representative at the exit interview and to report back afterwards. It is worth adding as a postscript at this point that the QA department should not be — as it too often is — exempt from the internal audit programme: it should be audited independently by senior management. Some companies perform such an audit once a year when the chief executive assesses whether or not the QA department is complying with the company's policies and performing the duties assigned to it. See also Chapter 27 — "The President's Audit".

Fig. 19.2 The lowest level of auditee management attending the exit interview

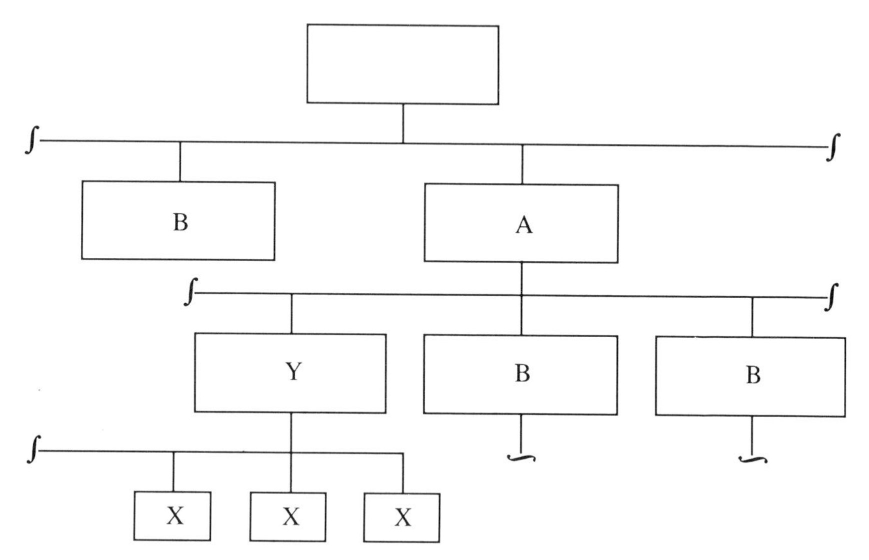

X = Work tasks audited.
Y = Level of management audited, in effect.
A = Lowest level of management that must attend the exit interview.
B = Does not attend because his/her subordinate area were not audited.

The audit team may feel it necessary to have other personnel from their own organization present, either if specific problems have been encountered or if specific investigations have had to be performed. These colleagues feature among the optional attendees listed in Fig. 19.1. Likewise, the auditee may wish to have certain others present at the exit interview for an external audit if their opinions are required or if topics particularly pertinent to their operations are to be discussed.

Preparation

Preparations for the exit interview are made continually throughout the audit. The auditor may consider himself prepared after he has gone through the following series of steps:

1. Write down the facts required in the original checklist, basing the answers on the objective evidence that has been examined.
2. Note who was present in each department audited and what discussions concerning deficiencies were held with the escorts.
3. Analyse the quality management systems, determining their strengths and weaknesses.
4. Discuss the findings and deficiencies with the audit team and investigate to find the root cause.
5. Obtain and analyse fresh evidence if this is necessary to arrive at the truth.
6. Hold a summary meeting between the audit team and the auditee each day in order to acquaint the latter with any problems, allowing him to institute his own corrective action if possible.
7. On the eve of the exit interview, discuss the position with the audit team and decide which findings, if any, must be presented as formal Corrective Action Requests.
8. Summarize these findings and write up the Corrective Action Requests on the company's standard forms.
9. On the eve of the exit interview, discuss and prepare the exit interview presentation (this applies to lead auditor and team leaders).

The audit team must take great care to choose its words wisely or misunderstandings — even litigation — may occur at a later date.

> One company reached the stage of its lawyers exchanging letters with its supplier's lawyers over a dispute concerning payment for contract completion and contract compliance. As part of their claim and counter claims, each party submitted the audit reports to their respective attornies.

When assigned to an external audit, the audit team, and particularly the lead auditor, must bear in mind that the audit reports may be used later on as a source of reference in order to resolve a dispute over whether or not the customer had been satisfied and, if not, whether it had discussed its dissatisfaction with its supplier. Since an external audit is normally concerned with the objective evidence to prove satisfactory contract compliance, it might be construed as an opportunity for "examination" of the goods involved. Most purchase orders do contain a clause to the effect that any examination of goods will neither preclude subsequent rejection if they are found to be unsatisfactory nor relieve the supplier of his obligations under the contract but there may be cases where such wording will prove insufficient. (The ISO 9000 series as issued under the British Standard 5750 — 1987[1] contains a warning to suppliers that compliance with the standard does not confer immunity from legal obligations. Obviously the term "legal obligations" permits liberal andextensive interpretation.) In the case of extrinsic audits performed by statutory bodies, the possibility of legal defence by means of audit reports will depend on the regulations involved, on the associated power and duties of the auditors and on the legal precedents set in the country concerned. The liability of third party assessors, to the best of my knowledge, has yet to be established but if history teaches one anything, it is that such liability will one day be clarified in a court of law. There are abundant examples of financial auditors being sued and prosecuted and I see no reason why third party assesors should — or will — remain immune from similar treatment.

> While preparing for an exit interview, a principal engineer of an auditee's design department approached me in the desire to impart some "vital" information, claiming that it could substantially affect the results of an audit I had been engaged to perform. He alleged that the company's chief engineer was overruling equipment selection and design decisions to such an extent that there was a resultant risk to safety at a particular petrochemical complex. To support these allegations, various documents were tabled before me. I decided that these allegations had to be investigated, that to do so was beyond the scope of my current activity (which had excluded that engineer's area) and that an independent investigation should be recommended. The statement made at the exit interview was carefully worded and considered beforehand. Furthermore, I resolved that the whole affair needed to be brought to the personal attention of the chief executive officer.

To ignore that type of allegation would be to fail in one's legal duty of care. The statement made at the exit interview is described in page 20-3.

If the audit has been properly performed, the exit interview becomes little more than a formality.

> In many governmental institutions, many issues are discussed and resolved prior to meetings between the senior people. Everybody is informed of each other's stance and of the necessary compromises that may be proposed and agreed at the meeting. The meeting itself is little more than a rubber stamp session. This is a wise practice since top management time is always at a premium. No top manager wants to be party to a brawl (and nor, indeed, should anybody else). What they want is an agreed summary of the facts and concrete, constructive proposals.

Duration

The duration of the exit interview varies according to the audit type, scope and objectives, as well as the extent and seriousness of any problems encountered. An hour should be adequate in most cases. Occasionally the meeting may run to an hour and a half if there is a considerable list of deficiencies to discuss, as may well happen if the auditee is just embarking on a new QA system. The only occasion I have ever been engaged in an exit interview that lasted for one and a half hours was for a company where there was a language problem and, consequently, communication difficulties.

Attendance list

In the case of an external audit, the audit team should always initiate an attendance list and request that everyone present signs. There should be a record of those who were present, just as there is at any normal meeting that is minuted. In the case of an extrinsic audit, if the audit team does not initiate an attendance list, the auditee should do so instead. Moreover, the audit team must then be requested to sign it.

Auditee speakers

The audit team should make a mental note of those who speak and attend on behalf of the auditee. It is extremely valuable to note the atmosphere, response and reactions of the auditee's personnel since these may indicate stormy waters ahead. The management audit is not finished until the auditor's organization has verified that any corrective action requested has been implemented efficaciously. Every so often, this may give rise to a major battle. It is not unknown for an auditee to procrastinate about implementing corrective action in the hope that the auditor's organization will be forced to overlook problems if delivery of the product becomes critical. If the audit team picks up warning signs of such difficulties at a later stage, they must pass the information on to their own management.

The sequence of the proceedings

The suggested sequence for conducting the exit interview is set out in checklist form in Fig. 19.3. The following points should help the audit team get through the business efficiently.

a) When presenting the results, it is recommended that the strengths of the auditee's systems and practices are mentioned first. This is good psychology. On hearing a barrage of criticism that seems endlessly to point out the problem areas, management tends to "switch off". One can even read their thoughts, "We know we have problems but surely not everything is bad?" As those thoughts develop, folk are not paying attention, resentment and communication barriers are building up. However, if the

Fig. 19.3 Proceedings for the exit interview

Lead auditor	*Auditee*
1. Initiate attendance list.	
2. State that the critique is based on objective evidence presented and does not mean that areas not seen or mentioned are considered satisfactory.	
3. Request all questions be held until presentation is completed.	
4. General impressions.	
5. Strong/impressive systems.	
6. Deficiencies and presentation of Corrective Action Request(s) and recommended corrective action(s).	
7. Position statement.	
8. Explain CAR form layout and use.	
	9. Questions/clarification of CARs, etc
10. Resolve points raised by auditee.	
	11. Sign CARs to indicate concurrence with non-conformity description(s).
12. Ensure that everyone has signed the attendance list.	
13. Thank auditee for hospitality, courtesy and assistance.	

strengths are tabled first, the auditee's personnel will be more receptive to hearing of any weaknesses that were uncovered. In these circumstances, people tend to think "Fair enough, we have got problems but at least the auditor has recognized that we also have our strengths". The auditee will consequently be more willing to consider and hasten through the improvements required. Using this ploy, the auditor will present the good news first to ease the transition to the "bad" news (if any),

With the proviso that the auditor has held a daily meeting and kept the auditee constantly informed of his findings, good and bad, as the audit has progressed, people will be in the correct frame of mind to recognize that the "bad" news presents an opportunity for improvement and possible cost reduction.

b) Group similar deficiencies together (under each of the task elements, for example, or by department). This helps the auditee to concentrate and to comprehend the extensiveness of the problems encountered and is a useful technique in getting corrective action undertaken.

c) Report all deficiencies but ignore trivia. Instances of ''human error'' (see Chapter 17) need only be mentioned in one umbrella statement, such as ''A few cases of isolated human error were encountered but these are not considered significant and have been acted on to the satisfaction of the audit team'' (provided, of course, that this is actually the case).

d) Report deficiencies that *are* being acted upon and about which the auditee knew before the audit team discovered them. However, such deficiencies must *not* be reported as formal Corrective Action Requests. It is enough to say that the audit team have considered the corrective action which the auditee is attempting to implement and will verify its implementation at a later date. Remember to compliment the auditee for having acted properly in that he initiated corrective action.

e) If the auditee was able to resolve some deficiencies promptly before the exit interview, say so and praise the auditee's personnel for their prompt action (see Chapter 17). An umbrella statement such as '' The audit team is pleased to report that some deficiencies we noted during the audit were promptly resolved and not need to be reported here'' consequently should do.

f) When presenting the CARs, describe, as a minimum: the non-conformity; the justification for issuing the CAR (i.e. the particular part of the statute, code, standard, regulation, procedure, manual or whatever that has been violated) and the audit team's recommendations for corrective action. The auditee is asked to sign the ''concurrence'' box on the CAR form immediately after the Position Statement has been made by the lead auditor (see below).

g) If necessary, report favourably or unfavourably on the attitudes of the auditee's personnel although it may be better to discuss sensitive issues privately with the top management. If a private discussion seems desirable, the lead auditor should discreetly indicate this to the auditee's senior management. I have never known the latter to refuse.

h) Remember that the prime responsibility is to present a ''true and fair view'' of the status of the management systems, procedures, equipment or whatever, in relation to the audit objectives. It follows, therefore, that the audit team *must* mention the good points and impressive areas, as well as the bad, in order to present a balanced view. Too many auditors present only the gloomy side of the picture at the exit interview.

Method of approach

Many exit interviews are ruined because of poor presentation by the audit team. Some key rules to follow are detailed below.

1. Be prepared: the audit team must have its facts at its fingertips.
2. Base the presentation on objective evidence, not subjective opinion. Most people are willing to bow to the force of facts. As Rensis Likert wrote:—

   "People seem most willing and emotionally able to accept, and to examine in a non-defensive manner, information about themselves and their behaviour, including their inadequacies, when it is in the form of objective evidence."[2]

3. In making the presentation on behalf of the audit team, speak clearly, calmly and audibly. This is particularly important when the auditee's mother tongue is not that of the audit team. The auditee cannot be expected to implement efficacious corrective action if he can't understand what is being said.
4. Remain cool and unemotional. Do not get provoked into any heated arguments that would allow the auditee the chance to complain to the auditor's organization and declare the audit null and void (see Chapter 15).
5. Be constructive and helpful if the auditee has questions or queries concerning the problems uncovered or if he wishes to propose certain actions. When asked, the audit team must indicate clearly whether or not the auditee's proposals for corrective action would be acceptable to their organization.
6. Be polite, firm, fair and reasonable.

Stop work decisions

Occasionally stop work may be considered necessary. When requesting that work be stopped, the audit team must explain the reasons that have led them to this decision. The issue can occasionally produce a fairly unpleasant situation, with much resistance from the auditee, which is why it is important for the auditors to have consulted with their own senior management beforehand (see Chapter 17). The limitations on the auditor's authority are described in page 20-3. When requesting stop work the lead auditor must state:

— the extent of work that has to be stopped;
— the reasons that led to the stop work decision;
— the suggested corrective action to be taken (this will be descibed on the CAR form);
— the full extent of the problem, including the costs and risks of maintaining the status quo;
— the circumstances under which work could be restarted;
— the anticipated time required to accomplish the suggested corrective action.

Fresh evidence

If at any point during the exit interview, the auditee wishes to present fresh evidence, the audit team must go back and re-audit the contentious area or analyse the evidence presented.

In being allowed the opportunity to offer fresh evidence, the auditee is reassured that the auditor is genuinely concerned with obtaining a true and fair view. The auditee, therefore, has less justification to complain about the conduct of the audit and has been given "a fair go", as Australians would say.

The auditor should remain firm, however, if the fresh evidence does not obviate the original findings. It is beneficial to explain why the fresh evidence remains unsatisfactory because the situation could herald confusion within the auditee as to what the deficiency actually is.

If the evidence disproves the audit team's findings, they must:

1. apologize for the wrong conclusions that were drawn.
2. thank the auditee for presenting the fresh evidence so that the truth could be ascertained.
3. strike the previous findings from their checklists and notes.

The third point is especially noteworthy. The reason why I generally complete my checklist in pencil is to make it easy to delete items if fresh evidence turns up to discredit the first findings. To let false findings stand in the checklist and notes is grossly unfair to the auditee: a third party, not actually involved in the audit, may subsequently review the checklist and notes and thereby gain a false impression of the auditee. In the case of over-zealous or officious extrinsic auditors, the discredited findings may provide grounds for lengthy arguments: deleting the relevant notes eliminates all chance of this occurring.

Position statement

Whatever the type of audit, the audit team MUST ALWAYS include a position statement in the exit interview. In the case of third party assessments, this is a formal necessity.

The position statement must be absolutely clear and unambiguous. A statement like "The systems as documented and implemented fulfil/do not fulfil the requirements of the such and such regulation" will leave the auditee's management in no doubt about where they stand and whether or not their systems have achieved their objective or not. It is bad practice and bad manners to leave the auditee in the dark.

An alternative and unequivocal statement would be:

"On the basis of the objective evidence presented and with the exception of those matters that are the subject of Corrective Action Requests and with the exception of those areas that were not audited,
— the company does meet the requirements of (the code/standard/ specification);
— the company's systems do comply with the (XXX) regulations
— the company is complying with its quality assurance manual/ directives".

(The above can be modified by the auditor to reflect the objective of the audit.)

If, during an extrinsic audit, the audit team does not offer a position statement, the auditee should first ask politely for one. If this is refused, the auditee should then declare the audit null and void as far as he is concerned and communicate this in writing to the auditor's organization. The auditee should refuse to sign any formal Corrective Action Requests presented by the audit team until the position statement is forthcoming. *The auditee is entitled to know where he stands.* This is especially true for a third party assessment.

The hidden tape recorder

Auditors must not be afraid of allowing people to make a tape recording of the exit interview, whether this is done openly or surreptitiously. If they are not prepared to stand by their statements or if the statements are in any way incorrect, then the auditors are not prepared for the exit interview, they have not performed a proper audit and they have failed in their duties. If an audit team is confident that the audit has been performed in a professional, thorough, and honest manner, then it is presenting a true and fair view and need not be concerned by such tape recordings. A similar attitude should be adopted towards video recordings of the proceedings.

> During one audit, I became aware that someone was secretly attempting to make a tape recording of the exit interview. In accordance with my normal procedure, I was myself quite openly recording the exit interview, only switching the tape off when certain remarks were to be made off the record or in confidence. Upon becoming aware of the activities of the person who was attempting to make a clandestine tape recording, I invited him to put his tape recorder on the top of the table beside mine and perhaps to sit nearer to me so that his recording would be of better quality. The person concerned went crimson with embarrassment and certain of the auditee's representatives went crimson with rage at his behaviour.

Before making a tape recording of the exit interview, I always inform the auditee that the tape recording is only being made in order to help me when it comes to writing the audit report and that, should anyone wish to make any remarks off the record, the recording will be switched off at that point. In my experience, no one objects to tape recordings made upon these conditions. When I have finished with the tape, I use it for another audit; I do not keep them.

Interruptions

Before presenting the audit team's findings and conclusions, the lead auditor should request that any questions be reserved until the presentation has been completed, adding that the team will be delighted to answer them then.

If the auditee interrupts the presentation, ask whether or not the query can be saved until the end: if not, deal with it swiftly on the spot and carry on with the presentation. In my experience, it is rare for the presentation to be unduly or excessively interrupted. The most common cause of interruptions is difficulty in communicating when the auditee and audit team do not share the same mother tongue.

Corrective Action Requests

The completed Corrective Action Request forms are presented to the auditee at the exit interview. The audit team must make quite clear that, whilst they will be pleased to receive one, they do not expect a commitment to corrective action at that time, only an acknowledgment that the description of the non-conformity is accurate and truthful. (The CAR form should include space for a concurrence signature from the auditee's representatives — see Chapter 17.)

The auditee must be told how long he will be allowed to consider the commitment he is prepared to make to corrective action. A period of 30 days for consideration and commitment is generally satisfactory. However, urgent cases, such as stop work decisions, may call for speedier decisions. The audit team must consider each case on its merits.

If the auditee is unwilling to concur with the non-conformity description as presented on the CAR form, the problem must be resolved there and then and, if necessary, fresh evidence sought. It is seldom that an impasse is reached.

Auditee questions

Auditors must answer or attempt to answer all the questions that the auditee may wish to pose. If they lack any of the information needed to produce an answer, they must promise to find out the facts for the auditee and must be as good as their word.

Copies of the auditor's checklist.

Some auditees request that the auditor leaves a copy of his/her marked up checklist. There need be no objection to this since it will only contain details of the auditee's own objective evidence accompanied by the auditor's doodles, flow charts, scribbles. It is always disappointing to receive such a request because the auditee's escort should have been taking the same details as the auditor on his own checklist. See also Chapter 23: Note taking.

Good manners

At the end of the exit interview, the audit team should thank the auditee for the assistance and hospitality they received throughout the audit, making it clear that achieving a meaningful and thorough audit depends most crucially upon the response of the auditee's organization. Even if there were some contentious issues and the parties had to agree to differ and try to resolve their problems at a later date, the team should still indicate that it has appreciated the auditee's co-operation.

Private conference

If the managing director, chief executive officer, president, or other senior management cannot get to the exit interview (for an external audit), the lead auditor should try to arrange a short conference with them in private. Similar remarks apply in the case of internal audits if the requisite manager was unable to be present. This is particularly important if some points of contention have arisen or if obstructive behaviour has been encountered during the audit. A short talk with senior management gives the auditor the chance to put these points across discreetly.

> A few individuals had been adopting a beligerent attitude both towards an audit team and towards the audit being performed. The lead auditor decided to seek a meeting with the auditee's chief executive officer. This was arranged and the CEO's prompt response to the question was that he most certainly did not condone the attitude of those employees and that the auditor organization's contract requirements would willingly be honoured

since they were perceived as most beneficial for the company's future. He was as good as his word. It is worth recalling that an audit does remove the rose coloured spectacles! That CEO was not fully aware of the manner in which customers might be treated by isolated individuals.

Occasionally the top man may wish to convey to the audit team information that is highly confidential and that cannot be aired in public at the exit interview (see the example in page 14-9). At this sort of private conference, only the lead auditor (perhaps accompanied by his organization's contract manager) should attend on behalf of his organization. Any information transmitted in these circumstances must obviously be treated as strictly confidential.

The auditee

The auditee must be prepared to discuss the auditor's findings and, if necessary, to refuse to sign or accept in any way a formal request for corrective action if he is unhappy about the construction which the audit team has put upon the objective evidence. He must be prepared to pursue the matter with the audit team's senior management, particularly if he feels that the audit has been performed unfairly, incorrectly or by untrained or incompetent personnel.

Some auditors are guilty of exceeding their terms of reference, of going beyond the actual requirements of the codes, regulations or standards concerned, and of trying to enforce their own subjective interpretation of the texts. In the long term, it is of benefit to the auditor himself to have these mistakes corrected. The situation can hardly improve unless the auditee is prepared to let the auditor's senior management know about their representatives' errors. A servile attitude towards the auditors is quite out of place, no matter what the organization to which the auditors belong.

References:

1. BS5750: Part 1: 1987, *Quality Systems, Part 1. Specification for design/ development, production, installation and servicing*. British Standards Institution, 2 Park Street London W1A 2BS.

2. Likert, Rensis, Harvard Business Review July/August 1959 pp 75-82.

20. The Audit Report

Let us admit it fairly, as a business people should,
We have had no end of a lesson: it will do us no end of good.
Rudyard Kipling.

The audit report is virtually a written transposition and summary of the exit interview. It summarizes the audit team's findings and conclusions as to the status and efficacy of the auditee's management policies, systems, procedures and instructions. If the exit interview has been properly conducted, there should be no problem with the audit report.

This chapter covers the content of the audit report and suggests a format for it.

Responsibility for preparation and timing

The lead auditor, together with the individual team leaders (if there were any), prepares the report. Before it is released and distributed, the entire audit team should review it to check that the statements it makes are fair, complete and true. After this review, the lead auditor signs the audit report on behalf of the entire audit team since he is ultimately responsible for both the conduct of the audit and the veracity of the audit report. The report must always be written and distributed immediately upon the return to the auditor's premises.

Content and layout

These depend on company policy, the type of audit performed, and the lead auditor's practice. As the organization and the auditors themselves become more experienced in conducting internal and external audits, both content and layout tend to evolve. One typical audit report is shown in Fig. 20.1. As a minimum, the report should state the following details.

1. The auditee's name (internal department or external company name); the dates during which the audit was performed; the location(s) at which the audit was performed (in the case of geographic dispersion, there may be a number of locations not involved in the audit) and the contract or product identification (number, name, or code).

2. The objectives of the audit; the names of the particular departments that were audited and the basis or justification for performing an audit (e.g. QA standard, regulation/statute, code).
3. The key personnel contacted during the audit.
4. The names of the audit team members and their "rank" during the audit.
5. The auditing qualifications of each auditor. (Some standards require that an auditor be qualified: ISO 9001[1], for example, requires this by virtue of the fact that auditors are performing "a specifically assigned task" whilst both API Q1[2] and BS 5882[3] require auditors to be "qualified").
6. The identification of the checklist/procedure/flow chart that was used to guide performance of the audit.
7. The results of the audit, including details of the CARs issued (these should, in any case, be attached to the report), the date of the exit interview and the attendees, any recommendations for improvements to the management policies, manual or systems, as well as any particular observations made at the exit interview.
8. A "true and fair" position statement (see Chapter 19) that is consistent with the audit objectives.
9. The audit team's appreciation for the hospitality and help received from the auditee during the audit.
10. The distribution list for the audit report.
11. A list of the attachments such as CARs, if any.

There are a number of things that *MUST NOT* figure in the audit report. These include the details listed below.

1. Deficiencies that were discovered, acted upon, and corrected by the auditee during the audit.
2. Confidential information provided during a private conference.
3. Anything that was neither discussed nor mentioned during the exit interview.
4. Trivia.
5. Subjective opinions: the report must deal only with verifiable facts.
6. Information that is to be confidential to the auditor's company, in the case of external audits (on the basis of the two-edged sword principle, requirements for corrective action in house, for example; or remarks about the performance of individual auditors during the audit).
7. Ambiguous statements.
8. Antagonistic words or phrases (avoid pointless adverbs and adjectives).

The audit report needs to be written in clear, concise and unambiguous language. If the auditee's mother tongue is not the same as the auditor's, it is particularly important to keep the wording simple and to avoid using words that could be misinterpreted. The auditor's organization will not achieve the required actions if it fails to communicate these to the auditee.

It is a very dubious practice deliberately to include — as some organizations do — loopholes that will enable the auditors to alter their position later on. If the auditor is not prepared to stand by the audit report, he has not carried out a proper management audit, and has not based his conclusions solely on objective evidence.

The audit report must *not* be a "snow job" that tries to cover up significant deficiencies still in existence when the audit team left the auditee's facilities. The "snow job" damages the auditor, the auditor's organization and the auditee.

Stop work

The audit report must state the reasons for requiring work to be stopped, the circumstances under which work can be restarted as well as the other matters listed in Chapter 19 on this matter. It is most unusual for an entire project or contract to be stopped as a result of deficiencies discovered during an audit. More often the deficiencies are confined to a particular area or set of activities. Hence the audit report must state exactly what work must be stopped (e.g. machining operations, painting, purchasing, computer aided design).

Limitations on the auditor's authority

a) Stop work:

When the auditor does not have the authority to stop work, when he has been engaged, for example, as a consultant to perform an internal audit, any situations that are serious enough to warrant further action by the auditee management must be drawn to its attention.

In Chapter 19 mention was made of an audit during which an auditee's senior engineer made some serious allegations with severe legal implications. It was not the auditor's prerogative to make judgements. Accordingly, the matter was brought to the attention of the auditee's CEO and the audit report contained the following statement:

> A senior engineer has made serious allegations that essential designs have been altered without the knowledge or consent of the senior engineer responsible, such that installed equipment could present a hazard; design codes and material standards have been misapplied; recommendations made by an expert external to the company have been disregarded such that certain equipment may be unsafe.

> It is most strongly recommended that a full and totally independent investigation be undertaken immediately by a competent person or organization external to the company to determine the veracity or otherwise of these allegations and to identify any unsafe situations that might exist.

If the auditor had not brought the situation to the attention of management he would have been failing in his legal duty of care. In this type of circumstance, it is essential that such matters be put in writing.

b) Corrective Action Requests:

If the auditor does not have the authority to issue CARs, deficient situations must be stated in the audit report together with the auditee's recommendations for rectifying them and curing the root cause. In other words the auditor records the "Non-conformity", justification reference and "Recommendations for corrective action" parts of the CAR form in the "Results" section of the audit report.

Naturally both of these situations will have been presented at the exit interview.

Supplier ratings

The audit report is generally not the place to state the supplier rating. This should be reserved for a separate communication, for the following reasons:

1. Audit reports may, in the case of some contracts, be auditable by third parties. The supplier rating system is not generally the concern of such third parties: it is a matter between the auditor's company and the supplier.
2. Most quality assurance standards (including ISO 9000 series) do not require the use of supplier rating schemes, so such schemes are not auditable.
3. The omission helps to forestall pointless and time-consuming arguments with extrinsic auditors about the company's methods of supplier rating.

Distribution channels

The audit report, its attachments and copies thereof are forwarded via the *correct* formal channels (see Chapter 9) by the lead auditor, who may attach a covering memorandum or letter, according to company practice. The master copy of the audit report should be retained by the QA department: this enables further copies to be produced at a later date if they are needed.

Fig. 20.1 Example of an audit report

HYPER-QUALITY COMPANY LIMITED

AUDIT REPORT

Auditee: S.C. Rap Metal Products Ltd
Location: Stonehenge, England
Dates: 13-15 January 1988
Purchase Order No: 1234
H-QCL Project: Candle Power Wotnots
Audit performed by: H-QCL QA department
Previous audit: 16-20 February 1987

Basis: The basis of the audit was the requirements of B.G.P.V. QA specification ABC 123 Revision 4 and the S.C. Rap QA manual.

Audit scope: A full audit comprising all S.C. Rap departments involved in execution of the purchase order.

Checklist: H-QCL standard checklist 3 was used to facilitate auditing of discrete departments of S.C. Rap.

Persons contacted: The following key S.C. Rap personnel were contacted during the audit:—

S.C. Rap	Managing director
A. Brown	QA manager
C. Dawson	Chief engineer
E. Fowler	Contracts manager
G. Hawkins	Purchasing manager
I. Jones	Works manager
K. Llewellyn	QA engineer

All of the above ladies and gentlemen attended the exit interview which was held 15 January 1988.

Audit team: Two sub-teams were formed as follows:

Team A	J. Smith	Lead auditor	H-QCL
	G. Thomson	Auditor	H-QCL
	D. Bailey	Observer	Candle Power Corp.
Team B	B. Jones	Team leader	H-QCL
	P. Davidson	Auditor	H-QCL
	R. Robertson	Observer	Candle Power Corp.

Auditor qualifications: J. Smith and B. Jones are qualified lead assessors as per the British Institute of Quality Assurance's Registration Scheme.

Page 1 of 2

Fig. 20.1 Example of an audit report (cont).

Results:

Performance of the audit resulted in the generation of one (1) corrective action request (CAR). This CAR is numbered SCR/88/1/01. No corrective action was provided at the exit interview but S.C. Rap committed to respond, within 30 (thirty) days of the exit interview with a proposal for corrective action; this is considered to be a reasonable period of time.

The following recommendation was made at the exit interview:

— Increase the internal audit frequency in all departments. Although the present practice is in compliance with contract requirements it is considered that an internal audit frequency of once in two years is inadequate.

H-QCL position statement:

On the basis of the objective evidence presented and with the exception of the matter raised in the corrective action request those departments involved in the execution of Purchase Order 1234 meet the requirements of that order and of CAN 3 Z299.1

The design control and special coatings systems are particularly impressive. The co-operation and helpfulness of all S.C. Rap personnel was most appreciated throughout the audit.

Lead auditor H-QCL

Distribution
Purchasing department (3)
H-QCL QA manager (1)
H-QCL Q.C. Representative (1)
Candle Power Corporation. (1)
Supplier file (1)

Attachment: CAR SCR/88/1/01

Page 2 of 2

The auditee's response

If the auditee does not agree with any part of the report, he must pursue the matter *promptly* with the auditor's organization. In the case of an external audit, there may be difficulties if the auditee delays his raising of objections beyond a "reasonable" time. It may be sufficient simply to notify the auditor that the auditee *will* disagree in due course and that he wishes to discuss the contentious issues in order to reach an amicable solution.

References:

1. ISO 9001 — 1987 *Quality systems — Model for quality assurance in design/development, production, installation and servicing*. Published by the International Organization for Standardization.
2. API Spec. Q1, First edition, January 1, 1985, *API specification for quality programs*. Published by the American Petroleum Institute, Production Department, 211 N. Ervay, Suite 1700, Dallas TX 75201-3688.
3. BS 5882 :1980, *Specification for a total quality assurance programme for nuclear installations*, published by the British Standards Institution, 2 Park Street, London W1A 2BS.

21. Follow-up and Close-out

It's a long road from the inception of a thing to its realization
Moliere.

There would be little point in performing audits, requiring corrective action or having a quality management system at all, if the auditee knew that the auditor would never verify that the corrective action has been efficaciously implemented.

Follow-up action

There is a commonly held and mistaken belief that the only acceptable method of performing follow-up action is by means of a re-audit of the areas found to be deficient (and known, logically enough, as a follow-up audit). This is not so and it is encumbent on the lead auditor to choose a cost effective method of verification based on the circumstances. Most quality assurance standards including the ISO 9000[1] series do not stipulate that a follow-up audit must be performed. Depending on the nature of the real root cause of the problems, the auditor's organization can check the implementation of corrective action in many ways including those listed below.

1. A re-audit of the deficient area(s).
2. Reviewing revised/new documents (e.g. procedures, training records, specifications, reports) submitted by the auditee, if such information was the problem.
3. Verification performed at the next periodic management audit (if the original findings do not demand urgent action).
4. Verification performed on the next occasion at which a representative of the auditor's organization is present at the auditee's workplace or premises.
5. Verification performed by a specialist from the auditor's organization (although depending on the nature of the corrective action required), during a routine meeting with the auditee.
6. Verifying, on receipt of the next lot of products forwarded by the auditee to the auditor's organization, that the quality problems have been eradicated (by, for example, performing a receiving inspection of items: or by checking the correctness and completeness of work before further use).

Fig. 21.1 A completed corrective action request form (CAR)

HYPER-QUALITY COMPANY LIMITED

CORRECTIVE ACTION REQUEST

Issued to:	Issued by:	No:
S.C. RAP METAL PRODUCTS LTD.	H-QC LTD.	SCR/88/1/01 Date issued: 15th Jan. 88

Non-conformity description
Stored consumables have deteriorated and are unusable. J. Smith

Auditee concurrence with non-conformity description	Non-conformity at variance with:
Signed: A. Brown Position: QA MANAGER Date: 15th January 88	CAN 37299.1 PARA 3.5.12 (b)

Recommendation(s) for corrective action
Document and implement a system for recording and monitoring of shelf life of stored items. Train staff in importance of shelf life control and in the use of the procedure. Verify proper implementation during internal audit.

Corrective action commitment As per the 'Recommendation'; system will be documented in SC Rap. QA Manual; training will be performed by QA Department and recorded in Store's Personnel Records.

Date for completion of CA: End Feb. 1988
Signed: A. Brown
Position: QA MANAGER
Date: 22/1/1988

Follow-up and close-out action
H-QCL QC Representative to check during hold point #7.

The corrective action is verified as efficacious and this CAR is now closed out.
See QC Report 88/26 of 15th March 1988
Signed: J. Smith
Position: Lead Auditor
Date: 16th March 1988

Record and acknowledgement of close-out

This is the responsibility of the lead auditor. The corrective action is closed out upon receipt of objective evidence that the corrective action has been verified as efficacious. The objective evidence may consist of an audit report, an inspection report, minutes of a meeting, a memorandum from another department with the auditor's organization or anything similar.

When this evidence has been received and found to be satisfactory, the lead auditor completes the "closed out" section of the Corrective Action Request form, specifying the objective evidence received (see Fig. 21.1). He sends a copy of the closed-out CAR (or a letter, telefax, telex, memorandum or telegram stating that the corrective action is acceptable and closed out) to the auditee via the correct formal channels. Copies are also sent to all other recipients of the audit report so that they are properly appraised of the auditee's actions. This is especially vital if there has been a regulatory body or a customer involved during the audit as observer(s). If stop work had been ordered, the lead auditor states that work may now resume. Finally, after updating the Corrective Action Request log, the lead auditor files the closed out CAR form with the audit report.

Timing

The amount of time which the auditee should be allowed in order to propose, commit himself and complete corrective action depends on many factors, among them the following:

1. the urgency of the situation (stop work, for example, is always an urgent situation).
2. the severity of the findings that require corrective action and failure costs.
3. the work status (there may, for instance, be little time left before the scheduled delivery date).
4. financial and legal considerations.

Some companies have a policy of allowing the auditee only 30 days to propose and commit himself to corrective action but generally this should be sufficient. This does *not* mean that the auditee has to *implement* corrective action within thirty days. He only has to state *when* corrective action can be completed and *what* corrective action is proposed.

If, after careful consideration, the audit team decide that the auditee's proposals for corrective action should prove efficacious if implemented, they must signify their agreement to the auditee immediately. The schedule for completion of corrective action is more likely to be a point of contention, depending on the situation at hand. If any aspect of the auditee's proposals is not satisfactory to the auditor's organization, the matter must be promptly discussed and resolved.

The schedule for verifying the implementation of corrective action will naturally follow from the agreement between both parties as to what corrective is suitable, and when it should be put into effect.

Gestation problems

If a company implements a quality assurance programme, the number of deficiencies existing at any one time in the auditee's area eventually reduces. During the gestation or development phase, however, it is quite common for the auditee to run into teething problems. The number of deficiencies that an audit would pick up during this phase may increase rather than fall in relation to the first audit. Personnel will still be learning how to work with the new systems and mistakes of the human error kind will probably heavily outnumber grave deficiencies. In the circumstances, it is asking for trouble to audit during this phase. Allow the auditee a reasonable time to get over the teething troubles without outside interference. It is good practice, however, to let the auditee know that the auditor's organization is happy to make help available if this is requested.

Fig. 21.2 General situation during a quality improvement campaign

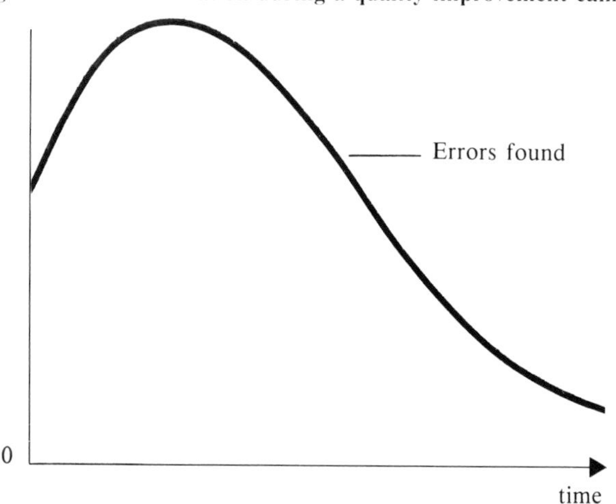

Figure 21.2 depicts the typical situation I have encountered over many years, that of a company which decides to embark on a quality assurance programme that necessitates the introduction of revised quality management systems. This curve shows what inexperienced "consultants" often do not tell the auditee or do not know themselves!

As time elapses, the number of errors found initially increases as opposed to decreasing. It is crucial for the auditor and auditee to comprehend this phenomenon fully because managers tend to complain that they have more problems than they did before the campaign started: they prefer the "old way" and do not realize that the errors are being found because the system is doing its work. Many problems that would previously have been accepted as "the way things are in our business" become highlighted as quality problems. The responsibility for reporting problems has been defined as has the responsibility for curing them; there is a standard for acceptability and rejection of a situation; there is a nonconformity and corrective action system specifically designed to bring such situations to the attention of management.

As the problems are unearthed, management has the opportunity to eradicate them permanently. Eventually the breakthrough point is reached and the number of errors found in any time period diminishes.

It is unwise and also unfair for a follow-up audit to take place during this "gestation" period since the auditee management is fully occupied in achieveing improvements. Give the auditee the chance to get through this busy time.

Fig. 21.3 Typical failure cost trend during a quality improvement campaign

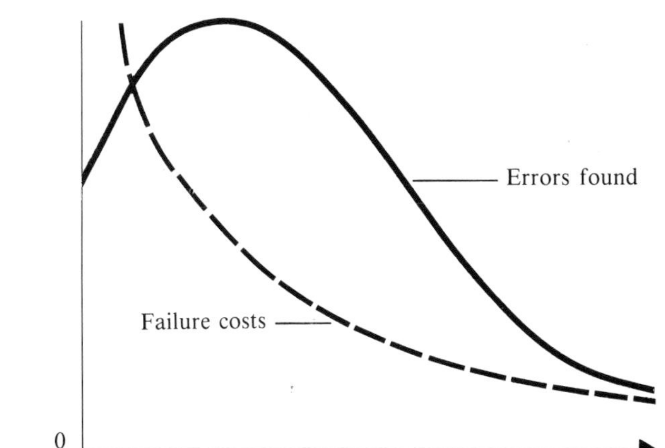

Figure 21.3 is Fig. 21.2 superimposed with the typical effect of the new systems on failure costs. These show a virtually immediate drop as soon as the system starts to operate properly. This effect has to be drawn to the attention of the auditee management (and also the auditor's management, who may not be able to understand the benefits of the audit and the quality management systems either). It is always advisable for the introduction of a quality improvement campaign to be coupled with the advent of a quality cost capture

system so that the auditee's personnel at all levels can be reassured that real benefits are indeed occurring. The risk that management may give up before the breakthrough point, a development which is unhelpful to all concerned, means that the auditor should recommend an appropriate system for obtaining the improvement performance data.

Subsequent audits

Unless there have been major changes, company re-organizations, take-overs or senior appointments, for example, subsequent audits seldom produce such dramatic results as first audits. The deficiencies they reveal tend not to be so major or so numerous. If the first audit was able to deal only with the auditee's systems (i.e. a systems audit), the next audit must deal with compliance with those systems.

When an audit team next visits an organization, it would be well advised to follow a different method of proceeding. It could, for instance, look at different areas or different sorts of objective evidence, consider different members of the same department or different product ranges or it could follow a trace-back rather than a trace-forward method. The audit team must check *quickly* that closed-out corrective action is still being implemented. The check should not take too long and the auditors should not dig around in any area with a view to finding trouble. The auditee's internal audit system should be particularly closely checked if the first audit revealed widespread problems. The internal audit system can investigate the auditee's quality programme far more thoroughly than an external audit team (see Chapter 2) and so it is extremely important to establish that it is working properly.

References:

1. The ISO 9000-1987 *Quality systems* series of standards is comprised of ISO 9000 to ISO 9004 inclusive and is published by the International Organization for Standardization (ISO).

22. The Auditor

If you can fill the unforgiving minute
With sixty seconds run,
Yours is the Earth and everything that's in it,
And — which is more — you'll be an auditor, my son!
(with apologies to Rudyard Kipling).

This chapter describes what makes a good auditor and points out some traits that do not. Figure 22.1 lists the desirable and undesirable attributes of an auditor and is in some respects quite daunting. Nobody is so perfect as to possess all of the desirable characteristics but the more the auditor has, the better.

Fig. 22.1 What to look for in an auditor

Characteristics and abilities	
Desirable	*Undesirable*
Good judgement	Injudicious
Open minded	Closed mind
Resilient	Gives in
Diplomatic	Argumentative
Self disciplined	Undisciplined
Honest	Dishonest
Unbiased	Opinionated
Listens	Deaf
Patient	Impatient
Articulate	Inarticulate
Industrious	Lazy
Can communicate to all levels	Uncommunicative
Professional	Unprofessional
Interested	Apathetic
Inquiring mind	Gullible
Analytical	Accept things at face value
Unafraid of unpopularity	Wants to be liked by all
Human	Unreasonable
Sober	Drunk/drug addict

Knowledge

The auditor must have the proper sorts of knowledge to be able to perform the audit concerned. The type of things he must know include:

1. The quality management criteria applicable for the product concerned.

These criteria may be invoked by the auditor's customer, by legislation or by his own organization: those which are applicable will depend on the audit objectives.

2. The actual words of the codes, standards and regulations.

The auditor must not read into these words his own prejudices or past experiences. It is the actual words that matter.

3. Quality management practices for the auditee's industry or business sector.
4. Contractual and legislative requirements that apply to the auditee's product.
5. The work processes that the auditee would use.

If the lead auditor does not possess this knowledge, then specialist help and guidance must be obtained for the audit.

There is a school of thought which says that if one is acquainted with the principles of auditing, one can audit any activity or department. According to this theory, a floor cleaner trained in the principles of auditing could audit, say, an accounts department or a factory. In fact, the unfortunate person would be almost certain to run into difficulties directly stemming from a lack of background experience in the area being audited. The "auditor" might not be able to interpret accounting systems or product specifications sufficiently well to judge their adequacy. An unscrupulous auditee would be able to capitalize on this situation. For this reason, the person chosen to carry out any audit should have a background of experience and expertise in the area concerned.

6. How to organize himself and plan activities.

Unless the auditor works to a plan, the audit will be chaotic and haphazard.

7. How to audit.

A person may understand all of the above points and still be unable to perform an audit because he knows nothing about the style of questioning, auditing methods, conduct and preparation required. No matter how knowledgeable the auditor may be in other respects, unless he has been properly trained in auditing, the money spent on the audit is wasted.

Training

Attendance at a formal course on auditing is one obvious method of training but this should always be supplemented in one way or another.

The value of on-the-job training depends upon the efficiency of the "experienced" auditor who is providing the training. Working with an experienced and competent auditor, either as an observer or as a member of an audit team, is extremely valuable although the trainee auditor will, in any case, probably pick up bad habits as well as good ones.

Before assigning someone to perform an external audit, it is sensible to have him participate in an internal one first, giving him a critique of his performance during that internal audit. This critique of performance should also be provided during the subsequent external audits to which the trainee is assigned. These reviews should always be given in private and not in front of the auditee.

Independence

The auditor should be independent of the activity being audited, the only exception to this being the "self-audit" which forms part of the tiering of audits, as mentioned in Chapter 2. There is often some concern about the issue of an auditor being involved in the development of the quality management systems, the contentious point being that the auditor's independence might thereby become compromised. This debate has frequently descended into arguments about whether or not the auditor is, in reality, a policeman or a consultant. If the former is the case then the audits generally are perceived as being witch-hunts and confrontational positions rapidly develop which are not conducive to progress. Both auditor and auditee erect their own Chinese walls and prepare to do battle while the product and all associated with it suffer the consequences.

From my own experience, the consultancy role has been proved time and again to be preferable. The auditor has certain concerns and knowledge that should rightly be brought to bear when the auditee is developing his systems. This has the considerable advantages of ensuring that the auditee's and auditor's legitimate interests are balanced at the outset, are appreciated by each whilst the systems become fit for purpose earlier than would otherwise be possible. The auditor has not relinquished any authority to require corrective action and the responsibility for achieving quality and implementing effective quality managemenmt systems still rests with the auditee. In fact, the auditor finds himself in an even stronger position if his audit reveals that the auditee has not heeded his advice and requirements with the effect that quality problems have emerged: the auditee was, after all, forewarned of the factors to be considered. It is the knowledge that the sanction to require corrective action exists that provides a deterrent. The mature auditor will not become compromised by giving assistance and advice.

Politics

An auditor must not allow himself to be "used" for the auditee's own political ends. His function is to assist in sorting out the auditee's systems, not to be enrolled in some covert power struggle.

Achievement

While it is not always possible to reward high achievement financially, a job well done should carry its own reward. The satisfaction of knowing that his work has been carried out professionally and thoroughly should be sufficient for any auditor.

23. The Auditee

From lowest place when virtuous things proceed,
The place is dignified by the doer's deed
William Shakespeare (All's well that ends well).

It is just as appropriate for the auditee to adopt a set of guidelines to govern his conduct as it is for an auditor to do so. Where an extrinsic audit is concerned, the auditee should ideally display as many as possible of the characteristics listed as desirable in an auditor in Fig. 22.1.

Attitude towards the audit

While it is quite natural for an auditee to feel a degree of anxiety about being audited (particularly the first time), he should try not to become too tense and nervous. The higher levels of management can set an example to their staff by being as relaxed and calm as possible throughout the audit. This will help matters to proceed smoothly and efficiently.

Extrinsic audits can assist the auditee in several ways. The audit team not only provides fresh eyes which may see a new solution to familiar problems but can also help to convince the management that action is necessary. Extrinsic auditors can also provide very useful clarification of obscure requirements in the codes, standards or regulations affecting the auditee. The auditee should recognize the potential benefits of being audited and try to ensure by his conduct that these benefits are realized.

Such guidelines apply each and every time an organization is audited. Simply because no deficiencies were found at a previous audit, it does not follow that the management systems will be passed with a clean bill of health on a subsequent occasion. Practices, standards and legislation are all subject to change, and sooner or later the time will come when the systems operating within the organization will also need to change. Hence an extrinsic auditor's findings should never be ignored, however many other auditors have found no deficiencies. No organization should consider itself above reproach: every adverse finding should be taken seriously and welcomed as providing an opportunity for improvement.

Answering the questions

Do not volunteer any information that the auditor has not requested but do not be unco-operative. Only the question in hand should be answered and it should be answered in full. Be prepared for the auditor to use silence as an interrogative tactic (see Chapter 13), and don't talk yourself into unnecessary trouble.

Bluff

It is always risky to try to bluff your way out of a tight corner. It is far better to admit ignorance if you don't know the answer to a question. Bluff is very rarely convincing and it can cause a great deal more trouble than it cures. If an auditor realises that he is being duped, his respect for the auditee will disappear: the auditor will no longer trust the auditee and will probably start to take larger samples of objective evidence, which is both time consuming and costly.

Taking action on the spot

If problems are discovered during the audit, the auditee should try to take corrrective action immediately and show *genuine* concern about addressing the real root cause. By taking action on the spot, the auditee can save embarrassing revelations being made at the exit interview or in audit reports that will be submitted to the auditee's senior management. Of course, if the problem is such that only top management can resolve it, then the auditee should forewarn the appropriate level of management of the situation before the exit interview. They may well appreciate some suggestions for corrective action.

> A peculiar and undesirable example of prompt action happened to me whilst auditing a manufacturer in a Mediterranean country. The checking of a material certificate revealed that the product's chemical composition was incorrect as per the specification. The auditee manager concerned looked aghast and put his hands to his face expressing shock. After a few moments, however, he regained his composure and, with a face of pure joy, proceeded to mark up the certificate with the specification's figures! His elation was shortlived as he was politely informed that life is not so simple.

Challenging the auditor

If it seems that the auditor has made a mistake, perhaps by scrutinizing an inadequate amount of objective evidence, the auditee should offer to show him further objective evidence to correct the misinterpretation. If in doubt about the interpretation of requirements, the auditee should ask for the contract, regulation, standard, specification or code to be re-read, in order that he may establish exactly what they are. (This is a variant of the auditor's "Show me" request.) Do not automatically assume mal-intent on the part of the auditor: auditors are only human and they *do* make the occasional mistake. As soon as it is apparent that the auditor is in this position, the auditee must draw the error to his attention. If the auditee does not do so, the auditor may be entitled to ask why the findings were not corrected at the first opportunity. It is in the interests of both the auditor and the auditee that a true and fair view is obtained.

Note taking

The auditee should make and retain his own notes, detailing the objective evidence seen by the auditor (e.g. document numbers, item identities, persons involved etc., as discussed in Chapter 11). These will be most important when the auditee has to follow up with corrective action, to answer the senior management's questions at the exit interview or to explain the nature of the deficiencies and why they *are* deficiencies to the individuals responsible both for the quality of their work and for taking corrective action to improve it. The notes will also serve to refresh his mind at a later date.

Preparation

It is important that the auditee is properly prepared for each day's auditing activities, a rule which applies especially to the escorts who will be on the spot during the audit.

Before the audit team arrives, the auditee and the escorts must be familiar with:

1. the basic references that will be encountered e.g. regulations, contract/specification or their relevant parts;
2. the relevant quality management systems and where objective evidence of their implementation is to be found;
3. the objective evidence available to demonstrate those systems' results in each of the various departments or units to be audited;
4. the auditor's checklist and programme (so that the various activities are forewarned of the auditor's concerns and approximate time of arrival and so that they can prepare accordingly).

At a later stage, the auditee must prepare for the exit interview. This involves checking up on corrective action proposals and on the result of purges, so that these do not come as an unwelcome revelation to the senior management who will attend the exit interview.

Auditee's personnel

A responsible member of a department that is being audited should try to help the proceedings along. It is *not* helpful to intervene when the auditor is interviewing a member of staff (unless it is apparent that communications have broken down). The auditor needs to talk to the person on the job to find out how well he or she knows the job, what training has been provided and so on. The department head should stay in the background unless specifically asked for some information or help. Department managers who are inexperienced in being audited commonly and mistakenly believe that in answering the auditor's questions, they are helping the situation. This is erroneous for not only is an untrue and unfair view of the actual state of things at the ordinary workplace being but they are also deluding themselves about their departments' real effectiveness and needs.

If a deficiency is found, the audit should not be allowed to develop into a witch-hunt. The head of department should not try to allocate blame or ask for excuses there and then.

> An auditee's manager started describing his schedule for the internal audits for the coming year. He had only been talking for a minute or so when a subordinate challenged him. A heated argument flared up immediately. It was obvious that the two individuals disliked each other intensely and were continually feuding. I had to ask the ''gentlemen'' to quieten down: ''Please don't spill blood on the table, it will make a mess of my checklist and not look good in the file''. This type of brawl is embarrassing for all concerned and must be prevented at all costs.

Obstructive tactics (see Chapter 15) should be stopped immediately, before they have time to sour the proceedings.

Corrective Action Requests

When a justified CAR appears to be coming the auditee's way, it is a good idea for him to prepare some proposals for discussion with the auditor at the exit interview. If the nature of the findings makes this impossible, the auditee should try to elicit an opinion from the auditor as to what the corrective action might be.

Marketing statements

The auditee must ensure that he can live up to the statements and commitments made by his salesmen. If salesmen are over-zealous and make rash representations and commitments, a company may find itself embarking on a contract which it lacks the resources to meet or which it can only fulfil by resigning itself to a loss (which may turn out to be worthwhile if it carries the promise of profitable business in the future). Whatever the company's motives, an extrinsic auditor will still expect the codes, standards and product requirements to be satisfied. It will be no defence to plead the high cost of doing what is required — if the cost of compliance is too high, the auditee should not have become enmeshed in the first place.

Obvious deficiencies

Before the audit team arrives, the auditee would be well advised to carry out a purge of the areas concerned. There is nothing worse than to receive Corrective Action Requests for obvious deficiencies such as superseded documents still in use, uncontrolled material and the like. The auditor will quite rightly assume that if the obvious is deficient, the not-so-obvious is also likely to be in a poor state. This can provide good grounds for suspecting that the auditee has a negligent attitude towards quality achievement and has a poor internal audit system.

Escorts

If at all possible, the auditee should have a trained auditor available to escort the audit team. The benefits of making such a person available are that:

1. Someone will be on hand who is able to talk the auditor's language.
2. The escort will understand what is going on, what the auditor's method is, and what the auditor is looking for.
3. The escort will be able to learn from watching another auditor in action.
4. The escort will be able to see whether or not the internal audit system needs amendment and, if so, where.

> A large company was being audited. The management decided that there would be no constant escort present at each location: each area audited would in turn accompany the audit team to the next area and leave it there to do its work. This rapidly proved to be unwise because when corrective action was required, the auditee's staff experienced difficulty in understanding the reasoning behind the auditor's request fully since the true extent of the objective evidence studied was not appreciated or recorded by them.

Regrettably, there is no guarantee that the auditor aspires to professional standards of auditing. This can obviously cause much upset to innocent staff and a knowledgeable escort can prevent this sort of occurrence. If, however, the audit team is known to be particularly proficient, an inexperienced person could also learn a lot by participating as an observing escort. The auditee should consider these points when selecting the escorts.

24. Auditing Software and Computer Applications

for all our power and weight and size,
We are nothing more than children of your brain!
Rudyard Kipling.

This is a subject that has become of increasing importance to management and to auditors. Given that in itself it is a very large subject, the following is only intended to provide some basic guidelines on how to approach an audit of a software supply project or an operating computer installation. The chapter must assume that the reader has basic knowledge of a typical computer configuration and the various pieces of equipment that it comprises such as the central processing unit, disk drives and terminals, the function of each one and how they link together.

The importance of software

Software is the life blood of a computer and if it is not fit for purpose, the computer's performance will be impaired. A computer is totally inoperative without software, which is the master for whatever work is done on it such as design or accounting calculations or the control of complex equipment. In the control of hazardous equipment, the quality of the software dictates safety, efficiency and operability. The potential size of failure costs of software quality are considerable and if one considers the product liability costs that might arise in the event of an accident, one can speculate that inadequate control of a computer installation or its software could have disastrous results for a company and could financially jeopardize it.

Problems of procurement

Most organizations tend to purchase software from software houses which now proliferate in response to the enormous demand for their products. As in every walk of life, some are of doubtful integrity. They all allege that their product is of high quality but customers often find that the software does not quite fulfil their needs and bugs are constantly being found. Quite commonly bugs are found by "user groups". (These are quasi-clubs set up by some software houses and comprise a forum at which their customers come together to discuss how to use the product. People exchange information about the operational limitations discovered in the software and how their inconvenience was avoided or mitigated. The software house will often then release a new version of the software which addresses those problems that the original version was intended to.) As in any type of purchase, the risk of using a disreputable source remains. What redress does a customer have if the software is unfit for purpose and there is a consequential loss? Most suppliers refuse to accept a consequential loss clause in their software contracts. Plainly, there is a need to control the procurement activities carefully in respect of computer installations and quality. Pre-award surveys and audits will help but many customers may find they are in no position to perform these.

This chapter is addressed to those customers who are in a position to audit their software suppliers and, although it is written in the context of a contractual situation, the principles still apply to internal audits of software development and computer usage.

The role of the auditor

Occasionally, there is some confusion between audits and reviews. A review is really an inspection of work performed in the supply of software, conducted for the purposes of acceptance or rejection, and is therefore a quality control. An audit, on the other hand, is aimed principally at ascertaining whether or not the management systems proposed for use on a software supply project will prove effective in practice and/or the compliance with those systems and the determination of their efficacy. Auditing is a preventative action taken on behalf of management to determine that the release or use of resources is justified.

If a systems audit is being performed prior to commencement of the entire project or of any phase therein, the auditor will be verifying that:

— the project is organised properly;
— the quality management systems have been properly considered;
— the necessary resources have been fully and properly budgeted;
— the time required has been carefully and properly allocated.

These last two points assist management in deciding whether or not to allocate the time and resources requested for the project, to commence the project or any particular phase and to know if the risk of loss or of avoidable failure costs has been minimized. The systems audit should be planned sufficiently ahead of the commencement of each phase to enable the project management to take any major corrective action revealed as being desirable or necessary before the initiation of the phase or project. See also Chapter 3.

If the project is required to act in accordance with the supplier's standard project control procedures, the auditor will also:

- verify compliance with those procedures;
- obtain objective evidence from the project's performance in order to determine its efficacy and, of course,
- require any corrective actions to that procedure that are considered necessary.

Depending on the audit objectives, the auditor will, during a compliance audit, verify that the management systems are being carried out such that:

- fitness for purpose is being achieved;
- fitness for purpose will be achieved;
- the contractual and legal obligations are being met and
- time and resources are being properly managed and justified.

The auditee's procedures may refer to various standards with which the personnel must comply. In this event, the auditor will also spot check to verify that the requirements of those standards are being met: this may entail obtaining and using the advice of a specialist on the audit team. One must stress again that such audits are not being performed as quasi-inspections: one purpose of the compliance audit is to ensure that one can have sufficient confidence that the auditee is complying with basic project requirements, procedures and standards. The auditee should also be monitoring his own observance of those by means of quality controls and audits and by implementing his own non-conformity and corrective action systems, if problems arise.

Conduct of the audit

Many people become very concerned and anxious when they are asked to lead an audit in a computer environment. The essential point to remember is that computer controlled operations can still be split into work phases and tasks from which the task elements and sub-elements can be extracted. Whereas the lead auditor may not have the competence or experience to determine whether, say, the content of a software design specification or of some lines of code are adequate or not, he will recognize from the task elements that they are types of information whose content must be correct. This being a key matter that the audit must address, the lead auditor can then turn to a specialist on the audit team and ask that he or she confirms whether or not the information content is correct and complete. The specialist will then use his or her skills and advise the lead auditor accordingly.

The audit method and question technique will both be as discussed in Chapters 11 and 13. Each department involved in the software supply project will be analysed as per Chapter 7; management systems will be treated as suggested in Chapter 16. Careful audit preparation as described in Chapter 9 is obviously beneficial as is the creation of a checklist or flowchart as discussed in Chapter 8.

So, for any particular task being performed in any phase of the software supply project, the basic checklist described in Fig. 8.5 or the matrix shown in Fig. 8.12, both of which are based on the four elements listed in Chapter 5, non conformity and so on should be usable.

There is no reason for an auditor who is inexperienced in computer applications or software developments to feel any more anxious than an auditor who is inexperienced in, say, food manufacturing. All this means is that specialists must be co-opted onto the audit team and directed by the lead auditor. Software development and the running of a computer installation, regardless of its size, are activities that require proper management and, as we have seen throughout this book, need to be subject to a management audit.

In performing the audit, the auditor will need to look for various controls that are peculiar to projects and to computer installations. The following sections attempt to give basic guidance on particular features to be studied.

The need for controls

Software creation has been regarded as something of a black art for many years but nowadays software engineering techniques are extensively recognized and documented. Their associated basic procedures are well understood by the professional software engineers and there remains little excuse for producing poor quality software.

In order to ensure software quality and that the computer installation function properly, it is essential that various management controls are put into place. These are:

1) controls implemented during the supply of new or revised software;
2) controls implemented during the operational life of the computer installation and the software;
3) loss controls.

Loss controls (my own phrase) are an overriding discipline that are necessary during software development, supply and operations. It is essential that consideration of loss be taken into account from the inception of a software development project so that the loss controls that will be required for the operational life will be effective.

1. Controls implemented during the supply of new or revised software.

The supply of new or revised software can be considered to be a project which passes through various discrete phases. These can be depicted as shown in Fig. 24.1 which can be seen to be very similar to the Figs. 3.2 and 9.3. It is therefore clear that a software supply project can be properly planned, indeed, if the quality of software is to be assured, it is vital that proper planning does take place. Each of the phases can be further divided into task units and hence into the various task elements and sub-elements of Chapters 5 and 25.

The auditor must verify that the software project has been broken down into the various phases, such as those shown in Fig. 24.1. (It matters not what method of planning has taken place whether it be by the use of a simple Gantt chart as shown in Fig. 24.1 or by PERT or CPM means). Each of these phases will take a certain period of time for satisfactory completion. Remembering that lack of time is a real cause of quality problems, the auditor will examine objective evidence to verify that:

— management systems for the estimation of the time budget really needed for each phase have been defined and communicated to the project management;
— the basis for planning and budgeting of time is consistent with the project objectives and customer requirements;
— the project has defined its systems for monitoring and recording its use of time and has communicated them throughout the project;
— all the foregoing management systems are implemented and are effective;
— the project analyses the areas of opportunity for time savings which are not to the detriment of quality achievement.

Fig. 24.1 A software project gantt chart

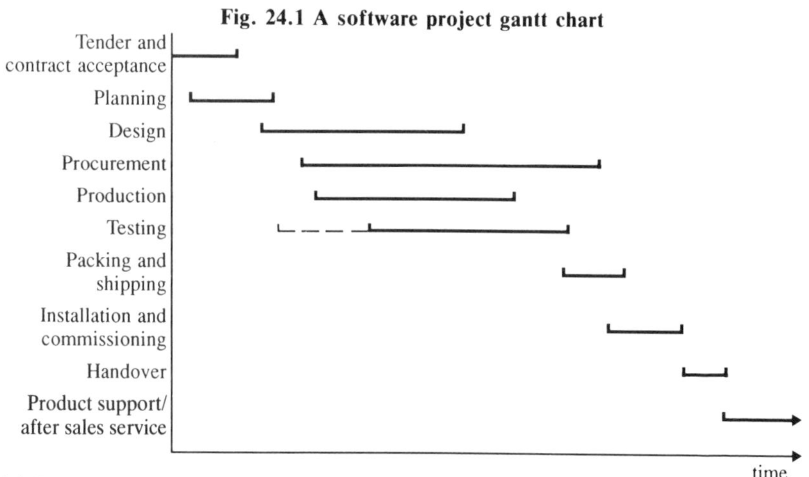

Tendering and contract acceptance

This will include the auditee's receipt of a specification from the potential customer, his decision to tender or not, his conduct of commercial negotiations and his decision to accept or reject a contact offered. To check that this phase is properly managed, the auditor will look for the documents depicted in Figure 24.2. The most important documents affecting quality are the Requirements Specification and those defining the milestones and payments. The Requirements Specification will fully describe what the customer is seeking in terms of performance and function of the software or computer installation.

Fig. 24.2 Contract documents and information required

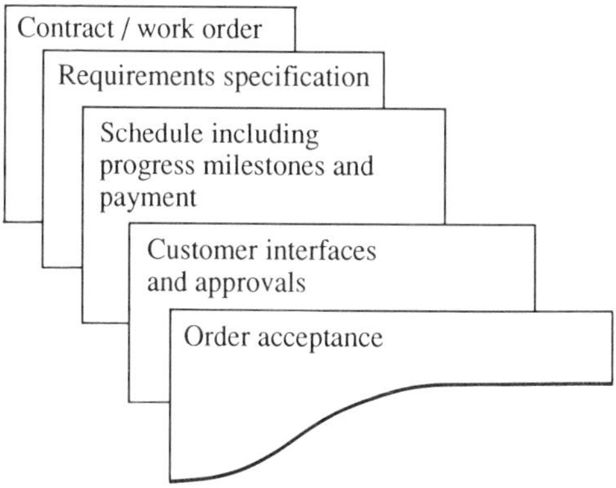

Contract / work order
Requirements specification
Schedule including progress milestones and payment
Customer interfaces and approvals
Order acceptance

One must bear in mind that many customers do not have the technical know-how to prepare an adequate Requirements Specification fully. In such circumstances, it is incumbent on the software supplier to institute a procedure whereby all of the key questions which need to be addressed (to obtain a complete and correct Requirements Specification) have been raised with the customer in an honest fashion: this should be done as normal part of the tendering procedure. Regrettably, there has been a tendency over the years for rogue software suppliers to regard an unsophisticated customer as an open cheque book. Responsible and reputable software suppliers have a procedure whereby the customer's operational use and user environment circumstances are carefully analysed. Such analysis is performed together with the customer and enables the supplier to prepare an adequate specification from which the cost and time impact for successful supply can then be accurately estimated and provided to the customer. It is of no help to either the vendor or the customer to find that the Requirements Specification had been inadequately conceived such that extra costs are incurred to the detriment of all. The Requirements Specification also forms key information upon which the supplier will decide whether or not he has the capability of satisfying the customer's needs and whether or not to enter into a contract. The decision to enter into a contract must be based on the supplier being fully aware of his capabilities in relation to the customer's needs.

The auditor will look for objective evidence demonstrating that:

— a system, for ensuring that careful review of customer enquiries is performed, has been developed and communicated to the project;
— that system is followed and that commitments made to customers are consistent with the auditee's known capabilities;
— only authorized competent persons are able to negotiate with the customer.

The various milestones for marking the progress of the project and the payments associated with each one must be properly defined. This enables both customer and supplier to predict their respective cash flow requirements and for each to know the circumstances under which they will agree that fitness for purpose is being achieved. The customer may wish to become involved with the software supplier as the project proceeds. These interface arrangements, which may be for the purpose of reviewing design work or witnessing performance tests, must be adequately defined and will probably be linked to milestone payments.

The auditor will examine objective evidence to show that:

— contractual milestones and interfaces have been properly considered, defined and agreed between the respective parties.

For a contract to be legally binding, there must be both an order placed by the customer and the supplier's acceptance of that order returned to the customer. The terms and conditions of contract offer and acceptance should be consistent and agreed. In the event of any differences between either parties' terms and conditions, the courts of law will normally uphold those definitions furnished last, whether by customer or by the software supplier, to be the ones to prevail in the event of a dispute arises. For this reason, the auditor will examine objective evidence to verify that:

— a system has been developed and communicated to the project, to ensure careful review of the contract prior to acceptance in order to verify that only the features tendered for and negotiated are included in that contract;
— that system is followed and contractual commitments made to customers are consistent with the auditee's known capabilities and
— only authorized, competent persons are able to commit the supplier to supply software.

One can readily see that for software supply contracts, the management controls are no different from those in normal commercial contracts involving the supply of hardware or services. The auditor will use the unit concept and task element analysis when auditing each of the tasks involved in the tendering and contract acceptance phase.

Planning

Most of the planning should have occurred before the contract signature — after all, if the supplier has not planned how the project will be run, how could an honest tender be made? Fig. 24.3 shows the principle matters that the auditee should have considered and planned if the software development project is to be properly executed. The overall schedule, discussed above, will indicate the major milestones that have been agreed between customer and auditee: from these milestones the particular internal ones used by the project for monitoring its progress should have been defined. The auditor must always be wary if the main schedule shows a lengthy "maintenance" phase since this is often a sign of an auditee who intends to finish developing and de-bug his product while the customer's operational phase proceeds and consequently to charge the customer for the privilege of doing so. Frequently, this has the effect of the customer paying more than once for the same product and is a common form of fraud in the software business. Legitimate product support and aftersales service are entirely different matters since they help the customer to obtain better service from, and understanding of, a product which is fit for purpose and has complied with the agreed requirements.

Fig. 24.3 Principal matters to be planned

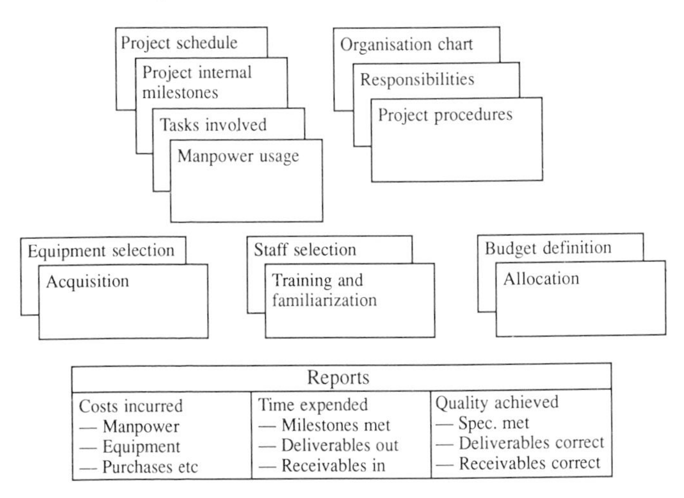

The various phases will contain specific tasks to be performed which should be properly defined. Associated with each one, the responsibilities and limits of authority should have been documented. The auditor will examine objective evidence and verify that the organizational matters raised in Chapter 4 have been performed by the auditee. This includes verifying that:

— the auditee has planned his organization by producing a chart which contains all of the principle functions needed and their relationship to each other;
— job descriptions and specifications for each of those key tasks have been produced and communicated to the persons assigned to them.

Detailed planning of each task should be by means of procedures describing the quality management systems which are to be used in accomplishing the tasks. The auditor will verify that that these have been produced and that they appear effective. The reader will remember that proof of efficacy can only be obtained by compliance auditing.

Principle matters concerning organization are shown on Fig. 24.4. When reviewing the organizational arrangements, the auditor should verify that those features have been incorporated into the project procedures and set up. An example of an organization chart is shown in Fig. 24.11.

Fig. 24.4 Principal matters for the project's organization

Management	*Independence*
• Determines policies and budgets • Reviews and approves plans and procedures • Selects and appoints staff • Reviews and approves controls' results • Requires management audits • Authorizes corrective action	• In review and approval of information/documents • In testing and approval of new/changed software • Of audits • In following-up corrective actions identified

A major reason for quality problems in the development of software is inadequate consideration of the manpower build-up that will be required as the project progresses. Professional and modern project management practice is to summarize graphically the planned and actual build-up of manpower. This is often called "S Curve" and an example is shown in Figure 24.5. The cumulative total can be seen to form an elongated "S".

The auditor will examine objective evidence to verify that:

— systems for the estimation of the manpower budget really needed for each phase have been defined and communicated to the project management;
— the basis for manpower planning and budgeting is consistent with the project objectives and customer requirements;
— the project has defined its systems for monitoring and recording its use of manpower and has communicated them throughout the project;
— all the foregoing management systems are implemented and are effective;
— the project analyses the areas of opportunity for manpower savings which are not to the detriment of quality achievement.

The timing necessary to create availability of manpower, as and when required, must be carefully thought through by the auditee and based on solid estimates that are consistent with the tasks to be performed. As stated in Chapter 18, lack of resources is a real cause of quality problems and this is particularly true for software development projects, many of which have failed over the years because their managements did not adequately consider manpower build-up, with the result that cash flow requirements had been underestimated.

Fig. 24.5 A typical project 'S'-curve

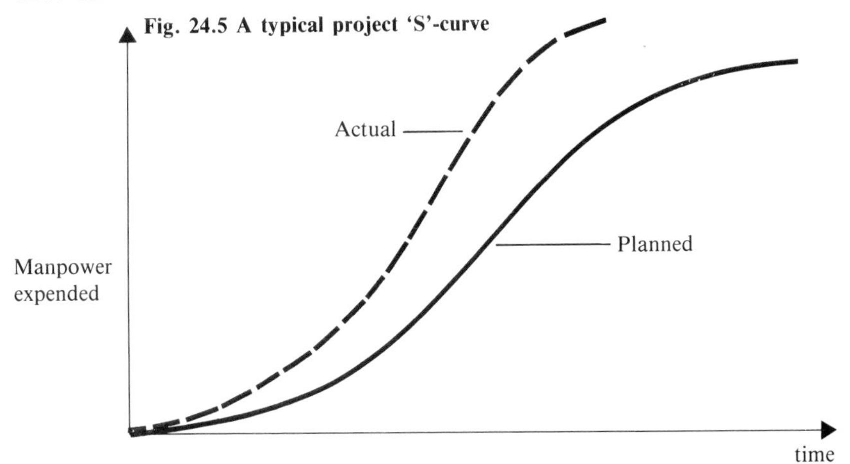

A person should have been assigned to each task and the "PERSON" sub-elements of Chapter 5 can be applied. Prior to commencement of work, it is often advisable for the project team to be given training and familiarization not only with the project and contract requirements but also with the specific techniques, management systems and skills that will be used on the project.

Just as for any other audit, the auditor will examine objective evidence and confirm that those matters raised in Chapter 5 and 25 have been planned and implemented.

In some cases, the customer or end user may want the software to run on equipment of a different type or make to that which the vendor has. It is important to verify that the auditee has correctly selected the computing equipment which will be used to assist with the software development. If the equipment does not have the same capability, condition, configuration etc. as the user's, the auditee will need to have made provision for the acquisition either by purchase, lease or rent of the right type of equipment. This will incur expenditure of money which should have been properly estimated and allocated.

The auditor will examine objective evidence to verify that:

— management systems for the estimation of the equipment budget really needed for each phase have been defined and communicated to the project management;
— the basis for equipment planning and budgeting is consistent with the project objectives and customer requirements;
— the project has defined its systems for monitoring and recording its use of equipment and has communicated them throughout the project;
— all the foregoing management systems are implemented and are effective;
— the project analyses the areas of opportunity for equipment savings which are not to the detriment of quality achievement.

The sum total of all these aspects of planning, namely, personnel build-up, equipment utilization and acquisition costs will form a major part of the overall budget that the auditee will require in order to develop the software correctly for the customer. The auditee will examine objective evidence to verify that:

— management systems for estimating the overall budget for all the resources really needed for each phase have been defined and communicated to the project management;
— the basis for planning and estimating that overall budget is consistent with the project objectives and customer requirements;
— the project has defined its systems for overall monitoring and recording of its use of those resources and has communicated them throughout the project;
— all the foregoing management systems are implemented and are effective;
— those resources and budget have been allocated by management that is authorized to do so (i.e. management that is acting within the constraints and authorities of its own job descriptions);
— the project analyses the areas of opportunity for overall resource savings which are not to the detriment of quality achievement.

Vital aspects of planning concern the performance monitoring of the project as it progresses. This includes planning feedback reports not only on cost achievement, schedule achievement but also on quality, as depicted in Figure 24.3. It is peculiar that many project managers avidly specify reports concerning the cost and time expended but rarely preplan feedback to tell them whether or not that expenditure is achieving the desired effect. It is futile to believe that one is within budget and time if the quality is wrong. To execute its duties properly, the project management must know whether fitness for purpose is constantly being achieved at each milestone, as the project progresses and whether it will be achieved when the project concludes. This fitness for purpose must be achieved as far as possible on a right first time basis. Naturally this means that management need to be forewarned of any quality problems that can result in wasted cost or wasted schedule. The type of feedback required, therefore, not only derives from inspection or test of completed work (which is after the fact and, as the saying goes, cannot put quality into a product) but also from quality management audits which will inform the project manager whether any problems either exist or are likely to develop by virtue of the manner in which the project team is working. The auditor will look for proof that:

— the project has defined its management systems for overall monitoring and reporting of its actual quality achievement and has communicated them throughout the project;
— the particular points at which quality achievement will be ascertained have been defined;
— the detailed methods to be used for each monitoring activity have been defined and that responsibilities for that monitoring have been assigned and communicated throughout the project;
— the foregoing management systems are implemented and are effective.

Fig. 24.6 Various software design considerations

System architecture	*At module level*	*General*
• Hierarchy of software modules • Program/Data flow charts* • Data dictionary* • Definition of each module • Interfaces with other software systems • Hardware configuration • Central processing unit constraints • Data storage requirements • Response and performance levels	• Screen layouts • Keyboard commands • Response times • Reports, queries, print-outs needed • Authorities/security • Priorities • Interfaces, data transfer protocols • Data files involved • Hardware requirements • Central processing unit constraints	• Audit trail to Requirements Specification • Programming language • Standards & Conventions • Design quality controls (reviews, approvals, walkthroughs etc) • Control of design changes • Corrective actions • Procedures and proforma • Library controls

* if used

Design

This might be the first major phase for which an audit team needs, within its midst, appropriate specialists who can provide advice on whether or not the content of information, for example, is correct. Various features that need to considered in the design of software are listed in Figure 24.6. It is beyond the scope of this book to describe the content of each one and the reader should peruse any of the standard texts that are available. The auditor can consider design to be a process and then analyse its task elements (which will generally consist of person, equipment and information only) and the sub-elements for each, as stated in Chapter 5.

The auditor should also verify that the auditee's design management systems ensure that the loss and software controls outlined later in this chapter are fully considered and incorporated into the software design. Depending on the audit objectives, the auditor will, naturally, then verify that those systems are both implemented and effective.

Procurement

If the software project team needs to procure any hardware or services in order to perform its duties, then the normal types of control used in any commercial procurement situation should have been carried out. Once again the auditor is well advised to remember that procurement constitutes a set of tasks each of which can be broken into the applicable task elements, described in Chapters 5 and 25. Whereas there may not be a physical item involved at the workplace of certain of those tasks, the remaining ones and their sub-elements will still apply. Figure 24.7 summarizes the principle information that is usually created.

Fig. 24.7 Principal procurement information

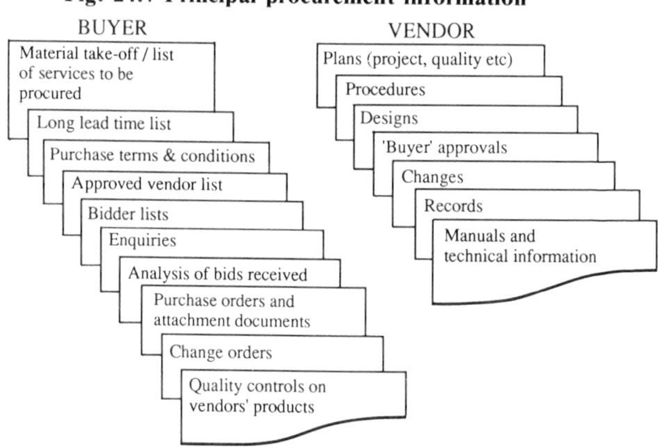

Production

The production phase principally involves the coding of the software in accordance with the design output. It consists of a set of tasks each of which can be broken into the applicable task elements etc. Assistance and support from a specialist on the audit team may be required to audit the sub-elements involved in this part of the software development project.

Testing

Since software cannot be seen, its testing is a vital check on quality achievement. The problem in relation to software testing was neatly encapsulated in the saying attributed to Edsger Dijkstra:

"Software testing reveals defects but not the absence of defects".

As for any other type of test, a test plan is essential. The software test plan should, however, specify:

a) tests designed to verify that the software does what it is meant to do;
b) tests designed to verify that the software does not do what it is not meant to do.

The latter is particularly important because unforeseen peculiarities could be most inconvenient or could, perhaps, result in an unsafe situation (in the case of control of hazardous plant, for instance.) As a minimum, the test plan must state who performs each test; the testing methods to be used; equipment required for each test (perhaps a simulator may be involved) and the reports to be generated. It must contain or reference detailed procedures that describe each particular test and the method of performance. The content of reports required, authority for preparation and approval might be contained in auditee's procedures as a standard: the auditor should verify this point.

It is extremely beneficial for the auditee to develop the test plan in conjunction with the design so that as a particular feature of the software is designed, the designer is constrained to state how that design feature will be verified as being efficacious. It is important that the auditee plans before performing tests. If this is not done, there is the risk that the software testing will descend into a mish-mash of people playing at computer terminals. Test plans are required for each level of the software being developed or changed. Those levels are:

a) tests on individual modules;
b) integration tests;
c) tests on the software system;
d) tests to verify compatibility and effectiveness of the software and hardware interfacing.

The auditor must examine objective evidence to ascertain that each level of test and each test is covered by a procedure. If the auditor is performing a systems audit prior to any design or testing being performed, then it is important to verify the existence of a set of plans and procedures describing how these activities are to be controlled and accomplished, as described above.

Packing and shipping

The auditor should verify that the arrangements for packing and protecting the software during shipping and delivery to the customer have been properly considered and planned. The auditor can use the task elements when analysing the efficacy of the tasks and their associated management systems.

Installation and commissioning

As with the other project activities, installation and commissioning contain functions that can be broken into the task elements and thereupon thoroughly planned, executed and audited. The auditor should look for plans which will describe how the software is to be installed onto the customer's or user's computer and how it will be commissioned. This is particularly important if both customer and auditee are to be convinced that the software quality is as required.

In some circumstances, the customer may have to install and commission the software without the supplier's presence. If this is so, the supplier should have provided the necessary information (for example, user manuals, instruction sheets, procedures, "help" facilities within the software) that will enable the customer to do so successfully. That information should have been controlled as per its sub-elements, contained in Chapter 5. The auditor will verify that the quality management systems required to furnish that information have correctly addressed those sub-elements.

Handover

The auditor should verify that handover activities have been carefully planned and agreed between the customer, user and supplier. This is because the results obtained from handover tests will establish a base line from which any warranty claims or deterioration in the computer system itself can be monitored and, as such, normally has a considerable influence on the final payments to be made by the customer to the software supplier. A smooth handover which reveals fitness for purpose in the software and its compliance with the contractual requirements is the acid test of the project's quality management systems. Handover is the point at which each party will want to be convinced that everything is right. The handover activities also establish a datum that will be of great assistance to the user or customer in maintaining an effective loss control system, described later in this chapter.

Product support and after sales service

All five task elements are present during this phase. The auditor will ascertain that the after sales service has been designed and that the quality management systems that will be required to support the foreground activities are efficacious, as described in Chapter 25.

2. Controls implemented during the operational life of the computer installation and the software.

During the operational life of software and the computer installation, controls are required for hardware, software, data and documents. The principle process controls for hardware amount to correct running and operation of the computer and its peripherals, together with the management systems required to support and maintain its correct condition. These include condition monitoring and planned maintenance.

Since much operational software is retained on magnetic media, a principle feature to require attention relates to the care of master tapes and disks, as well as copies used for day-to-day operation. It is bad practice and extremely risky to use the master copies of software in a day-to-day environment although in certain circumstances, particularly in small applications, this is not an uncommon practice. Where programs are of high value, the auditor should verify that there is proper protection of the masters. Then, in the event that the operating copy should become damaged in some way, a new working copy can be promptly made from the master. In the case of data, the auditor should verify, for batch processing in particular, that regular back-up copies are made so that if some transaction data has been lost, it will only be a loss restricted to the time period extending back to the previous back-up. As is touched upon later in this chapter, the auditor must ascertain that proper library controls are being implemented to prevent the risk of loss to software and data.

The major concern in the day-to-day running of the machine is that the correct and complete output is obtained. In a batch processing environment, this is totally dependent on the completeness and correctness of the input, once the fitness for purpose of the actual software and hardware has been proved. It is only in exceptional circumstances that incorrect output might be obtained even though correct input has been supplied. For present purposes, it is assumed that the process hardware and software is completely reliable. The auditor will verify that the quality management systems for the maintenance of that reliability exist, have been communicated to those that need them, are implemented and are effective.

Fig. 24.8 lists various methods that are used to ensure completeness and correctness of input and output. These types of controls are fully described in standard basic texts on data processing, which the reader who wishes to know more should study. The principle matters that the reader should note are that:

a) various of these methods require human intervention (known as MANUAL controls) such as the checking of a printout to verify that the output is consistent with the input;
b) certain of these methods are performed by the software itself (SOFTWARE controls). (An example of the latter might be in relation to validity parameters: if, for example, some technical software has been designed to calculate the flow rate of a fluid through a pipeline, the software can be programmed to reject an input which states the pipeline to be of negative diameter; in the case of dates of purchasing transactions, the software can be programmed to reject a date such as 45th September.)

Fig. 24.8 Various methods for ensuring completeness and correctness of input and output during the operational phase

Method	*Completeness*	*Correctness*
Batch totals	i o	i o
Checks of print-outs	i o	i o
Computer sequence checks	i o	
Matching	i o	i o
Verify data preparation		i
Edit checks		i
Validity parameters		i
Control totals	o	o
Rejection control	o	o
Reconcile master & transaction files	o	o

Audit methods that can be used in the case of manual controls and software controls are shown in Fig. 24.9. When preparing for the audit, the lead auditor must determine the methods that he will use. The first three, relating to manual controls, have been outlined in Chapter 11 within the section "Obtaining objective evidence". A brief description of the last three audit methods that relate to software controls is detailed below.

a) Visual comparison:

By this method, the auditor will compare a printout of the actual software used with a master copy of the correct software which is kept in a secure environment and used solely for the purpose of auditing. This can be a rather lengthy process which entails a risk of error by the auditor in missing differences between lines of codes of the two copies. An alternative method is to load an audit copy of the software onto the computer with an instruction for the computer to highlight any differences between the audit copy and the one in use.

Fig. 24.9 Audit methods for manual and software controls

Audit Method	*Manual controls*	*Software controls*
Visual examination of objective evidence	●	
Manual reperformance	●	
Observe reperformance	●	
Visual comparison with audit copy		●
Reperformance		●
Audit pack		●

b) Re-performance:

By this method, the auditor asks the auditee to re-run the software in his presence. The correct data is loaded into the machine and the auditor then verifies that the same results are obtained. This can also be done by loading that data and comparing the results obtained when it is processed, using an audit copy of the software with that obtained from the software edition that is in use. This method is not always suitable for auditing of computer operated plant.

c) Audit pack:

By this method, the auditor uses special software which has been produced solely for the purpose of auditing. This software comprises a set of data or programs to be processed by the computer, the results of which are pre-known to the auditor. Alternatively, a simulation pack which creates known situations is used. If there are any irregularities in the results, the auditor will investigate the matter further. One particular problem with this method is that audit packs can cost a lot of money to develop and it is often only large companies or computer applications which can justify their creation. This particular method is much favoured these days by accountancy firms.

3. Loss controls.

Loss is an overriding discipline that must be an integral part of both the software supply project and the operational life of the software and computer installation. I have found it convenient to categorize loss as being comprised of six principle types, each of which is further described below. They are:

a) damage;
b) deterioration;
c) sabotage;
d) theft;
e) fraud;
f) change.

Each of those six can afflict the hardware, software, data and documentation used. Plainly, loss controls are important.

Damage

One must not only consider damage that can be caused by fire, flood or tempest but also damage which can be caused by the working environment. This might include nuisances in the form of high or low humidity; dust or airborne particulate matter; stray electro-magnetic fields that can damage magnetic media; high static electricity levels; high temperature or low temperature; vibration, which damages disk drives and other mechanical pieces of equipment. The reader will recall that "environment" is one of the sub-elements of "equipment": see Chapters 5 and 18.

At various points of operation and development, the auditor will check the arrangements that are designed to prevent any environmental nuisance from occurring. (The number of points at which the arrangements will be checked will depend on the audit objectives.) This activity will include:

— checking the management systems that control the support utilities required to maintain correct environmental conditions;
— checking the arrangements for fire protection and detection.

The latter will be required at each work station, in the computer room (in the case that the auditee is operating a mainframe or large mini computer system) and also within the library itself (where magnetic tapes, disks, master listings, print outs and log books are retained). Any damage in such areas can obviously lead to a high degree of financial loss both directly and indirectly as a consequence of the value of the software's, information's and data's content.

Deterioration

Things gradually deteriorate or wear out with use. This is particularly true of disk drives and magnetic tapes that may be continually loaded and unloaded from a computer. Disk drives and printed circuit boards have a finite life and they require constant maintenance. The auditor should verify that the auditee is operating a satisfactory, planned maintenance system, as well as a condition monitoring system, to cover all equipment used.

A log should be maintained by the auditee so that the number of times that a particular magnetic tape has been loaded on and off the computer is known. There should be arrangements to ensure that prior to the predicted end life of the tape, its contents are copied onto a new tape to prevent the risk of loss.

Sabotage

One is not dealing here primarily with sabotage caused by explosive devices although this must not be overlooked (particularly in the case of military or other types of secure installations that could be a prime target for terrorism). A more insidious type of sabotage occurs through the "software bomb" which takes the form of someone gaining access to a computer program or data, leaving some coded instructions designed to do damage to that software at a future point in time. Software bombs may be an action by a disgruntled employee. It is, therefore, generally desirable that any disaffected employee or any person who appears about to resign from a company, have his or her authorization to use the computer system or to access any part of the software, withdrawn immediately. If an employee decides to resign, the auditee may well be advised to ask the person to leave immediately and provide him with the appropriate remuneration due. These actions are as much to protect the innocent employee from the finger of suspicion as they are to protect the company from the risk of a software bomb. Accordingly, this will affect the auditee's personnel policies.

The auditor will examine objective evidence that demonstrates that:

— an effective policy exists, concerning the authorization or removal of access to software in the case of new employees or resignations;
— an effective policy exists, concerning positive vetting of new staff prior to engagement and assignment to sensitive situations;
— an effective policy exists, regarding constant monitoring of staff in sensitive situations;

— quality management systems have been developed for implementing each of those policies and have been communicated to those charged with implementing them;
— those policies and quality management systems are implemented and are effective.

Apart from careful monitoring and selection of staff, other essential controls include the maintenance of log books and signatures of personnel authorized for access to or use of specific tapes, disks, print outs, programs and so on. These should all be maintained in a secure environment within the library and there should be a regular check by the auditee to ensure that unauthorized alterations to the software have not taken place. In the event that access to the computer or its software can be obtained from an external site via a telecommunications link, there must be careful control over the issuing and security of passwords and over the authorization that each potential user might have to access any part of the system. The points to verify have been outlined below under "Theft".

Theft

Theft of hardware and hard copy can be prevented by normal security controls at a reception desk, for example. However, software or data theft can also occur by unauthorized transmission. Industrial espionage is a genuine problem these days and it is somewhat irritating to find that a new suite of software, a new design for a product or the company's accounts have been stolen by or on behalf of somebody outside one's own organization.

The auditor will verify that:

— unauthorized printouts of programs and data are prevented;
— there are controls as to who can log into the computer, which include the use of the security clearances, confidential passwords and user names;
— unauthorized transmission of data or software through telecommunication links is prevented;
— alterations to programs, standing data or transaction data are only performed by authorized people on the basis of signed management approvals. This in turn means a close monitoring of access to libraries to obtain master disks, tapes and other media that contain software;
— there is controlled access to every part of the computer installation and controlled use of the programs and data that the system may contain;
— management systems to achieve the above have been defined, documented and communicated to those who need them;
— those systems are implemented and are effective.

Theft can also occur by electronic eavesdropping on stray electro-magnetic radiations that are caused whenever a computer is operating or a data transmission line is working. This has particular significance for military and high security installations. With this in mind, the software development or computer operation might need to take place within a secure bunker, for example, that is completely electro-magnetically screened and secure; transmission may need to be scrambled. In these circumstances, the auditor may also wish to assess the protection systems that prevent the stray radiations being picked up by a foreign or potentially hostile power. Other matters that may require verification by the auditor have been listed in the section "Sabotage" above.

Fraud

Fraud is recognized as being a modern white-collar crime and is purportedly a "business" with one of the highest growth rates. It can occur either by alteration of master tapes and programs or by alteration of standing data: it can also occur through improper use of, or access to, the computer.

To deter fraudulent acts, the auditee should maintain log books recording who has had access to any part of the software or data as well as formal authorizations for such access. Naturally, the auditee should also be regularly checking that programs and data have not been altered. The auditor must verify that such arrangements are being made and are properly maintained. The other points which are listed under "Theft" and "Sabotage", above, should also be checked by the auditor.

Where fraud could occur during actual use of a computer through batch processing, the operational controls, described earlier in this chapter, must be verified.

Change

Software and data can be changed either deliberately or inadvertently. Deliberate change is for the purposes of fraud, theft or sabotage which have already been mentioned. Inadvertent change often arises from good intentions: it is not uncommon, for example, to find that a programmer, trying to help the users, may alter a program, but in so doing has introduced other problems into the running of that software. Hence there is a need to maintain a tight control on the configuration of the software. Inadvertent loss arising from change also requires:

— the implementation of rigid controls in the library;
— planned authorizations regarding change to the software;
— the maintaining of log books;
— strict control over personnel authorized to alter standing data that is maintained by the system;
— independent auditing of all of these controls.

Loss can also occur when parts of the hardware such as printed circuit boards are changed. Accordingly, when the computer system is being maintained, it is important that the auditee ensures that the same type of spare parts as in the original machine have been used. Without such control, there is the possibility that the software and hardware interface may become impaired.

Organization requirements for loss control

Figure 24.10 lists various organizational requirements that should have been considered by the auditee in preventing loss. These features need to be verified by the auditor when looking at organization charts, job descriptions, job specifications and procedures. The various loss controls, the four task elements and the associated sub-elements are interrelated. Controls over the distribution of information, for example, are identical to analysing the problem of controlling access to that information, which helps to prevent several of the categories of loss; control over the checking and the edition of information reduces the risk of loss caused by change; an important attribute of the people working on the system, or developing the software, is honesty and integrity. The reader will by now appreciate that applying the four task elements and considering the implication of the key sub-elements is essential if the risk of loss is to be minimized.

Fig. 24.10 Principal organizational features for loss control

Management	*Authority*	*Independence*
• Determines policies and budgets • Reviews and approves plans and procedures • Selects and appoints staff • Reviews and approves controls' results • Requires management audits • Authorizes corrective action • Authorizes development of new/changed software and documents	• Operators not permitted: — to write/amend programs or system software; — access to program listings • Development staff not allowed unauthorized use of computer • Controlled access to: — library — computer room — terminals	• Library staff independent of operations/ development staff. • Independent audit of library controls • Independent tests of new/changed software • Independent audits • Independent follow-up of corrective actions identified

Organization charts

Fig. 24.11 depicts a rather large data processing department. Various of the organizational features described in this chapter can be seen in that diagram. An example of this would be to study the functional independence between the between the operations staff, the programming staff and analysis staff and to compare the independent positions of the audit and the library from each other. Of course, it is not adequate to just to look at such a chart, the auditor also needs to ascertain the names of the people charged with the responsibilities of each position in order to check that the same person has not been assigned tasks that could lead to a conflict of duties.

Fig. 24.11 Organization chart — a large data processing department

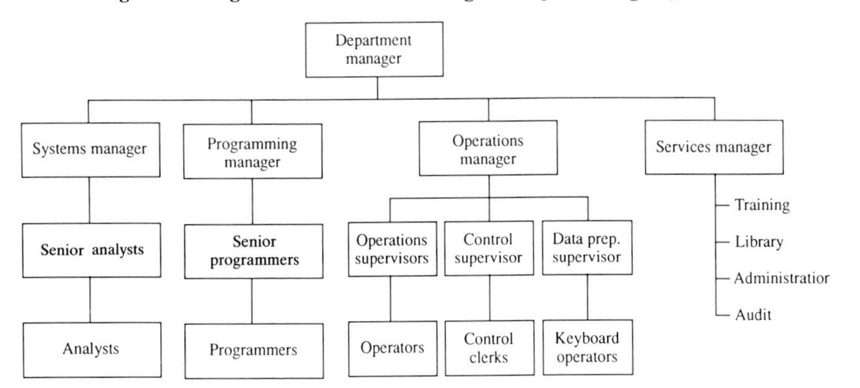

25. Auditing Service Companies

Serve and thou shalt be served.
If you love and serve men, you cannot,
by any hiding or stratagem, escape the remuneration.
Ralph Waldo Emerson.

Introduction

Services are prevalent in all companies regardless of the industrial sector in which they operate. They permit specialization and are intended to reduce unit costs, thus increasing efficiency for the customer/user. To achieve this state of affairs, they must be efficient in themselves. They can only succeed by not incurring failure costs and are thus obliged to prevent quality problems associated with their own work, just as manufacturing functions are constantly required to.

Service companies are no different from any other. They have their quality problems, company-wide and in individual departments. Those problems also have their roots in the six real causes described in Chapter 18 and, just as for any other industry, services can benefit from management audits.

The importance of service quality

The service sector of all nations' economies forms an ever increasing percentage of most countries' gross national product and, since it is comprised of human beings possessing all the usual frailties, it creates an ever increasing percentage of each nation's failure costs. In the civil services, the failure costs are funded by the tax burden and one can only speculate how much one's own nation's income taxes could be reduced if those failure costs were reduced by 10%, 20%, 50% or whatever, if only as much attention were paid to quality improvement in these sectors as has been the case in many manufacturing industries. Alternatively, one might wonder how many more hospital beds and surgical operations would be possible if the money saved invested immediately in a nation's health service.

The quality of service received from departments within one's own company and from external companies is a major factor in deciding competitive advantage. A better service can mean a better price; reduced marketing; repeat business; increased market share; increased profit and return on investment;

increased share value. Concentrating on service is an area of opportunity for every company. Auditing can help to identify the opportunities.

What is a "service"?

The traditional view of services is that they are comprised of activities such as banking, insurance, postal delivery, entertainment, tourism, transportation and the security sectors of the economy. Many other businesses also provide services including for example, design, storage, specialized manufacturing, product repair, all of which would have been found at one time in-house at manufacturers' premises — indeed, many still are. Some activities are called services but comprise the delivery of a tangible product. Vending machines, for example, deliver a product and are more accurately described as process equipment in the way that power station boilers are. A vending machine is a robot that acts as a shop, delivery system and factory combined. It requires human tending and servicing just as a production line robot does. Plainly, services are "work done for someone else"[1], regardless of any particular economic sector. One could view a motor manufacturer as a service company in that it does something for someone else. There is a tangible "item" involved.

Not all services result in a tangible product, however. Transportation of items or people does not cause them to exist, it merely removes them from one location to another; an insurance company does not cause its customers to exist. It does provide them with certain knowledge, information about which can be communicated in a document called a policy whilst contractual agreement about this information can be denoted by the issuing of a certificate.

At the time of writing this book, no definition of "services" was available from the ISO 9000[2] series of quality systems standards or the available ISO 8402[3], which is at least consistent with its omission of a definition for the term "product". These omissions are curious in that both products and services are supposed to be the raison d'etre for quality achievement efforts and quality management systems. The Oxford English Dictionary, however, contains the useful explanation that "service" is "conduct tending to the welfare or advantage of another", which contains obvious overtones of a quality including safety, price and timeliness. Bearing in mind that both a company and an individual are each considered in law to be a "person" and putting together the above, I consider a service to be:

> "Work performed for someone else in a manner that tends to the welfare or advantage of that person".

This definition provides some useful guidance for both auditor and auditee alike, containing a prescription that can be applied to everybody's work in all companies by denoting a desirable attitude to adopt. The definition does not restrict its application to contractual instances and is, thus, also consistent with my long standing view that customers are those who receive the result of one's efforts and suppliers are those whose efforts are directed at satisfying one's needs. (The reader will recall that any task unit must define its suppliers and its customers: see Chapter 7.)

What is "quality"?

As always, quality can be considered as comprising an amalgam of fitness for purpose, compliance with customer requirements and realization of customer expectations. Quality and price are not synonymous: they never are, even in the case of manufacturing. In all businesses, quality and price are inextricably entwined to form the concept of value for money which is a perception of the customer: so too with services, hence the importance of customer expectations. When considering value for money, the customer certainly expects the service to tend to his welfare and advantage for if it does not, the service will not be sought. Value for money and his own welfare and benefit are, therefore, important constituents of customer expectation. As in any business, the provision of services imposes contractual and legal obligations. In the final analysis, all of these considerations are, as ever, vital features of the service which must be defined.

The role of the auditor

An audit is aimed principally at ascertaining whether or not the management systems proposed for use in the development and supply of a service will prove effective in practice and at determining both the extent of the compliance with those systems and the systems' efficacy. As always, auditing of services is a preventative action taken on behalf of management to determine that the release or use of resources is justified. The audits assist management to make sound decisions by providing them with factual information.

If a systems audit is being performed prior to commencement of a service product's life cycle or before the start of any particular phase of that life cycle, the auditor will be verifying that:

— the service organization has been properly conceived;
— the quality management systems have been properly developed and communicated to those who will use them;
— the necessary resources have been fully and properly budgeted;
— the time required for the product to become fully operational has been properly budgeted.

Such knowledge helps management both when it is deciding whether or not to allocate further resources and to proceed with the subsequent activities as planned and when it is trying to judge if the risk of loss or of avoidable failure costs has been minimized. The systems audit will, as always, be planned sufficiently ahead of the scheduled start of each phase to permit any corrective action, revealed by the audit as being necessary, to be accomplished. The audit objectives will be determined as outlined in Chapter 3. If those responsible for the service are required to implement any company standard procedure the auditor will also:

— verify compliance with those procedures;
— obtain objective evidence of performance in order that the efficacy of those procedures can be ascertained;
— inform those responsible for authorizing those procedures of any corrective action to them that is considered necessary.

Depending on the audit objectives, the auditor will, during a compliance audit, verify that the quality management systems are being met fully, such that:

— fitness for purpose is being achieved;
— fitness for purpose will be achieved;
— contractual and legal obligations are being met;
— time and resources are being properly managed.

The auditee's procedures may refer to various codes and standards with which the personnel must comply. If so, the auditor will spot check the auditee's compliance with them. Should this necessitates the presence of a specialist on the audit team, then this must be arranged. The auditee should be monitoring his own adherence to those standards etc. by means of quality controls and audits and should also be pursuing his own non-conformity and corrective action systems when he discovers problems. The auditor's spot checks are primarily aimed at obtaining confidence in the auditee's diligence in such matters and are not in themselves intended as quality controls for the auditee's use.

Conduct of the audit

The various QA standards mentioned throughout this book can still apply but only once substantial changes have been applied to them. Some specifically mention the need for control of services but speak mainly in the context of service functions which support manufacturing operations. In so doing, they outline various basic controls and systems to consider but, whilst they do contain a few useful precepts for service companies, they all require too much interpretation to be of direct use for organizations such as banks, insurance companies, travel agents, postal companies and the like. They are of some use to those organizations, though, when procuring manufactured equipment and items.

If the audit's objectives include ascertaining the auditee's state of compliance with any particular codes, standards or regulations, then, as part of the audit preparations, the auditor must obtain the interpretation that has been imposed on or agreed by the auditee. Regardless of the use or otherwise of a QA standard, the four elements described in Chapter 5 will still apply to individual tasks in the service operation. Fig. 25.1 shows the four elements and their sub-elements as listed in Chapter 5 together with the sub-elements for the fifth task element which applies to services only. I derived the fifth element from "ITEM" which is one of my original four.

The auditor will split the auditee's work into phases and tasks in order to investigate the systems, as described earlier in this book. The audit method and question technique will be as per Chapters 11 and 13 respectively; each department can be analysed as described in Chapter 7; and systems can be considered as per Chapter 16. The vital importance of thorough preparation remains (see Chapter 9) as does the advisability of using a checklist, matrix or flowchart etc., as per Chapter 8.

Certain aspects peculiar to services are described in the following sections of this chapter. These aspects are concerned with:

- organizational matters;
- designing of services;
- quality controls.

The auditor should address these matters as required.

ORGANIZATIONAL MATTERS

In organizing his operation, the auditee should have analysed his business and potential markets and then defined the following:

- customers and their associated market locations;
- the services to be offered to each customer at each location;
- the market share, penetration and timing of that penetration at each selected market location.

These are the key strategic decisions that should be made within the framework of a management system which ensures that:

- the basic information which has to be obtained to assist the strategic decision makers is defined;
- the information on which the strategic decisions are based is reliable, up-to-date and recorded;
- that information includes details of current finance, management, staff and technical capabilities available within the company;

— the information includes all relevant legislation and other restraints that would affect the company and its product at the individual market locations;
— the information is presented to those decision makers at the time required and in the manner specified;
— the absence of information required by those decision makers but not available is recorded;
— the constraints imposed on the decision making process are recorded;
— the people making the decisions are competent and trained in the skills and techniques required;
— security of the information, its acquisition and the decision making process is maintained.

The auditor will look for objective evidence that such a management system exists, has been communicated to all concerned, is implemented and is effective. This may involve the consideration of matters which are best treated during a President's audit. (See Chapter 27.)

Once the decision has been taken to proceed with the supply of the service, it has to be designed and there will often be some iteration between the actual designing and the strategic decision making process. The strategic decisions constitute key input to the design team and help to formulate its terms of reference. Accordingly, the auditor will check that this design input has been effectively communicated to that team and is consistent with the information provided to the strategic decision makers, thereby verifying the existence of an audit trail.

At this point or when the design has been approved, the auditee management should:

— define the tasks involved in performing the service;
— define the organizational structure including reporting levels, job descriptions, as mentioned in Chapter 4. both for
  a) the central corporate body, such as a business profit centre (if any),
  b) each service product,
  c) each market location to be served;
— analyse and specify each task (as described below);
— design the management systems and work sequence;
— communicate these features to all concerned, perhaps by means of manuals or procedures.

The auditor will look for proof that these things have been done and are consistent with the needs of the service as designed and approved.

Remembering that lack of resources and lack of time are real causes of quality problems, the auditor will also look for proof that the auditee:

— has developed a management system for the estimation of time required for the development and introduction of the service;
— has developed a management system for the estimation of resources needed for the development and introduction of the service;
— has developed management systems for the monitoring of time and of resources;
— has communicated those systems to the staff involved in the development and introduction of the service;
— has implemented those systems;
— can demonstrate that those systems are effective;
— has allocated the resources necessary for the development and introduction of the service;
— has allocated the time required to introduce the service at each location;
— analyses areas of opportunity for saving time and resouces which are not to the detriment of quality achievement.

Foreground and background activities

There are two distinct sets of activities involved in service companies and departments. I refer to those which come directly into contact with customers and end users as "FOREGROUND" activities and I call those which are behind the scene, supporting the foreground, "BACKGROUND" activities. Both require organization and integrated quality management systems.

Examples of tasks that might be encountered in a company are:

FOREGROUND TASKS	BACKGROUND TASKS	
Reception	Personnel	Purchasing
Marketing	Advertising	Materials management
Sales	Storage/warehousing	Distribution/transport
Telephone enquiries	Staff training	Packaging
Customer support advice	Accounts payable	Item processing
Customer equipment servicing	Technical library	Computing
New installations	Plant maintenance	Management information systems
Delivery to customers	Plant design	Quality control
Customer training	Plant procurement	Security
Accounts receivable	Fleet maintenance	
Contract/project management	Legal	
Technical information	Cleaning	
Customer complaint	Finance	
Customer equipment design	Records	
	Research	
	Product development	
	Product design	

Fig. 25.1 The five task elements for services

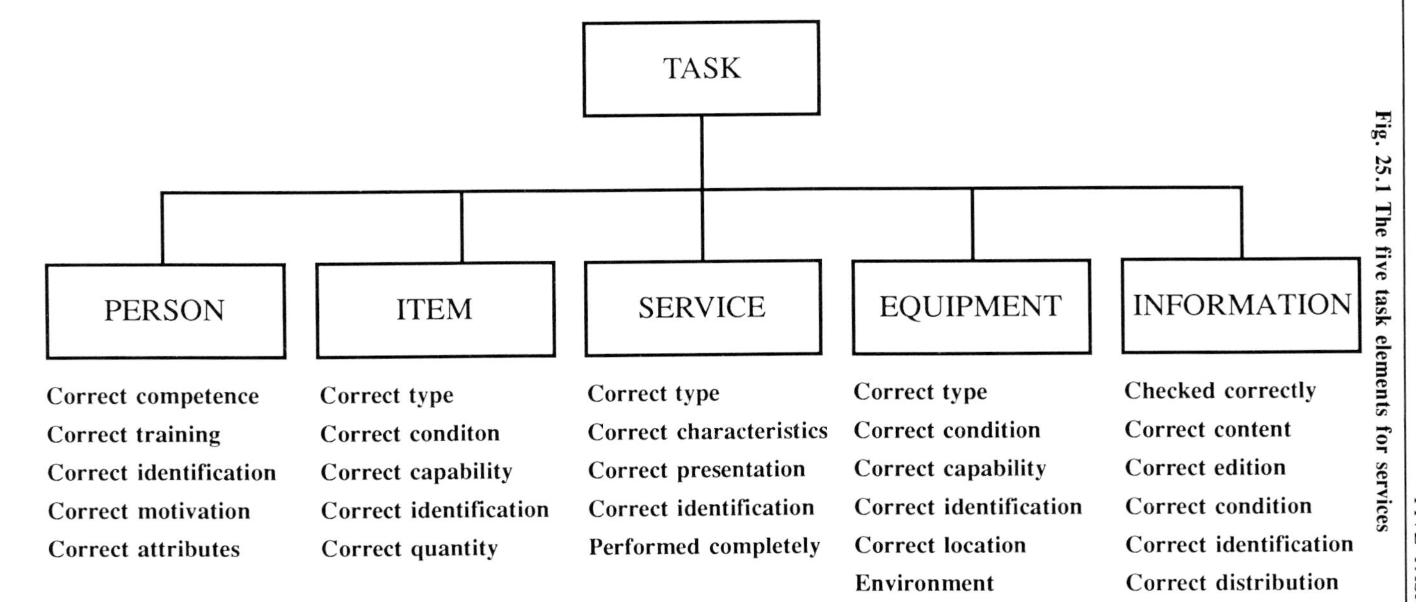

Every company will have its own individual differences, shades of gray and overlap between the foreground and background tasks listed above. Company image is especially sensitive to lapses in those who interface directly with the customer and personnel must be carefully selected, trained and assessed accordingly. The exposed nature of foreground tasks dictates the need for special care in their accomplishment which can only be achieved as a result of thorough designing and planning of the tasks before they are introduced. Company image can also be affected by the way in which individuals and departments interface and deal with other external bodies who are not customers. If, for example, purchasing officers are unpleasant with supplier staff, this can affect the company reputation. In this context, one can see that virtually everyone in a company has to be aware of the service aspects of his or her performance and that the precepts contained in the fifth task element "SERVICE" could, therefore, apply to all.

The five task elements for service activities

Each of the five task elements listed in Fig. 25.1 is now enlarged upon. The points raised are complementary to those made under the same headings within Chapter 5 and the reader should cross refer to them.

SERVICE

Correct type

The auditee must be providing the correct type of service for the customer. The type of service may be expressed in general or specific terms. As examples, general types of service may be the provision of insurance or provision of a civilian police force. Both will have their own specific types of service such as, respectively, providing private motor vehicle insurance or performing a police street patrol. Fig. 25.2 presents a hypothetical example of an insurance service and has been expressed in fairly broad terms. The auditor must ascertain the specific type of the service the auditee is performing; must verify that the person responsible is informed of the correct type of service required and ensure that the correct type of service is being carried out.

Correct characteristics

The quantity of service that a customer receives in relation to the price affects the value for money perception of the customer. Price is in itself a characteristic that requires consideration by the auditee. The overall price charged to a customer incorporates the true costs of the auditee's task, its associated failure costs incurred through waste and a charge levied to provide for profit. True cost is unavoidable, failure costs are avoidable but are seldom the result of a conscious decision to waste money deliberately. Profit level is discretionary, though, in that the management will decide upon the margin. Clearly, this decision is of importance for charging too much cannot be considered as tending to the customer's welfare or to his advantage since it reduces value for money which is a matter of concern for business customers and general public customers alike. Getting the price wrong affects goodwill which is of vital concern for any company, particularly when the customer is captive, as in the case of compulsory state education, a national health service or other nationalized industry: loss of the public's goodwill can affect the particular concern's ability to survive the vicissitudes of political fashion. Investigating matters of pricing policy may be a topic that can only be covered during a president's audit: it is a matter unlikely to be explored by the external auditor but could well be a topic of interest to an extrinsic auditor, such as a regulatory body.

In tending to the customer's welfare and advantage, the auditee must recognize that, when the service is performed, the customer will also be influenced by the way in which it is performed. Of concern to a customer will be such characteristics as safety, legality of method, the reliability with which the auditee performs the task and the consistency of its outcome in satisfying the customer's needs. Cases in point include a customer using an airline's services naturally wanting personal safety to be secured at all times during his trip; a customer seeking a home insulation service wanting to know that the materials provided comply with legal regulations dealing with fire retardant capability and absence of carcinogens such as asbestos; a company using the services of a chartered accountant wanting the financial audit and account preparation to comply with statutory requirements; a person buying a house wanting his attorney to ensure that all legal necessities governing the acquisition and registration of the property and the transaction are met.

Reliability and consistency are two further key characteristics. Travellers, for instance, always desire a service that can be relied on to depart from and arrive at the places advertised and at the times stated on all occasions. Similarly, customers always want to be able to trust the consistency of the task results: the processing of holiday photographs, for example, will not be entrusted to a someone who is known to produce variable results.

The service may need to cater for the individual requirements and circumstances of the customer. This may not always be possible and it is vital that the foreground task is informed of the extent to which the service can be customized. This is rather similar to placing tolerances onto a manufacturing drawing and is a matter to which the designers of service should have paid special attention as the management should have done in formulating the job descriptions and procedures. I refer to this important service characteristic as its "bandwidth".

Customer satisfaction can be influenced by the after-care characteristics which occur when the central part of the task is completed. Illustrations of this include a chimney sweep, a house builder or a plumber who does not remove his debris and mess: a surgeon who omits to remove all the surgical instruments used in an operation will be unpopular with the patient or residual relatives — according to the results. After-care and control of by-products are characteristics that require planning, training of the staff, and provision of the equipment to facilitate the process of cleaning up.

The outcome of the service is another key characteristic. In many cases, the outcome is a tangible entity. The entity may be a document containing information (an insurance policy, for example, a bill of lading, a will, mortgage deeds) or an item supplied (a cooked meal, for example, a cleaned garment of clothing, transfused blood or a transplanted kidney). Equipment may have been subjected to the service and, so, for example, a repaired refrigerator, an office that has been painted or a car that has been cleaned could each constitute the entity; equally a person who has undergone an examination might be that entity. Each of these are, of course, instances of the other four task elements: their own sub-elements must be in accordance with a specification laid down by the customer or by the auditee as well as by regulatory bodies. To do so is in itself an important characteristic of the service.

The outcome of the task can in some cases be intangible: the excitement a customer feels after a roller coaster ride, for example, or after watching a football match, a ballet, a rock concert or other spectacle. Another intangible is the knowledge obtained by the customer when a task has been completed. This knowledge can take several forms: in the case of an airline trip, the customer knows fairly quickly whether or not he has arrived at the right destination; in the case of training services, the customer will sense the extent to which a foreign language has been learned from a language teacher or the degree to which the rigging on a boat is understood after attending a training course on sailing. A customer will also know if any part of the service caused personal annoyance.

The major difference between the tangible and intangible outcomes of a service is that the tangible ones can be subject to quality control actions by the auditee either before or during delivery of the service to the customer. Intangible aspects can only be judged by the customer and the auditee must devise mechanisms whereby feedback from the customer is obtained. Quality controls and customer feedback are discussed later in this chapter.

The auditor will look for objective evidence to verify that:

— the characteristics of the service have been defined and communicated to the workplace;

— those characteristics are consistent with the needs of the customer and market location concerned;
— those characteristics are achieved correctly by that workplace prior to completion of the task.

When there is a tangible outcome, the matters to be investigated by the auditor have already been described in Chapter 5. When there is an intangible outcome, the auditor will investigate the quality controls and customer feedback mechanisms described later in this chapter.

Correct presentation

A crucial feature of service presentation is the image which is projected. Colours, logos, design and layout of facilities as well as packaging all help to satisfy the customer's expectations. They affect the appearance of equipment such as delivery trucks, aircraft and premises; uniforms; information and documents as well as items delivered to the customer. All must be kept in smart order so that a desirable image is maintained. The auditee should be wary when designing logos that another company's trade marks or copyright have not been infringed.

The style of presentation also affects the perceived image and it must reflect the social issues, values and tastes of the target audience. Advertisements involving say, the human female form clothed solely in a bikini may be unacceptable in one country but acceptable in another; consideration for the environment by avoiding the use of packaging materials that are thought to pollute or otherwise damage it may be highly desirable; apparent failure to care for the environment when the target audience perceives a greater degree of care for others' environments could provoke a negative response. Of course, society is constantly changing and circumstances can impose a need for swift action to protect image.

> A few months after the "Herald of Free Enterprise" passenger ferry disaster in 1987 in which nearly two hundred people were killed, that same vessel was still featuring in an advertisement for Townsend Thoresen, the vessel's operator. The advertisement was carried in one of the UK's Automobile Association's brochures which advertised the latter's "5 Star Service", claiming Townsend Thoresen to be the "No.1 CAR FERRY COMPANY".

The speed with which the actual service is offered or accomplished characterizes the attitude of the company towards customer satisfaction. The speed of response to the customer's requests and the promptness of delivery of the service could involve, in the case of a telephone company, for example, matters of queue time, time to answer the telephone or the time required for the customer to have the number connected. In certain activities, however, over-promptness can be a bad thing: restaurant diners do not wish to be rushed through their meals, for example; people attending a doctor's surgery might not appreciate hasty diagnoses of their ailments; trainees attending a course may wish to have time spent on difficult matters.

Key features of the presentation involve the conduct of staff and the way in which the customer is treated. Helpfulness, pleasant and polite manners, personal hygiene and habits, body language, improper language, eye-to-eye contact, patience, tenderness, sympathy and understanding could all warrant consideration as would the sincerity with which the auditee expresses those factors — is the smile genuine or contrived, the sympathy patently false, the delivered speech reminiscent of that obtainable from a trained parrot? Achievement of such expressions is largely dependent on the auditee's competence and basic attributes which would be enhanced by training. The service must not only possess the characteristics of safety and legality but also must be presented in a way that appears safe and legal. This consideration affects the visual condition of equipment and the methods used by the auditee in performing the duties.

The auditor will look for objective evidence that:

- the features for correct presentation have been defined and communicated to the workplace;
- those features are consistent with the needs of the customer and market location concerned;
- those features are accomplished properly prior to completion of the task.

Complete performance

A vital characteristic in the case of services such as electricity supply authorities or telephone/telex companies which do not have a physical item, is the quantity of service supplied. Telephone companies sell time and distance; electricity supply companies provide, of course, electric power. The meters placed to record the power units or period of time over which the customer has used the service, require proper calibration performed by instruments whose accuracy and precision is known and is traceable to national measuring standards. Most countries have enacted legislation concerning weights and measures which will probably govern this matter. Alternatively, where a public service has been created by the government, its charter or Act of Parliament might place restrictions on fair trading and accuracy of measurements. In some cases, full traceability of meters to national standards may not be necessary provided reasonable accuracy can be established. This will vary according to the nature of the measurements to be taken, a computer bureau that charges its customer on the basis of computer connect time and processing power used, for example may only have to demonstrate accurate logging and reliability of the machine.

The particular circumstances must be ascertained by the auditor who will investigate further and as necessary in the manner contained within Chapter 5 in the discussion about ''Equipment''.

When the service involves human effort, the auditee will need to devise a system for the accurate and honest recording of manpower used. The units might be logged to the nearest man-day, man-hour or quarter-man-hour but whatever they are, the personal attribute of honesty is central to customer satisfaction. The auditor will investigate the system accordingly.

Certain of the service's aspects cannot be measured to determine if they have been performed completely in relation to what the customer will pay. Quality controls can, however, help the task, verifying that everything has been done. Visual inspection of information for completeness, using a checklist as an aid to ensure that all pertinent details have been covered might help. Quality controls are discussed further later in this chapter.

The auditor will look for proof that:

— the service's aspects that would constitute its complete performance have been communicated to the workplace;
— the service is performed completely for the customer.

Correct identification

Some aspects of a service cannot be identified by a label or sign but their availability can be denoted by logos, labels, shop signs, advertisements or by the self evident appearance of what is being done (a cleaner polishing a table, a refuse collector handling garbage). The existence of the service and whether or not it is the right one can be gleaned from verbal announcements (air crew announcing the correct flight number and aircraft's destination, for example). All of these constitute information, which is one of the other four task elements, and the auditor will investigate the matters relating to it as described in Chapter 5.

An alternative way of identifying the service is by virtue of the the equipment used or worn by the auditee, uniform and badges, for example. These can be investigated as described in Chapter 5 under ''Equipment''.

PERSON

Competence

Formal educational qualifications can be irrelevant or of secondary importance to the person's achieved abilities and attributes. In services such as sports and entertainment, the competence of players and performers is of paramount importance since their abilities are a major attraction of the service, affecting customer satisfaction and business success: nobody pays to see a loser. In other services functions, such as serving in a hamburger store or selling insurance, the competence levels can be defined in terms of experience, formal educational qualifications, vocational certificates and the like, and can be prescribed in a job specification.

If the service involves the actual supply or hiring out of staff, the auditee must ensure that the candidates' competence and other personnel accomplishments are consistent with the customer's needs. This will necessitate a management system for the review of customer requirements, scrupulous attention to the selection of staff and a policy of ensuring that only those staff who meet the customer's needs are offered to that customer. Even though an employment agency or recruitment consultant may not actually employ the candidates, they are equivalent to foreground staff who reflect the quality of the service provided. Not only must the competence and other sub-elements relating to the persons responsible for selecting and interviewing the staff be controlled, so too must the procedures for selecting candidates offered to the customer. These considerations apply equally well to the work performed by personnel departments when screening job applicants. The auditor will pay attention to these points.

Training

As ever, training is of vital importance. Special aspects of training that a person may require are mentioned throughout this chapter. The individual is responsible for the quality of his or her work and that of the staff for whom he or she is assigned responsibility. This is especially important in foreground activities and is a point that must be impressed upon the individual during training programmes.

Considerable assistance can be given to foreground staff in the form of training programmes which present the expected standard of performance in matters such as courtesy, customer handling, personal appearance and so on. Adequate performance in these matters should be a part of the assessment process to determine staff competence; regular re-assessment and training must also be considered and performed as necessary. The auditor can verify whether or not the auditee implements an effective system for the achievement of these aims.

Motivation

The same factors raised in Chapter 5 apply.

Attributes

The exposed position of foreground tasks means that special attention must be paid to defining the attributes that the ideal person would possess. Amongst them might be behaviour; articulacy; the ability to work in a team; the ability to work under pressure; personal appearance and hygiene; self discipline; self-confidence; ability to take criticism, both warranted and unwarranted; patience; flexibility/adaptability. Certain attributes such as behaviour, courtesy, presentation and attitude of staff can also be most important but can be improved by the process of training.

> During the early 1980s British Rail (the UK's national rail transport company) completed its customer care school programme through which all staff had undergone training in dealing with customers. Although others might have had experiences to the contrary, as an infrequent user of British Rail's services, I must say that I noted a marked and pleasant improvement. If they can do it so can anyone else.

ITEMS

Many services actually provide finished items for consumption or use by the customer. Fast food stores, restaurants, airlines, shops, supermarkets, photo studios, dry cleaners all do so, some of them actually making the item (e.g. snacks or meals), others using chemical or physical processes to provide the service (e.g. dry cleaners, photo studios). Attention to the quality of the item provided is, of course, a central part in achieving customer satisfaction. Obviously the sub-elements for "Item" require the auditee's careful consideration and control. A simple example of how item sub-elements might apply to a hamburger is shown in Fig. 25.2.

Legislative constraints on the item must be obeyed and the management systems must ensure that their edicts are satisfied. Weights and measures regulations, for example, govern the quantity controls for the items provided to the customer. Compliance with them will depend on other sub-elements including personnel honesty; equipment condition; correctness of information. The equipment, staff and information to which they relate might be either in background or in foreground activities and the auditor must ascertain which.

Correct type and correct capability

See Chapter 5.

Correct condition

The condition of the item might have been specified by the customer (glossy finish to a photograph; ice cold beer; sharp creases in pressed trousers) or it might be specified by the service company and advertised as such ("ice cold beer on tap"; "photographs ready mounted"; "cleaning includes pressing"). For various services, the law may stipulate certain minimum conditions that the item must possess, most frequently in respect of health and safety (e.g. non-toxic food; insulation that contains no asbestos).

Care of customer property must be ensured at all times and, so that the company's liability position can be safeguarded, the condition of the items should be established on receipt. Any apparent damage should be pointed out and agreed with the customer, a note being made to that effect. If the condition is such that the service may cause damage or would not be effective, the auditee staff should make this known to the customer and if necessary decline to accept the work. Examples include badly packed parcels that the customer wishes to post; torn or stained garments sent to a dry cleaning agency; out-of-date film that the customer wishes to have processed. The auditor will check that the auditee has a management system to ensure these points receive attention and that the staff are trained accordingly.

Correct quantity

Excess or short measure is always unacceptable. The meters, gauges, scales and other measuring devices used in background and foreground activities have to be true and accurate: in most countries, there is legislation affecting these matters. Hence, traceability to a recognized national standard is prudent and essential from product liability and reputation standpoints. Certain quantities require equipment maintenance as opposed to conventional calibration of gauges: in the case of a cash dispensing machine, for instance, there would be no thanks for short change. The auditor will ascertain the quantity control required and use this information when considering "Equipment", discussed below.

Correct identification

The customer wants to receive the items that he has selected. Identification might be by visual appearance which makes the identity of the item self evident; it could equally well be on a package, as, for example, take-away food may be labelled or contained in a pre-printed package. Tags, ticket stubs, counterfoils, labels etc. could all be acceptable means of identification provided that they do not damage the item, reduce its quality in any way or present a risk to the customer.

The background and foreground staff must understand and use the same identification system. Embarrassment can be caused when the actual status of processing the item is not known by foreground staff and it is handed over to the customer incomplete, unready, unfinished or whatever. Where background and foreground staff work in close proximity to each other, these situations can develop when things get busy. The auditor should investigate how those embarrassments are prevented.

Fig. 25.2 Simple comparison of tast elements "ITEM" and "SERVICE"

TASK — Serve Hamburger	*Task — Provide Insurance Cover*
ITEM: Hamburger *Type:* ¼lb Cheeseburger	SERVICE: Insurance sales *Type:* Motor vehicle insurance
Condition: As delivered to serving tray by kitchen. Fresh cooked within last 10 minutes; Meat hot; Cheese melted; Uncrushed; Absence of oil or grease stains; Ingredients stacked as per company standard; Packaged in company standard 'cheeseburger' carton.	*Characteristics:* Nationwide availability; Office sale (face to face with customer); Accurate premiums as per insurer's tables A selection of insurers for customer to choose from, but also catering for customer's other personal preference; Credit card or cheque payment All company outlets to operate in consistent manner.
Quantity: Single unit comprising 1 Hamburger slice of ¼ pound uncooked weight; Standard sesame seed bun; 2 slice tomato; 4 pieces pickle; 2 slice lettuce; 2 onion slices; 1 slice cheese.	*Presentation:* Max. waiting time 5 mins. Customer care during wait; Individual attention without interuptions; Private consulting room if requested; On-the-spot written quotes; Immediate cover facility; Pleasant and friendly atmosphere; Smiles, eye contact, calm, confident manner and absence of raised voice; Do not rush the customer; Helpful — "nothing is too much trouble"; Comfortable clean rooms with soft background music; No discrimination at all. Standard local office hours.
Capability: To retain a temperature of at least 110°F up to 10 minutes after cooking and packing.	*Perform completely:* Provide all information the customer requests; Transaction forms filled in; Customer receipts provided; Mailing list up-date, if requred; Customer welcome procedure; Privacy procedure if needed; Refreshment and courtesy procedure; Customer farewell procedure
Identification: Position in serving tray; visual appearance and pre-printed cheeseburger carton.	*Identification:* Company colour and logo to identify offices, staff uniforms and documents. Labelled sign on motor insurance officers's desk. Motor insurance documents to be titled as such.

EQUIPMENT

Correct type

See Chapter 5.

Correct condition

The condition of the equipment used in foreground activities can affect the company image. It must be in a presentable condition that is properly maintained. Cleaning, painting, lubricating, overhauling may each be necessary to some extent and the frequency at which these actions are undertaken will depend on usage rate and service conditions. Passenger transport vehicles may require cleaning prior to each journey; sales office desks may require cleaning, polishing and dusting every day and repainting every six months with carpets being replaced at least yearly; decorative plants may need weekly tending.

Similarly, background equipment will also require its own maintenance programme for daily, weekly, monthly actions or for routine maintenance every so many running hours. Hotel kitchens, for example, may require nightly cleaning whilst air conditioning equipment may require an overhaul every 5,000 hours of operation.

In certain instances, the equipment condition might affect safety of customers and/or of staff. There will probably be various regulations and codes that the auditor must consider when covering this matter.

Correct capability

The same factors raised in Chapter 5 apply here but the consistency of performance and reliability of the service are greatly dependent on the reliability of the equipment used by the customer or by staff. The equipment must work correctly under all operating conditions and even under abnormal circumstances, such as when there is peak demand for the service or when there has been a failure in another part of the service. Such latter considerations must be taken into account when the service is being designed and equipment is being specified for procurement.

Higher levels for safety, faster transportation, better snow clearance in a municipality, entertainment machines capable of providing the customer with greater excitement or mental stimulation and similar demands for better services constantly necessitate higher specifications for the equipment. The auditee will render himself liable to increased failure costs if these matters are not considered.

The auditor will investigate the matters raised in Chapter 5 on this subject.

Many service operations rely on computers. They are often a convenient scapegoat for staff who cannot admit their own fault or their own sloppy work. The computers must be capable of processing the volume of information required within a time frame that is acceptable to the customer.

> In October 1986, the rules governing the buying and selling of stocks and shares in London were changed. The event was known as the "Big Bang". As these rules were changed, so were the computer systems used to present information to the dealers. When trading began, the systems crashed because the demands on them exceeded expectations. Acute embarrassment and frustration was incurred by those responsible as well as by the users.

When programmed properly, computers can reduce the likelihood of error because of their ability to permit consistency of quality. Further discussion of controls on computer software and installations is contained in Chapter 24.

Correct identification

The same considerations explored in Chapter 5 apply.

Location

Customers are seldom impressed when the necessary equipment for performing the service is not available at the right place at the right time. The auditee should consider the need for issuing complete sets of equipment to each of its foreground staff since sharing might cause inconvenience, delay or frustration.

Closely allied to this, is the consideration of availability of equipment by virtue of its capability. This has been further discussed in Chapter 5.

Environment

This has been examined in Chapter 5. The key principle is to ensure that nuisances do not arise: whereas in a manufacturing environment, a nuisance is one that affects the performance of staff, the condition of items or equipment, in foreground activities of the same sector, however, the "condition of the customer" also can be affected. Lighting levels, temperature and humidity controls, dust and dirt, noise levels, crowded conditions each play a part in customer satisfaction. Customer expectations for the environment must be considered since, if the environment does not meet the standards set by competitors or similar industries, business may be lost. It is wise to remember that the ready availability of international travel affords the opportunity for customers to compare standards with those set in other countries.

The auditee must take these factors into account when the environment is being designed and maintained. The auditor will investigate whether or not the auditee has done so.

INFORMATION

Content

All members of staff and all customers want correct information. Some information can be especially critical or sensitive, particularly when it relates to personal details. Customer records must be correct and complete and one can easily imagine the damage and upset caused if, for instance, a hospital's medical records are inaccurate (allergies are not listed; blood types are wrongly recorded; drugs prescribed to the patient are incorrectly stated; physical or mental ailments are listed incorrectly). Similarly, customers do not wish to settle someone else's account, to be billed for services which were not required or not received to be billed without due discounts being applied or receive incorrect tickets or reservations.

The precepts concerning loss control described in Chapter 24 are also important in service operations and the auditor should investigate such matters.

Correct edition; correct condition; correct distribution and correct identification

See Chapter 5. The auditor should investigate the matters raised in that chapter in the context of the service being audited.

DESIGNING OF SERVICES

Designing anything is a task itself whose outcome depends on the quality of the input, the task elements involved and avoidance of the six real causes of quality problems. The latter two have been previously discussed in Chapters 5 and 18 respectively.

Design input

Typical information that comprises design input is listed in Fig. 25.3, much of which should have been the result of the strategic decisions described earlier in this chapter. Some matters obviously require particular attention. In considering "who is our customer", for example, the auditee should bear in mind that customers may be manifold and that the term does not just include the person who pays for the service. "Customers" could be end-users; those who see the effects of the service and its results i.e. bystanders; regulatory bodies, banks, insurance companies, with which the company has to deal to secure loans or execute its business; colleagues in the chain of supply/consumption/system; even vendors who receive the results of the service, as in the case of the company's own purchasing service. Any or all of these must receive due consideration.

The fact that there can be many different customers involved can be illustrated by considering those telephone users who experience the quality of service offered by a telephone company. They could include:

— domestic subscribers; private and business;
— international visitors; private and business;
— international recipients; private and business;
— international interfacing organizations such as foreign telephone companies;
— international callers; private and business.

Each customer has its own particular needs, some or all of which may be identical to others': these must be subject to careful analysis by the designers. The auditor will verify that the auditee has a system which:

— provides the correct input information to the designer prior to commencement of the design;
— ensures that the input is incorporated into the design.

Fig. 25.3 Summary of service design, input, factors for consideration and design actions

Design input from management	*Factors for consideration*	*Principal design action*
• Who is our 'customer'? • What is our product • Where is the customer located? • What would constitute fitness for purpose? • Anticipated customer and market expectations • Contractual obligations • Legal obligations • Target selling, price volume and market share • Current company capabilities • Available resources • Time scale for introduction of the service • Budget available	• Assisting the customer in specifying requirements • Customer behaviour • Assumptions can be wrong • Customised services • Potential non-conformities • Customer complaints • Product liability	• List the foreground tasks • Define task elements and sub-elements for each • List the background tasks, task elements & sub-elements for each • Design the quality management system that links the foreground and background tasks • Define acceptance criteria for tasks • Define quality controls for tasks (i.e. produce quality plan)

Assisting the customer in specifying requirements

The foreground staff could be faced with a customer who is not completely sure about what he wants, cannot provide a detailed specification or merely wishes to explore the various options available. In these situations, the customer can be helped if presented with some choice or menu. A questionnaire form, checklist or set of prompts on a visual display unit which the foreground staff can discuss with the customer may aid the latter's decisions. The auditor will look for proof that the auditee:

a) has developed a design control system to ensure that:

— mechanisms for assisting the customer to select and specify his particular requirements are designed;
— those mechanisms are properly checked prior to issue;
— those mechanisms are communicated to the foreground staff.

b) has communicated that design control system to those that will use it;

c) has implemented that system and that the system is efficacious.

Customer behaviour

Customer behaviour can affect the employee response desired under normal circumstances. The customer's perception of that response and of the service might make his behaviour even more unpredictable. A vicious circle could develop leading to a breakdown in communication, antagonism and hostility, the effects of which might extend far beyond a lost customer. Customer actions and questions must be anticipated and planned. A dummy run with a member of staff assuming the role of a difficult customer can help the design process by highlighting unforeseen factors. This is similar to prototype testing which is often practised in manufacturing industry as part of design control.

The design should, therefore, strive towards exploring and removing possible causes of unpredictability by ensuring that the customer will be managed from the time when initial contact is made. Layout of premises, of forms, provision of instructions and signs all help. A good example of managing the customer is to be found at Disneyland with its marvellous queueing and help systems. The environment in which the service is delivered also affects and conditions the customer to react in the desired way. Attention to nuisance avoidance is important. The way in which the customer is managed helps to prevent product liability claims.

The auditor will look for proof that the auditee:

a) has developed a design control system to ensure that:

— the customer's possible questions and actions are carefully considered;
— measures to deal with those questions and actions are developed such that customer dissatisfaction is prevented as far as could be reasonably foreseen;
— those measures are checked properly prior to issue;
— they are communicated to the foreground staff.

b) has communicated that design control system to those that will use it;

c) has implemented that system and that the system is efficacious.

Assumptions can be wrong

Without a market survey or other feedback it is impossible to know completely what the customer's acceptance criteria are or will be. Even with this information, it is easy to misjudge the relative importance of individual features of the service to the customer. It is always possible that values within the auditee's company have influenced the market information obtained as the result of a failure to address certain matters which the customer considers important but which were neglected by the auditee or dismissed by him as being trivial. The company may have also misjudged how the customers regard the competitor's performance. The auditee must recognize that customer expectations develop from competitors' products, technological and other advances in the market or environment. A classic example of the impact of technological advances is the market change caused when television started to compete with cinema. Although film companies competed with each other, there came a time when they were competing also with technology — if convenience foods provided convenience eating, television provided convenience entertainment. Many failed to realize this. Amusement parks, that rose in popularity during in the early 20th century, suffered a similar decline as competition from motor cars and television increased, both developments drawing customers away. It took a new concept to revive such parks. This was due to Walt Disney's "theme parks" initiated in 1955 with the opening of Disneyland in California. The auditor will investigate whether or not the auditee's design control system ensures that the design considers and allows for erroneous assumptions.

Customized services

Customers always like to feel that they are receiving personal attention and are considered to be important. Foreground staff will want to be as accommodating as possible in satisfying the customer's particular needs or whims. It is obviously sensible that they do not commit others to a customized service which is beyond the company's resources or capability. Staff training and good communications are vital if the "Yes, we can do that for you" promise is to be honoured. The bandwidth will establish the limitations.

In order to customize the service, it is essential that its "core" is defined at the outset. From this the bandwidth, or range of options possible, must also be defined. The bandwidth necessary can be based on the experience and feedback obtained during a rehearsal or from a market survey. The service designer must receive this information and study it. Similarly, the input information concerning the existing capabilities must be reviewed and the designers should consult with as many members of staff as possible to determine what really is possible as well as the particular requirements of each.

The auditor will look for proof that the auditee:

a) has developed a design control system to ensure that:

— detailed information of the core of the service is produced by the designers and is properly checked prior to release;
— detailed information of the service bandwidth is produced and properly checked prior to release;
— all of such detailed information required by the foreground and background staff is communicated to them for their own further action.

b) has communicated that design control system to those that will use it;

c) has implemented that system and tht the system is efficacious.

Non-conformity

An effective service must recognise that things can go wrong without warning and that "Murphy" can strike, when, for example, equipment fails or in the case of an airline luggage is lost. Alternative causes of action must be available immediately for there will be no time to process a conventional non-conformity report form and no time to train the staff in how to handle the situation.

The auditee should have defined "What-if" situations and designed solutions for them into the service and into the quality management systems that will support the foreground staff in dealing with the difficulties. Flow charts, fault trees, Ishikawa charts, failure modes and effects criticality analyses (FMECAs) are all excellent tools that the auditee can employ when analysing non-conformity scenarios and their associated risks. These tools help identify the need for alternative actions.

Contingency plans, along with the arrangements and resources required for them are essential. Their associated details must be part of the training and competence level of staff. The auditee's design must specify what is entailed. When properly considered and prepared, contingency plans can head off loss of business or reputation as well as a product liability claim but even with all this effort the sad fact is that Murphy's Law can still prevail.

The auditor will examine proof that the auditee:

a) Has developed a design control system to ensure that:

— the design defines the operational situations that could lead to non-conformity;
— each situation is analysed to determine its likelihood and risk;
— those that must be catered for have been specified;
— alternative actions, contingency plans and arrangements, readiness requirements and the requirements for dealing with each of those specified situations and their non-conformities have been developed;
— those contingency plans etc. are properly checked prior to issue;
— they are communicated to the foreground and background staff with details of responsibilities for making them work successfully;

b) has communicated that design control system to those that will use it;

c) has implemented that system and that the system is efficacious.

Customer complaint

The design can help to reduce the likelihood of customer complaint but for those unforeseeable occasions when complaints do materialize, there should be a system for dealing with them courteously and promptly.

The auditor will examine proof that the auditee:

a) has developed a design control system to ensure that:

— the design defines the situations that could lead to customer complaint;
— guidelines for dealing with each situation have been specified;
— those guidelines are properly checked prior to issue;
— they are communicated to the foreground and background staff, together with details of responsibilities for dealing with those complaints successfully.

b) has communicated that system to those that will use it;

c) has implemented that system and that the system is efficacious.

Product liability

The designer must consider the breaches of contractual and legal obligations which could give rise to a product liability claim and then "design out" potential causes. Obviously it may not be possible to foresee everything that could happen but the risks can be minimized by performing the analyses previously outlined in the section concerning non-conformities. Contract notices, warning notices, descriptions, advertisements, security, equipment and information safety, tort, health, trespass, weights and measures are but a few of the matters to be considered. Legal experts must review the design and plans.

The auditor will examine proof that the auditee:

a) has developed a design control system to ensure that:

- legal requirements are defined;
- product liability risks are defined;
- these are communicated to the designer prior to the design work being started;
- the design defines the operational situations that could lead to infringement of legal requirements or incur a product liability risk;
- the possible causes of those situations are analysed;
- the likelihood of those causes arising is prevented or minimized;
- arrangements for dealing with any such situation that might arise have been specified;
- those arrangements are properly checked prior to issue;
- those arrangements are communicated to all staff, together with details of responsibilities for preventing such situations and for dealing with them successfully.

b) has communicated that design control system to those that will use it;

c) has implemented that system and the system is efficacious.

Service characteristics

The characteristics required to ensure the achievement of quality and customer satisfaction must be defined and it is essential that careful consideration is paid to defining them during the design process so as to develop a service specification. Service characteristics have already been outlined in this chapter.

The auditor will look for proof that the auditee's design control system ensures that:

— the characteristics are defined and checked prior to issue;
— acceptance criteria for each characteristic are defined and checked for adequacy prior to issue;
— those characteristics and their acceptance criteria are communicated to those foreground and background areas affected by them.

The auditor will also look for objective evidence that the system is implemented and is efficacious.

Service presentation

A selection of features which constitute correct presentation have been mentioned earlier in this Chapter. The design effort will involve specifying the presentation required and then defining how each feature will be achieved by foreground tasks and by the management systems that direct the efforts of background staff in support of their foreground colleagues.

The auditor will look for proof that the auditee's design control system ensures that:

— the presentation features are defined and checked prior to issue;
— acceptance criteria for each feature are defined and checked for adequacy prior to issue;
— those features and their acceptance criteria are communicated to those foreground and background areas affected by them.

The auditor will also look for objective evidence that the design control system is implemented and is efficacious.

Service performance

In order for the service to be performed completely, the foreground task needs to know precisely what would constitute complete performance. The design must state those details and devise methods which can be used to assist all concerned in checking for complete performance. (This matter has been discussed earlier in this chapter.) A major problem is that when the service requires customization, the designers cannot readily allow for the completeness of performance although details pertaining to the core of the service will remain immutable and require their attention. The auditor will look for proof that the auditee's design control system ensures that:

— the aspects constituting complete performance of the service are defined and checked prior to issue;

— those aspects are communicated to those foreground and background areas affected by them.

The auditor will also look for objective evidence that the design control system is implemented and is efficacious with regard to these matters.

Service identification

Methods for identifying the service were described earlier in this chapter. They will be achieved by means of organizing the other task elements viz. ITEM; EQUIPMENT; INFORMATION; PERSON. The auditor will look for proof that the auditee's design control system ensures that:

— the methods for identifying the service are defined and checked prior to release for use;

— those methods are communicated to those foreground and background areas affected by them.

The auditor will also look for objective evidence that the design control system is implemented and is efficacious with regard to these matters.

Design output

The preceding paragraphs have outlined design output information, all of which has consequences upon both the time needed to introduce the service and the actual resources that will be needed to introduce it and to operate it successfully. When the design is complete, the foreground and background departments must organize themselves for their contribution to the overall service effort. They will be linked together by quality management systems that contribute to the common objective of assuring that the service will be of quality.

The auditee should have considered the design output and then planned the entire delivery cycle/process. The delivery cycle should then have been broken into interlinking tasks and the task elements and sub-elements defined for each. These in turn can be used to determine:

— efforts needed to introduce the service;

— time required to develop and introduce the service;

— resources needed to develop, introduce and provide the service.

These activities have been mentioned to earlier in this chapter, in the section entitled "Organizational matters".

QUALITY CONTROLS

Quality control always provides useful management information in the form of feedback so that areas for improvement can be detected. However, control is similar to the examination of accounts: it deals in history. Items, equipment and information that are supplied as part of the service can all be assessed by means of conventional quality controls, such as inspection or statistical quality control. All quality control involves measuring, testing, inspecting, examining a product in order to decide whether or not it complies with its acceptance criteria and(which might be stated in a specification or a standard) and a decision either to release the product for further processing, for use, for repair/rework and then further examination or to scrap the product and make a new one.

Acceptance criteria

Performance standards are needed. Certain aspects of presentation and service characteristics can be measured, common examples of this being response times versus response rates; errors per transaction/document. The acceptance criteria for both background and foreground activities must be specified since without this, management will never be in control of their departments.

Performance levels of background and foreground tasks mutually affect each other. The existence of an integrated quality management system linking them together naturally has the effect that they reinforce each other's needs. Poor performance in a background task, however, will quickly result in poor performance in a foreground one whereas the opposite is not automatically true. The effect of the tasks on each other can be estimated with the help of fault trees etc., as described previously in this chapter and the auditee should not hesitate to use them when determining acceptance criteria for each task in the quality management system.

Some targets for performance can be specified and information may be readily available as a basis for setting improvement goals. Examples of data frequently available, if only the auditee were to take the trouble of analysing them, are defective documents or data entries, customer complaints, records of average response time, equipment failure rates, maintenance costs, warranty claims and refunds. All constitute simple measurements which can be used to establish acceptable levels of service performance for customers and between departments. These can be further estimated during rehearsals. The target levels of performance and deviation limits permissible could well be 100% and 0% respectively, particularly where health and safety are concerned.

Although the intangibilities of service characteristics and presentation cannot be be assigned units of measurement, the standard for acceptance can be indicated by means of audio cassettes, tapeslide programmes, photographs, training videos, visual demonstrations and the like. Unacceptable standards can be portrayed also by similar means.

Auditee quality control techniques

A major problem with a service is that because certain of its characteristics and presentation are intangible, one canot totally "inspect" them before delivery. For this reason, services also have to rely on prototype assessment, rehearsals, staff training and competence tests as well as feedback from customer surveys. Staff knowledge and skills can be regularly tested and certificates of recognition can be awarded. Performance based incentive schemes or promotions are used by some auditees to signify an acceptable level of achievement. Service activities can be observed whilst in progress but observation may affect performance. Some auditees may use anonymous assessors to act as customers in order to appraise the level of performance.

Foreground and background staff can check the state of readiness, of the equipment, of information and of items that they require both before and during the working day. Planned and periodic checks can also be performed by them. Records of completed activities and routine checks can be reviewed or audited.

Customers are the final arbiters on service quality and if their experience and views are obtained, a better guide becomes available. One must, however, appreciate that customer feedback is still only available after the event and does not present REAL TIME control on quality performance. A wide variety of customer feedback mechanisms are used by auditees in service companies and operations, the most common include: questionnaires delivered by mailshot or with the "product"; telephonic follow-up and personal interview; customer complaints obtained from regular contact with the clients or from "hotline"/emergency calls; repeat orders used to analyse each customer's buying trends, market share trends and media reports derived from product surveys, test reports, complaints, comparisons with competitors' products. The results of these techniques must be promptly fed back to the staff and can form a part of the personnel performance appraisal process.

Clearly, many quality control options are available to the auditee and, by examining proof, the auditor should verify that:

— the auditee has developed quality management systems which ensure that quality control activities are planned and used;

— those systems ensure that acceptance criteria for the various tasks are defined and communicated to the workplaces at which those tasks are performed;
— those systems have been communicated to the areas responsible for performing those activities;
— those management systems are implemented and are efficacious.

Self-control in foreground tasks

Service locations might be geographically dispersed to the point that the service is actually performed in the customer's home or office. Although the auditee could be tempted into producing voluminous procedure manuals, these are often of little help and are unlikely to be read by the foreground staff. A better approach used by some auditees is to give foreground staff more discretion and freedom. This can lead to a higher estimation of the service quality in the eyes of the customer and is an approach that is good for motivation as it is a form of job enlargement. If the increased motivation also leads to lower staff turnover, this in itself is a saving of the failure costs to the company. On balance, it is preferable to pursue the concept of self help and self inspection/control, provided that safety and quality are not jeopardized.

Error analysis

Although it makes little sense to develop a quality control system to specify acceptance criteria and to capture information as a result, only to ignore the opportunities presented, a surprisingly large pecentage of auditees do precisely that. Often the problem rests in a failure to analyse the information and present it in a form that is easily assimilated. Pareto charts, graphs, pie charts, flow charts are all simple devices which can help.

With these points in mind the auditor will check the improvement opportunity system mentioned as STEPS 6 and 7 in Chapter 11.

References:

1. Juran, J.M., *Quality Control Handbook*, Third edition, 1974, published by the McGraw-Hill Book Co., New York, USA.

2. The ISO 9000-1987 *Quality systems* series of standards is comprised of ISO 9000 to ISO 9004 inclusive and is published by the International Organization for Standardization (ISO).

3. ISO 8402 *Quality — Vocabulary*. Published by the International Organization for Standardization.

26. Safety, Resources and Energy Audits

Our wasted oil unprofitably burns,
Like hidden lamps in old sepulchral urns.
William Cowper.

Safety, resources and energy are often the focus of audits dedicated specifically to their investigation. Bearing in mind their increasing importance, from a cost or potential liability point of view, prudent managements have derived substantial benefits from paying attention to them. This chapter is intended merely to emphasize, by highlighting certain matters, the auditing aspects that have have been studied throughout this book.

Role of the auditor

The auditor's role will depend on the specific objectives of the audit. That role may be to determine the efficacy of the systems which affect the use of energy or resources; it may be to determine the status of safety practices and procedures in the company; it may be as a consultant engaged specifically to recommend improvements and cost savings.

Whatever the objectives, the auditor is still representing management and must approach the audit with an absence of preconceived ideas.

Conduct of the audits

The preparation, performance and reporting of each of these types of audit remain as described throughout this book. The audit objectives, as ever, require most careful definition if the audit is to be successful. This is a point of particular importance because each area of investigation, be it energy, safety or resources, calls for specialist knowledge and expertise in the auditor. In the case of safety, a strong familiarity with legislation, case law and its interpretation as well as with acceptable preventative systems are vital.

The audit can and must only be based on the examination of objective evidence. Facts are vital, hearsay inadmissible.

Whether or not Corrective Action Requests should be issued is a matter of policy that must be determined at the outset of each audit and the position of the auditor will, clearly, have some effect on this. If, for example, an outside consultant or specialist is engaged, the management may require a report which only states areas for which corrective action is recommended. It will then be the decision of the company's management to issue Corrective Action Requests or not. If the auditor is performing an extrinsic audit, as in the case of safety audits, it is probable that the statute which empowers the auditor to enter the auditee's premises for these purposes will also be translated into the authority to issue a formal Corrective Action Request (or, more likely, a Corrective Action Requirement).

Whichever type of audit is being performed, however, the auditor can use the task elements of PERSON, ITEM, EQUIPMENT, INFORMATION and SERVICE with their corresponding sub-elements (all of which are shown on Figure 25.1) to considerable effect.

The following sections seek to provide some additional guidance to the points raised elsewhere in this book.

Safety audits

Safety is a large subject, even more so if the additional context of health is introduced, but all in this realm can ultimately be reduced to the task elements etc. and the way in which they are or might be used, abused or misused. The reader will recall that fitness for purpose means careful consideration of the use, abuse and misuse to which a product may be subjected in service. Since fitness for purpose is a prime constituent of quality, it is clear that efficacious quality management systems incorporate safety management systems, that, in fact, the two are synonymous and inseparable.

The systems must be based not only on the requirements of legislation but also on the hazards inherent in the work task, equipment, item etc. that is involved. Legislation is necessarily couched in the most general of terms and the auditee must have interpreted those terms accordingly. The general legislative climate is also important. Some countries operate more extensively on a strict liability basis than do others and this has a considerable effect on the depth of thought required in the designing or auditing of a quality management system. It is precisely for this reason that special expertise is required of the auditor: safety audits are not trivial matters in which amateurs may dabble.

Person:

Safety is directly affected by the person performing a task. Lack of competence and training in the equipment used, items used or processed, the process itself or quality management systems can give rise to risks as can failure to inform others of what is required or of risks involved.

Items:

The condition of the item(s) being processed or handled has to be considered. Items can be inherently dangerous (nuclear isotopes, acids, explosives etc.) or unsafe only when abused. Similarly, items can be inherently safe until they are mixed, combined or brought into contact with other items (such being the case in chemical reactions). The auditor needs to consider the operational circumstance and decide on the risks that could be involved: these factors set the objectives of the quality management system and of the corresponding audit. Naturally, the auditor will verify that the auditee has exercised the same thought process and acted responsibly on the results.

Item quantity can also give rise to risks. Excess quantities of items, for instance, can lead to unacceptable forces, weights, heat or other loads; in the case of certain nuclear substances, too much can lead to a critical mass; in chemical reactions, similar scenarios can develop. A variation on the problem of quantities is one of excess concentrations: the auditee should have considered these possibilities, designing and implementing his systems accordingly. The auditor will need to determine the correctness and completeness of the auditee's determination of acceptable quantities and then analyse the efficacy of the resultant systems and measures in use to control their potential effects.

Items need to be correctly identified in order to keep the user or bystander properly informed of their existence and status.

The correct type of item must be issued to the user and the auditee needs to develop systems to ensure that this is done. However, supplying the correct type also entails careful analysis of the circumstances in which the item will be used or placed. The auditee should have determined this as a prerequisite in developing quality management systems to ensure issue of the correct type of item.

Equipment:

The reader will recall that in Chapter 5 I stated that the workplace's equipment was at one time someone else's item since it has first to be made or created before it can become equipment.

The selection of the correct type of equipment depends on the operational circumstances that it will encounter. It must be fit for purpose along the lines described earlier in this chapter.

Accordingly equipment must possess the correct capability for the task involved. It cannot be securely expected to operate beyond the limits of safety for which it was designed. Abnormal circumstance must have been considered in the selection process, together with transient conditions which can occur. The working loads, duties and stresses should each have been thoroughly scrutinized and their effects calculated prior to specification of the equipment itself. The operational circumstances might include maintaining items or containing them so as to retain a particular condition (e.g. canisters, nuclear containment buildings, heat shields) or it may be to maintain a particular environment (e.g. fume extractors, heating and ventilating plant). The auditor needs to verify that these circumstances were properly considered, built into the equipment's capability and that the equipment is maintained so as to retain that capability. Naturally, the operating conditions must be such as to avoid exceeding those designed conditions.

Equipment must be identified to inform the user and bystander of its existence and its condition. The auditee must have ensured that the right equipment reaches the right location at the right time, otherwise unsafe equipment might be substituted. Associated with this aspect is the requirement that safety and protection devices be available physically and operationally. The auditor will pay attention to these points.

Environmental nuisances must be controlled. Dangerous (slippery, explosive, badly lit etc.) or toxic atmospheres (fumes, leaked radiations, sour gas etc.) must be prevented. They can affect operator performance or the innocent bystander and might result from the condition of items or equipment in the area or perhaps from inadequate information or operator carelessness. The risks associated with undesirable atmospheres, as well as the potential sources, should have been analysed by the auditee. The auditor will verify the completeness and correctness of the auditee's analyses and subsequent actions.

Information:

When information is unchecked there is a risk that its content is unproven or unfit for purpose. Content could mislead, be ambiguous, dangerous or false. A user can also be misled and come into contact with unsafe conditions of equipment, items or practices if the incorrect edition of information is available. Likewise, when the valid period of personnel competence certificates or licences is exceeded without reaffirming ongoing competence, safety can become compromised.

Information must be presented in a usable condition which means that illegibility of documents due to damage, deterioration or small print sizes (in relation to the distance from which someone is expected to read the information) must be avoided by the auditee. A particular and unsafe condition of information is the instance where it is presented in the wrong language. The auditee should have based the information on the user's needs and circumstances but this can only be achieved if he has first ascertained what they are. The auditor will verify the validity of the premises on which the information has been created before going on to determine the efficacy of the auditee's resultant actions.

Closely associated with the last point is the necessity for proper distribution of the information. Improper or inadequate distribution that can cause people to be ill-informed or un-informed is unacceptable. The auditee must have analysed exactly who needs to know the information, such analysis not being satisfied by his stating his opinion of who needs to know. The auditee should also have considered extraordinary cicumstances and planned the distribution of information accordingly: product recall situations, for example, place particular demands on information distribution and the prudent auditee will have determined not only the distribution required but also the method of distribution in relation to the speed with which information needs to reach the target audience. The auditor will investigate the thoroughness and efficacy of the auditee's actions.

Services:

The characteristics of the service place particular demands on the interfacing task elements. If, for instance, a certain level of safety risk is required, this will have a direct impact on the selection of the type of equipment and its capability. The auditee must have defined the safety characteristics and risk levels as a basis for determining the stringency of the supporting quality management systems. The auditor will investigate the decision making process surrounding this basis as well as the efficacy of those systems.

The method of presentation can also give rise to or reduce the risks to safety. The presentation and potential safety risks have a particular effect on the training of the foreground personnel, as discussed in Chapter 25. The auditor will verify that the presentation and possible attendant risks have been analysed, defined and effectively communicated to the personnel involved.

Failure to perform a complete service can also be unsafe. The auditee needs to ensure that his quality management systems prevent the attendant risks associated with incomplete performance. If, for example, a company is engaged to perform a cleaning or sterilization process, a risk to safety can arise if there is anything less than total thoroughness. Or, in the case of an airline, it really is rather inconvenient for the passengers to have the flight element of the service cut short in mid-air!

The six real causes:

In addressing the need for corrective action, when it is found necessary, the auditor will trace through to the real root cause(s), a process which was described in Chapter 17. Just as other quality matters, safety problems have their root in the six real causes that were mentioned in Chapter 18, some common examples of cause and effect being:

— inadequate resources leading to inadequate training, staff levels, equipment and so on;
— inadequate time leading to a lack of due care and attention to the work in hand;
— lack of discipline in following procedures that affect health or safety having obvious results;
— lack of organization leading to unsafe conditions or to difficulties in controlling them when they do arise;
— lack of training in the safety aspects of a task and in the sub-elements causing accidents. Inadequate training in the handling of non-conformities can mean situations getting out of control;
— lack of top management support for safety having potential repercussions that are unthinkable.

Resources audits

The audit team might be of rather mixed origins in that it could comprise systems analysts and technologists from various disciplines, chosen because of the help and advice that they could bring to bear.

Resources are required for providing the five task elements and their attendant sub-elements as well as to support the quality management systems.

The auditors are, in essence, looking at the waste prevention attitudes and associated management systems of the auditee. Waste can result from any of the following all of which have been discussed previously in this book:

— overcomplex quality management systems that waste time or manpower;
— non-conformities derived from any of the six real causes;
— excessive handling of items;
— inadequate quantity control of items;
— superfluous information content or distribution;
— equipment of the wrong capability;
— incorrect decisions;
— obsolete decisions being maintained;
— competence mismatch between personnel assigned to perform a task and the needs of the task itself;
— poor utilization of space;
— failure to modernize or reinvest in equipment of improved efficiency or capability;
— failure to update attitudes or practices in line with developments.

Several of the foregoing derive from failure to change or from a resolute and irrational defence of the status quo. The audit must check that the auditee has a policy and practice of self-help and thereby has a system which defines, allocates and monitors resources, also encouraging the identification of opportunities for improvement. That system must ensure ongoing and continuous input of new ideas based on technological trends and developments. Of vital importance is the support of top management towards a willingness to change.

Energy audits

Two separate issues must be considered by the auditor the first of these being the selection of the energy source, the second the actual usage of energy. Together they ensure that energy costs are optimized or are wasted.

a) Energy source selection:

The key questions that the auditee must regularly address are as follows:

— are we using the right type of energy?
— would it be more economic to use a different source such as oil or gas (if, say, electricity is currently being used)?
— would it be more economic to alter the work pattern to take advantage of off peak tariffs?
— if we were to change, what would be the pay back period?
— are we too reliant on one type of energy source, a particular vendor, for example?
— should we look for an alternative vendor source, perhaps an international one?
— if we are purchasing our energy from international sources, are we ensuring that our exposure to exchange rate fluctuations is minimized?
— do we need an alternative type of energy source to minimize our exposure to risks of strikes, power cuts (which might affect manufacturing processes, computersor telecommunication links)?
— should we install our own generators to reduce those risks?

As all engineers know, energy can be high grade or low grade: high grade energy sources can be completely transformed into other forms of energy, low grade sources cannot and result, therefore, in energy wastage. Electricity, for example, is a high grade source because it is completely converted into other forms of energy at a conversion rate that depends on the equipment efficiency; heat is a low grade source since a portion of it always remains unavailable, thereby constituting a loss. Such are the laws of thermodynamics.

b) Energy usage:

Energy is required to operate equipment, maintain environmental conditions, perform processes, distribute items and information. The auditor will generally have an engineering background because energy balance and optimization form an important part of professional engineering training. Various points for consideration are detailed below.

— The auditee needs to monitor energy usage at all points of his operations. It is also important that process capability together with equipment and workplace layout are carefully considered because they can affect energy consumption dramatically.

— The selection of particular equipment should always be based on the efficiency with which it converts energy to serve a useful purpose. Electric lamps, for example, can have greatly different light outputs for a certain energy consumption; electric motors can have different efficiencies over a given power range. The equipment will have been constructed from various materials whose inherent capability may or may not be conducive to energy efficiency. Cases in point might be the characteristics of insulating or conductive property or of reflective ability. When selecting equipment, the auditee should be considering such matters and obtaining suppliers' performance curves and other data.

— The process is affected directly by the capability of the items being used and their energy demands. Such properties as melting point, viscosity, specific heat, freezing point, hardness and other chemical and physical properties all have their effect on energy consumption. In designing the product, the energy conscious designer should have considered them all for they will constrain the processes required, the energy consumption levels and hence the unit costs, price and profitability. As part of the auditee's design control system, the features should have been analysed.

— When the items or services have been designed, the processes which will be used to furnish them must be determined. The equipment that will be used and the interrelationship of the processes will affect the layout of premises in which particular environmental conditions will need to be maintained. Space and layout affect energy loads directly and the design must have considered this fact.

Thus the auditor will look for an audit trail between what exists and what was designed. Challenging the basic assumptions and the design decisions generally reveals the greatest opportunities for energy savings.

Briefly, designing is a decision making process whose product is controlled primarily by the PERSON and INFORMATION task elements. The auditor should verify that the auditee's design control system ensures that the design process is based on complete and correct input information and is executed by designers who are competent, trained etc. If the design process uses equipment such as computers supported by software, the auditor should investigate computers by considering them to be EQUIPMENT, as described in Chapter 5 and should consider the software to be INFORMATION. Where the software is used or has been developed in-house, the precepts of Chapter 24 should be considered also.

The usage of energy can be measured and the auditee should be measuring consumption as well as input levels. The difference will represent a loss and reveal the inefficiency: it is thus a measure of the opportunities available. However, it must always be recognized that opportunity can only be realized by energy recovery and/or by initial savings born of improved equipment, processes or the demands made on them. Recovery is limited by the laws of thermodynamics and depends on whether the waste takes the form of high or low grade energy. The usage of energy can be reported in various forms, either descriptive or graphic. One graphic method that has been used by engineers for many years is the Sankey diagram (the origin of which has been attributed to Captain Riall Sankey[1] or by means of a pie chart. The auditor will check that the auditee has a system for capturing and analysing data on energy usage.

Six real causes:

Once again, the six real causes can have effects on energy efficiency. Wastage of energy is just another example of failure costs born of decisions of bad quality. Energy wastage is anathema to a quality professional just as much as scrap items.

Top management needs to support energy conservation programmes both by expressions of encouragement and by direct action in the form of demanding regular energy usage reports and energy audits. It should appoint someone to be responsible for monitoring energy usage and sources who must report back on a regular basis.

Lack of discipline over the use of energy leads to dissipation and waste.

Lack of resources to obtain energy efficient equipment and practices will, ironically, lead to avoidable costs.

Lack of training in energy conservation and awareness can lead to profligate attitudes caused by ignorance of the importance and cost of energy.

Lack of time devoted to analysing energy usage and sources means that valuable opportunities will remain hidden.

Lack of organization in estimating, allocating, and monitoring energy leads to hidden costs derived from unknown waste.

References:

1. Lyle O. *The efficient use of fuel*, H.M.S.O. Third impression.

Author's note: *Although technological advances have rendered obsolete some of its content Oliver Lyle's book is a veritable tome of timeless wisdom about the economic use of energy. Its companion "The efficient use of steam" (an H.M.S.O. publication also written by Oliver Lyle) similarly contains precepts that energy auditors will find valuable.*

27. President's Audit

Facts when combined with ideas, constitute the greatest force in the world. They are greater than armaments, greater than finance, greater than science, business and law because they are the common denominator of them all.
Carl W. Ackerman.

Introduction

President's audits are gaining rapidly in popularity. As the name suggests, they are authorized by the president or chief executive officer (CEO) of the company and in some cases are actually performed by that person. Generally, however, the audit team is hired from outside the company in order to ensure genuine independence as well as an absence of the inbred habits and beliefs which would inevitably occur if the audit team were to be derived from within the company's own ranks. These audits enable the CEO to determine that corporate policies and strategic decisions have been properly delegated throughout the company and are being implemented. In addition, they obtain factual evidence concerning the current validity and correctness of earlier strategic decisions, also serving to determine the efficacy of these decisions. President's audits can reveal the true capabilities of the company factually. Clearly, they provide a most valuable input for successful management at the top of any company.

Role of the auditor

The reader will recall that I regard the fundamental product in a company to be "decisions". The most important decisions are the ones that are made at the top because everyone's actions stem from those decisions. The president's auditor investigates the quality of the decision making process as well as the management actions that result from those decisions, verifying that an audit trail exists between strategic decisions made at the top and the actions taken at all levels. If no such trail exists, the possibilities of bad communications, incompetence, anarchy, but principally the suspicion that the management and workforce are out of touch with each other, are raised.

Certain matters cannot be effectively addressed by the regular auditor who is appointed from middle management or lower ranks of a company. Auditing the structure and membership of the board of directors, for example, is a job which must be left to the president or his directly appointed auditor. This is because some auditees would consider it to be either an impertinence or an embarrassment to be audited by someone from a lower level in the company. It is also unfair on the auditor himself since the sense of self-preservation and embarrassment surrounding the questioning of those who hold superior positions in the company could render his performance less than adequate.

Auditees

The president's audit, by definition, is at the highest level within the hierarchy of the company's audits as described in Chapter 1. The primary auditees are those managers who report directly to the president or CEO but, depending on the audit's objectives, the auditees they may be found at any level in the company whose participation is necessary to obtain the requisite facts.

Conduct of the audit

The audit is prepared, performed and reported using the same principles that have been described elsewhere in this book. It can only be prepared and performed successfully within the framework of well known and carefully defined objectives which will be different to those set for normal management audits. The effect of those objectives will be to enlarge the scope of the audit by taking into account a larger proportion of the company departments and operations.

In those cases where the president/CEO is to be a member of the team, it is important that he or she sets an example to all by being properly trained since without this, a lack of discipline in the performance of the regular management audits could easily ensue.

It is crucial that the right attitude be adopted during these audits. The president's audit must not only *be* a fact finding exercise that will present a true and fair view but it must be *seen to be* such otherwise much damage can be done. The audit has to be performed with a good degree of sensitivity as some auditees imagine hidden motives behind everything and their instincts of self preservation emerge at the slightest (imagined) provocation. Accordingly, the audit team must be especially careful to adopt the consultancy role that I have advocated throughout this book. They must make suggestions and be helpful to the auditees at all times. Given that, the audit team is representing the president of the company, its actions and attitudes can easily be interpreted to be those of the president/CEO himself. Much damage to team spirit can result if an insensitive, incompetent and ill-trained audit team is let loose: such a disgrace can severely damage a corporate team spirit that has been carefully nurtured over a number of years. For this reason, one cannot recommend that the audit team be comprised of anything other than auditors who have considerable experience of making such audits. The audit team must act responsibly, never adopting the attitude that it has a special position and extensive powers of censure, for it does not. It is merely a group of people authorized to go and gather facts, that is all.

The auditors must remember that they will obtain valuable results by challenging the decisions made by the particular auditees and by challenging the framework within which those decisions are made. They must never challenge the person for to do so merely raises barriers. It is counterproductive and gives totally the wrong impression about the president's psyche. The president's audit is not an inquisition and it is vital that this is remembered because there will be natural apprehensions, fears and defensiveness to overcome in the auditees.

In most president's audits an element of auditee politics, personal motives and malicious attitudes surface. Phrases such as "Well, of course, its not for me to say what his department is doing, I have no doubt you will see it for yourself" which are accompanied by a "knowing smile" can easily inject subtle poisons into the mind of an inexperienced auditor but they are to be ignored. The audit team must be particularly scrupulous to ensure that it works only on rock solid objective evidence and that it does not report hearsay for some auditees try to seize on the president's audit as an opportunity to do harm to others and benefit to themselves. The "dirty dozen" tactics can occur (see Chapter 15) and the auditor needs to deal with them effectively. When auditing senior managers, there can be a tendency for the trial of strength to take the form of a manager trying to browbeat the auditor by virtue of the seniority of his position (although clearly this does not work when the auditors come from external sources). Implied bribes which stem from hints about using the auditor's company's skills for future contracts can occur — the auditor should simply ignore them and continue with the job in hand.

> I was engaged to perform a particular president's audit and one of the auditee's top managers stated that he was a great believer in quality and the value of such audits. He further ventured the opinion that I was just the kind of person that his company needed at the top and that he would express those sentiments to his managing director. However, once the exit interview was completed, he remarked that I was clearly not the type to work effectively in "his" team and that I was unsuited to be one of his managerial colleagues. The audit had revealed that his particular office was at the root cause of various quality management problems.

Attitude of CEOs

With the exception of matters of honesty, conventional financial audits, whilst checking for the existence of an audit trail between vouchers and the accuracy and verity of accounts, do not investigate and are not really designed to investigate, the performance realities that lie behind the figures. The president's audit is specifically intended to do so. They remove the hypocrisy involved in most internal management audits which only consider the efficacy of subordinates' actions whilst steering well clear of uncovering facts about the effectiveness of the work (i.e. decisions) performed by the top management. A major benefit of these audits is their ability to increase staff motivation by demonstrating genuine leadership for the company wide quality programme since they set an example for all to see.

Corrective action requests (CARs)

Whether or not formal Corrective Action Requests should be issued to cure problems identified during an audit is a policy matter which tends to vary between companies. Some enlightened CEOs willingly receive CARs placed on themselves if the root cause of problems is identified as resting with them. In authorizing the performance of such audits, the president/CEO must realize that there is always a possibility that particular inadequacies in the company may be directly traceable to his own efforts or lack of them. Honestly and openly to admit any personal shortcomings or inactions that the audit may identify, as opposed to counter-productively "shooting the messenger", is an act that requires personal stature and integrity. It does, however set a model that is of enormous benefit to the company's operational and quality objectives. Not everyone possesses such worthy attributes.

Frequently the audit team will describe shortcomings and the recommended solutions in the audit report, not in CARs.

Audit reports

The precepts of Chapter 20 still apply. The reports must be concise and to the point. The audit team must not be afraid to state the facts plainly because that is precisely what they have been engaged to do. The Aldous Huxley quote in Chapter 1 should be borne in mind by auditor and auditee alike. Often the president's audit report will have a restricted circulation although it may be sent to the senior management and to the board. This will depend on the policy for such audits and also on the audit's objectives of the audit. If, for example one of the objectives has been to examine the performance of a particular senior manager, it would be singularly inappropriate for his colleagues to receive a copy of the report. If, however, the objectives are not of a particularly sensitive nature then restricting the distribution of the report could in itself be a demotivator.

Follow-up actions

Should the audit identify various corrective actions as being required it is essential that follow-up action be taken to determine the effectiveness and completion of those actions. When the audit has identified the need for corrective action on the part of the president/CEO, the latter should ensure that follow-up action is seen to be taken to verify the efficacy of the results. Those who are prepared to act in this way set a shining example to their company.

Typical objectives and topics raised

The following provides a selection of various objectives and matters which often arise in or from president's audits.

Audit trail between strategic decisions and actions

President's audits are fact finding exercises. They verify that the plans, policies and procedures set or authorized at the top of a company have been accurately translated throughout the various levels of the company and consequently implemented. They determine that there is consistency within the organization at the lower levels of the company. Like any other audit, they remove the rose-coloured spectacles to reveal the way things really are as opposed to the way that the president might have believed them to be, a general impression based on information provided by his immediate subordinates.

Some of the matters raised during the president's audit will have been topics for discussion at top management in companies for many years. Those discussions can be of dubious value when they do not base themselves on reliable information obtained directly from the "coalface" where the work is actually being performed in the company. The president's audit fills the information gap that frequently exists between those discussions and the conventional management audit (quality assurance audit) which often focuses on management issues but assumes the key decisions about the way the company is organized and operating to be correct and consistent with the corporate objectives.

To be genuinely integrated, the management systems must not only integrate with each other but also with those used to make strategic decisions. There must be an audit trail between those decisions and the operational management systems. The president's audit will, amongst other things, verify the existence of such an audit trail.

The main product of any level of management is "decisions". Decision making is a task that principally involves the task elements "PERSON" and "INFORMATION". In investigating the efficacy of the decision making system, the auditor will pay attention to those elements and their sub-elements.

The basic premises under which decisions have been made need to be re-ascertained and evaluated in the light of changing circumstances. The issues are:

— was that original decision right at the time? — is it still correct?
— have the basic premises changed and if so what should be their impact?

Management of resources and time

The audits are often aimed at ascertaining whether or not resources and time are allocated, used properly and are properly controlled. They can verify whether or not quality costs are constantly monitored at all levels in the company and whether or not efforts are made to reduce avoidable costs by the identification of opportunities. Associated matters raised normally resemble the following:

— do we know what our costs really are?
— do we know how much time is really needed to satisfy the customer's needs?
— if not, what must we do?
— what improvements are possible?
— what do our budgets really need to be?
— if we took X% of the cost reduction opportunities identified during the audit, by what amount would this reduce the company's financing or borrowing needs?
— alternatively by taking those opportunities what would our pricing levels be and what impact could this have on market share?

Long range plans

Vital to such audits is the fact that they verify that the operational plans at all levels of the company are consistent with the corporate objectives set by the president. These objectives may have been defined in long range plans. The audits can ascertain the actual capabilities available in the company in order to assist the formulation of corporate strategy. To promote the determining of long range plans, the president's audit can also report:

— how quickly do the departments respond in practice?
— how quickly could they respond to decisions made at the top of the company?

Legal obligations

The president's audit can question whether or not legal considerations are really respected at all levels, in areas concerning health and safety, trade descriptions, weights and measures, employee discrimination and the like.

Organizations

Henri Fayol spoke of the need to audit the organization of any enterprise regularly. The value of his shrewd advice remains undiminished over the years. He wrote:[1]

> "It would be most improvident not to make periodic inspections of all parts of a machine, especially a complex one. There would be a risk of poor output, accidents, even catastrophes. Daily (somewhat superficial) inspection is no adequate guarantee. No less great is the need for periodic overhaul of administrative machinery .... The following rule meets this need — 'Every year, in connection with the drawing up of the annual plan, a scrupulous study of the constitution of the organization is to be made with the assistance of summarized charts'".

The foundation for the company's effectiveness is laid by the organizational decisions taken by top management. The typical management auditor has little opportunity to investigate the rationale behind a particular organizational structure and conventional management auditing consequently tends to ignore this vital aspect which determines the quality performance of the company. Naturally this must be addressed during the president's audit. The decisions behind a particular organization must be questioned in terms of the basic information upon which they were originally made. Trading circumstances and product needs are constantly changing and no company can assume that a particular organizational structure will adequately serve its purposes for ever without any change. Organizational features which can be investigated have been described in Chapter 4 and 18. The key questions that must be asked are:

— if we still had only the facts on which the original organization was based, would we still structure it the same way?
— in light of the facts now available concerning our product range, business objectives and so on, would we structure the organization in the same way?
— if not, how would our decisions be affected?

The information obtainable from the president's audit creates such reflections as:

— are our direct sell or licensing policies still valid?
— considering the current status and capability of our equipment, our financial strengths and people resources, not neglecting commercial and technological trends, should we re-invest or buy in basic goods or services? i.e. should we revise our make or buy decisions and change our vertical or horizontal integration status?
— is the way in which we are organized consistent with the needs of the marketplace and the customer? How well does the existing organizational structure respond (in terms of speed and cost opportunity) to their needs?

Management systems, effectiveness and information

The audit will examine the company management systems to determine if:

— cross-company management systems are compatible;
— they are implemented in a consistent manner across the company;
— they are effective in securing the company's objectives.

Management effectiveness issues often raised consist of questions such as

— are individual managers effective?
— if not, what training or other actions should we take?
— do those managers avoid decisions? If so, why?

At the executive management levels the following questions are exceedingly valuable in helping the CEO and top management put their own actions and achievements into perspective:

— is the company executive/am I responsive to department needs or are we/am I out of touch?
— do I/we really know what they need?
— do I/we serve them properly and on time?
— do I/we engender fear or defensiveness?
— do I/we communicate with them effectively? or do I/we communicate AT them?
— what must I/we do to improve my/our performance?

These audits frequently investigate motivation and team attitudes by addressing such matters as:

— what is the real state of motivation throughout the company?
— what is the real state of motivation in a particular department?
— do we really work as a team?
  — is information communicated effectively?
  — is integration of interfacing systems really achieved?
  — what is the timeliness of inter-department supply?
  — is there joint effort on problem solving?
  — do we work by personal contact or through petty minded memos?
  — do we have too many meetings and, if so, why?
  — how well do we conduct our meetings?
  — are assigned actions really taken and followed up?

Every executive likes to believe that he or she is in touch with what is really happening and that his or her information systems achieve those laudable aims, but the president's audit can look to the truth of the situation by addressing matters such as:

— how effective or accurate is the normal reporting system?
— do we and our managers really know what the shop floor problems are?
— are their management reports accurate, reliable and timely?
— how quickly do we and our managers respond to quality problems?
— can that response be improved?
— are we preventive minded or are we fire-fighters? In other words, are we managers or are we fixers?

References:

1. Fayol H. *General and Industrial Management*, Pitman.

Index

Index learning turns no student pale,
Yet holds the eel of science by the tail.
Alexander Pope.